Ukraine and Russia in Their Historical Encounter

 University of Alberta

compliments of

Canadian Institute of
Ukrainian Studies
352 Athabasca Hall
University of Alberta
Edmonton, Alberta
Canada, T6G 2E8

Telephone (403) 492-2972
Fax   (403) 492-4967

Ukraine and Russia in Their Historical Encounter

Edited by
Peter J. Potichnyj, Marc Raeff,
Jaroslaw Pelenski, Gleb N. Žekulin

Canadian Institute of Ukrainian Studies Press
University of Alberta
Edmonton   1992

Copyright © 1992 Canadian Institute of Ukrainian Studies Press
University of Alberta
Edmonton, Alberta, Canada

Canadian Cataloguing in Publication Data

Main entry under title:
Ukraine and Russia in their historical encounter

Papers from the first Conference on Ukrainian-Russian Relations held on Oct. 8-9, 1981 in Hamilton, Ont.
ISBN 0-920862-84-5

    1. Ukraine — Relations — Soviet Union — 2. Soviet Union — Relations — Ukraine — Congresses. I. Potichnyj, Peter J., 1930- II. Conference on Ukrainian-Russian Relations (1st: 1981: Hamilton, Ont.)

DK 508.57.S65U4 1992   327.47'71047   C92-091407-1

PRINTED IN CANADA

Table of Contents

Culture and Religion

Economy and Demography

Conclusion / *Nicholas V. Riasanovsky*   327

Appendix: On Ukrainian-Russian Relations

Contributors   343

INTRODUCTION

Omeljan Pritsak

The Problem of a Ukrainian-Russian Dialogue

One of the great tragedies of our time is the sad fact that Ukrainians and Russians—or, to put it more precisely, the intellectuals and politicians of these two nations—have had in the past and present very little opportunity to talk openly with each other and to discuss frankly their respective and mutual problems. This kind of discussion is essential, since after the Ancient Greeks discovered the uniqueness of the human being (all other civilizations first discovered God), with pensive intellect as his distinctive feature, the only productive way to solve problems between two parties has been the *dialogue*, also an ingenious Greek invention.

There are many historical reasons for the lack of Ukrainian-Russian Russian dialogue. The first actual meeting between these two peoples, which occurred in 1654, was indeed ill-omened. To the tenor of Professor Torke's paper, I add that event's appraisal by a scholar of the stature of Vasilii Kliuchevsky, who wrote: "Not comprehending each other and not trusting each other, both sides [Ukrainians and Russians in 1654] in their mutual relationship did not say what they thought and did what they did not wish to do..."[1]

The limitations imposed on the two peoples by pre-secular convention were soon blurred by the strange, secular phraseology and terminology of the first two West European intellectual currents, which almost simultaneously reached the two peoples during the Napoleonic wars, when both were part of the empire based in St. Petersburg. These currents were the Enlightenment and Romanticism, especially the latter, which proved to be a two-faced "gift." On the one hand, Romanticism elevated folklore and the vernacular to the rank of the only true literary creation, thus giving birth to modern Ukrainian national culture. But on the other hand, it stimulated the creation of Nicholas I's "Official Nationality," studied in an exemplary way by Professor Nicholas Riasanovsky, with its emphasis on mystical and bureaucratic patriotism.[2] Romanticism also introduced the Hegelian concept of non-historic nations, which, as adapted by Marx and Engels, became such a dynamic force among the youth of the Russian Empire at the threshold of our century.

Although the Russian Empire's old regime was much more "liberal" than its "proletarian" successor, under tsarism certain boundaries were not to be crossed and certain problems not to be raised. Among them was the Ukrainian question, especially after the prohibition of Ukrainianism in 1861 and 1876.

In 1905, not coincidentally in the wake of the first occurrence of revolution, the Imperial Academy of Sciences in St. Petersburg published its famous report stating that the Ukrainian language was not a Russian dialect, but an independent Slavic language with a sizable literature (printed mainly in Galicia because of the previous prohibitions) and recommending that the prohibition against the Ukrainian printed word be terminated. This report was due primarily to two Russian philologists and academicians of very great stature: Aleksei Alexandrovich Shakhmatov and Fedor Evgenievich Korsh. Not only had they devoted their skills to the study of Ukrainian philology for decades, but they also had the courage to defend publicly, against all odds, the right of Ukrainians to their own culture.

But even such an idealist as Shakhmatov (whose friends called him "St. Alexis, the Man of God") had limits as far as Ukrainianism was concerned. An independent Ukrainian culture—yes! But when his Ukrainian friends, encouraged by his proven Ukrainophilism, spoke with him about the concept of Ukrainian political autonomy, they found staunch resistance. Shakhmatov would accept no such possibility. His reasoning was very simple: he objected to any "separatism" because it would "cut us Russians off from the warm sea" (meaning the Black Sea). Shakhmatov's reaction to the First Universal issued by the Central Rada (23 June 1917) was very definite and negative. According to his Ukrainian friend Petro Stebnytsky, Shakhmatov angrily cried: "Non possumus!" (We cannot allow it!).[3] As elaborated by Professor John Reshetar,[4] Lenin, like the majority of Russians from Russia, was originally unaware of any Ukrainian issue; he wrote exclusively of and to the "Russian working class". Lenin discovered the "peoples of Russia," among them the Ukrainians, only during the revolution of May 1905. From that time he often dealt with the Ukrainian problem because of its increasing significance, but always in his typical dialectical manner: one day acknowledging the right of the Ukrainians to independence, and the next denying them equality with the Russian workers in Ukraine, who were to be treated as the only decisive group there. Lenin was ready to grant the Ukrainians a limited statehood and their own limited government and limited culture, but he reserved supervisory rights to his new form of empire centred in Petrograd. He would emphatically deny establishing the separate national Ukrainian Communist Party, the only real authority in Ukraine after the October Revolution.

Throughout this century, only a very few Russian intellectuals ever dealt seriously with the Ukrainian problem. And even in our own time, the Ukrainian problem is not on the list of important matters considered by Russian intellectuals.

One rare exception was Petr Berngardovich Struve (1870–1944). But the perception of the Ukrainian problem by this "liberal on the right" (former "liberal on the left"), so aptly analyzed by Professor Richard Pipes,[5] was anything but attractive to the Ukrainians. Struve's starting point was the concept that as a nation Russia was still *in statu nascendi*. Unlike Austria-Hungary, which Struve classified as a "multinational empire," Russia should be viewed as a "genuine national empire," because it had the potential to assimilate non-Russian cultures. "National unity" was to be achieved not ethnically (as in Austria-Hungary), but culturally. Only one high and dominant Russian culture was to be permitted in the empire, with the Russian language elevated to the status of the *koine*, comparable to the Ancient Greek *koine* and German *Hochdeutsch*. For the Ukrainians, Struve foresaw a modest regional development, a phenomenon whose culture was to be confined largely to elementary education and patois literature.

Peter Struve has not officially entered the Soviet pantheon, and he is not acclaimed as one of the communist Founding Fathers. In the first edition of the Ukrainian Soviet Encyclopaedia,[6] the entry "Struve, P. G." states that he was originally a "legal Marxist," but later, as a Kadet, became the ideologist of Russian imperialism and denied Ukrainians the right of autonomy. Significantly, in the *Ukrainian Soviet Historical Encyclopaedia*, published ten years later, after the Shelest period,[7] Struve is not even mentioned. Yet since the mid-1960s the official Soviet policy toward Ukraine, apparently spearheaded by Mikhail Suslov, has been nothing other than the realization of Struve's concept of two cultures, that is, the implementation of the dominant Russian high culture and the unattractive patois Ukrainian "culture." The concept of a "new historical entity—the [uniform] Soviet people," launched in 1976, is the most recent version of an idea that can ultimately be traced back to Struve.

Why is this so? Apparently the Russians are still unable to overcome a basic blind spot in their vision of reality: they still insist on the integrity of their empire. This is very painful for Ukrainians to live with, but one must deal with that fact and look ahead, beyond it. It was only in the writings of the Decembrists in the 1820s that, as Professor Marc Raeff points out,[8] a shift in allegiance from the patrimonial ruler to the state, as an entity separate from the person of the ruler, occurred for the first time in Russian intellectual history. The secularization of the concept of a sacred, indivisible empire, and the freeing of the Russian nation from the burden of maintaining a universal empire (again, the two entities, *empire* and *nation* are still perceived as a *oneness*), will one day reach even Russia. To be sure, it will be a traumatic experience for the Russians at first (as it was after World War II for the older colonialist nations— the Portuguese, Spaniards, Dutch, British and French), but also a necessary and liberating one.

Now let me turn to past and present-day Ukrainian intellectuals. Apart from political populists of the brand of Mykola Kostomarov and Volodymyr Antonovych, two basic types have developed: one in interwar Galicia, which continues in the emigration (especially in North America), and the other in Soviet Ukraine.

In the interwar period, owing to the activity of the political thinker Dmytro Dontsov (Dontsov, a Russian renegade), a blind hatred of all things Russian developed among the young generation of Ukrainians. This was a reaction against their father's ideas: Mykhailo Drahomanov's liberal confederationism and differing shades of socialism. To the young Ukrainians precisely these "decadent" teachings were responsible for defeats in the struggle for Ukrainian independence. From the point of view of Dontsov's followers, nothing good could ever come from the Russians, hence there was no need for any dialogue with them.

The totalitarian Stalinist and post-Stalinist regimes have created a unique human creature in Ukraine—the eternal younger brother who has no right to mature and is consigned to perpetual mediocrity. He has no right to an independent existence; he must forever be attached to his older Russian brother. Only a Russian has the right to be an original thinker, poet, scholar, politician, etc. The Ukrainian's duty is simply to imitate him. Any originality on his part is regarded as an unforgivable crime and is punished mercilessly.

A Soviet Ukrainian is a citizen of the Ukrainian Soviet Socialist Republic, theoretically an independent state, a founding member of the United Nations. There is a Ukrainian government and a foreign ministry, but only one Ukrainian ambassador abroad: a representative at the United Nations. This "independent" state cannot make any decision, even in a trivial matter, without the prior approval of the All-Union (Russian) Older Brother. His native language is constitutionally recognized as the official language of his republic, but that language is denied any *dignitas*. In order to survive, a Ukrainian has to use Russian in his daily and professional life; otherwise he would be accused of nationalism or cretinism. If he is a scholar, he has no right to use original sources. Only Russian translations may be used, since only Russian is the window to the world.

Although there are ten Ukrainian universities (where the primary language of instruction is Russian), every dissertation has to be written in Russian and defended and/or attested in Moscow.

No institution in Ukraine can exist independently. Even the Ukrainian Academy of Sciences is now a branch of the Russian ["All-Union"] Academy. Although the state is atheistic, it maintains tsarist policies of co-operating with Russian [official] Orthodoxy in support of Russian imperialism. An independent Ukrainian Orthodox church is denied the right to exist. Even the Galician Uniate church was "reunited" with the Ukrainian branch of the Russian Orthodox church.

Certainly, in the Soviet Union there is no need for the older brother to be engaged in a dialogue with his Frankenstein-like creation, the proverbial younger brother who is far from his equal.

This means that a Russian-Ukrainian dialogue, at least at the present time, should and must be conducted between those of us living in the free world. But the prerequisite is, in my view, that both sides free themselves from all complexes of the past (mentioned only in part in this short article) and turn their outlook and intellects toward a vision of the future.

The Ukrainian-Russian problem is not unique. As mentioned above, other colonial empires and their "second-rate" subjects experienced a similar day of reckoning. Both the Russians and the Ukrainians should learn a lesson from such experiences. What is needed most is courage and frankness. As an example let us look at the courage and frankness of de Gaulle's France, which brought about the decolonization of Algeria.

The historical Muslim Algerian government was brought to a violent end by French intervention in 1830–48. Colonization of the conquered territory started as early as 1840. By 1843, Algeria was declared French territory and divided into three departments, like the rest of France. There were some rebellions by the native Algerians, the last of which began in 1954.

But even in 1958, the French government reassured the several generations of French colonists who had their homes in Algeria that that country was an "inseparable part of the French republic" (a formulation so familiar to Ukrainians!) By that time Algeria's population consisted of 9,240,000 Muslim Algerians and 1,035,000 Europeans, mostly Frenchmen; the ratio was 9:1. The cities and industrial areas were all populated mostly by the French; only 15 per cent of their residents were natives. Even the capital city, Algiers, had the character of a French city. Four years later, as a result of a courageous decision by de Gaulle, against the will of Algerian-born Frenchmen, who even revolted, Algeria was offered the opportunity to settle her future by a free vote. On 1 July 1962, the majority voted for separation from France, and the country in its entirety, without the establishment of any "non-Muslim" enclaves, was proclaimed an independent state. Although many French Algerians were descendants of settlers who had arrived a century or more previously, 90 per cent of them left the country. Their places were immediately taken by natives. Soon foreign enclaves disappeared, and Algerian cities and industrial areas became national Muslim Algerian. In the ensuing years, France and Algeria, as two sovereign states, settled all their remaining affairs (e.g., expropriation of abandoned property). Today they continue to maintain close cultural and economic ties. For instance, France continues to provide more than one-third of Algeria's imports.

This example suggests a possible solution for Ukrainian-Russian relations. If the Russians recognize—but this time in all seriousness—the sovereignty of Ukraine (within the present boundaries of the Ukrainian SSR), a reasonable exchange of population could settle and end forever the tensions between these two peoples. This resolution would certainly facilitate the establishment of co-operation by two *equal partners*.

Can Russia produce a great statesman of the stature of de Gaulle? I pray it will!

I therefore believe that after such a catharsis of liberating distance, the two peoples, Ukrainians and Russians, will definitely free themselves from their paralyzing complexes: Ukrainians from their inferiority complex and Russians from an imperial "older brother" complex. Then the two rejuvenated peoples will find a true partnership and enter a new period of their relationship, that of two equals.

I regard this symposium as the first step in that direction.

Notes

1. Vasilii O. Kliuchevsky, *Kurs russkoi istorii*, Part 3, in *Sochineniia* (Moscow, 1957), 3: 118.

2. Nicholas Riasanovsky, *Nicholas I and Official Nationality in Russia, 1825–1855* (Berkeley and Los Angeles: University of California Press, 1967).

3. Oleksander Lototsky, *Storinky mynuloho* (Travaux de l'Institut Scientifique Ukrainien, vol. 12; Warsaw, 1933), 3: 357.

4. John S. Reshetar, Jr., "Lenin on Ukraine," *Annals of the Ukrainian Academy of Arts and Sciences in the United States* 9 (New York, 1961): 3–11.

5. Richard Pipes, "Peter Struve and Ukrainian Nationalism," *Eucharisterion: Essays Presented to Omeljan Pritsak* (=*Harvard Ukrainian Studies*, vols. 3–4 [Cambridge, Mass., 1979–1980]): 675–83.

6. *Ukrainska Radianska Entsyklopediia* (Kiev, 1963), 14: 133.

7. *Radianska Entsyklopediia Istorii Ukrainy* (Kiev, 1969–72), vol. 4.

8. Marc Raeff, *The Decembrist Movement* (Englewood Cliffs, N.J.: Prentice-Hall, 1966), 15.

HISTORY

Medieval and Early Modern History

Jaroslaw Pelenski

The Contest for the "Kievan Inheritance" in Russian-Ukrainian Relations: The Origins and Early Ramifications

The contest for the inheritance of Kievan Rus' has represented one of the oldest bones of contention in the history of Russian-Ukrainian cultural and political relations. It began among the Eastern Slavs in the second half of the eleventh century and culminated in the famous controversy between the "Northerners" and the "Southerners," that is, between Russian and Ukrainian scholars.[1] This controversy over the question of who are the legitimate heirs to the Kievan tradition—the Russians or the Ukrainians, which has continued until the present day, has had a profound impact on the development of the cultural perception, historical awareness, modern national consciousness, and the national mythology of the intelligentsias and even common people of the two sides involved.

The three major theories or schools of historical interpretation formulated by modern scholarship about the Kievan inheritance are as follows:

1) The monolineal and exclusivist Russian national theory developed already in the late eighteenth but basically in the nineteenth century in the works of Russian historians of the national-imperial school, such as V. N. Tatishchev, M. N. Karamzin, S. M. Solovev, and V. O. Kliuchevsky. Resting largely on historical-ideological claims and political-juridical theories formulated in Muscovy between the 1330s and the late 1560s, this theory was founded on the transfer of the ecclesiastical institution of the Kievan metropolitan see from Kiev first to Vladimir and eventually to Moscow, the uninterrupted dynastic continuity of the "Riurikides," and on the Kiev—(Rostov-Suzdal)—Vladimir—Moscow *translatio* theory.[2]

The notion that Muscovy is the only legitimate heir to Kievan Rus' has influenced the interpretations not only of Russian, but also of Western historiography. Views critical of Muscovite theories about the Kievan inheritance and the canons of Russian nineteenth-century national historiography generally, even if expressed by such distinguished Russian scholars and intellectuals as A. N. Pypin, P. N. Miliukov, A. E. Presniakov, and M. K. Liubavsky, have been conveniently disregarded.

2) The monolineal and exclusivist Ukrainian national theory advanced by Ukrainian national historiography between the 1840s and the end of the 1930s. It was summarized most clearly by Mykhailo Hrushevsky in his *Istoriia*

Ukrainy-Rusy and in his seminal article on the "rational organization" of early East Slavic history.[3] This Ukrainian theory found its own line of continuity, i.e., Kiev—Galicia-- Volhynia—Lithuania-Rus'—Cossack Ukraine, and utilized mainly territorial, ethnodemographic, social, and institutional arguments.

3) The official Soviet theory, which in ideological terms allots equal rights to the claims to the Kievan inheritance of the three East Slavic nations—that is, the Russians, the Ukrainians and the Belorussians—but which in fact is much closer to the traditional Russian theory and its forceful advocacy of Russian national interests than it is to the Ukrainian one. This Soviet theory also comes coupled with a distinct preference for research on Kievan Rus' conducted in Russia proper and by Russian scholars primarily. Thus the major studies of Kievan Rus' history since World War II have been written by Russian scholars, such as B. D. Grekov, B. A. Rybakov, M. N. Tikhomirov, M. K. Karger, and D. S. Likhachev. The last of these was the first to deal specifically with the origins of Muscovite preoccupation with the Kievan succession, again from an exclusively Russian perspective. It is significant that contemporary Kiev is not the principal centre for the study of the history and culture of Kievan Rus'.

The Soviet theory was first articulated in the late 1930s, but was not elevated to the status of an official state doctrine until the Tercentenary of the Pereiaslav Treaty in 1954. Then it was enunciated in a document of extra-ordinary importance entitled "Theses Concerning the Tercentenary of the Re-unification of Ukraine with Russia (1654–1954) Approved by the Central Committee of the Communist Party of the Soviet Union."[4] According to it, "the Russian, Ukrainian, and Belorussian peoples stem from one root, which is the Old Rus' nationality that formed the Old Rus' state—Kievan Rus'."[5] The formation of the three East Slavic peoples, or, in Soviet terminology, "national-ities" (*narodnosti*), took place, according to this theory, in the fourteenth and fifteenth centuries, when the Russian (or Great Russian) nationality played the most important role of guarding the Kievan tradition, not only during that formative period, but also in the two succeeding centuries.

Although there are serious differences of opinion among the protagonists of each of the three schools of thought, with a few exceptions like M. Hrushevsky and A. E. Presniakov, they all share several assumptions about the nature of the Kievan Rus' state. One of them is that Kievan Rus' was a well integrated polity based upon a unified Old Rus' people or nationality (*narodnost*) of East Slavic ethnic origin inhabiting the "Rus' land," which allegedly nurtured an inherent proclivity for territorial, ethnonational, and political unity.[6] They therefore stressed the ethnic homogeneity, political unity, and cultural coherence of Kievan Rus', familiar concepts in all nineteenth-century national ideologies. From this perspective, it was not difficult for both Russian and Ukrainian historians to go a step further and develop coherent and well-integrated continuity theories that linked their own latter-day nationalities with ancient Kievan Rus'. To do so they had only to modernize and refine earlier versions and couch them in appropriate academic terminology.

This image of a unified, integrated, and even ethnically defined Old Rus' which has been handed down to us by several generations of scholars, however, reflects the ideological concerns of the authors and editors of the Kievan chronicle, *Russkaia pravda*, Metropolitan Ilarion's *Sermon on Law and Grace,* and the *Vitae* of the Kievan rulers more than it does the political, cultural, and ethnic realities of Rus'. Kievan Rus' was never really a unified polity. It was a loosely bound, ill-defined, and heterogeneous conglomeration of lands and cities inhabited by tribes and population groups whose loyalties were primarily territorial, *landespatriotisch,* and urban but not national in the modern sense of the term. They were ruled for a time by a dynasty which very soon dissolved into several rival subdynasties which fought each other more fiercely than they battled the much-maligned nomadic "heathens" of the East. Although the decline and dissolution of Kievan Rus' are usually attributed to "bad neighbours," internal factors played a larger part. Among them were the victory of patrimonial territorial states and city-states over multiterritorial and heterogeneous empires or protoimperial polities.

Kievan Rus' was a transitional polity which exhibited some of the characteristics of an empire, but it lacked a well-structured imperial framework. Comparing it to the Carolingian Empire or the Holy Roman Empire of the German Nation is, therefore, not quite justified, not only because of differences in ethnic and territorial composition, but also because Kievan Rus' lacked a hierarchy of dynasties and an administrative superstructure. The "Riurikide" dynasty and the ruling elite of Kiev and the Kievan land—the most developed patrimonial-territorial unit and for a time the senior principality within the broader multiterritorial conglomerate of Kievan Rus'—attempted to impose on their highly diverse polity the integrative concept of *russkaia zemlia* ("the Rus' land") and the unifying notion of a Rus' people. In the long run they failed, however, for both concepts soon took on entirely different meanings. The concept of Rus' did, however, refer to a relatively integrated cultural entity based on the Orthodox religion, a Slavicized Byzantine culture, and a transplanted *lingua franca* in the form of Church Slavonic. This cultural unity was elevated to an ideal which, in the realm of ideology, was applied to the political and ethnic spheres as well. The city of Kiev and the Kievan land were among the oldest and richest in that part of the world and Kiev had long been the actual or nominal capital of Rus'. This lent prestige to Kiev from the perspective of the new polities that were emerging from the amorphous superstructure known as Kievan Rus'. The new polities could emancipate themselves so easily not because an artificially invented Old Rus' nationality had disintegrated into three new nationalities, but because the old cities and lands provided a foundation for transforming ethnoterritorial groups into peoples or nationalities. For a variety of reasons their elites then laid claims to what they perceived as their rightful inheritance, and these claims ultimately assumed the status of national myths.

The first phase of the contest between the claimants of the Kievan inheritance, or more specifically the senior capital city of Kiev itself and Kievan Rus', lasted from the late eleventh to the late thirteenth century. Until the mid-1260s it was characterized by political and ideological succession struggles between the subdynasties that ruled the four patrimonial entities of Chernigov, Suzdal-Vladimir, Smolensk, and Galicia-Volhynia. These struggles were followed by the transfer of the Kievan metropolitan see from Kiev, first to Vladimir from around 1250 to 1300, and then to Moscow in 1326, and by the establishment in the first half of the fourteenth century of the Halych metropolitanate. This unprecedented division of the Kievan metropolitanate marked the beginning of the conflict between Vladimir and Galicia over the Kievan ecclesiastical legacy.

Of the four contenders, the house of Chernigov conducted the most protracted struggle, the beginnings of which can be traced all the way back to the 1070s.[7] From that time until the Mongol invasion of the Rus' states in the 1230s-40s, several princes of the Chernigov dynasty managed intermittently to ascend the Kievan throne and rule with varying degrees of success. Their aim, it appears, was to govern Rus' from Kiev using the practices and customs observed in their own patrimonial-territorial principality. Since the principality of Chernigov disintegrated after the Mongol invasion, its competition for Kiev had no lasting historical consequences. The Chernigov dynasty did not die out until the beginning of the fifteenth century, and some of its rulers even retained the title of "Grand Prince" of Chernigov. The title had no real significance at that time, however, and no evidence suggests that the Chernigov dynasty perpetuated its claims to be legitimate Kievan heirs in that later period.[8]

Until the end of the 1160s, the contenders for the Kievan inheritance aimed at full control of Kiev and the adjoining land and at reestablishing the traditional relationship with other parts of Rus' that existed in the reigns of Volodimer I, Iaroslav I, Volodimer Monomakh, and Mstislav I Harold. Throughout that early period, the takeover of Kiev itself was regarded by the contenders as the goal to be achieved, since Kiev was considered the most prestigious city and the proper capital from which to govern the Rus' polity.

That perception changed dramatically with the sack of Kiev in 1169 by an army acting on the orders of Andrei Bogoliubsky. That event especially shifted the attitude toward Kiev of the Russian ruling elite in the then emerging Suzdal-Vladimir principality from respect to ambivalence.[9] In its formative years, the Suzdal-Vladimir principality, especially during the reigns of such rulers as Andrei Bogoliubsky (1157–75), Vsevolod III Iurevich (1176–1212), and Aleksandr Iaroslavich Nevsky (1252–63), was torn between the need to retain dynastic and historical ties with Kiev, on the one hand, and the desire to diminish its status and enhance that of the rising patrimonial-territorial Grand Principality of Suzdal-Vladimir on the other. The desire to enhance first Vladimir, its capital on the Kliazma River, and later Moscow at the expense of

Kiev is evident in both practice and theory, as can be detected in contemporary ideological writings.[10]

Vladimirian rulers claimed the Kievan inheritance through dynastic connections to the Kievan dynasty. This provided them with the justification to refer to Kiev as their "patrimony and ancestral property," and to develop a set of ideological justifications to substantiate their "rights" to Kiev, based on the assertion that the Christianization of their land and the founding of the city of Vladimir had been accomplished by Prince Volodimer I. Using this assertion, parallels could then be drawn between Bogoliubsky and Volodimer I, who had aspired to be the senior prince of all Rus'. Andrei Bogoliubsky attempted to subordinate the other princes of Old Rus' by referring to them as his vassals (*podruchniki*).

At the same time, the Vladimirian rulers were responsible for two sacks of Kiev—directly for the sack of 1169 ("for three days they plundered the entire city of Kiev with churches and monasteries; and they seized icons and books and chasubles")[11] and indirectly for the sack of 1203. They also reduced the status of Kiev as the capital and the centre of Rus' in order to elevate Vladimir to the status of principal city of Old Rus'. Under Bogoliubsky an attempt was made to establish an independent metropolitanate in order to undermine Kiev's position as the ecclesiastical centre of Rus', but it was not successful. At the same time, an ideological program was developed to supersede Kiev and replace it with Vladimir. It included undertakings such as the building of new impressive churches, the development of the cult of the Icon of Our Lady of Vladimir (an icon originally taken from the Kievan land), the celebration of the Feast of the Veneration of the Virgin Mary, a new Feast of the Saviour, and the veneration of the newly discovered relics of Bishop Leontii of Rostov.[12]

An ambivalent attitude toward Kiev is also evident in the political program advanced by Aleksandr Nevsky, as reflected in contemporary chronicle writings and in the ideological statements made in his *Vita*. Nevsky was credited by some chroniclers with having succeeded in obtaining from the Mongols "Kiev and the whole land of Rus'."[13] According to his *Vita*, written from a devotional point of view, he was linked dynastically with the saintly *srodniki* Boris and Gleb and Iaroslav I. These references may be later interpolations in the text. The crucial opening passage of the *Vita* states only that his dynastic lineage reached back to his father Iaroslav Vsevolodovich and his grandfather Vsevolod III Iurievich, both of Suzdal-Vladimir. The same *Vita* refers to a eulogy allegedly delivered by Metropolitan Cyrill at Nevsky's funeral in which the Metropolitan proclaimed that upon Nevsky's death, "the sun has set in the Suzdal land."[14] Curiously enough, the *Vita* emphasizes the Suzdal-Vladimir dynastic lineage of Aleksandr Nevsky and extols the image of the Suzdal land, but refrains from mentioning Kiev and the Rus' land.

The Vladimirian claims to Kiev were, therefore, not formulated with the purpose of supporting a Kievan revival or in anticipation of its glorious future.

On the contrary, Kiev was to be subordinated to the rising capital city of Vladimir. The Kievan inheritance would serve as a convenient tool for gaining hegemony for the Suzdal-Vladimir principality over the lands of Old Rus'. That ambivalent attitude toward the Kievan inheritance has remained a Russian tradition, regardless of the changing nature of the Russian state or the capital city of the Russian Empire. In 1482, for example, when the Crimean Tatars sacked Kiev at the instigation of Ivan III, the Grand Prince committed blasphemy by accepting from Khan Mengli–Girei a gift of the sacred vessels plundered from the Saint Sophia Church. Significantly, this happened during a gap in the development of the governmental Muscovite theory concerning the Kiev—Suzdal-Vladimir—Moscow *translatio* formulated between the mid-1450s and 1504.[15]

The last principal claimant to the Kievan inheritance was Galician-Volhynian Rus', a patrimonial-territorial state.[16] Its dynasty raised claims to the Kievan succession about half a century after the princes of Suzdal-Vladimir. Originally the intentions of the Galician-Volhynian dynasty were not even in direct conflict with those entertained by Suzdal-Vladimir, but they were more on a collision course with an older contender, the house of Chernigov.

Similar in several respects to their northern competitors, rulers of Galicia-Volhynia such as Roman Mstyslavych (1199–1205) and Danylo Romanovych (1237–64) succeeded for brief periods in controlling Kiev and, by extension, southwestern Rus'. Their ultimate aim was to claim succession to all Rus' in order to attain an exalted status for their principality among the lands of Old Rus'. Like Andrei Bogoliubsky and Vsevolod III Iurevich, Roman and Danylo were not interested either in ruling Kiev or in ruling from Kiev, according to the old tradition. They preferred to exercise the power of investiture and install minor princes or later, in the case of Danylo, even a governor. Danylo's replacement of a vassal prince by a governor can be interpreted as an additional contributing factor to the decline of Kiev in both the political and judicial spheres.

The Galician-Volhynian dynasty devised its own ideological program vis-à-vis Kiev and the all-Rus' inheritance based on the law of investiture, on patrimonial ties with the Kievan dynasty, and on the special relationship to Kiev of religious objects. This program is set forth in the Galician-Volhynian Chronicle, the third major component of the Hypatian Codex.[17] Of particular significance is the special "Introduction" to the Hypatian Codex, which explicates the exclusive historical and dynastic rights of the Galician-Volhynian house to the Kievan succession:

> These are the names of the Kievan princes who ruled in Kiev until the conquest of Batu, who was in [the state of] paganism: The first to rule in Kiev were co-princes Dir and Askold. After [them followed] Oleg. And following Oleg [came] Igor. And following Igor [came] Sviatoslav. And after Sviatoslav [came] Iaropolk. And following Iaropolk [came] Volodimer, who ruled in Kiev and who

enlightened the Rus' land with the holy baptism. And following Volodimer Sviatopolk began to rule. And after Sviatopolk [came] Iaroslav. And following Iaroslav [came] Iziaslav. And Iziaslav [was succeeded] by Sviatopolk. And following Sviatopolk [came] Vsevolod. And after him [followed] Volodimer Monomakh. And following him [came] Mstislav. And after Mstislav [followed] Iaropolk. And following Iaropolk [came] Vsevolod. And after him [followed] Iziaslav. And following Iziaslav [came] Rostislav. And he [was followed] by Mstislav. And following him [came] Gleb. And he was [followed] by Volodimer. And following him [came] Roman. And after Roman [followed] Sviatoslav. And following him [came] Riurik. And after Riurik [followed] Roman. And after Roman [came] Mstislav. And after him [followed] Iaroslav. And following Iaroslav [came] Volodimer Riurikovych. Danylo installed him in his own place in Kiev. Following Volodimer, [when Kiev was governed by] Danylo's governor Dmytro, Batu conquered Kiev.[18]

This narration was composed either just after the conquest of Kiev by Batu in 1240, or after Danylo had made his final attempt to reclaim Kiev from the Tatars in the late 1250s, or just after Danylo's death in 1264. The line of Kievan rulers it provides from its origins to Danylo and his governor Dmytro is intended not only to demonstrate an uninterrupted dynastic line from the Kievan to the Galician-Volhynian rulers, but also to show that at the beginning of the thirteenth century the centre of power was transferred to southwestern Rus'.[19] According to it, the last legitimate overlord in Kiev before the Mongol-Tatar invasion was none other than Danylo, who invested the last nominal ruler, a vassal prince, and ultimately a governor. Therefore, any attempt to lay claim to the Kievan succession on the part of other Rus' rulers, including the Suzdal-Vladimir line, which for a brief time between the early 1240s and the early 1260s succeeded with the help of Mongol-Tatars in obtaining the title to Kiev,[20] was illegitimate and invalid. This "Introduction" to the Hypatian Codex reflects the contents of many parts of this work, especially the Galician-Volhynian Chronicle, and provides evidence that both the codex and the chronicle were compiled to justify, among other things, the Galician-Volhynian claims to the Kievan inheritance.

The ideological programs of the two dynasties differed in several respects. The compilers of the Galician-Volhynian Chronicle, in contrast to their Suzdal-Vladimirian counterparts, did not attempt to diminish the image of Kiev in favour of any one of their principal cities (Halych, for example), nor did the Galician-Volhynian rulers engage in a sack or plundering of that ancient city. The compilers of the Galician-Volhynian Chronicle treated Halych as an important centre of Galicia-Volhynia, but they did not try to substitute Halych for Kiev. Nothing in the Galician-Volhynian Chronicle suggests that it advocated any idea of Halych as a "second Kiev."[21] Steps were taken to attribute religious significance to the founding and rebuilding of towns such as Kholm and Volodymyr-Volynsky, but never with the aim of undermining the status of Kiev. They were simply meant to show that the Galician and Volhynian lands also had towns worthy of note. An attempt was even made to link those cities with Kiev, as attested, for example, in the account of the rebuilding of Kholm following Batu's invasion. When the Church of St. John was erected, it was said that Danylo brought icons and a bell from Kiev and donated them to the new church.[22]

Although the two territorial states observed many of the same religious conventions, including a providential interpretation of history, religion played a much greater role in the Suzdal-Vladimirian ideological program than it did in the Galician-Volhynian counterpart. Religious practices such as the veneration of icons, celebration of religious feasts, and adoration of relics of saints constituted an important part of the Suzdal-Vladimirian ideological program. The Galician-Volhynian elite was more pragmatic, as evidenced by data in the Kievan Chronicle pertaining to Galicia-Volhynia and in the Galician-Volhynian Chronicle itself. It did not involve itself in developing a system of religious ideological justifications, and its outlook remained more worldly.

Comparable differences can be seen in the relations between the secular power and ecclesiastical authority of the two states. Almost from the beginning, Vladimirian rulers aggressively interfered in the affairs of the church, first by attempting to organize an anti-Kievan metropolitanate, somewhat later by endeavouring to dominate the Kievan metropolitanate and, finally—just like the later Muscovite rulers—by making every possible effort to retain exclusive control over the Kievan metropolitan see, which was eventually moved to the north. Such a transfer was accomplished easily, because the Metropolitan See of Kiev and All Rus' was still an ecclesiastical province of the Byzantine patriarchate.

The Galician and Volhynian rulers also had their conflicts with ecclesiastical authorities, especially after two of their appointees to the metropolitanate, Cyrill and Peter, proved to be "turncoats." Those two metropolitans did not hesitate to accommodate themselves to the political and ecclesiastical designs of the Vladimirian and Muscovite rulers, the Golden Horde, the Patriarchate of Constantinople, and the Byzantine Empire, all of whom were interested in maintaining the unity of the Kievan metropolitan see and its centre, first in Vladimir and later in Moscow.[23]

When this new ecclesiastical arrangement proved intolerable, because the metropolitans of Kiev had become tools in the hands of the rising Muscovite rulers and the religious needs of the southwestern Rus' were competely neglected, the Galician-Volhynian rulers simply curtailed their contacts with the Vladimir and Moscow-based Kievan metropolitanate and negotiated with the Byzantine Patriarchate for the establishment of a separate Halych Metropolitanate of "Little Rus'."[24] In contrast to their Vladimirian and Muscovite counterparts, who clung tenaciously to the administrative link with the Kievan church, the Galician-Volhynian ruling elite was more inclined to seek pragmatic solutions to religious and ecclesiastical problems and to abandon its ecclesiastical administrative claims to Kiev.

When it came to secular claims, however, the Galician-Volhynian dynasty and elite retained their claims to the Kievan inheritance through historical and legal arguments. In them, the interchangeable use of the concepts *Rus',* *russkaia zemlia,* and *vsia zemlia russkaia* played a significant role. The term "Rus'" and its variants, "the Rus' land" and "all the land of Rus'," lost their original ambiguity and acquired geographically and politically clearly defined meanings that pertained from about the mid-twelfth century to the Kievan and Pereiaslav lands and subsequently to the southwestern Rus' in general.[25] In the thirteenth century and throughout the first half of the fourteenth these terms referred to the Kievan, Galician and Volhynian lands, and at approximately the same time began to converge geographically with the emerging concept *Ukraina* (Ukraine), which appears for the first time in the Hypatian Codex under the year 1187.[26]

The concepts *Rus', russkaia zemlia,* and *vsia zemlia russkaia* were also used to mean Suzdal-Vladimir, though less frequently than they were applied to Galicia-Volhynia. In fact, the preponderance of available evidence suggests that over extended periods the use of these terms began to decline in the north-eastern regions in favour of other terms. For example, during the reigns of Andrei Bogoliubsky, Vsevolod III Iurevich and Aleksandr Nevsky, the terms "Suzdal land" and "Vladimir" were more commonly used, while following the death of Aleksandr Nevsky and until approximately the mid-fifteenth century, the concepts "Suzdal land," "Grand Principality of Vladimir," and eventually "Moscow" were employed to denote the territories of northeastern Rus'. The traditional terms *Rus', russkaia zemlia,* and *vsia zemlia russkaia* were revived and applied to Russia proper beginning in the second third of the fifteenth century, but by then they acquired still different connotations.

The Galician-Volhynian dynasty and elite, on the other hand, continued to advance claims to "Rus'," "the Rus' land," and "all the land of Rus' " and adamantly to restate their historical and dynastic pretensions to those entities until the very end of the state's existence. Beginning with the rule of Iurii Lvovych (1301–8) and during the co-reign of his sons Andrii and Lev (c. 1309–c. 1321–2), and subsequently of Iurii II Boleslav (1324–40), the application of these concepts and claims to the inheritance in question were recorded in documentary sources, in the titles on charters, and even affixed on a seal. The seal used by King Iurii and his successors, for example, portrayed the king *in maiestatis,* crowned and seated on a throne with a sceptre in his hand. The inscription in Latin surrounding the central image read: *s(igillu) domini georgi regis rusie.* The reverse side of the seal, which depicted a mounted warrior with a shield in his hand, contained the inscription in Latin: *s. domini georgi ducis ladimerie.*[27]

The use of Latin in these inscriptions and in documents is indicative both of the Westernization of the conduct of business affairs in the ruler's chancery and of the evolution political thought had taken in Galicia-Volhynia. It had already manifested itself in the Galician-Volhynian state under Danylo, the first native king of Galicia,[28] whose (and later King Iurii's) royalist conception of rule is unique in the history of the East Slavic world. Iurii's sons Andrii and Lev continued in traditional fashion to claim Rus' in their titles, as attested in their charters: *Dei gracia duces totius terrae Russiae, Galiciae et Ladimeriae*, and *dux ladomiriensis et dominus terrae Russiae.*[29] The same can be said about Iurii II Boleslav, who in 1327 referred to himself as *Dux Terre Russie, Galicie et Ladimere*[30] and who, apparently under Byzantine influence, applied the name of Rus' exclusively to Little Rus' in the Charter of 1335, where for the first time he styled himself *dux totius Russiae Minoris.*[31]

This brief analysis of the early history of the contest to claim the legacy of Old Rus' can yield some conclusions concerning its origins and its early ramifications. The role of the Kievan inheritance in Russian-Ukrainian relations defies convenient generalization. The complexity of the problem is compounded by its elusive quality, by its involvement in the sociocultural conditioning of the two peoples' intelligentsias and other segments of their population, and by its absorption into the scholarly paradigms of linguists, ethnographers, and historians of various backgrounds and methodological approaches. Under such circumstances, historians, instead of asking popular "new" questions, might do well to reopen old ones and offer some "unpopular" tentative answers.

The contest for the Kievan inheritance is neither an invention of the contending Russian and Ukrainian national historiographic schools, nor does it fall into the category of traditional territorial disputes, although certain parallels can be drawn with other historical, religious and national controversies from the Middle Ages to the present day. The notion that national legitimacy rests in tracing one's heritage back to Kievan roots is deeply imbedded in the historical consciousnesses of Ukrainians and Russians alike, though originally it had no nationalistic implications in the modern sense. For this reason, projecting contemporary national concerns into the history of Old Rus' or speaking of a conflict between "nationalities" in the early medieval period, followed by assumptions about the existence of a unified Old Rus' state, is erroneous and misleading.

There should be no misunderstanding about the realities of the period under consideration. Both hard and circumstantial evidence suggests that little unity or harmony existed in the Old Rus' polity and that the desire of its component parts to go their separate ways manifested itself early in its history and prevailed before the Mongol invasion. Following the reign of Iaroslav I the Wise, the dynasties, the lands, the cities, and the people of Old Rus' apparently had no real feeling of unity or need for East Slavic "togetherness." Some of them interacted with the nomads of the southern steppes, some with the Poles and the Hungarians, others with the Meria and the Ugro-Finnic tribes. Early in its history, Old Rus' displayed all the features of a multi-civilizational and proto-imperial polity. Two of its territorial entities, Suzdal-Vladimir and Galicia-Volhynia, followed separate roads of *Staatsbildung* to form two clearly defined and independent monarchical states. These two states shared a common religious and cultural heritage and even found themselves confronted with some similar sociopolitical domestic problems, such as the conflict between the monarchical power and the strong *boiar* groups aspiring to greater political influence, and their elites continued to maintain contacts.

However, the two states differed in their relationships with other powers, entered into alliances with different partners, belonged to different civilizational and commercial communities, and were in more intimate contact with neighbouring states and societies than with each other. Furthermore, the evolution of their two political systems and their general ideological outlook diverged markedly and the two states were founded on dissimilar ethnically mixed strata, which, in fact, contributed to the definitive internal consolidation of the two separate peoples.

The two states displayed contrasting attitudes in their political responses to the Mongol-Tatar supremacy in the *ulus* Rus'. The Suzdal-Vladimirian rulers were ready to co–operate with the Mongols and to serve in the Horde's administration of the Rus' lands. The southwestern rulers, such as Danylo of Galicia-Volhynia and Mikhail of Chernigov, actively opposed the Mongol domination of their states.[32] When Danylo's anti-Mongol policies suffered defeat, his successors managed to contain Tatar influences, and as a result their lands apparently were not integrated as effectively into the Horde's tax collection system as those of northeastern Rus'. For obvious reasons, the Suzdal-Vladimirian chronicles are rather circumspect in their treatment of the Mongol-Tatar rule and the active co-operation of its dynasty with the Golden Horde.

Similarly, opposite approaches were taken by the rulers of the two states with respect to participation in the anti-Mongol coalition and the related issue of the union of churches, both sponsored by Pope Innocent IV. Danylo of Galicia-Volhynia, like Mendovg of Lithuania, was inclined to join the anti-Mongol coalition and, although he actually did not accept the union, he was involved in the negotiations. As a result both rulers were rewarded, in 1253 and 1251 respectively, by Pope Innocent IV with royal crowns for their support of his initiatives. Aleksandr Nevsky was evidently not interested in joining an anti-Mongol coalition, just as he firmly rejected papal overtures concerning the unification of churches.[33]

When Suzdal-Vladimir and Galicia-Volhynia departed on their separate courses they joined two different civilizational communities. Suzdal-Vladimir became part of a northeastern community of Russians, surrounded by other Eastern Slavs in the southwest, west, and northwest, Ugro-Finnic tribes in the northeast, and Volga Bulgars in the east. Its rulers were chiefly interested in controlling the Novgorod commerce and the Volga trade route. Following the conquest of the Rus' state by the Mongol-Tatars and their takeover of the Volga commerce, Suzdal-Vladimir became their junior partner in the Volga trade. Their geographic location made the Suzdalians and Vladimirians the natural partners first of the Volga Bulgars and later of the Mongol-Tatars. Thus, their state was incorporated into the imperial structure of the Golden Horde and became part of a new civilizational entity along the banks of the Volga River.

Galicia-Volhynia, on the other hand, constituted an integral part of the East Central European civilizational community that included Polish territorial states, Hungary, Bohemia, and even Austria, and belonged to the southern commercial complex which embraced those countries. The borders of this complex were defined by the Dnieper River in the northeast and the Danube in the southwest, with access to the Black Sea in the southeast. The famous old "route from the Varangians to the Greeks" had ceased to function effectively before the Mongol invasion of Rus', not only because salt routes had been cut off by the nomads, but also—and primarily—because the commercial interests of the territorial states found new avenues and better opportunities outside the old framework.

Just as distinct were the differences in the development of their monarchical models, although at the outset they shared common conceptions of rulership (prince, principate) and utilized analogous (nominal reverential) titulature (grand prince and even *tsar*). In Suzdal-Vladimir the conception of rulership emphasized the senior grand princely position enjoyed by the rulers of that state, and its authors even made use of the Byzantine author Agapetus to buttress the exalted nature of the ruler's status.[34] That status was based on a combination of East Slavic, Byzantine, and later Mongol-Tatar models. Unlike its northeastern counterpart, Galicia-Volhynia derived its notion of rulership from the East Slavic principate and the European royal tradition in its Hungarian and Polish manifestations.

Even though the two monarchical systems were based on the theory of the divine right of rulers and both elites shared an Orthodox providential worldview, certain ideological differences were obvious even in the formative stages of their development. In the official ideology of the Grand Principality of Suzdal-Vladimir, for example, the Orthodox religious component played a greater role than it did in Galicia-Volhynia, which was relatively tolerant of other peoples, even those belonging to the Catholic fold. They displayed an open-minded approach toward the vexed issue of the union of churches under papal auspices.[35] The only villains, according to the Galician-Volhynian ideology, were the "heathens," that is, the various nomadic peoples of the steppe who lived in a symbiotic relationship with the people of the Old Rus' lands. But even this attitude was not rigid, for it was no coincidence that some nomadic folklore (the moving legend of the *ievshan zillia*, for example) found its way into the Galician-Volhynian Chronicle.[36]

Developments on the territories of Old Rus' ultimately led to the formation of two separate nationalities, that is, the Suzdal-Vladimir Russians and the Ruthenians, or, in other words, the proto-Russians and the proto-Ukrainians. Many factors were instrumental in transforming a population into a relatively integrated people in medieval times: territorial integration and continuity, consolidation of a territorial monarchical state, conduct of dynastic politics, participation in a civilizational community, development of a common religious culture and of secular attitudes, social changes and economic interests, intermingling of elites and population groups. The histories of the Suzdal-Vladimirian and Galician-Volhynian states provide good examples of the formative processes of the two medieval territorial states and of the two peoples.

Which of them was more justified in claiming the Kievan inheritance? The answer depends on the significance one wants to attribute to normative value and on the weight one wants to ascribe to the various pieces of available evidence. If one were to answer it on the basis of the religious evidence exclusively, or on a combination of that and some aspects of dynastic politics, the Principality of Suzdal-Vladimir would have to be credited with having a serious claim. If, on the other hand, all the other factors, such as territorial continuity, ethnic identity, common social and institutional traditions, dynastic politics and religious or cultural evidence are added in, the Galician-Volhynian competitor emerges as the more legitimate successor. Since it was precisely this contest for the Kievan inheritance that significantly contributed to the splitting off of the Russian and Ukrainian peoples and to their consolidation as two separate entities to begin with, the debate over the Kievan succession that has followed since the nineteenth century can in itself be regarded as a further step in the protracted process of building a nation.

Notes

1. For an introduction to this controversy, see A. N. Pypin, *Istoriia russkoi etnografii*, vol. 3, Etnografiia malorusskaia (St. Petersburg, 1891): 301–38. A Soviet perspective is to be found in N. K. Gudzii, "Literatura Kievskoi Rusi v istorii bratskikh literatur," *Literatura Kievskoi Rusi i ukrainsko-russkoe literaturnoe edinenie XVII–XVIII vekov* (Kiev, 1989), 13–43.

2. On the origins of this theory and the literature on the subject, consult J. Pelenski, "The Origins of the Official Muscovite Claims to the 'Kievan Inheritance'," *Harvard Ukrainian Studies* (hereafter *HUS*) 1, no. 1 (1977): 29–52; *Idem.*, "The Emergence of the Muscovite Claims to the Byzantine–Kievan 'Imperial Inheritance'," *HUS* 7 (1983): 520–31; *Idem.*, "The Sack of Kiev of 1482 in Contemporary Muscovite Chronicle Writing," *HUS* 3–4 (1979–80): 638–49;

Idem., "The Origins of the Muscovite Ecclesiastical Claims to the Kievan Inheritance," to be published in the Acts of Congress devoted to "The Origin and Development of the Slavic–Byzantine Christianity: the Baptism of 988 in the Long Run," (Rome, 3–6 May 1988), *Studi storici* of the Istituto Storico Italiano.

3. M. Hrushevsky, *Istoriia Ukrainy-Rusy*, 10 vols. (3rd rep. ed., New York, 1954–8); "The Traditional Scheme of Russian History and the Problem of a Rational Organization of the History of Eastern Slavs 1909," in *Annals of the Ukrainian Academy of Arts and Sciences in the U.S.* 2 (1952): 355–64.

4. *Tezy pro 300–richchia vozziednannia Ukrainy z Rosiieiu (1654–1954 rr.) skhvaleni Tsentralnym Komitetom Komunistychnoi Partii Radianskoho Soiuzu* (Kiev, 1954).

5. Ibid., 16.

6. For an antithetical view, see the study by O. Pritsak, "Origins of Rus'," *Russian Review* 36, no. 3 (July 1977): 249–74, as well as his *The Origin of Rus'*, Volume One (Old Scandinavian Sources other than Sagas), (Cambridge, Massachusetts, 1981).

7. The history of the Chernigov land and dynasty has been treated by P. V. Golubovskii, *Istoriia Severskoi zemli do poloviny XIV stoletiia* (Kiev, 1881); D. Bagalei, *Istoriia Severskoi zemli do poloviny XIV stoletiia* (Kiev, 1882); R. V. Zotov, "O Chernigovskikh kniaziakh po Liubetskomu sinodiku i o Cherni-govskom kniazhestve v Tatarskoe vremia," *Letopis zaniatii Arkheograficheskoi Kommissii 1882–84 gg.*, Vypusk 9 (St. Petersburg, 1893), 1–327, 1–47; "Cherni-govskie kniazia," *Russkii biograficheskii slovar* (St. Petersburg, 1905), 22: 231–67; Hrushevsky, *Istoriia Ukrainy-Rusy*, 2: 312–38; O. Andriiashev, "Narys istorii kolonizatsii Siverskoi zemli do pochatku XVI viku," *Zapysky istorychno-filolohichnoho viddilu Vseukrainskoi Akademii Nauk u Kyivi*, kn. 20 (1928), 95–128; V. V. Mavrodin, "Chernigovskoe kniazhestvo," *Ocherki istorii SSSR* (Period feodalizma IX-XV v.v. v dvukh chastiakh), Part 1 (Moscow, 1953), 393–400; A. K. Zaitsev, "Chernigovkoe kniazhestvo," in L. G. Beskrovny (ed.), *Drevnerusskie kniazhestva X-XIII vv.* (Moscow, 1975), 57–117; M. Dimnik, *Mikhail, Prince of Chernigov and Grand Prince of Kiev 1224–1246* (Toronto, 1981); B. A. Rybakov, *Kievskaia Rus' i russkie kniazhestva XII-XIII vv.* (Moscow, 1982), 498–508.

8. Hrushevsky, *Istoriia Ukrainy-Rusy*, 3: 175–81. The last document of ideological importance bearing on the activities of the house of Chernigov was the *Vita* of Mikhail of Chernigov. A. N. Nasonov advanced a plausible hypothesis that the execution of Mikhail by the Mongols in the Horde was the ultimate act in the struggle between the houses of Chernigov and Vladimir for seniority in the lands of Rus' (*Mongoly i Rus'* [Moscow-Leningrad, 1940/1969], 24–8). In his political biography of Mikhail, Dimnik advanced the hypothesis that the principality of Chernigov had definitely won the contest for Kiev and had actually become the principal force in Rus' politics on the eve of the Mongol invasion (*Mikhail, Prince of Chernigov*, pp. 136–9). Dimnik's hypothesis is based on the situation in the years 1235–6, which could easily have changed later even if the Mongols had not invaded Rus'. The fact that the principality of Chernigov ceased to be a serious factor in Rus' politics after Mikhail's death supports the established view

that the principality was internally weak. The title phrase of the *Liubetskii sinodik* refers to the grand princes of Chernigov and Kiev, only in a factual manner, but, significantly, gives precedence to Chernigov (Zotov, *O Chernigovskikh kniaziakh...*, p. 24).

9. For general accounts of the history of the Suzdal-Vladimir principality, see D. A. Korsakov, *Meria i Rostovskoe kniazhevstvo*; *Ocherki iz istorii Rostovo-Suzdalskoi zemli* (Kazan, 1872); A. E. Presniakov, *Obrazovanie velikorusskago gosudarstva: Ocherki po istorii XIII-XV stoletii* (Petrograd, 1918), 26–47; A. N. Nasonov, *"Russkaia zemlia" i obrazovanie territorii drevnerusskago gosudarstva* (Moscow, 1951), 173–96; *Idem*, "Vladimiro-Suzdalskoe kniazhesto," *Ocherki istorii SSSR* (Period feodalizma IX-XV vv. v dvukh chastiakh), Part 1 (Moscow, 1953), 320–34; N. N. Voronin, "Vladimiro-Suzdalskaia zemlia X-XIII v.," *Idem.*, *Problemy istorii dokapitalisticheskikh obshchestv*, V-VI (1935); *Idem.*, *Pamiatniki suzdalskogo zodchestva XI-XIII v.* (Moscow-Leningrad, 1945); *Idem.*, *Zodchestvo Severo-Vostochnoi Rusi XII-XV vv.*, 2 vols. (Moscow, 1961–2); *Idem.*, *Vladimir, Bogoliubovo, Suzdal, Iurev-Polskii*, 3rd ed. (Moscow, 1967), and his concise article "Vladimiro-Suzdalskoe kniazhestvo," in *Sovetskaia istoricheskaia entsiklopediia*, vol. 3, cols. 528–33.

10. Ideological writings pertaining to the age of Andrei Bogoliubsky have been discussed by N. N. Voronin, "Andrei Bogoliubskii i Luka Khrizoverg: Iz istorii russko–vizantiiskikh otnoshenii XII v.," *Vizantiiskii vremennik* (hereafter *VV*) 21 (1962): 29–50; *Idem.*, "Zhitie Leontiia Rostovskogo i vizantiisko-russkie otnosheniia vo vtoroi polovine XII veka," *VV* 23 (1963): 23–46; *Idem.*, "Povest ob ubiistve Andreia Bogoliuskogo i ee avtor," *Istoriia SSSR*, 1963, no. 3: 80–97; *Idem.*, "Skazanie o pobede nad Bolgarami 1164 g. i prazdnike Spasa," *Problemy obshchestvenno-politicheskoi istorii Rossii i slavianskikh stran (Sbornik statei k 70–letiiu akademika M. N. Tikhomirova)*, ed. V. I. Shunkov (Moscow, 1963), 88–92; *Idem.*, "Iz istorii russko-vizantiiskoi tserkovnoi borby XII veka," *VV* 24 (1965): 190–218; W. Vodoff, "Un 'parti théocratique' dans la Russie du XIIe siècle?" *Cahiers de civilisation médiévale* 17, no. 3 (1974): 193–215; Iu. A. Limonov, *Letopisanie Vladimiro-Suzdalskoi Rusi* (Leningrad, 1967); E. S. Hurwitz, *Prince Andrej Bogoljubskij: The Man and the Myth* (Studia Historica et Philologica 12, Sectio Slavica 4) (Florence, 1980); J. Pelenski, "The Contest for the 'Kievan Succession' (1155–1175): The Religious Ecclesiastical Dimension," Proceedings of the International Congress Commemorating the Millennium of Christianity in Rus'–Ukraine, *HUS* 12–13 (1988–9): 761–80.

11. This statement was made by the compiler of the Suzdal–Vladimirian Chronicle (*Polnoe sobranie russkikh letopisei* [hereafter *PSRL*] 1, issue 2 (1927): 354. On the events of 1169, confer J. Pelenski, "The Sack of Kiev of 1169: Its Significance for the Succession to Kievan Rus'," *HUS* 9, no. 3/4 (1987): 303–16.

12. For a discussion of the various aspects of this program, confer the literature enumerated in note 10. E. S. Hurwitz concludes that "Vladimir on the Kliazma was a second Kiev..." (*Prince Andrej Bogoljubskij...*, 50), but contemporary sources make no such explicit claim.

13. *PSRL* 1, issue 2 (1927): 472.

14. For the critical edition of the *Zhitie Aleksandra Nevskogo*, see Iu. K. Begunov,

Pamiatnik russkoi literatury XIII veka "Slovo o pogibeli russkoi zemli" (Moscow-Leningrad, 1965), 159–80, especially pp. 159, 165, 178.

15. J. Pelenski, "The Sack of Kiev of 1482 in Contemporary Muscovite Chronicle Writing," *HUS* 3/4 (1979–80): 638–49.

16. The most comprehensive modern treatments of the history of the Galician-Volhynian Rus' and of the literature on the subject have been provided by Hrushevsky, *Istoriia Ukrainy-Rusy*, vols. 2 and 3; Josyf Pełeński, *Halicz w dziejach sztuki średniowiecznej* (Cracow, 1914); V. T. Pashuto, *Ocherki po istorii Galitsko-Volynskoi Rusi* (Moscow, 1950); K. A. Sofronenko, *Obshchestvenno-politicheskii stroi Galitsko-Volynskoi Rusi XI-XIII vv.* (Moscow, 1955); P. Hrytsak, *Halytsko-Volynska Derzhava* (New York, 1958); I. P. Krypiakevych, *Halytsko-Volynske kniazivstvo* (Kiev, 1984).

17. For a convenient English translation of the Galician-Volhynian Chronicle and for the literature on the Chronicle, confer *The Galician-Volhynian Chronicle* (The Hypatian Codex, Part Two), an annotated translation by G. A. Perfecky, *Harvard Series in Ukrainian Studies* 16, 2 (Munich, 1973).

18. *PSRL* 2 (1908²), cols. 1, 2. Confer also *The Galician-Volhynian Chronicle* under the years 1245/46 for the relevant statement, which reads as follows: "Danylo Romanovych, the great prince who ruled the Rus' land, Kiev, Volodymyr and Halych,..." (58).

19. Pashuto, *Ocherki...*, 17.

20. Nasonov, *Mongoly i Rus'*, 26–33. Available evidence indicates that Danylo attempted to reconquer Kiev in the mid-1250s (*The Galician-Volhynian Chronicle*, 73).

21. A. I. Hensorsky's hypothesis, as well as his comparison of the alleged theory of Halych, "the second Kiev," with Moscow, "the Third Rome," should be regarded as artificial constructions (*Halytsko-Volynskyi Litopys* [Kiev, 1958]), 86–7.

22. *The Galician-Volhynian Chronicle*, 75–6.

23. A partial treatment of Cyrill's political adjustments has been provided by J. T. Fuhrmann, "Metropolitan Cyrill II (1242–1281) and the Politics of Accommodation," *Jahrbücher für Geschichte Osteuropas*, 24 (1976): 161–72. For a study of Russian-Byzantine relations in the fourteenth century, especially the ecclesiastical aspects, and the literature on the subject, see J. Meyendorff, *Byzantium and the Rise of Russia* (Cambridge, London and New York, 1981).

24. Ibid., 91–5, including the literature on the subject.

25. For introductory discussions of these concepts, see Nasonov, *"Russkaia zemlia...,"* especially 28–9 and L. V. Cherepnin, "Istoricheskie usloviia formirovaniia russkoi narodnosti do kontsa XV v.," in *Voprosy formirovaniia russkoi narodnosti i natsii (Sbornik statei)* (Moscow, 1958), 61–3, 81–2. A definitive study of this problem has not yet been written.

26. *PSRL* (2nd rep. ed., 1908), 653.

27. *Boleslav-Iurii II, kniaz vsei Maloi Rusi (Sbornik materialov i issledovanii)* (St. Petersburg, 1907), 249; Hrushevsky, *Istoriia Ukrainy-Rusy*, 3: 113.

28. The Hungarian kings, who at certain times advanced claims to Galicia, were the

first to use the title *Rex Galaciae* (1189) and *Galiciae Lodomeriaeque rex* (1206 and later) (Hrushevsky, *Istoriia Ukrainy-Rusy*, 2: 449 and 3: 18).

29. *Boleslav-Iurii II, kniaz vsei maloi Rusi*, 149–50.

30. Ibid., 4, n. 2.

31. Ibid., 154.

32. Nasonov, *Mongoly i Rus'*, 26. Dimnik argues that Mikhail of Chernigov was the strongest opponent of the Mongols and was therefore executed on orders of Batu (*Mikhail, Prince of Chernigov...*, 130–35).

33. *Novgorodskaia Pervaia Letopis starshego i mladshego izvodov*, ed. A. N. Nasonov (Moscow-Leningrad, 1950/1969), 305–6.

34. I. Ševčenko, "A Neglected Byzantine Source of Muscovite Political Ideology," *Harvard Slavic Studies* 2 (1954), 142–4.

35. *The Galician-Volhynian Chronicle*, 67–8.

36. Ibid., 17.

Edward L. Keenan

Muscovite Perceptions of Other East Slavs before 1654 — An Agenda for Historians

It is the objective of the present brief essay to draw attention to certain aspects of Muscovite perceptions of other East Slavs, and of the nature of the shared historical experience, that seem to me still poorly understood even by specialists and usually misrepresented in the general literature. I offer what follows as an "agenda," both as a means of indicating that what I shall have to say is not the finished result of systematic researches on the various matters treated, and in order to imply that historians have—or should have—tasks of understanding before them that must be accomplished if they are better to comprehend the reality of Moscow's attitudes toward other East Slavs in the period before roughly 1650. I must apologize for the scrappiness of the list; what I offer is intented not as a comprehensive new understanding but rather as a cluster of puzzled observations.

My puzzlement arises from the observation that, contrary to the expectations generated by the commonly accepted notion of a shared East Slavic cultural development leading, in early-modern times, to the "emergence" of the three fraternal nations, our sources seem to reveal a *greater* "cultural distance" between Muscovites and other East Slavs in, say, 1600 than was the case a century earlier *or* later. And when I observe that, surprisingly, Muscovite elites in the latter part of the sixteenth century appear to be poorly informed, and unconcerned, about the dramatic national-cultural struggles taking place in non-Muscovite East Slavic territory. And when I consider the evidence that, in particular, the confessional polemics and politics that are so passionate and all-embracing for Orthodox citizens of the Commonwealth seem to have had little resonance in Muscovy, especially in court circles. And, finally, when I find that the serious and profound Muscovite awareness of both confessional and East Slavic national-historical matters that is characteristic of the latter half of the seventeenth century bears the mark of a *new* development, involving new actors, new texts, new languages, and new conceptual categories.

I shall turn in a moment to a more detailed discussion of the reasons why I question generally accepted notions about how well Muscovites understood other East Slavic societies and how much they cared about them. But first let me pose the larger problem differently in a series of questions that would seem to constitute the minimum agenda for those who would either reject or embrace the views I put forth below.

How did sixteenth- and early seventeenth-century Muscovites— particularly those actively engaged in politics[1]—conceive of their relationship to other East Slavs? How much contact and social interchange was there among East Slavic elites? What was the "quality of communication" as measured by the ease and efficiency of linguistic and cultural mutual comprehension? How did Muscovite politicians react to the information that they *did* obtain from their East Slavic neighbours, and what attitudes or considerations determined their reaction?

These plain questions, fundamental to an understanding of Muscovite policies vis-à-vis the non-Muscovite East Slavic lands, seem never to have been addressed with appropriate specificity. It would appear that the explanation for this oversight lies in the fact that they are questions about how Russians of the period perceived their Ukrainian and Belorussian contemporaries, whereas historians have been primarily concerned with Muscovite military and diplomatic (including ecclesiastical/diplomatic) activities, or with treatments of the East Slavic, primarily Kievan, historical tradition, as transmitted in the shared chronicles and certain other works. But did Muscovite politicians read their own chronicles? Did they understand them? What did they make of them? How, in particular, did they conceptualize the Kievan period and later events in Ukraine and Belorussia in relation to their own Muscovite history? We know, for example, that Ukrainian historical consciousness as concerns the Kievan past developed in unexpected ways and not without significant periods of interruption in the tradition[2]—what of the Muscovites?

Our response to these questions must depend in part—particularly as concerns interpretation—on the answer to another deceptively simple question: How did leading Muscovites—members, let us say, of the most eminent political clan—see *themselves*? That is, how did they construe their own history and, in particular, how did they conceptualize their own society? Did they, for example, think of themselves as part of a "nation"? How was that "nation," if it existed for them, defined?

Finally, we may ask whether, and how, the answers to these questions would change if we were to pose them with regard to different stages of Muscovite cultural history—1550, 1600 and 1650, for example. In what follows, I shall stress the earlier period first, moving gradually to the later.

I have already indicated my consternation at the apparent contradiction between what I see in the sources and certain widely accepted views on the subject; I should begin, perhaps, with a characterization of these views that will necessarily be brief and schematic, but not, I hope, unfair. In enumerating the following points that I think we must consider most critically, I do not intend to imply that I think accepted views utterly erroneous and pernicious, but rather to point out that they are, in many cases, insufficiently justified by the sources or are, to some extent, based upon what I think to be anachronistic modes of understanding.

I think it quite questionable, to begin, that Muscovite politicians during most of the early period of Muscovite expansion possessed a culturally innate and spontaneous awareness of a shared East Slavic heritage and tradition, powerful enough in itself to make them irredentists and—to use a graceless term—"pan-rus'ists" as regards East Slavic lands to the west. I think it by no means demonstrated—and perhaps indemonstrable—that the noble cavalrymen who made decisions in the Kremlin about military and foreign-policy matters were, in framing their approach to relations with the Commonwealth, critically influenced by what we would now call religious, historical, or ethnic considerations. I think it quite unlikely that many—if any—of them had any extensive understanding of contemporary cultural and social process in the other East Slavic lands. I doubt that most of them—and at the beginning *any* of them—could "understand," i.e., interpret and respond to, the remarkable dynamic of renaissance of Orthodox—and non-Orthodox—culture that was taking place among non-Muscovite East Slavs in this period.

It is probably most appropriate to begin consideration of the range of problems I have raised by dealing with the self-conception of Muscovite politicians, and with the obvious but necessary caveat that one must be cautious in applying modern conceptual categories to the study of pre-modern mentalities. Muscovite politicians did not, at the end of the sixteenth century, think in terms of "nation" as we have come to construe that term since the eighteenth century. (Indeed, I would argue that they had no equivalent term in their lexicon.)[3] And since, for example, these noble cavalrymen appear not to have considered particularly significant, as determinants of their status of self-conception, the bonds of religion and vernacular speech that linked them to the great mass of Russian agriculturalists, it seems highly unlikely that they were particularly sensitive to the importance of their lesser similarities to Ukrainians and Belorussians as representatives of a more inclusive ethnic or religious category. To be sure, Muscovite elites perceived that other East Slavs—particularly "Lithuanian" noblemen to whom some of them were related by remembered ancestry—were more like them than, say, Englishmen or Persians, but it is very difficult to extract from the record evidence that Kremlin courtiers responded to "Lithuanian" East Slavs in some way that was functionally different, or as different as we would expect, from their treatment and perception of, e.g., Swedes, Poles or even Cherkessians.

Further—even if we must acknowledge that sixteenth-century Muscovites had some operative sense of, let us say, *svoi* vs. *chuzhoi*, I think it very possible that they had so little information about other East Slavs in the middle of the sixteenth century that they were unsure to which category "Lithuanians" should be assigned.

In order to understand how these systems of perceptions operated in the later sixteenth and earlier seventeenth centuries, we must begin by recalling that the culture areas of which we speak were, in several critical respects, significantly more "distant" from one another, and more different from one another, than they had been in earlier centuries, or than they became in more modern times. There is something counter-intuitive about such a conclusion; we tend to think in vaguely evolutionary terms about the history of the East Slavs, about the "emergence" of the modern Ukrainian and Belorussian and Russian nations from a common source, and the like. But the fact of the matter is that an enormous share of what is now "common" to these communities is the result of relatively modern processess: the growth, migration and convergence of populations; the spread of Muscovite political and social institutions; improved communications; various waves of educational standardization; and others. To be sure, these processes of assimilation were greatly facilitated by the existence of shared traditions of religion and culture, and they drew much of their formal aspect from the common heritage, but these facts should not obscure the differences and discontinuities of the pre-modern period.

Centuries of separate development had produced, by the early-modern period, significantly divergent cultures and institutions in several East Slavic lands. These may, for the sake of brevity, be typified by the purely linguistic differences between, let us say, the vernaculars of Lviv, Polatsk and Moscow as of 1550, when these differences were still unintermediated by bands and pockets of bilingualism and by the learned diglossia of education and communications. [4]

Perhaps even more significant regional variation was produced, toward 1600, by the differential impact on the separate East Slavic regions of the various influences of Balkan, Bohemian and Polish high cultures, and of social structures and political institutions of these neighbouring societies.

Indeed, it might be argued that the period between the middle of the sixteenth century and the middle of the seventeenth was the time of greatest differences between Muscovy and other East Slavic societies as regards social and political structures. Both before and after, for various reasons, Muscovite elites and other social groups had more in common with their cousins, but in this period, from the Union of Lublin until Pereiaslav, very clear differences separated them. One need only consider, for example, the differences between Muscovy and the commonwealth as regards the role of the royal establishment, the legal status and corporate self-conception of the nobility, the position of townsmen, or the relations between church and state in order to become aware of these distinctions. All these differences made it difficult for Muscovites to understand, let alone to identify themselves with, the legal and political struggles of other East Slavic elites, or to comprehend adequately the significance that the notion of a "national" culture was beginning to have in these struggles.

Moreover, even *within* these culture areas significant—and growing— distinctions among social groups meant that the idea of "nationhood," which we apply so automatically today, meant very little; more, certainly, among the

Orthodox population of the Commonwealth than in Muscovy, but less even there, I think, than we might assume. In Muscovy itself, status and self-perception were still determined, as they had been for centuries, almost exclusively by heredity; among other East Slavs these critical aspects of self-awareness were shaped by a combination of heredity, an increasingly complex social reality, and the legal systems of a determinedly supranational Commonwealth.

Finally, in approaching the problem of how Muscovites perceived their distant cousins in the western regions of East Slavic settlement, we must distinguish quite precisely among the attitudes of several distinct groups: the court, which we must divide into the grand-princely establishment and the oligarchy of boyar clans; the amorphous but increasingly important service gentry; the Church, which we must separate into metropolitan and parochial groups; and others. Of these others—the great bulk of the population—we have, of course, little account.[5]

One may well ask why, if Muscovites—and, in particular, Muscovite politicians—were so distinct from the dynamic events and processes that were changing the life of other East Slavs in the late sixteenth century, historians have typically assumed that they were well-informed and concerned about them. I would suggest that the answer is that historians have extracted modern meanings from pre-modern sources. Let me elaborate, very schematically.

Kievan and Muscovite chronicles are, of course, the progenitors of modern historiographic tradition, and they are the sources to which historians of Muscovy must inevitably return. In particular, the Primary Chronicle, which describes events of the Kievan period, often forms the introductory or earliest part of even very late Muscovite chronicles. This fact has led historians to assume that Muscovites in general, and not only chroniclers, read, studied, and were moved by the tale of the common East Slavic Golden Age of Volodymyr and his immediate successors.

But, while there is no denying that these Kievan annals were copied and incorporated into all manner of Muscovite historical compilation, before we assume that Muscovites—and in particular the Muscovite secular elite—drew from these annalistic accounts some compelling sense of historical East Slavic unity, we must consider two aspects of sixteenth-century Muscovite culture. First, we should demand more positive evidence than has heretofore been presented before we conclude that the chronicles—especially those that dealt with the early period of Kievan hegemony—were widely read outside the circles of the monastic clergy who were their copyists and authors. I personally find it quite helpful to think of the Muscovite secular court and the ecclesiastical establishment as distinct cultural spheres, each with its own literary language, social structures and cultural traditions.[6] Even if such a sharp division is not to be accepted, it must be said that the Muscovite secular elite was not distinguished by literacy, especially in the literary Slavonic in which many (and especially the older) portions of the chronicle texts were written. It

is also true that the manuscript tradition does not support the view that any significant number of Muscovite cavalrymen owned or read such texts until the
middle of the seventeenth century, when all secular elites began avidly to read
native and foreign histories.

Second, as one considers the Muscovite historiography of the later sixteenth
century—the great Nikon Chronicle and subsequent original texts—it is
difficult not to be struck by what we could call their Moscow-centrism; it is the
events that are specifically important to the Muscovite princes and to the
emergence of Muscovy that are elaborated upon in literary tales like the
Zadonshchina; the fate of Kiev itself and the history of the more westerly East
Slavic lands, while mentioned in entries borrowed from earlier sources, do not
often attract the attention of Muscovite elaborators. The Mongol destruction of
Kiev, or raids on Kiev by Mengli-Girei and other Tatar khans, are treated most
matter-of-factly, without the kind of literary excursions that accompany, for example, the entries about attacks on Moscow or Riazan. And in general, this
later, original, Muscovite historiography for a time—until well into the
seventeenth century—develops as a new national historiography, or historiography of the Muscovite dynasty, revealing little concern for the Kievan
heritage and even less for the later fate of other East Slavs.[7] Later, of course—a
convenient landmark is the *Synopsis*—Ukrainians themselves begin to re-
introduce the sense of a unitary Rus' historical experience, but this is a matter
for later discussion. As to the beginning of the period we are considering, it
should be said that, in the area of historiography, it is one of *divergence* in the
tradition—one finds, e.g., the emergence not only of specifically Muscovite
chronicles and chronographs with the point of view I have described, but also
distinctively non-Muscovite compilations, the so called "West-Russian" chronicles.

Another important source that has exercised considerable influence upon the
traditional interpretation is, of course, the diplomatic correspondence of the
period, especially the various exchanges between Moscow and Vilnius
concerning disputed lands and towns in Belorussia and Ukraine. The critical
phrase, often repeated in such documents from the times of Ivan III if not earlier, is "such-and-such a town (say, Smolensk) is our patrimony (*otchina*)." Now
the modern interpretational predispositions of statist and national historiography
have led scholars to make much of this diplomatic cliché: to some it has been
taken as evidence that the boundaries of a Muscovite nation-state were
"legally" construed as extending as far as the given town or territory; others
have seen it as evidence that the Muscovite Grand Princes saw themselves as
custodians of a national territory so defined.

I would question whether the preponderance of the evidence permits such
interpretations. First, let us remember that the Grand Princes were the kingpins
of an oligarchic political system based in significant part upon genealogical
relationships; no one knew better than the very *diaki* who wrote these

diplomatic texts that scores of Riurikids had some reason to consider Smolensk their *otchina*, and that the claim of the Daniilovichi (the princes of the Moscow house) was not necessarily the strongest. Second, as I mentioned, the notion of the Grand Prince as custodian of some national destiny in anything like our modern sense is quite alien to this period. Of course, in the diplomatic phases of the struggle for control of these contested territories, Muscovites attempted to justify their political objectives with the aid of whatever historical claims came to hand. (One could hardly, after all, begin negotiations by declaring that one coveted Smolensk for its good fortifications and strategic location). And since Muscovites apparently knew that their state—or, rather, their ruling dynasty—a historical entity that they *did* construe as meaningful, had no recent historical claim, those who were at pains to justify Muscovite policy were constrained to broaden the context of discussion until it embraced some category that included both Muscovy and these clearly non-Muscovite lands. The general (and, *nota bene*, not necessarily juridicial) notion of "patrimony," then, served this purpose. I suggest that the formula be read, in modern parlance, "we have certain historical interests in this region."

Another point upon which the modern interpretative stance has misled us in reading documentary sources, in my view, is the matter of religion—or, more specifically, what we might call confessional politics. Much has been made, since the very beginnings of historiography on these matters, of the mentions of religion that are found in diplomatic and other sources. But there is, I would argue, something slightly paradoxical about any discussion of religion in sixteenth-century Muscovite diplomatic sources, since, in that period, the court itself (by contrast, e.g., with the chronicle-writers) seems to have been rather secular-minded and tolerant about confessional matters (as, for example, in its attitude toward Muslims). Such a statement, while unorthodox, should not be surprising, in view of the fact that Muscovy was still distant from the great confessional struggles of the age in more western lands.

Indeed, what is surprising is the fact that religious matters do indeed find their way into the diplomatic sources, whence, as I have said, I think scholars have drawn the wrong conclusions. Wrong, because, if we look at the sources in the light of what we know about Muscovite court culture of the time, and not from the point of view of what came much later in Moscow's cultural development, we can interpret these discussions of confessional matters quite differently. What we must keep in mind is the fact that, from the discussion of Ivan III's marriage to Zoe/Sofia to the great arguments about the betrothal of Peter the Great's Aunt Irene to Valdemar of Denmark in the 1640s, the great majority of such discussions of religious matters is elicited by questions of marriage, an institution that was by its nature specifically religious—confirmed by a sacrament—whatever other considerations may have determined the choice of partners. At the same time, marriage was, for Muscovite courtiers, the link that held the clan-based patronage organizations of the oligarchy together and bound them to the Great-Princely family.

Betrothals, in and around the royal family, were the crucial events of domestic politics in the Kremlin. The marriages of the heirs to the throne, and the associated lesser pairings that usually followed closely upon these, established, reinforced and symbolized the political arrangements of a whole generation. Muscovite politicians realized that if the Great-Princely family were to spring itself loose from that affinal web that made the leading clan elders the brothers-in-law and uncles of the Great Prince, the base of their power would be diminished, and a configuration like those of other states would arise, in which the royal establishment, with its non-noble and dependent bureaucracy and clients, would stand apart from and opposed to the hereditary nobility. The potential consequence of such a development for boyar families was clear: they would be deprived, in a system based upon clan seniority and formulated in the system of *mestnichestvo*, of both their only mechanism for orderly change in their own relationships and of their best guarantee against political chaos. Any betrothal, in Kremlin circles, pitted those who stood to benefit from the prospective marriage against those whom it would place at a greater distance from the throne. When faced with the dangers of such a potential match within their own group, the opposition resorted, as the record amply demonstrates, to backstairs intrigue, poison, and black magic. In dealing with the greater, external, threat to the whole political system, they employed the additional weapon of religious arguments. That they did so, however, cannot be taken as proof of their religiosity or—in the present context—of their participation in or understanding of the confessional politics of the Orthodox lands of the Commonwealth. About such matters, I submit, in this early period they were surprisingly indifferent and ignorant.

Let me detain you with a single well-known and historiographically very influential example. The famous "disputation" between Ivan the Terrible and Antonio Possevino has often been cited as an example both of Ivan's theological erudition and sensitivity and of the anti-Catholicism and Orthodox militancy of the Muscovite court. Indeed, Possevino's own report of that encounter leaves the strong impression that, although the Italian Jesuit was particularly eloquent in his exposition of the contemporary position of the Vatican in matters of faith and ecumenicity, the Muscovites were obdurate in the defence of their heretical ways. If, however, one compares Possevino's *ex post facto* report to his superiors in the Vatican with the far more prosaic and detailed contemporary records of the Muscovite *Posolskii prikaz*, there emerges a rather different impression of that encounter. For the Muscovite record, with the dogged meticulousness, love of the letter, and fond embrace of verbatim repetition that characterizes *prikaz* documents, reveals not only that many of the complex religious questions dealt with in Possevino's account were not even recorded—and probably not discussed—but that Ivan IV demonstrated a decided lack of interest in matters of religion. Ivan did, it is true, have some curiosity about such unnatural Roman practices as the shaving of beards, but he quite explicitly and repeatedly told the Italian Jesuit that he had no wish to discuss what he called "major matters of religion" with him. There does, of course, arise a question here of the reliability of the two accounts; but I think it quite clear, on the basis of what we know both about the conventions of the *Posolskii prikaz* and about Possevino's literary activity, that the *diaki* left us a trustworthy account, while Possevino embroidered his narrative with texts prepared in advance for the occasion and perhaps even read aloud, but which, however, had little effect. During this period, I would argue, even in the context of important peace negotiations with Stefan Batory concerning the fate of Orthodox Belorussian and Ukrainian populations, Muscovite politicians, and in particular Ivan, were simply not interested in theological jousting. Little more than a generation later things would be quite different—but that is another matter.

The Possevino materials in the Muscovite records reveal something else that is of interest to us today: the texts of the *posolskie knigi* are here, as in many other cases that have to do with relations with Moscow's western neighbours, linguistically quite heterogeneous. That is, although much of the description and formal matter is presented in what was by the 1580s the highly standard-ized and purely Muscovite *prikaz* language, the passages that represent translations of what Possevino said or presented in written form are full of what we might call "Lithuanianisms," that is, the lexical and grammatical features that distinguish the chancery language of Vilnius and the Orthodox lands of the Commonwealth. It is not difficult to conclude, upon close reading, that, to the extent that Ivan and Possevino spoke to one another at all, they were speaking through one and one-half interpreters, that is, Possevino was speaking some kind of Latin to a Belorussian or Ukrainian (whom he calls his "young inter-preter"), who rendered his speeches in a mixed East Slavic not unlike what one hears even today when uneducated Ukrainians and Russians converse. What is quite clear, whatever the actual process of translation might have been, is that mutual comprehension was far from perfect: the portions of Possevino's account that corresponded almost verbatim with the Muscovite record provide some rather humorous examples, including the discussion of beards, from which it is clear that Possevino remained under the impression that Ivan was talking about the Pope's beard, while the Muscovites record that Possevino claimed that he—Possevino—did not shave his *own* beard!

This linguistic detail is no isolated curiosity. It draws attention to an important fact that the linguistic process of intervening centuries tends to obscure from us: Muscovites had significant linguistic difficulties with both vernacular and literary Belorussian and Ukrainian in this early period; they misunderstood; they had few experienced interpreters; they could not even "clean up" a macaronic text when it was recopied for inclusion in important official records. This difficulty was alleviated during the following period, but the process was slow and not necessarily "natural."

Other examples might be adduced; the point I should like to make is that the record does not, in my view, support the conclusions that the ruling elite in Moscow was well-informed about events in non-Muscovite East Slavic territory, that some sense of historical unity moved Muscovites to become involved in those events, or that they were inclined to be responsive to the religious-cultural struggles that were taking place to the west.

There were, however, those in Muscovy who were much more aware of what was happening in non-Muscovite Orthodox communities, more aware of the chronicle traditions, and more concerned about matters of confessional politics. These were the clergy, and in particular, in the earliest period, the clergy of Novgorodian and Pskovian monasteries and centres in the vast northern Novgorodian hinterland, the *Pomore*. By proximity and historical experience, these centres were at first more closely associated with Belorussian and Ukrainian lands than was Moscow itself, and they seem to have been differentially receptive to the literature, both manuscript and printed, that began to emerge from the west in the last decades of the sixteenth century. It was in these areas, apparently, that many of the first translations of Ukrainian and Belorussian works were made, and it was through these networks—later, it appears, to become Old Believer networks—that they were spread in Muscovy itself.

Mention of the Old Belief brings me to one of the most complex and perplexing aspects of our subject. The unfortunate neglect of the Old Believer tradition in Russian scholarship, on the one hand, and the indiscriminate inclusion of Old-Believer works in the mainstream of Muscovite texts, on the other, have created a great deal of confusion in the study of the cultural relations between Muscovy and other East Slavic centres. The problem is caused, in part, by the fact that as they became increasingly alienated from the established church, Old Believers became increasingly dependent upon translations from pre-Nikonian printed books published on Belorussian and Ukrainian territory, whose provenance they disguised by omitting title-page information, and spread in numerous copies through rural Muscovy. These were, of course, texts in which the anti-Catholic and, to a lesser extent, anti-Protestant arguments (Muscovites confused the two on occasion) that were generated in the cultural struggles in the western lands were eloquently set forth; as a rule, they reflected an earlier "Vilnius" (pre-Brest) stage of that struggle. The Old Believers used them against the official Orthodoxy of the Nikonians, itself heavily influenced by the post-Mohyla Kievan theology, which Old Believers saw with some justification as dangerously tainted by Catholicism. Scholars have relied on these Old Believer texts as evidence that Muscovites in general were keenly involved in the confessional disputes of their East Slavic cousins in the earlier period; the matter is more complex than has been realized, and still awaits discriminating study.

I should mention here a paradox, or rather a neat symmetry: after roughly the middle of the seventeenth century, older texts from the East Slavic areas of the Commonwealth, the so-called *knigi litovskoi pechati*, were for the Old Believers the repository of the "Old True Faith," much as Muscovy had been, for Ukrainians and Belorussians a century earlier, the source of "old and authentic" manuscripts—such as that used for the Ostrih Bible—and of "unspoiled" icons.

Let me conclude our discussion of the problems of the names of Muscovite understandings of the other East Slavs with some remarks on the Moscow expedition of one such antique hunter, a monk from Kamianets by name Isaiah. Born in Ukraine, educated in Moldavia, Isaiah seems to have been one of the bright young men of his time and place. In 1560 he was chosen to make an expedition to Muscovy, in order to obtain there some hagiographic literature and icons that were not available in Ukraine. (He may have had some other assignment, but the evidence is ambiguous on that count.) In Moscow he fell into deep trouble for reasons unknown, and apparently he never returned home. Isaiah is interesting in many respects, but those that concern us particularly today are two: first, it appears from his petitions for release that some part in his incarceration was played by confessional differences—he says at one point that "I did not come to raise questions about belief." One must assume from this that at least some Muscovites, long before the Union and the unleashing of the Jesuit-led Counter-Reformation, felt that Ukrainians were somehow heretical, or at least dangerously different. The second reason that Isaiah is interesting is that it was probably he who, in a sense, re-imported Maksim Grek into Muscovy. It seems that it was in part thanks to his efforts that interest in Maksim, which was surprisingly insignificant at mid-century, began to grow, and it seems quite logical that it would be such a person, educated in the monasteries of Moldavia, where the new Greek humanism that would soon sweep into Ukraine was already establishing itself, would hold Maksim in higher esteem than the Muscovites had originally done. Isaiah, about whom we should be able to learn a great deal more than we now know, is a fine example of how paradoxical, at times, the cultural history of these two East Slavic centres becomes upon close examination.

But I must move on. To summarize these brief remarks on the state of Muscovy's perception of the other East Slavic lands in the latter part of the sixteenth century, then, I would say that, for the most part, the political elites had surprisingly little information about, interest in, or concern for what we would today consider the most important aspects of cultural-political life in the main centers of Ukrainian and Belorussian culture. Of course, the situation was changing as the century came to an end, and these relationships were transformed particularly by the events of the turbulent decade we call the *Smuta*.

When I say "transformed," I have in mind for the most part the longer-range effects of the *Smuta*; in the context we are examining here one of the most remarkable aspects of this period is what *did not* happen between and among East Slavic elites. The events of the period provided numerous occasions for intimate and long-term contacts between Muscovite noble cavalrymen and their East Slavic counterparts within the Commonwealth; *Litva*, both Catholic and Orthodox, came to Moscow in force for the first time. This period was, moreover, one in which the first stirrings of what might properly be called a Russian national sentiment, transcending class and traditional regional boundaries, made themselves felt. Finally, at least some writers, in some contexts, construed the battles of the period as battles between Orthodoxy and its enemies. What better context for the awakening of the interest of Muscovites in the cultural life of their East Slavic coreligionists?

And yet here, too, the record disappoints those who would look for such interest among Muscovite politicians, or even for an awareness of the complexity of life in the Commonwealth. It appears, for example, that contemporary Muscovite writers frequently made no distinction between Ukrainians and Poles in the Commonwealth forces, or between Catholics and Orthodox. They are *Litva*; of the Polish occupation of the Kremlin one chronicle says simply, "*A byla Moskva za Litvoiu tri gody.*" In general, the Time of Troubles provides another example of how our Muscovite sources can lead us astray if we are not careful: the most influential narrative accounts, the so-called *Povesti o smutnom vremeni*, so ably studied by Platonov and others, would lead one to believe that there was more national and religious sentiment involved in the motivations of the main actors than there probably actually was. But these were written well after the event, and by churchmen—or churchly men—they are quite at variance with the documentary record and the memoirs of participants such as Żółkiewski. Certainly the various coalitions of boyars who treated with, and even supported, the First False Dimitrii, Władysław and Zygmunt, and even the Swedes, were not what we would call "up tight" about religion or East Slavic unity. The conversations between Żółkiewski and Prince Mstislavsky are particularly interesting in this regard. Here we have a Polish Catholic nobleman, owner of vast estates in Ukraine, dealing with a Muscovite boyar who is the son of a Ukrainian prince, and they seem to discuss only the most pragmatic political affairs, concluding a deal that is eminently practical, but owes little to the national or religious sentiments that the authors of the *Povesti* would have us believe were turning Muscovite hearts to ashes.

Żółkiewski, of course, had a model in mind—that of an expanded multi-ethnic noble republic—in which such sentiments, while certainly important, might find a *modus vivendi* similar to that then operating in the Commonwealth. Mstislavsky and his boyar colleagues, for their part, were willing to have Władysław as tsar—as they had been willing to have the False Dimitrii—because their primary objective was the restoration of the political stability of a system in which they could retain their oligarchic position under a nominal king. In the end, of course, the deal fell through—but *not* because of religious or national sentiments. (It should be remembered that, after Zygmunt failed them, the boyars made very serious overtures to the Swedes, and would have been satisfied, like the Poles earlier, with a tsar from the house of Vasa.) Of course, the Russians insisted that whoever became tsar convert to Orthodoxy—but this stipulation, as I see it, had to do with the marriage politics of the court; the example of the False Dimitrii had reinforced their insistence upon that linchpin of their political system.

But even if the immediate results of the *Smuta* experience had not fundamentally changed Muscovite attitudes about the supranational significance of Orthodoxy or about their historical relationship to other East Slavs, it did, as I have indicated, mark the beginning of a number of long-range processes that ultimately—rather late in the century—gave rise to the attitudes that are often thought of as typical for the earlier period. This change, I think, was brought about by several new factors, internal and external.

First, the experience of the Time of Troubles seems to have created, within the Muscovite court, a significant group of individuals who, for the first time since the influx of "Lithuanian" nobles in the early sixteenth century—i.e., before the major cultural developments in Ukraine and Belorussia—had some first-hand knowledge of the life and culture of their non-Muscovite East Slavic counterparts. The vicissitudes of the turbulent decade had, in addition, provided some Muscovites with the linguistic and literary experiences and skills needed to broaden that new knowledge.

Second, the Polish defeat, and successive evidences of the political might of Muscovy, turned the minds of Ukrainians and Belorussians, in a period of increasingly aggressive repression of their national and religious life in the Commonwealth, to Moscow as a potential ally and refuge.

Third, a broad array of social and cultural processes, stimulated in significant measure by the successful restoration of the Muscovite political system and the subsequent very impressive economic growth, made Muscovites of various social groups increasingly receptive to new external influences, including in the first instance those that emanated from the adjacent East Slavic lands.

Most of these processes reached their culmination only after the middle of the century, but it is nonetheless possible to trace their early stages as a means of understanding how Muscovite attitudes toward other East Slavs changed from the apparent relative indifference I have posited to the much keener interest of the time of Aleksei Mikhailovich.

It is not yet possible confidently to trace the evolution of that small group within the Muscovite nobility who, contrary to the long-standing boyar tradition, were actively literate in Slavonic and other literary languages, involved in religious and cultural disputes, and relatively *au courant* as concerns the cultural life of Orthodox centres in the Commonwealth. But that such a group emerged shortly after the *Smuta* there is no doubt. The names of Ivan Khvorostinin, Semen Shakhovskoi and Ivan Katyrev-Rostovsky come immediately to mind, and it appears that their experiences at the court of the False Dimitrii and in subsequent years had much to do with their formation. The return of Filaret and his colleagues from a long exile clearly also played a role, one that has still not been fully explored.

But while these individuals certainly were much more aware of cultural currents beyond Muscovite borders, and able to handle Polish and Slavonic texts from the Commonwealth, there are some caveats and paradoxical features to be noted in their reception of this new influence. First, we should note that, in this generation, Muscovite authors, even when translating from, let us say, texts produced in Ukraine, produced relatively pure Muscovite Slavonic, that is, they cleansed their translations of almost all evidences of their origin. One is stuck by this relative "purity" when comparing their work with texts from the latter half of the century, when, under the apparent influence of the massive emigration of Ukrainians and Belorussians, a kind of "Ukrainophilia" became almost a vogue. In this later period many texts, such as, for example, the later versions of works attributed to Andrei Kurbsky, became increasingly Ukrainized and Polonized with each editorial revision. One need not accept my hypothesis concerning the genesis and growth of the Ivan-Kurbsky "Correspondence" and related materials to acknowledge that the later texts of that corpus, which begins with Kurbsky's First Letter and Ivan's great First Letter, written in a Russian Slavonic almost free of Ukrainianisms, becomes increasingly "westernized," to the point that one can hardly read Kurbskii's "History" without some knowledge of literary Ukrainian of the period.

Second, we should note the striking fact that Muscovite authors of the *early* seventeenth century, in cleansing their models and originals of Ukrainianisms, also seem quite systematically to have suppressed specific references to Ukrainian *realia*. The study of such matters is just beginning, but it seems clear, for example, from comparison of the thousands of lines that Khvorostinin, apparently, translated line-for-line from Ukrainian poetical collections (and for which he has been acclaimed as the "originator of Russian verse") that, in addition to very careful deletion of lexical Ukrainianisms, he omits or changes numerous references to "Rus'," to Ukrainian magnates—and even to St. Volodymyr of Kiev![8]

Third, in this first generation of educated Muscovite noblemen one notes a very mixed attitude toward the new learning that was emanating in increasingly potent waves—borne primarily by the printed book—from Kiev. Filaret, here, is our exemplar, and it must be said that we still cannot—or at least I cannot—fully understand his attitudes in these matters. On the one hand, he seems to have been staunchly anti-Catholic and suspicious of these "Kievan" books; on the other, he manifestly allowed—and even sponsored—the emigration of a large number of Ukrainian churchmen, beginning a trend that, under Nikon, was to exert a massive influence in Russian cultural life.

This emigration, as I have noted, was one of the aspects of the second long-range trend that so changed Russian attitudes and awareness of other East Slavs in the seventeenth century. Scholars have been aware since Kharlampovich's great works of the massive influence of non-Muscovite East Slavs in Russian church life, and of the books that they brought with them, but I think that there are two aspects of this profoundly important process that, in the present context, call for comment.

First is the fact that it was these immigrants, apparently, who taught Russians to think in new terms not only about Orthodoxy and cultural authenticity, but also about East Slavic unity; it was they who brought to Russia the irredentist and national-historical modes of thought that in later times became so "typically" Russian. I would go so far as to say that it was they, directly and indirectly, who revived the notion of the "Third Rome" and other sadly remembered myths. They were joined in this by another group, about which we need to learn a great deal more—the itinerant and expatriate Greeks, who had, of course, their own reasons for fostering the ambitions of a great Orthodox military and political power, and had themselves, in all probability, acquired their notions of East Slavic history and cultural identity during sojourns of greater or lesser duration in Ukraine, on their way to Moscow.

The second component of this general wave of influence is, of course, the influx of printed texts from the Ukrainian and Belorussian presses that were so active in this period. This subject is by no means new or neglected, but it still requires a geat deal of study. We know, of course, that these books were everywhere, in Solovki, in Tobolsk, in monastic and private libraries—but what is, I think, still insufficiently appreciated is the massive influence of these texts, in variously disguised Russian Slavonic translations, throughout the manuscript tradition. These translations were disguised, of course, because of the ambiguous official and unofficial attitude toward "Lithuanian" books, but they were avidly read and copied in very large numbers, both by those who recognized their origin and by those who did not. There are thousands of such copies that have not yet been properly identified and compared with their originals, and until that work is well begun we cannot assess the impact of this powerful new technology of cultural diffusion and the way in which Russian attitudes were gradually changed.[9]

Let me mention a single, rather pertinent example. The "History of the Eighth Council," attributed to the "Klirik Ostrozsky" and printed in Ostrih in 1598, obviously had a wide circulation in Muscovy in subsequent decades, although mostly considerably later than one might expect. Indeed, it is another of the paradoxes of our subject that Muscovites seem not to have been particularly deeply affected, at first, by the church union of 1596. Be that as it may, at some time, perhaps in the middle of the century, the "History" was translated in a version that has been attributed to Ivan Khvorostinin, and it was independently retranslated a number of times throughout the century. At some fairly late date, a kind of Russian paraphrase was done, probably from the original, and attributed to Kurbsky (the earliest copy is ca. 1675). Now until we gather all of these variant translations, determine what they owe to the original and what to each other, establish the original Russian interpolations and glosses, and study their circulation and readership, we shall not really be able to speak of the evolution of Russian attitudes toward this critical matter of church union and the world-historical role of Russian and East Slavic Orthodoxy.

I mentioned a third set of long-range processes, the general trends of social and cultural development of Muscovy, as a final factor in the evolution of ideas about other East Slavs. I have in mind particularly the role of non-Slavic foreigners, Catholics and Protestants, Danes, and Dutchmen and Scots, in Muscovite court and military circles in the second half of the century. It was these communities, together with the Bohemian and other Jesuits studied by Antonii Florovsky, who, together with the Ukrainian and Belorussian immigrants, finally sensitized Russians to the cultural and confessional issues in the fast-changing and critical cultural turmoil of the 1670s and 1680s, issues that had so long dominated the lives of other East Slavs. Even then, however, I would point out that Muscovites were not so fully committed to the notion of East Slavic unity and historical identity as we might expect them to have been. I am struck, for example, that the capture of Polatsk, Vilnius and even ultimately Kiev did not seem to elicit an outpouring of national rejoicing and expressions of long-sought historical triumph among Muscovites. We should remember, for example, that it was not Muscovites, but the likes of Semen Polotsky who wrote the odes for such occasions, and that the "hero" of the ill-fated campaigns of the 1670s in Ukraine was Vasilii Golitsyn, a great friend and protector of Moscow Jesuits, and a noted lover of things Western. Whether he was motivated to any significant degree by historical notions of East Slavic common destiny and Orthodox unity remains, in my mind, an open question.

I propose, then, an unorthodox and fundamentally exploratory hypothesis, as follows: in the century before—to take the date for convenience only—1654, leading figures in the Muscovite political establishment, and to a different degree in the ecclesiastical establishment, were passing through a period of learning and development of the notions about East Slavic cultural history and relationships whose results, apparent only later, we wrongly attribute to them over the whole period. At the beginnings of the period, in the middle of the sixteenth century, only a precious few Muscovites had much of an inkling either about what was taking place in Ukraine or about any notion of shared historical experience. Around the time of the *Smuta*, when the cultural turmoil in Ukraine was at its height, Muscovite politicians came into meaningful contact for the first time—largely through chance encounters—with representatives of the most important and dynamic Ukrainian elites that were influenced by the cultural revival. Even then, however, most Muscovites remained at first surprisingly ignorant and indifferent about the nature of the cultural and national-historical struggle that was taking place. Even after the mid-century wars that ultimately led to the inclusion of vast amounts of Ukrainian and Belorussian territory into the Russian state, one looks in vain for substantial evidence that influential Muscovites were guided, in personal or official acts, by notions of East Slavic unity or common heritage. Moreover, until after the *Smuta* the most significant influence in Muscovy of the Ukrainian and Belorussian cultural-religious experience was felt in peripheral and non-elite areas, such as the terrain that eventually gave rise to the "Old Belief," and in the "white" clergy generally, while the established church, on the one hand, and the political elite, on the other, were more influenced by a later wave of the most profoundly Catholicized and Polonized representatives of western East Slavic culture.

I am not so mad as to fail to realize that these are somewhat questionable propositions; I shall not cling tightly to them. But I do think that they are well worth considering, and that in any case, even if eventually we must re–embrace the former mistress of our minds, the historiographic tradition, we must first test these or similar hypotheses. In order to dismiss them, reaffirm the tradition, and set our minds at ease, we must reconsider the base upon which that tradition rests in the light of what we know about Muscovite society. We must, in the first instance, restudy the abundant texts, identify their origins and evolution, and assess their influence. We must devote renewed attention to the old agenda of the philologists in order to be able to identify and analyze a great variety of translations, imitations and registers on the basis of their language. We must separate, analyze and ultimately re-integrate the vast and mysterious Old Believer tradition. We must once again reconsider the role of Ukrainian and Belorussian immigrants as cultural intermediaries and as bearers of new ideas about Slavic unity.

We must, finally, consider Muscovite society not as a homogeneous and integrated "national" entity, but as a pre-modern society whose still distinct elites responded differentially to the cultural stimuli of the time, and in particular to a new conception of the historical role and destiny of Muscovy as an East Slavic Orthodox society. In sum, we must set aside modern notions of nation, ideology and society, but apply modern social-science and humanistic techniques, in order better to understand, on its own terms, a complex and still obscure past reality.

Notes

1. Here and below, by politics I mean the process of assigning and maintaining power, property, and status at court, and the associated foreign- and domestic-policy decision-making. I shall often use the term "politicians" to designate

members of the small coterie of clans of cavalrymen—often called "the boyars"—who participated in that activity.

2. For an interesting discussion of this aspect of the matter, see Omeljan Pritsak, "Kievan Rus' and Sixteenth-Seventeenth-Century Ukraine," in Ivan L. Rudnytsky, ed., *Rethinking Ukrainian History* (Edmonton, 1981), 1–28.

3. I discuss this problem, from a slightly different point of view, in "Royal Russian Behavior, Style and Self-Image," Edward Allworth, ed., *Ethnic Russia in the USSR. The Dilemma of Dominance* (New York, 1980), 3–16.

4. One should mention here the traditional notion of the unifying role of Slavonic; in my view Slavonic played almost no role in the lives of the secular elite I am calling "Muscovite politicians." Very few of them knew Slavonic at all, and almost none could write it; until the seventeenth century and the advent of the printed book there was for practical purposes no communication in any form of Slavonic between Muscovite and other East Slavic *secular* elites. The failure of Church Slavonic as a general cultural "lingua franca" is easy to document, and has to do with the highly unstable relations among vernaculars and languages of literary use in the various territories involved. The period with which we are dealing saw the emergence, in non-Muscovite East Slavic territory, of several literary languages based on Slavonic; texts in these languages, typically, became popular in Muscovy only after they had been translated into either Muscovite "plain style" or Muscovite Slavonic.

5. It has long been the practice, of course, to impute to the demotic majority "patriotic" views on the basis of modern interpretations of the *povesti i skazaniia* (to use Platonov's term) about the Time of Troubles. Such a practice, however, seems to me to lack sufficient justification, if only because the texts in question, still for the greater part of undetermined origin, remain ambiguous as concerns their original purpose and significance. Furthermore, such evidence as we do possess about such matters does not permit the conclusion that they expressed, or influenced, the thinking of the great illiterate mass of Muscovites.

6. This dichotomy is not, of course, absolute, but it is significant in comparisons of the Muscovite elites with their contemporaries in the rest of Europe; the boundaries are limned by the contrasts between Slavonic and *prikaz* language, between the stress on kinship in the secular elite and its rejection by the ecclesiastical hierarchy, and between the military and monastic traditions.

7. I have tried to open the discussion of this matter in "The Trouble of Muscovy: Some Observations upon Problems of the Comparative Study of Form and Genre in Historical Writing," *Medievalia et Humanistica. Studies in Medieval and Renaissance Culture*, New Series, No. 5 (1974): 103–26.

8. Compare, for example, Khvorostinin's texts as published in *Letopis zaniatii Arkheograficheskoi kommissii*, with the apparent originals, published in V. P. Kolosova and V. I. Krekoten, comp., *Ukrainska poeziia. Kinets XVI pochatok XVII st.* (Kiev, 1978), 115–36.

9. One must regret that the great work of Vladimir Peretts, *Istoriko-literaturnye issledovaniia i materialy* (St. Petersburg, 1900), has not found imitators in recent times. Peretts sketched convincingly the paths of development of certain forms of

poetry from their Western origins through Ukraine to the "folkloric" imitations collected by nineteenth-century Russian philologists; similar work would, doubtless, elucidate parallel developments in other forms as well.

Hans-Joachim Torke

The Unloved Alliance: Political Relations between Muscovy and Ukraine in the Seventeenth Century

The manifold relations between Russia and Ukraine in the seventeenth century were played out on at least three levels: official relations on the political, diplomatic and military level; semi-official relations in the ecclesiastical-pedagogical and commercial sectors; and unofficial relations concerned with spiritual and cultural influences. Both the latter complexes are related to the first and cannot be disregarded here, although this article focuses on political events and on the way in which they were understood by decision-makers.

My purpose here is not to employ well-known and frequently consulted sources in order to elicit yet another interpretation of the Pereiaslav Agreement of 1654 or the character of relations between Muscovy and the Hetmanate in the ensuing period. Concerning Pereiaslav, there exist at least seven different interpretations (temporary alliance, personal union, real union, vassalage, protectorate, autonomy and incorporation), and in regard to the second topic, there is also a range of interpretations from full independence to complete incorporation of the Cossack state. No Western scholar has yet written an account that goes beyond O'Brien's monograph to take in the whole century.[1]

The question remains whether the period from the first contacts of the Dnieper Cossacks with Muscovy in the sixteenth century to the end of the Great Northern War in 1721, examined as a whole, yields a perspective on Muscovite policy that can be reconciled with the formula "Russian Imperialism from Ivan the Great to the Revolution."[2] It may be recalled that the historical roots of Russian imperialism were discussed in the *American Slavic and East European Review* in the early 1950s. At that time, in the wake of political statements about Soviet foreign policy and letters to the editor of the *New York Times* by Russian and Ukrainian émigrés, Oscar Halecki began a scholarly debate in which Nicholas V. Riasanovsky and Oswald P. Backus also took part.[3] Halecki interpreted the conquest of Novgorod by Ivan III as the first clear manifestation of Russian imperialism and, naturally, applied the same concept to the Ukrainian problem, although he touched on the latter only briefly. Riasanovsky did not deny the fact of Russia's expansion, but regarded it as a policy intended to counteract Polish expansion and wrote in this connection: "It is interesting to note that Moscow was at first reluctant to come to the aid of the Ukrainians, and that it took both the desperate appeals of the latter and the decisions of its own *Zemskii sobor* to force the Moscow government to act."[4]

Notwithstanding this discussion, the above-mentioned book on "Russian imperialism," edited by Taras Hunczak, appeared two decades later. More than any other contributor to the volume, Henry R. Huttenbach applied the term "imperialism" to Muscovy, even though, in the strict historiographical sense, it should be reserved for the period prior to World War I. While W. Leitsch interpreted Moscow's actions in the light of policy considerations *vis-à-vis* Poland and Sweden, Huttenbach's remarks on Moscow's policy toward Ukraine may serve to exemplify the way in which foreign policy is sometimes viewed with the hindsight afforded by developments in later centuries.[5] In contrast, this article will not maintain that Moscow deliberately planned from the beginning to defeat first the Poles, then the Swedes, and finally the Ottomans, or that the year 1654 was preconceived as a turning-point in East European affairs. No one would deny that, in the subsequent period, Muscovy tried more and more to gain a foothold in Ukraine, but it did so half-heartedly and hesitantly, and certainly not as part of a conscious effort at incorporation until the reign of Peter the Great. Whereas the aloofness of most of the Cossack leaders toward Moscow is a well-known fact, this article undertakes to show the hesitancy of the Muscovite government, whose motives have been of less interest to researchers than the often vacillating and "colourful" actions of the vanquished party. Accordingly, the thesis of this article is that the most conspicuous feature of Muscovite-Ukrainian relations during the seventeenth century was *mutual reserve*. Neither the desire for "fraternal union" on the Ukrainian side nor the drive toward "imperialism" on the Russian side was dominant, and this holds true not only for the relatively well-known period of 1648–54.

*

Leaving aside the military expeditions of the administrator (*starosta*) of Cherkasy, Ostafii Dashkovych (1514–35), who marched with the Tatars on Novhorod Siversky in 1515 and on Muscovy in 1521,[6] it can be said that Ukraine came gradually into the Muscovite government's field of vision in the second half of the sixteenth century. The urgent project of incorporating the central and northern Russian principalities, as well as the struggle against the Tatars in the east and south-east, postponed the overdue settlement with Lithuania for a long time. Only after the middle of the sixteenth century, when the completion of the defensive line (*zasechnaia cherta*) made possible an orderly defence of the southern frontier, and when the incorporation of Kazan (1552) and Astrakhan (1556) ensured peace in the East, could Ivan IV orient his policy toward the West. Moscow's characteristic hesitation to move into the south-west was already apparent at the very beginning of this period: the tsar preferred to wage war against Livonia rather than to follow the advice of Adashev and other councillors to continue the Crimean campaign. The "wild steppe" (*dikoe pole*) in the Don region was not secured as a territory. Instead, its inhabitants—the East Slavic provincial (*gorodovye*) and service (*sluzhilye*) Cossacks—were put to work. Territorial ambitions in the direction of Ukraine were even less significant, although some contacts had already been established with the Dnieper Cossacks.[7]

These contacts began after the conquest of Astrakhan, when Ivan IV sent the secretary (*diak*) Rzhevsky with Cossacks from Putyvl to reconnoitre the Tatars along the Dnieper. Rzhevsky was aided by the famous Dmytro Vyshnevetsky (Wiśniowiecki), who hoped to obtain Muscovy's support for his plans regarding the Zaporozhian Sich. Vyshnevetsky, who had to conceal his contacts with the tsar from the Polish king, travelled to Moscow in 1557–8 and, in return for his oath "to serve Ivan faithfully until death" (*pravdoiu i do svoei smerti*), was granted the town of Belev, many villages in the Moscow area, and the sum of 10,000 rubles.[8] No lasting relations developed from this episode, which ended in 1561, but occasionally the Dnieper Cossacks provided their services. In the spring of 1577, for example, the tsar asked them to undertake an expedition against the Crimea and Kozliv, for which they were compensated with saltpetre and other products.[9] In the years that followed, an increasing number of Cossacks entered Muscovite service.[10] The leader of the revolt of 1591–3, Hetman Kryshtof Kosynsky, was prepared to place the entire Zaporozhian army under Moscow's command, but Fedor Ivanovich (i.e., Boris Godunov) refused his offer in the spring of 1593.[11] After the Oprichnina and the loss of the Livonian War, the Tsardom of Muscovy was too weak to engage in such adventures. Even so, the power of military command seems to have existed, for the Tsar "ordered" the army to wage war against the Crimea.[12] During the disturbances of the second half of the 1590s, a good deal of money flowed from Moscow to Ukraine.[13] It must be noted that Muscovy did not take advantage of the revolts of the Dnieper Cossacks against Poland-Lithuania, which can be traced back to 1573.

This reserve is easily explained by Muscovy's respect for the might of the Rzeczpospolita, although the no less cautious Grand Dukes of earlier centuries had not shirked conflict with Lithuania during the "gathering of Russian lands." The restoration of the old Rus' would have been justified in any case, especially as the election of the tsar in 1598 showed that the time of the appanage principalities (*udely*) had finally passed and that the principle of the unity of the tsardom prevailed even during a change of dynasty.[14] Whether it is a matter of loss of the historical memory of Kievan Rus' or of actual weakness is of no importance here: the Polish intervention during the Time of Troubles indicated the true balance of power. Incidentally, in this case the Cossacks fought on both sides, just as they did in the subsequent wars of the second decade of the seventeenth century. With the marauding Cossacks the Muscovites encountered for the first time the more troublesome characteristics of their southern neighbors, especially as the spirit of revolt began to make itself felt on their own territory. The Bolotnikov revolt broke out in the Chernihiv region in the autumn of 1606 and spread as far as Riazan.[15]

This revolt was crushed in a year, but Muscovy continued to observe the Ukrainian revolts of the first half of the seventeenth century without taking any action.[16] It availed the Zaporozhians little that, referring to their earlier services, they offered assistance to Mikhail Fedorovich in the spring of 1620: Petro Sahaidachny's envoys were merely praised for the registered Cossacks' official appeal to the tsar and given 300 rubles. They had, after all, employed the title of tsar, which the Poles considered Władysław's exclusive possession. Equally fruitless was the communication from the voevodas of Putyvl in the summer of the following year to the effect that some 50,000 Cossacks wanted to liberate Kiev and other towns from Polish rule and place them, as well as themselves, under the tsar's authority.[17] In the following decades only a few Cossack battalions with their colonels or hetmans resettled along the Don, and a number of rebels fled from the Poles.[18] Since the Poles regularly demanded the return of the refugees, whom the Russians called *perebezhchiki*, and since their flight was clearly illegal under international law, Muscovy was intimidated. Its frontier voevodas were ordered to allow refugees to enter only in small groups so that they would not be noticed and thereby disturb the peace with the Rzecz-pospolita. Officially it was argued that the Polianovka peace treaty (1634) contained no reference to this problem and that no one had asked the refugees to come(!).[19] But how could the emigrants disturb the peace if the treaty did not even refer to them? In any case, the newcomers were equipped quite well, as they were needed for the defence of the Belgorod line, a fortification 300 versts in length whose construction had been undertaken in the mid-1630s and was not completed until 1677.[20]

If, up to this point, it has been possible to interpret the Cossack refugee movement and the decision of some Cossack leaders to place themselves under Moscow's authority either as a response to the exigencies of practical politics or as opportunism, in the 1630s these two phenomena began to be based on an awakening political consciousness. In 1632 the Cossacks, led by their Hetman Kulaha-Petrazhytsky (1631–2), addressed a petition to the Sejm requesting that they be admitted to the King's election. This would have meant acceptance into the nobility, and therefore the senate rejected this proposed augmentation of the szlachta by 8,000 nobles.[21] It was a single step from this petition to the idea of a separate Cossack Ukrainian state, which materialized in 1648–54. This phase, too, is characterized by timid Muscovite policy.

Although Bohdan Khmelnytsky recognized the sovereignty of the Polish crown only during the few intervals of peace, Aleksei Mikhailovich took no advantage of Ukraine's six years of independence. What happened was simply that the refugees, now even more numerous, who saw no chance of being entered in the Rzeczpospolita's register, were readily welcomed in Slobodian Ukraine (*Slobidska Ukraina*). The welcome was extended in mid-1649, when the tsar ordered the voevodas of Putyvl not only to observe Khmelnytsky and developments between the Cossacks and the Poles, but above all to protect the refugees—from nobles down to boyars' servants—from any harm.[22] However, Muscovy's responses to Khmelnytsky's appeals for help ranged from dilatory to negative. The future hetman had anticipated one reason for this attitude in the autumn of 1647, when he declared at the meeting of the *starshyna* in the "Grove of Chyhyryn" that he saw no other solution than co-operation with Muscovy and proposed to appeal to the tsar because they shared the same faith. Khmelnytsky acknowledged, however, that the Tsardom of Muscovy had been ravaged by the Poles in preceding years, had lost Smolensk and other towns to them, and had not regenerated its forces completely. "In such a condition it can hardly stand up for us."[23]

Nevertheless, between 8 June 1648 and 3 May 1649, Khmelnytsky addressed seven letters to Muscovy and to the frontier voevodas asking for military assistance and offering the Cossacks' services to the tsar, i.e., to attach them to his forces.[24] Aleksei Mikhailovich agreed only to the provision of grain and possibly weapons,[25] as well as to a more frequent exchange of envoys. He rejected any direct involvement in Ukraine or even the attachment of Cossack forces to his army. The tsar merely notified the Hetman on 7 August 1648 that he was not his enemy and that, contrary to rumours, he did not intend to ally himself with Poland against the Hetman.[26] Khmelnytsky attempted in vain to arrange interventions on his behalf by a number of individuals, including Patriarch Paisios of Jerusalem, who spent the first half of 1649 in Moscow.[27] In a letter of 13 June 1649 to the Hetman, the tsar finally mentioned the peace treaty with Poland as a reason for his attitude. He declared his willingness to accept the Cossacks if the king would release them, thereby placing the responsibility for a decision on the Poles.[28] The Treaty of Zboriv of 8 August 1649 [29] gave the Cossacks a breathing space, but Aleksei Mikhailovich then became even more explicit in his instructions of 16 August 1650, which he sent with his envoy, Vasilii Unkovsky, who was travelling to Ukraine. The peace could not be broken "without reason" (*bezo vsiakie prichiny*).[30]

The maintenance of peace with Poland was certainly a welcome, if not an entirely feigned, pretext for Muscovy to keep out of Ukrainian affairs. It is more likely that, as Khmelnytsky had assumed, the decisive factor was the tsardom's military weakness, which was consciously recognized when the Smolensk campaign of 1632–4 failed to bring the expected victory over the Rzeczpospolita. Nevertheless, almost two decades had passed since that time, and the Muscovite army had already been partially modernized along Western lines with the formation of the regiments of the new order (*polki novogo stroia*). That Muscovy was now indeed in a position to defeat Poland and even to wage a two-front campaign for a time was soon to be demonstrated by the thirteen-year (second) Northern War. The reason for Muscovy's hesitation is therefore to be sought primarily in the domestic situation. During the century of revolts, two major urban upheavals shook the country: the first took place in the capital city in 1648, the second in Novgorod and Pskov in 1650. Between 3 June and mid-October 1648 the government was virtually incapable of action, and the effects of the revolt were felt well into the following year. The fear that state servitors (*sluzhilye liudi*) and townspeople (*posadskie liudi*) would make common cause paralyzed the autocracy and influenced its actions in subsequent years. This was also true of its policies with regard to Novgorod and Pskov, whose location on the western border made war an imponderable risk.

The tsar's personality and the situation of the new dynasty may also have played a certain role. Aleksei Mikhailovich was relatively young (born 1629) and his position decidedly weak, especially because of the affair involving his fatherly advisor, B. I. Morozov. Furthermore, another false pretender to the throne had laid his claim, the eleventh since the appearance of the first False Dimitrii and the most dangerous since the Time of Troubles. In reality an escaped clerk (*podiachii*) from a Moscow central office (*prikaz*) called Timofei Akundinov (variously spelled Akindinov, Ankudinov, Ankidinov), he pretended to be the grandson of Vasilii Shuisky and was kept in circulation by Moscow's enemies. In 1646 the Poles sent him across the Moldau to the Sultan, from where he reached the Cossacks by way of Italy, Germany and Poland. It certainly did not help Khmelnytsky in pleading to the tsar for assistance that in 1650 the Hetman refused the impostor's extradition and evidently attempted to use him as a means of putting pressure on the tsar. In November Khmelnytsky banished him to Wallachia.[31] The importance of this episode should not be underestimated, for the Romanovs' claim to the throne was not yet entirely uncontested. Still, it has been assumed that Ukraine was not annexed as early as 1651 because of the disturbing news about "Timoshka."[32]

Early that year it seemed as if Aleksei Mikhailovich would venture to take the long-deferred step. A meeting of the so-called Assembly of the State (*Zemskii sobor*) was held at the end of January 1651. Its agenda included the Cossack appeal, but this item was preceded by a discussion of Poland's treaty violations and of her abuse of the tsar's title.[33] Indeed, these latter points constituted the main issue; it was not for nothing that Muscovy's envoy in Warsaw had threatened the king a year previously that such an assembly would be convoked. This does not mean that the assembly had gained decision-making power. Like most assemblies of the state in the seventeenth century, it served only as a source of information for the government, but it could also be used very readily as an instrument of foreign policy. Unfortunately, only the vote of the clergy on 27 February 1651 has been preserved, but it may be assumed that the other groups expressed themselves with similar caution. In accordance with the government's wishes, the admission of the Cossacks was made almost completely dependent on the attitude of the Poles.[34] This changed nothing in Muscovy's relations with Ukraine. On 11 March 1651, Khmelnytsky addressed B. I. Morozov with a request for intercession—a futile gesture, as the latter had not regained the influence he exercised before the revolt of 1648.[35]

Because of the deteriorating military situation, the Cossacks, who were hoping for a joint campaign against the Porte, made ever more urgent appeals through a whole series of envoys in 1651–2. Nevertheless, the Hetman, conscious of his equal status, remained self-confident. On 20 September 1651 he gave assurances that the truce of Bila Tserkva, concluded two days previously, had changed nothing in his attitude to Muscovy.[36]

Although Kapterev has emphasized that the major role in bringing about union with Muscovy was played by the Greeks, who were also interested in a war against the Ottoman Turks, and especially by Patriarch Paisios of Jerusalem,[37] it seems that the tsar's hesitant attitude toward Ukraine was actually changed by the direct influence of the new Muscovite Patriarch, the tsar's paternal friend Nikon. There is no direct evidence for this, as Nikon's first friendly letter to Khmelnytsky is dated 14 May 1653, when the government's positive decision was already two months old.[38] But the more forceful demeanour toward Poland, especially with regard to the unresolved question of the Kiev metropolitanate (see below), corresponds directly to the energetic policies of Nikon. As a promoter of rehellenization, he naturally listened to the Greek clergy. Characteristically enough, the whole problem was subsumed under the rubric of Muscovy's concern for the protection of Orthodoxy. The talks which Khmelnytsky's envoy Ivan Iskra conducted in Moscow in the spring of 1652 resulted in a mere reaffirmation of the pledge that, if oppressed by the Poles, the Cossacks could resettle on Muscovite territory along the Donets or Medveditsa rivers, the farther from the border the better.[39] Muscovy was still very far from wanting to expand its territory. But after the failure to reach agreement between the Cossacks and the Poles on the religious issue, Khmelnytsky once again posed his oft-repeated question at the end of the year through his envoy, Samiilo Bohdanovych.[40] This time he did not immediately receive a negative answer: Nikon had taken up his appointment in mid-year. The decision was finally made during the tsar's long consultation with the boyar duma, which lasted from 22 February to 14 March 1653.[41]

Obviously, Moscow did not feel rushed, and it was certainly in keeping with its traditional reserve in this matter that the decision was not communicated to the Hetman until 22 June 1653, after he had threatened union with the Ottoman Empire.[42] Previously, agreement had been reached on the convocation of another Assembly of the State and, for the time being, of a meeting restricted to members of the service class, who gathered on 25 May and earlier.[43] The townspeople were not invited until much later, on 1 October, as the financing of the war had to be debated. This time the votes were affirmative, for once again the government's decision had already been made, and the assembly was only required to sanction it.[44] Again, the government made no haste. The envoys who had left for Poland on 30 April were expected to return in time for the meeting on 1 October, and actually returned on 25 September. V. V. Buturlin departed for Ukraine with the news on 9 October,[45] and war was not

declared on the Rzeczpospolita until 23 October.[46] It is well known that the actual annexation of Ukraine was not carried out until January of the following
year. These facts give rise to the strong impression that the question of the
tsar's title was much more important to the Muscovites than the Ukrainian
problem, which was handled in such dilatory fashion. In the autumn of 1654, a
Muscovite delegation in Vienna cited the question of the title as the sole reason
for declaring war.[47] In any case, Muscovy would have preferred the simple
resettlement of the Cossacks in Slobodian Ukraine to the incorporation of the
Dnieper region. As late as the summer of 1653, the above-mentioned delegation
visited Lviv to reconcile Poland with the Cossacks on the basis of the Treaty of
Zboriv![48] Even after the fact, Muscovy preferred to justify its action by citing
the persecution of the Orthodox Church. No territorial claims were made with
reference to the possessions of Kievan Rus'.

The tsar now took "Hetman Bohdan Khmelnytsky and the entire Zaporozhian Army with the towns and lands...under his sovereign high hand,"
according to the resolution of the Assembly of the State[49] which was ratified on
8 (18 N.S.) January 1654 in Pereiaslav.[50] Two and one-half months later the
"Articles of Petition of Bohdan Khmelnytsky," which had been prepared by the
Hetman(!), were approved in Moscow (21 March).[51] Despite the controversy
aroused by research on this "treaty," there is at least general agreement that it
was not formulated perfectly and that the future points of dispute were
therefore built in, so to speak. Yet it does appear extremely odd: here was a
state that in previous centuries had incorporated principality after principality;
whose rulers, from generation to generation, had refined their well-known
treaties with principalities as instruments to promote the rise of Moscow,
applying especially strict criteria for foreign relations and the collection of
tribute with reference to the sovereigns who were to be bound by these treaties.
Yet this very state refused until the last minute to take over the Kievan core
area of old Rus', and then, in 1654, acted with extreme negligence and
clumsiness when the questions of the hetman's foreign relations and the
stationing of Muscovite voevodas in Ukrainian towns (i.e., tax collection) were
at issue. Neither at Zboriv nor at Bila Tserkva had Khmelnytsky negotiated
such extensive privileges for the Cossacks as in "his" articles. The explanation
that Muscovy was weakened by the Cossacks' flirtation with the Sultan is
convincing only at first glance. It would hold true if Muscovy had had an
overwhelming interest in the incorporation of Ukraine. As has been shown,
however, this interest was weak, whether because of inertia or fear of Poland-
Lithuania. One could more readily conclude that Muscovy was not susceptible
to extortion and that, as a further consequence, the "treaty" was not negotiated
skillfully enough because of ignorance or lack of interest. Not even the poor
military situation in which the Cossacks often found themselves was exploited
at the right time.

In practice this meant that during the Khmelnytsky period Ukraine was only nominally under Moscow's control; it was in fact independent. Unfortunately, this difference between the document and the actual force of law has often been overlooked. The full text of the "articles" was never made public in Ukraine during Khmelnytsky's lifetime; they were known only in the form of Khmelnytsky's first draft.[52] Thus the Hetman was able to sign treaties with the Sultan, with Transylvania, and even with Sweden, which later found itself at war with Muscovy.[53] Compared with Khmelnytsky's excellent connections in the West, Muscovy seemed isolated. Kiev was the only place where a Muscovite voevoda was stationed, for the Hetman, who did not want to accept even a single voevoda "because of the turbulent times," stated in 1657 that only this one had been agreed with Buturlin and that the income, which was not very great in any case, had to be used for the upkeep of the army and the foreign legations.[54] Instead, the tsar guaranteed the Zaporozhians their traditional forms of administration, including even the Magdeburg Law for Ukrainian towns.

Khmelnytsky's defensiveness is characteristic of his new attitude after 1654. Previously he had insisted on an alliance with Muscovy, apparently thinking in terms of a federation defined by the concept of ancient Rus' in a pan-Orthodox framework[55] and regarding his relationship with the tsar as one of service. Now, however, Khmelnytsky and most of his successors devoted their energies to maintaining their autonomy, even to the point of separation. Conversely, a greater interest in Ukraine can be detected from this point on the part of Muscovy. A commitment to maintain property and to establish a religious protectorate is particularly apparent in the policies of Aleksei Mikhailovich, although the previous reserve did not disappear entirely. Even when considering the second half of the seventeenth century, one cannot speak of a fundamentally new Muscovite policy. The following one and one-half decades demonstrate very clearly that the idea of "eternal subjection" (*vechnoe poddanstvo*), on which Soviet historiography puts so much emphasis, was not taken literally even by Muscovy.[56]

Nevertheless, Aleksei Mikhailovich styled himself "Autocrat of all Great and Little Russia" (*vseia Velikiia i Malye Rusii samoderzhets*) as early as 5 February 1654.[57] When a truce was negotiated with Poland in Vilnius in 1656, it was explicitly stated that in the event of the tsar's participation in a personal union following the death of Jan Kazimierz, Ukraine would not be considered part of the Rzeczpospolita, for it had become subject to the tsar.[58] Muscovy held to this agreement and subsequently denied the rumour spread by the Poles that it intended to sacrifice Ukraine and return it to Poland for the sake of a lasting peace.[59] The tsar's assumption of the role of sovereign followed rather automatically from the superiority of the traditional concept of autocratic dominion to the newly arisen Cossack statehood. It was by no means recognized at the time that, by incorporating Ukraine, the Tsardom of Muscovy had become Russia (*Rossiia*) and had laid the foundation for its later status as a great East European power. Desire for such status was not at all evident.

Financially, the new situation was a great burden to Muscovy, which had to provide Ukraine with a good deal of money, arms and grain. In 1654 the register was increased from 20,000 to 60,000 men because of the impending war with Poland, without the required list of names being made available to Moscow. Such a list would have made it possible to limit entry into the Cossack host once and for all. But Khmelnytsky, who did not intend any limitation, promoted the recruitment of peasants and of the petty bourgeoisie (*meshchane*), so that the number of Cossacks shot up to more than 100,000.[60] The tsar could do nothing about it, just as he was unable to guarantee his generous gifts of land in Ukraine. The members of the starshyna who received land in Ukraine from Aleksei Mikhailovich had to conceal their property rights at home; otherwise they would have had to fear for their lives.[61] The peasant masses had already shown a preference for Muscovy, seeing it as a haven from oppression by the Polish nobility. Because the tsar, unlike the king, could not guarantee property in land or peasants to the nobility, and thus could not even carry out his function as legislator, the Ukrainian peasants were saved from complete serfdom, which had just been introduced in Russia, for well over a century.[62] This fact also demonstrates the true effectiveness of the tsar's sovereignty. From the beginning, Muscovy had failed to consolidate its position, so that the alliance with the Cossacks virtually broke down when the interests of the two sides proved incompatible. In 1656 Aleksei Mikhailovich declared war on Sweden, with which Khmelnytsky had been allied for six years, and shortly before his death the Hetman was again preparing to turn to the Ottomans.[63]

All these tendencies became stronger after the Hetman's death. The tsar's land grants in Ukraine were recognized only if they constituted an additional confirmation of the Hetman's universals, while the actual awards of land were made even by regimental colonels. Muscovy tacitly recognized the 300,000 Cossacks on the register[64] and completely lost control of the Zaporozhian Sich, which was only loosely bound to the Hetmanate. It allowed the new hetman, Ivan Vyhovsky, to be elected without previous consultation, and did nothing to prevent his negotiations with Poland and the Crimea. In May 1658, Buturlin, now voevoda in Kiev, reported this to Moscow and found it noteworthy "that nowhere in Ukraine are there any voevodas or soldiers of Your Majesty (the Tsar)."[65] Vyhovsky even intended to send all official Muscovite delegates home for the summer. Muscovy, for its part, attempted to station voevodas in some of the larger towns, and the autocratic tsar vested his hopes in groups of rebellious Cossacks. He could not prevent the Hetman's defection (i.e., the Treaty of Hadiach with Poland). The Muscovite government cannot be said to have reacted with particular dispatch in this situation. Not until November 1658 did G. G. Romodanovsky cross the Ukrainian border with 20,000 men, while A. N. Trubetskoi marched from Sevsk as late as March 1659. In June,

Muscovy's 100,000–man army suffered a crushing defeat at Konotop. What later saved the Russian presence in Ukraine was by no means a more energetic policy, but dissension among the Cossacks themselves, who paid the price of Ukraine's partition into Polish and Muscovite spheres of influence.

Afterwards, Muscovy tried to regain a foothold in Left-Bank Ukraine by trickery: in 1659 Trubetskoi presented the new Hetman, Iurii Khmelnytsky (1659–62), with articles which he identified as those of the old "Khmel" of 1654. Point five, however, which concerned the Cossacks' independence in foreign policy, was missing.[66] This was the first important step toward actual incorporation, but it was only *one* step. Moreover, it remained only theoretical, for the "articles," which had been accepted because of Muscovy's military pressure, created so much discontent that Iurii Khmelnytsky allied himself with Poland and the Muscovite army was once again defeated (at Chudniv).[67] At the end of 1662, when he was about to conclude his reign and enter a monastery, this hetman, too, warned against an alliance with either Muscovy or Poland and advised one with the Ottoman Empire.[68] It may have been a consolation to Muscovy that Poland, too, had its difficulties with the Right Bank (e.g., under Hetman Pavlo Teteria [1663–5]). Not until the de facto partition of 1663 did the tsar find a loyal follower in Hetman Ivan Briukhovetsky (1663–8), who slavishly called himself "the most servile Hetman-footstool of the throne of His Most Noble Tsarist Majesty" (*ego presvetlogo tsarskogo velichestva prestola nizhaishaia podnozhka-getman*), and whose rule brought administrative and fiscal benefits for Muscovy. But even at this time one cannot yet speak of the establishment of the voevoda system. The appearance of voevodas triggered rebellions in Chernihiv, Pereiaslav, Nizhyn, Poltava, Novhorod Siverskyi, Kremenchuk, Kodak and Oster; the Cossack authorities therefore continued to function as an administration. On the other hand, Muscovy refused to invest any more money: the Cossacks, whose distinction from the rest of the population continued to fluctuate, no longer received monetary salaries, but had to live off their land. In order to strengthen his position, Briukhovetsky had to go to Moscow in 1665 and personally request military and financial assistance. The fact that the first Hetman who travelled to the capital city was promoted to the rank of boiar and married a Dolgorukova on this occasion, and that the members of his General Staff (*heneralna starshyna*) were declared nobles (*dvoriane*), did not increase his popularity at home.[69] The rebellion against him, which broke out in the following year, spread over almost the whole Left Bank by the beginning of 1668 and was also fueled by discontent with the Treaty of Andrusovo (1667), which was interpreted as a betrayal of the Cossacks. Nor did it help Briukhovetsky that, in the end, he turned against Muscovy.

It is more than astonishing that the tsar did not succeed in establishing his authority more strongly in Ukraine with the assistance of a hetman who was initially loyal to Moscow. Or did the government continue to regard this area as negligible? Those in power certainly stood aloof from Ukraine at this time. The voevoda of Rzhevsk, B. M. Khitrovo, who was favourably disposed to Poland, was the first to regard the annexation of Ukraine as superfluous.[70] It was even more important that the guidelines for foreign policy were determined by A. L. Ordin-Nashchokin, who was convinced that the Cossacks were detrimental to the state. As Platonov showed, Ordin-Nashchokin was the first statesman of old Russia who shared responsibility for decisions with the tsar.[71] Since Muscovy's relations with Ukraine resembled foreign relations even after 1654 (legations with instructions, letters and relations), they came initially under the jurisdiction of the Foreign Office (*posolskii prikaz*) and, after 31 December 1662, under that of the Office for Little Russia (*prikaz Maloi Rossii, Malorossiiskii prikaz*), which oversaw everything from the import of religious books to trials of tobacco smugglers.[72] On 17 June 1667, relations with Ukraine were again transferred to the Foreign Office, which was responsible for Right-Bank Ukraine in any case. Thus Ordin-Nashchokin, who had become head of the Foreign Office four months previously, took charge of Ukrainian affairs as well. This turn of events can only be explained by the bureaucratic reorganization, for Ordin-Nashchokin's pro-Polish attitude and opposition to "Muscovite Ukraine" were well known. He had been prepared to break all ties with the Cossacks as early as 1658. "Unless we abandon the Cossacks," he wrote in a report of 1667, "no lasting peace with Poland can be achieved, and the Cossack towns taken from the Poles bring us no gains, but only great losses."[73]

If the Left Bank remained with Muscovy (while the Right Bank was prematurely abandoned) in the Treaty of Andrusovo, which was negotiated by Ordin-Nashchokin, and if Kiev was added, then this was certainly due to Aleksei Mikhailovich himself. There was some foundation to the rumours circulating among the Cossacks, which Briukhovetsky believed as well, to the effect that Ordin-Nashchokin had bartered them away to Poland. Thus, at the official announcement of the treaty, the Muscovite government prudently concealed the fact that Kiev was to be returned to Poland in two years. Nevertheless, the Hetman came to know of this and became even more distrustful when, in the autumn of 1667, Ordin-Nashchokin prevented his envoys from obtaining an audience with the tsar.[74] This explains Briukhovetsky's about-face, which he executed by means of secret negotiations with the Right-Bank Hetman, Petro Doroshenko (1665–76).

It does not speak well for Ordin-Nashchokin's knowledge of Ukraine that the crisis which began in February 1668 took him completely by surprise. Neither does the fact that the mediators and messengers whom he selected for his communications with the Cossacks were basically opposed to him: Bishop Metodii Fylymonovych of Mstsislav, Metropolitan Iosyf Neliubovych-Tukalsky of Kiev, and the archimandrite of the Kiev Cave Monastery, Inokentii Gizel. All three were afraid of being subordinated to the Patriarch of Moscow. It was already too late to avert the rebellion when Moscow offered to revise the decree concerning the voevodas in Ukraine, more or less as compensation for the Kiev clause.[75] This willingness to reduce the degree of its administrative sovereignty demonstrates once again how little the government cared to bring about a true integration of Ukraine when there was a conflict of interest with Poland. At that time, Aleksei Mikhailovich was eagerly pursuing a plan to make his son Aleksei a candidate for the Polish throne and to bring about a Russo-Polish union. If Moscow had given in on the religious question, Right-Bank Ukraine would have become part of the Russian Empire then and there, one hundred years before the first partition of Poland. But there was no overwhelming desire to possess all of Ukraine: the difficulties on the Left Bank alone were formidable enough. Muscovy's voevodas and garrisons remained only in Kiev, Chernihiv and Nizhyn, not even retaining authority over local justice and administration. This situation prevailed after the rebellion until the end of the century.

Ordin-Nashchokin's incompetence in Ukrainian affairs had become clearly apparent. As early as January 1667, Aleksei Mikhailovich began partially to ignore his "chancellor" in these matters, and in March, upon the election in Hlukhiv of Demian Mnohohrishny (1669–72) as Hetman by the grace of Muscovy, the tsar let the Cossacks know that Kiev definitely would not be returned to Poland after the agreed two years.[76] At the same time, on 9 April 1669, A. S. Matveev took over the Office for Little Russia, which was completely incorporated into the Foreign Office on 22 February 1671, and thus continued to be headed by the new "chancellor," Matveev, after Ordin-Nashchokin's complete retirement at the beginning of 1671. Matveev had participated in several missions to Ukraine and had an excellent knowledge of conditions there. This was important to Moscow during the troublesome period that witnessed the Razin revolt, the independent policies of Doroshenko, and Mnohohrishny's decision to oppose the tsar, who had him sentenced to death for this in 1672 and then banished him to Siberia immediately before the planned execution. Mnohohrishny was betrayed by his own *starshyna*—an indication of the tensions that would develop in later decades between the Hetmans and the growing upper stratum of landowners that still lacked the legal documents required for noble status. The increasing importance of the *starshyna* corresponded to the waning of internal Ukrainian autonomy, much to Moscow's advantage.[77] Matveev's takeover of the Office for Little Russia marked the inauguration of a more energetic policy toward Ukraine—the second step toward the consolidation of the relationship between the two countries.

As part of this policy, the new Hetman, Ivan Samoilovych (1672–87), was elected, for the sake of security, on Muscovite territory (between Konotop and Putyvl) at the end of May 1672, once again with the aid of Romodanovsky, and his powers were further limited. He was the first to stay at the top for a longer period of time—one and one-half decades. Most importantly, Muscovy began an active struggle for Right-Bank Ukraine two years later, thereby becoming involved in its first war with the Turks (1677–9), after having stayed clear of Western alliances for centuries. However, this first twinge of expansionist ambition was transitory. The new tsar, the sickly Fedor Alekseevich, did not hold out very long. He pulled back to the Left Bank in 1679 and arranged a settlement with the Sultan two years later in Bakhchysarai. It could be said that the earlier reservations with regard to the Left Bank were now applied to the Right Bank, for there is no doubt that this sparsely populated and partly desolate area could easily have been taken from the Ottomans or, later, from the Poles.

In any event, for Left-Bank Ukraine Samoilovych's hetmancy was a time of consolidation, with a simultaneous acceptance of Moscow's sovereignty. This was all the easier because there were no remaining difficulties with the Rzeczpospolita. In 1685, the hetman failed to persuade Moscow to annex the Right Bank, just as he had already been refused permission in 1679 to extend the borders of the Hetmanate to Slobodian Ukraine, to which many refugees had come from the Right Bank during the 1660s and 70s. On the other hand, his suggestion of the same year to subordinate the Kiev Metropolitanate to the Moscow Patriarchate was carried out with alacrity. Samoilovych thus enabled his relative, the bishop of Lutsk, Count G. Sviatopolk-Chetvertynsky (1685–90), to occupy the metropolitan's chair.[78] In 1686, the Treaty of Moscow brought the final incorporation of Kiev and the Zaporozhian Sich, but also the renunciation of the Right Bank of the Dnieper, thus setting the capstone on Polish-Muscovite relations. Samoilovych, too, ended his days in Siberia, also delivered up by his officers, because Moscow needed a scapegoat for the failure of its first expedition to the Crimea (1687).

During the return of this expedition, V. V. Golitsyn had I. Mazepa (1687–1709) elected as the new hetman at the Kolomak council in mid-1687. The "articles" ratified on this occasion, which, in contrast to the earlier "articles," scarcely retained the character of a treaty, further limited the rights of the hetman in favour of Moscow and the *starshyna*.[79] At the same time, the customs barriers between Muscovy and Ukraine were lifted. Mazepa came from the Polish service, was a stranger on the Left Bank, and had ingratiated himself with Moscow by his reports on Doroshenko and Samoilovych in 1674.[80] Residing in Moscow in 1689, he managed the transition from Sofia to Peter the Great superbly, but he was just as consistent—and this was due to an honest concern for the fate of Ukraine—in turning from the latter to Stanisław Leszczyński after 1705, and subsequently to Charles XII. The motives for Ukraine's secession are to be found in Peter's stricter policies, which were manifested—to give one example—by the fact that now, for the first time, money flowed from Ukraine to Moscow, once the tsar had separated the hetman's income and expenditures from those of the army. Peter had no more interest in the Right Bank than his predecessors.[81] The actual incorporation of

Ukraine followed the conclusion of the Great Northern War. Even by the time of Ivan Skoropadsky (1708–22), "articles" were no longer ratified, and with the decree of 29 April 1722—the third step toward the limitation of Cossack autonomy—General S. Veliaminov was sent to Hlukhiv as head of a board of control, over the Hetman's protests. Out of this board developed the Little Russian College (*Malorossiiskaia kolegiia*), patterned after the former Central Office,[82] but without the tardiness of response and allowances for the freedom-loving Cossacks that had marked the whole second half of the seventeenth century.

This response to Mazepa's "betrayal" was unquestionably more appropriate to an absolutist state; indeed, Moscow's steadily harsher policy toward Ukraine can even be seen as a measure of the development of Russian absolutism, whose provenance was Western.

Perhaps the tsars' attitude can be made more comprehensible by examining Moscow's seventeenth-century image of Ukraine and the Cossacks, i.e., Ukraine's significance for the Tsardom of Muscovy.

*

When a seventeenth-century Muscovite thought of Ukraine, two associations probably came to mind. Ukraine was the home of a few, mostly clerical, educators, the source of certain innovations, and thus a gateway to the West, i.e., a place of intellectual unrest. It was also one of the homelands of the Cossacks, the starting point of many rebellions and the refuge of escaped peasants, i.e., a place of social unrest.

To begin with the second point: the Muscovite government generally ignored the fact that Ukraine also had a non-Cossack population, especially as the tsar only negotiated with the hetman. Thus, the Dnieper Cossacks represented Ukraine, and its growth during the second half of the sixteenth century was essentially due to the slowly increasing wave of emigration from the core territories of Poland-Lithuania and Muscovy—a consequence of economic change. Once the colonization of the interior had been completed and a service nobility created, the governments of both states wanted to gain control of the peasant serfs—Zygmunt August by means of the land reform of 1557 and Ivan IV by his state reforms of the 1550s, as well as the land survey. But the increasing bondage only helped provoke a mass peasant exodus, which began toward the end of the century.[83] From Podolia to the Volga, Cossackdom stood for a revolutionary social program,[84] especially when discontent began to manifest itself in rebellions, first in Poland and then, beginning with Bolotnikov's revolt, also in the Tsardom of Muscovy. However much Moscow took advantage of an army that served almost free of charge for the defence of its frontiers, it regarded the "wild steppes" (*dikoe pole*), especially Ukraine, with great concern, especially after the Time of Troubles, a traumatic experience whose effects were felt throughout the seventeenth century. This ambivalent attitude can be detected in the decrees on runaways and seems to have been inherent in the peasant legislation, for the government's hesitation in ratifying the extended time limit for the recovery of fugitive serfs (*urochnye leta*) before 1649, which had been requested by the nobility, was certainly related to the fact that an expansion of the army in the south was not unwelcome.

After the enactment of the *Ulozhenie*, the peasants did not cease their exodus, even though they were legally bound to the soil. In fact, the exodus increased during the war of 1654–67. The ambivalence noted previously reappeared in the decrees on the return of runaways, especially with respect to Ukraine, for the "wild steppes" were now more nearly in Moscow's grasp. Accordingly, the "articles" contained demands for the return of runaways, and at the beginning of the war Aleksei Mikhailovich even had ten runaways hanged to set an example.[85] However, the more the significance of the old noble levy (*opolchenie*) decreased because of the introduction of the "regiments of the new order," and the less attention had to be paid to the service nobility, the more lenient the peasant legislation could become. The deadlines for the return of runaways were continually extended. On 5 March 1653, the due date was that decreed in the *Ulozhenie*, but in 1656 it was that decreed in 1653; in 1683, for example, it was that decreed in 1675, and between 1684 and 1698 the punishment of runaways was suspended and cancelled four times.[86] Thus, in practice the government reintroduced deadlines to serve its own interests.

If the Muscovite authorities were ambivalent, to say the least, about the problem of peasants and Ukraine, it is easy to imagine the desperate rage that the rebellions aroused in them. Their determination to combat the rebellions originating in the south is so self-evident that any elaboration on it would be superfluous. The Cossacks, with their anarchic conception of freedom, were an example to peasants and townsmen alike. It is no accident that the century of the Ukrainian problem was also a century of revolt, termed a "rebellious time" (*buntashnoe vremia*) by contemporaries.

But perhaps Cossack ideals also had a less radical influence on the Tsardom of Muscovy. Apart from rebellions, the period after 1598 was generally marked by an awakening social consciousness. Beginning in the 1620s, collective petitions were presented on behalf of whole social groups or regions, and during the rebellion of 1648 there were even joint petitions from two social groups, the nobility and the townsmen. Also, the traditional Assemblies of the State assumed a new political character during the Time of Troubles and in 1648–9.[87] It is not noted in the sources that the social unrest stirred up by the Cossacks served as an incentive, but this can be assumed. A little of this is apparent in the volatile polemics published by eyewitnesses to the Time of Troubles during the second and third decades of the century. What could have been the most subversive, if not contagious, influence was the Cossack practice of holding elections. It is true that elections had been an old legal institution on Russian territory as well, and that by the mid-sixteenth century Ivan IV had established locally elected administrations by fiat, but never had there been as many governing bodies elected as during the Time of Troubles, and it is well known that at times the army's Grand Council of War functioned as the government. Never before had a tsar been elected. The matter-of-fact (though not, of course, "democratic") fashion in which the first election was conducted in 1598, and most particularly the election of 1613, which was carried out with greater participation of provincial delegates, cannot be explained solely by the example of other states. Although this is pure speculation, there do exist several slight indications of the impression made by the Cossack administration.

During the Bolotnikov revolt, a contemporary described the territory affected by it as follows: "in every town the Cossacks, who emerged from the slaves (*kholopy*) and peasants, have again increased in numbers, and in every town they make [i.e., elect] their otamans."[88] Awareness of Cossack freedoms certainly spread in other ways as well. Their attractiveness is very clearly expressed in a document that dates from the end of the era under consideration. During their rebellion of 1682, the Muscovite Streltsy made a demand in their political programme of 6 June for the establishment of self-governing bodies to be known as *krugi* (circles), whose elected delegates were to be responsible to the Streltsy. These functionaries were then to present the wishes of the Streltsy to "their tsar," who would be obliged to heed them.[89] The explicit reference to Cossack models is further illuminated by the fact that at the end of 1682 and the beginning of 1683 the service registry (*razriad*) explicitly prohibited the Streltsy, who had been banished to various towns after the rebellion, from conducting meetings in the fashion of the Cossack organs of self-government.[90] If elections and self-government are indicators of heightened political awareness, then the Tsardom of Muscovy is indebted to Ukraine, among other sources, for a century of stimuli to social activity, which was then stifled by the development of absolutism. In any case, the government had long had good reason to regard Ukraine as a trouble spot to be treated with suspicion and kept at arm's length.

This was also the case with other imports from Ukraine, not only goods such as tobacco and vodka, which were smuggled across the border despite a prohibition (as was salt in the opposite direction),[91] but also intellectual and cultural influences. The origins of this chapter in Russo-Ukrainian relations date back to the year 1572, when the first Russian printer, Ivan Fedorov of Moscow, settled in Lviv, and the products of his print-shop began to find their way back to Muscovy. Soviet researchers have documented in considerable detail the travels of individual monks, artists, teachers and others between Muscovy and Ukraine. However, this provides no grounds for considering the "reunification" (*vossoedinenie*) of 1654 particularly predestined, and the cultural exchange was by no means equal: rather, the influence proceeded from south-west to north-east,[92] especially when the customs duty on Ukrainian publications was lifted soon after 1654. In reality, this initial appearance turned out to be a Trojan horse.

In this connection, relations within the Orthodox church, which had been restored in 1622, are of great significance.[93] They consisted mainly of requests for Moscow's assistance against the church union, as well as of the influence of Ukrainian brotherhoods and their schools. However, it was a large step from the suggestion made by Metropolitan Iov Boretsky (1620–31) in 1624 that Ukraine be united with Muscovy[94] to its actual realization, which was welcomed especially by the lower clergy after 1654, while the upper clergy feared the threat of subordination to the Moscow patriarchate, which became a reality after 1685. Metropolitan Silvestr Kossov (Sylvestr Kosiv) (1647–57) objected with particular vehemence to the union of churches. However, quite independently of the political act of 1654, the church was overwhelmed by an intellectual shock that signified the end of the Old Russian era. The Kiev brotherhood, modelled upon the Western Ukrainian brother- hoods which had been in existence since the fifteenth century, was established in 1615. Under the leadership of Metropolitan Peter Mohyla (1633–46), the "Ukrainian school" developed an original interpretation of Roman Catholicism and Protestantism. Its influence penetrated Moscow, the center of Orthodoxy, producing a crisis there. However much Patriarch Nikon may have desired the incorporation of Kiev, his successors, who were opposed to Latinizing tendencies, could not have been pleased by the fact that the Ukrainian theologians, who now came to Muscovy in increasing numbers, clashed with the "Greek tendency" promoted by Nikon. The Kievan influence became equivalent to that of the West in the spheres of religion, education, literature, art and crafts.[95] Although there was scarcely any more opposition to secular Western culture in the second half of the century, the clergy had to defend itself for a long time against charges of "heresy," as the indictments and sentences of the 1690s demonstrate. Patriarch Ioakhim demanded that the Kiev Metropolitan Varlaam Iasynsky (1690–1707) formally declare his acceptance of the doctrines of the Russian church, going so far as to threaten the reluctant Iasynsky with an ecclesiastical tribunal.[96] The rise of absolutism did not supress this conflict. Instead, the problem was solved by Peter the Great's radical Westernization, whose scope was far greater than that of the earlier Ukrainian influences, as well as by the neglect of religion during the early Enlightenment.

*

Thus, there were sufficient political and ideological grounds for reservations about establishing too close a bond between Ukraine and the Tsardom of Muscovy. Ordin-Nashchokin's objections, to which reference was made earlier, become even more understandable in retrospect. His example shows that reservations concerning Ukraine could be expressed even by one who was otherwise open-minded about the West. In this respect, as in many others, he turned out to be a forerunner of Peter the Great, whose attention was also directed more toward the north-west. Even greater reservations were held by the conservative Muscovites, whose static thinking had no place for Cossack freedoms or the Magdeburg Law, for Silvestr Medvedev's conception of transubstantiation or for free-flowing architectural forms (the so-called Cossack Baroque). The history of Russo-Ukrainian relations has been called "essentially a chain of misunderstandings," because the law and freedom of the Cossacks constituted a breach of faith and betrayal for the Muscovites.[97] The term "chain of mutual distrust" probably fits the situation even better. A characteristic expression of this view is Peter the Great's opinion that all Hetmans from Khmelnytsky to Mazepa had been traitors.[98] So is a statement made in 1658 by Aleksei Mikhailovich, who wrote to his friend Ordin-Nashchokin under the impact of Vyhovsky's actions: "It is impossible to trust the Cossacks. They cannot be believed, for they sway like a reed in the wind, and, if necessary, the Russians should immediately sign a peace treaty with the Poles and Tatars."[99]

It was this mutual distrust that made the act of 1654 an alliance unloved by both parties. In contrast to "misunderstanding," the term "distrust" implies an active element. Until 1648 at the latest, Moscow's behaviour was indeed more instinctive than consciously reserved. In the following period, only aversion can explain the fact that the Tsardom of Muscovy, which overcame even the Rzecz-pospolita, did not enforce its rights in Ukraine with greater determination. Incorporation in the true sense of the word occurred only in the eighteenth century. It is true that the act of 1654 did not remain quite so nominal as that of 1656 concerning Moldavia, which used very similar terminology, but Moscow achieved true "reunion" (Kostomarov's term) only gradually, by the steps taken in 1659 (limitation of Ukraine's independence in foreign affairs) and 1672 (Matveev's takeover of the Foreign Office), as well as the events of the Great Northern War of 1700–21. Until 1672, there was a latent willingness on Moscow's part to release the Cossacks from "eternal servitude," and the annexation of Ukraine was by no means perceived as an epoch-making event. After slipping into its new role rather unwillingly, the Tsardom of Muscovy became the Russian Empire without at first intending to do so, for essentially it had only concluded a military and defensive alliance with the Cossacks, not even with Ukraine, which existed only as a territory in the environs of Kiev, but with Little Russia. Even after 1672, the eminently feasible conquest of the Right Bank of the Dnieper was contemplated only in passing. Ideologically speaking, this general reservation about conquest corresponded to the status inherent in the doctrine of the "Third Rome," to which any idea of expansionism and "imperialism," even of mission, was alien.[100]

The change of attitude toward Ukraine began with the fall of the "Third Rome" caused by the schism of 1667 and with the slow acceptance of Western rationalism. Moscow's grip became stronger under the influence of the absolutist doctrine of the sovereign's exclusive power in the state. There was no longer a place for autonomous forces, and this meant the end not only of

Ukraine's political autonomy, but also of her domineering intellectual influence on central Russia, which was yielding pride of place to St. Petersburg in any event. However, before Ukraine was absorbed by Russian state centralism, it played an important role for the Tsardom of Muscovy for almost seven decades, accelerating the latter's initiation into the modern era. In so doing, Ukraine tragically lost her significance. Her actual *ruina* occurred not after Khmelnytsky's death, but in the eighteenth century.

Translated by Gisela Forchner
and Myroslav Yurkevich

Notes

1. C. B. O'Brien, *Muscovy and the Ukraine. From the Pereiaslav Agreement to the Truce of Andrusovo, 1654–1667* (Berkeley and Los Angeles, 1963).

2. See Taras Hunczak, ed., *Russian Imperialism from Ivan the Great to the Revolution* (New Brunswick, N. J., 1974).

3. O. Halecki, "Imperialism in Slavic and East European History," *American Slavic and East European Review* (ASEER) XI (1952):1–26; N. V. Riasanovsky, "Old Russia, the Soviet Union and Eastern Europe," ASEER XI (1952):171–88; O. P. Backus, "Was Muscovite Russia Imperialistic?" ASEER XIII (1954):522–34. For reprints of the three articles, see *Die Anfänge des Moskauer Staates,* ed. P. Nitsche (Darmstadt, 1977), 272–339.

4. N. V. Riasanovsky, op. cit., 313. Backus, in his article, was mainly concerned with the fifteenth century, but generally criticized Halecki for not defining imperialism, which Backus considered an inappropriate term for the period in question.

5. H. R. Huttenbach, "The Origins of Russian Imperialism" in Hunczak, ed., *Russian Imperialism,* 18–44; idem, "The Ukraine and Muscovite Expansion," ibid., 167–97. Cf. W. Leitsch, "Russo-Polish Confrontation," ibid., 131–66. It is also O'Brien's view that the tsar wanted to "encroach upon Ukrainian sovereignty" from the very beginning. O'Brien alleges *raison d'état* (which was completely alien to Muscovite ideology) and a desire for territorial gain (which cannot be derived from the sources) (*Muscovy and the Ukraine,* 127ff.).

6. N. Karamsin, *Geschichte des russischen Reiches* (Riga, 1825), 7:57, 86.

7. The first reports about Cossacks in the Dnieper region date back to 1492. See K. Pułaski, *Stosunki Polski z Tatarszczyzną od połowy XV w.,* vol. 1 (Warsaw, 1881), no. 24. At first the Cossacks were a mixture of Tatars and Slavs, with the latter gaining the upper hand during the first half of the sixteenth century. See G. Stöckl, *Die Entstehung des Kosakentums* (Munich, 1953), 152.

8. *Polnoe Sobranie Russkikh Letopisei* (PSRL) (St. Petersburg, 1904), 13, 1:286. Vyshnevetsky's expedition to the Crimea was a failure; in order to escape

Moscow's retribution, he fled to Lithuania. Cf. Zygmunt August's commendation of 5 September 1561 (*Akty Iuzhnoi i Zapadnoi Rosii* [AIuZR], 2, no. 142).

9. S. M. Solovev, *Istoriia Rosii s drevneishikh vremen* (Moscow, 1960), 4:28.

10. In 1578 Stefan Batory notified the Crimean Khan that the Sich would be very difficult to take, for he had no fortifications there and the Cossacks would always find protection in Muscovy (*Acta St. Batorei*, no. 23). Marcin Bielski also reported that many Cossacks went to the Don (*Kronika Marcina Bielskiego* (Warsaw, 1829), 3:13ff.). In the 1580s there were whole regiments under the Hetmans M. Fedoriv, T. Slipetsky and S. Vysotsky. See E. M. Apanovich, "Pereselenie ukraintsev v Rossiiu nakanune osvoboditelnoi voiny 1648–1654 gg." in *Vossoedinenie Ukrainy s Rossiei 1654–1954: Sbornik statei* (Moscow, 1954), 79. Fletcher wrote of 4,000 Cossack mercenaries (G. Fletcher, *Of the Russe Commonwealth*, ed. A. J. Schmidt (Ithaca, N. Y., 1966), 78), and Margeret also counted 4,000 Cossacks at the beginning of the seventeenth century (*Skazaniia sovremennikov o Dm. Samozvantse* (St. Petersburg, 1859), 1:281).

11. St. Żołkiewski, *Listy 1584–1620* (Cracow, 1868), no. 17. In 1596 Żołkiewski threatened Chancellor Zamoyski with the prospect of the rebels' emigration to Muscovy if the Sejm did not approve funds to fight them.

12. "*...po ukazu gosudarevu...veleno*" (*Sobranie Gosudarstvennykh Gramot i Dogovorov* (SGGD), 2, no. 62). The Austrian envoy confirmed this in his diary (*Memuary otnosiashchiesia k istorii Iuzhnoi Rossii* (Kiev, 1890), 1: 163, 178. Hetman Nalyvaiko probably also intended to ally himself with the tsar in 1596, but the Poles anticipated this, as can be seen from the report of an imperial courier (*Pamiatniki diplomaticheskikh snoshenii drevnei Rossii s derzhavami inostrannymi* [St. Petersburg, 1852), 2, col. 294).

13. There is a reference to this in a letter by the Zaporozhian Hetman T. Baibuza dated 1598 (St. Żołkiewski, *op. cit.* (n. 10), no. 60).

14. O. Hoetzsch, "Föderation und fürstliche Gewalt (Absolutismus) in der Geschichte Osteuropas im 17. und 18. Jahrhundert," *Zeitschrift für osteuropäische Geschichte* (ZOG) 8 (1934): 24.

15. See I. I. Smirnov, *Vosstanie Bolotnikova, 1606–1607* (Moscow, 1951).

16. At the beginning of the century and in 1615 in Oster; in 1605 in Korsun; in 1615 in the Dnieper region; in 1616 and 1622 in the Kiev area; in 1625, 1630–31 and 1637–8 in various places; in 1640 in Korostyshiv; in 1644 and 1648 in Sniatyn; in 1646 in Cherkasy, Korsun and Stebliv. See A. I. Baranovich, *Ukraina nakanune osvoboditelnoi voiny seredini XVII v. (Sotsialno- ekonomicheskie predposylki voiny)* (Moscow, 1959), 188ff.

17. *Vossoedinenie Ukrainy s Rossiei: Dokumenty i materialy v trekh tomakh* (henceforth *Vossoedinenie*), v. 1 (1620–47) (Moscow, 1954), nos. 1–3 and 7. In 1625 the Poles reprimanded the Zaporozhians for this relationship and especially for the use of the title. See K. G. Guslisty, "Istoricheskie sviazi ukraintsev s Rossiei do osvoboditelnoi voiny 1648–1654 gg." in *Vossoedinenie Ukrainy s Rossiei 1654–1954: Sbornik statei* (Moscow, 1954), 37. For 1621, see *Vossoedinenie*, 1, no. 8.

18. For example, after the rebellions of 1630–31 (ibid., no. 63) and 1637–8 (ibid.,

no. 114). In 1638 I. Ostrianyn came with 3,000 and V. F. Ivankiev with 10,000 men (Apanovich, "Pereselenie ukraintsev...," 80ff). Cf. also a report dated April 1638 by the Don Ataman Tatarinov (*Vossoedinenie*, 1, no. 121).

19. In 1637–8 it was stated: "There is nothing in the treaty which says that the deserters have to be returned; nobody has called them, and how can you return someone who came voluntarily?" (Apanovich, "Pereselenie ukraintsev...," 88). The border voevodas argued in the same fashion with the Polish-Lithuanian starostas, e.g., in a letter of 6 September 1638 from the voevoda N. Pleshcheev of Putyvl to the elder M. Długcki of Hadiach (*Vossoedinenie*, 1, no. 147).

20. After having sworn an oath in Putyvl, the port of entry, most of the refugees were sent to live as far away from the borders as possible in special settlements (*slobody*). They were given money (five to eight rubles for the men, one and one-half rubles for other family members over 15 years of age, one ruble for children between 11 and 15 years of age, and one-half ruble for younger children); grain (from 8 quarters of rye for a large family to 3 quarters for a single person); seed (5 quarters of grain per family, 3 quarters for a single person); salt (2 puds per family, 1 pud for a single person); and, of course, land, i.e., virgin or state-owned land as service estates (20 quarters for a peasant, 40 quarters for a leader of a hundred men). Furthermore, if they were Cossacks, they received an annual salary, arms and ammunition (Apanovich, "Pereselenie ukraintsev," 89 ff).

21. S. Velychenko, "The Origins of the Ukrainian Revolution of 1648," *Journal of Ukrainian Graduate Studies* 1 (1976):23ff.

22. *Vossoedinenie*, v. 2 (1648–51) (Moscow, 1954), no. 101. While Polish nobles were sent back (ibid., no. 196), the Cossacks now received an average of 4 to 10 rubles per family. In February 1652, for example, almost the whole town of Konstantyniv came to Muscovy, as did the Cossacks of the Hlukhiv battalion and many inhabitants of Konotop; in March of the same year, Colonel I. Dzikovsky came from Chernihiv with more than 2,000 families. See I. D. Boiko, "Osvobo-ditelnaia voina ukrainskogo naroda 1648–1654 gg. i vossoedineie Ukrainy s Rossiei" in *Vossoedinenie Ukrainy s Rossiei 1654–1954: Sbornik statei* (Moscow, 1954), 132.

23. This comment was handed down by the later Hetman I. Vyhovsky (1657–9). See S. Grondski, *Historia belli cosacco-polonici* (Pestini, 1789), 49.

24. *Vossoedinenie*, 2, nos. 12, 20, 25, 34, 52, 68, 74. Colonel S. Muzhylovsky also delivered a petition on this matter to Moscow on 4 February 1649 (ibid., no. 50).

25. On 22 November 1649 Khmelnytsky thanked the Muscovite envoy G. Neronov for the deliveries of grain (ibid., no. 118). In January 1651 the Polish king's secretary complained to the Muscovite envoy V. Starogo about Muscovy's delivery of arms. See V. A. Golobutskii, *Zaporozhskoe kazachestvo* (Kiev, 1957), 279.

26. *Vossoedinenie*, 2, no. 39. On 13 March 1649 the tsar praised Khmelnytsky for the Cossacks' desire to become Muscovite subjects (ibid., no. 58).

27. Ibid., no. 46. Later, Metropolitan Gabriel of Nazareth (on behalf of Paisios), Metropolitan Joasaph of Corinth, and Metropolitan Galaktion of Macedonia attempted in vain to serve as mediators. Paisios himself and even the ecumenical

patriarch became involved once again in 1651. See R. Stupperich, "Der Anteil der Kirche beim Anschluss der Ukraine an Moskau (1654)," *Kirche im Osten* 14 (1971):68ff.

28. *Vossoedinenie*, 2, no. 90. Kliuchevskii called this argument "a cruel, malicious joke" (*zhestokaia nasmeshka*). See V. O. Kliuchevskii, *Kurs russkoi istorii* in his *Sochineniia* (Moscow, 1957), 3:118.

29. AIuZR 3, no. 303.

30. *Vossoedinenie*, 2, no. 173. Khmelnytsky mentioned his discontent with the tsar on 8 November 1650 in a conversation with Prior Arsenii Sukhanov of Moldavia, who was on his way from Moscow to Jerusalem, where he was to collect Greek sources for the Muscovite dispute about the correction of books. He accompanied Paisios (cf. n. 27) and was also to mediate in Ukrainian affairs, e.g., in the case of the false pretender to the throne, Akundinov (see below). Khmelnytsky complained that the tsar was unreliable. The Ukrainian envoys had been told good things and welcomed in friendly fashion, "but the next time he said something different, namely that he was at eternal peace with the king" (*Vossoedinenie*, 2, no. 76).

31. Cf. Khmelnytsky's letter of 11 November 1650 to the tsar (ibid., no. 190). The clergyman Arsenii Sukhanov had acted as a mediator on this issue (cf. n. 30; also S. A. Belokurov, *Arsenii Sukhanov (1632–1668 gg.)*, 2 vols. (St. Petersburg, 1891–3). Akundinov continued his flight to Sweden, through Livonia, Holland and several German principalities to Holstein, from where he was extradited to Moscow only in August 1653. There he was executed in the presence of the Polish envoy. For further information see H. J. Torke, *Die staatsbedingte Gesellschaft im Moskauer Reich. Zar und Zemlja in der altrussisschen Herrschafts-verfassung, 1613–1689* (Leiden, 1974), 23ff.

32. H. Neubauer, *Car und Selbstherrscher. Beiträge zur Geschichte der Autokratie in Russland* (Wiesbaden, 1964), 119.

33. *Vossoedinenie*, v. 3 (1651–4) (Moscow, 1954), no. 1; V. N. Latkin, *Materialy dlia istorii Zemskikh soborov XVII stoletiia (1619–20, 1648–49 i 1651 godov)* (St. Petersburg, 1884), 77ff.

34. *Vossoedinenie*, 3, no. 2.

35. Ibid., no. 11. Later on Khmelnytsky also wrote to Morozov (cf. n. 41).

36. Ibid., no. 60. Additional letters to the border voevodas confirm this attitude.

37. N. F. Kapterev, *Kharakter otnoshenii Rossii k pravoslavnomu vostoku v XVI i XVII stoletiiakh* (Moscow, 1885), 353. Cf. n. 27.

38. *Vossoedinenie*, 3, no. 165. This letter is a response to a communication that was not received from the Hetman. For the period from 9 to 13 May, there exists only one letter from the Hetman's envoys to the Patriarch requesting intercession with the tsar (ibid., no. 162). On 23 April, K. Burliai and S. Muzhylovsky had been received by Nikon (ibid., no. 154). Later, on 9 and 12 August 1653, Khmelnytsky asked the Patriarch to request speedier assistance (ibid., nos. 183 and 186). On Nikon's attitude, see also K. Zernack, "Die Expansion des Moskauer Reiches nach Westen, Süden und Osten von 1648 bis 1689" in *Handbuch der Geschichte Russlands* 2, no. 2 (Stuttgart, 1986), 129.

39. *Vossoedinenie*, 3, no. 101.

40. Ibid., no. 133 (letter of 12 November) and no. 138 (minutes of the negotiations in Moscow).

41. A. I. Kozachenko, "Zemskii sobor 1653 goda," *Voprosy istorii*, no. 5 (1957): 152. Just at this time, on 23 March, Khmelnytsky wrote four more letters to Moscow addressed to Aleksei Mikhailovich, B. Morozov, I. Miloslavsky and G. Pushkin in order to present his request (*Vossoedinenie* 3, nos. 147–50).

42. Ibid., no. 169. The Hetman received notice of the decision at an audience with the Muscovite envoys A. S. Matveev and I. Fomin on 4 July. His letter to the voevoda of Putyvl, Count Khilkov, testifies to his threat concerning the Ottomans: "...if the grace of His Majesty is not granted, I will become the servant and slave of the Turks." See P. A. Matveev, "Moskva i Malorossiia v upravlenie Ordina-Nashchokina Malorossiiskim Prikazom," *Russkii arkhiv* 39 (1901):221.

43. On the dates of the meetings in 1653, see Torke, *Die staatsbedingte Gesellschaft*, 199ff.

44. *Vossoedinenie*, 3, no. 197; SGGD 3, no. 157; V. N. Latkin, *Zemskie sobory drevnei Rusi, ikh istoriia i organizatsiia sravnitelno s zapadno-evropeiskimi predstavitelnymi uchrezhdeniiami: Istoriko-iuridicheskoe issledovanie* (St. Petersburg, 1885), 434ff.

45. *Vossoedinenie*, 3, nos. 203–6. R. Streshnev had already departed on 6 September with the preliminary decision (ibid., 191ff). Meanwhile the Akundinov affair had also been concluded satisfactorily (cf. n. 31).

46. *Polnoe Sobranie Zakonov Rossiiskoi Imperii* (PSZ), Series 1 (St. Petersburg, 1830), 1, nos. 106, 111.

47. W. Leitsch, *Moskau und die Politik des Kaiserhofes im XVII. Jahrhundert* (Graz and Cologne, 1960), 1:27.

48. V. A. Miakotin, "Die Vereinigung der Ukraine mit dem Moskauer Staat," ZOG 7 (1933):326. The Muscovite envoy R. Streshnev (cf. n. 45) was instructed to confirm the Russian guarantee only if Khmelnytsky insisted obstinately or if his war with Poland had already commenced (*Vossoedinenie*, 3, no. 194). Even when the Muscovite envoys had already reached Viazma on their way back from Poland, a special courier was sent from Moscow to Streshnev as late as 20 September in order to ensure that the latter would only guarantee Muscovy's support if war had already broken out (ibid., no. 196).

49. "*Getmana Bogdana Khmelnitskogo i vse Voisko Zaporozhskoe z gorodami i z zemliami...pod svoiu (gosudarevu) vysokuiu ruku*" (ibid., no. 197).

50. Cf. Buturlin's account of this (ibid., no. 205). Cf. also Khmelnytsky's letter of thanks to the tsar, dated 8 January (ibid., no. 225).

51. Ibid., no. 245.

52. Miakotin, *Die Vereinigung*, 329.

53. Hoetzsch's observation that the tsar's original patent made no mention of foreign relations, indicating that Moscow had decided to reserve foreign policy entirely to itself ("Föderation und fürstliche Gewalt," 27), can also be interpreted in the opposite sense: foreign relations were not mentioned because the Hetman had

been granted complete liberty in this sphere.

54. AIuZR, 3, no. 369. However, Khmelnytsky's envoy P. Teteria, who was in Moscow in 1657, admitted the opposite: a larger sum was at issue, sufficient to cover the upkeep of the whole army. For the time being, however, the army was not paid out of this fund, part of which the colonels kept for themselves (ibid., 2, Appendix, no. 2).

55. O. E. Günther, "Der Vertrag von Perejaslav im Widerstreit der Meinungen," *Jahrbücher für Geschichte Osteuropas* (JGO), New Series 2 (1954):243. However, what Khmelnytsky really thought and wanted is strongly disputed in the literature. See also H. Fleischhacker, "Die politischen Begriffe der Partner von Perejaslav," ibid., 222ff.

56. Evidently the expression *vechnoe poddanstvo*, used by Aleksei Mikhailovich in a letter to Khmelnytsky on 27 March 1654 (*Vossoedinenie*, 3, no. 248), belongs to the same category of fine political phrases as "eternal peace." V. Prokopovych suggests that "eternal" should not be interpreted to mean "aeternus," but rather "perpetuus" in the meaning of "unlimited" or "permanent." See V. Prokopovych, "The Problem of the Juridical Nature of the Ukraine's Union with Muscovy," *Annals of the Ukrainian Academy of Arts and Sciences in the U.S.* 4 (1955):926ff. and 946.

57. On the occasion of the birth of his first son, Aleksei, Khmelnytsky had addressed the tsar in this fashion as early as 8 January (cf. n. 50), but this letter exists only in Russian translation. In 1656 the tsar even called himself "sovereign of Kiev" *vis-à-vis* Poland (PSZ, Series 1, 1, no. 192). Such changes of title occurred rapidly and were sometimes temporary, as is shown by the titles assumed with respect to Georgia and Moldavia (Prokopovych, "The Problem of the Juridical Nature," 970ff.).

58. SGGD 4, 4. The same was true of the newly acquired Belorussian regions. See I. B. Grekov, "Iz istorii sovmestnoi borby Ukrainy i Rossii za osushchestvlenie reshenii Pereiaslavskoi rady (1657–1659 gg.)" in *Vossoedinenie Ukrainy s Rossiei: Sbornik statei* (Moscow, 1954), 311.

59. In early 1657 A. Lopukhin was delegated to inform Khmelnytsky that, *inter alia*, a treaty between Muscovy and Poland would not affect Ukrainian interests. See AIuZR 8, 386 ff. See also ibid., 7, 191.

60. Cf. the report by Protasev (ibid., 11, Appendix, no. 2).

61. A typical case is that of P. Teteria, who, as Khmelnytsky's envoy, made mention of these conditions in August 1657 and presented himself and the brothers I. and K. Vyhovsky as examples. Not even the Hetman was to know of the gifts, and preference was given to grants of land in Lithuania and Belorussia (ibid.).

62. A kind of "bondage of mutual consent" was introduced only gradually by the Cossack upper stratum. This system involved personal freedom for the peasants in exchange for the assumption of social responsibilities, with service estates distributed to the officers. See K. Kononenko, *Ukraine and Russia: A History of the Economic Relations between Ukraine and Russia (1654–1917)* (Milwaukee, 1958), 1 ff.

63. Fleischhacker, "Die politischen Begriffe," 231.

64. This was communicated to the lord high steward (*stolnik*) Kikin (AIuZR 11, Appendix, no. 3).

65. "...*a tvoikh de velikogo gosudaria...voevod i ratnykh liudei...na Ukraine nigde net*" (ibid., 4, 116).

66. Günther, "Der Vertrag von Perejaslav," 232. For a long time, scholars took these articles to be the actual "treaty," which survived only as a concept.

67. The Cossacks delivered the Muscovite commander-in-chief, Sheremetev, to the Tatars. Because the tsar did not consider him worth the ransom, he had to spend 20 years in Bakhchysarai.

68. Z. Wójcik, "The Early Period of Pavlo Teteria's Hetmancy in the Right-Bank Ukraine (1661–1663)" in *Eucharisterion: Essays presented to Omeljan Pritsak on his Sixtieth Birthday by his Colleagues and Students (Harvard Ukrainian Studies III/IV)*, (Cambridge, Mass., 1980), 2:965.

69. The Army Otaman Roh wrote to him: "The Army does not know what a boiar is; it knows only the Hetman." (Matveev, "Moskva i Malorossiia," 235). A Colonel (D. Iermolenko) made this comment on the wave of ennoblement: "I do not need the nobility; I am a Cossack of the old school." (AIuZR 6, no. 41).

70. This was reported by the tsar's personal physician, an Englishman. See S. Collins, *The Present State of Russia, in a Letter to a Friend at London: Written by an Eminent Person Residing at the Great Tzars Court at Moscow for the space of nine years* (London, 1671), 107.

71. S. F. Platonov, *Moskva i zapad* (Berlin, 1926), 120ff.

72. K. A. Sofronenko, *Malorossiiskii prikaz russkogo gosudarstva vtoroi poloviny XVII i nachala XVIII veka* (Moscow 1960). The office employed up to four secretaries (*diaki*) and between 15 and 40 scribes (*podiachie*) (ibid., 43).

73. Matveev, *Moskva i Malorossiia*, 226. As early as 1658 Ordin-Nashchokin had wanted to return Ukraine, as well as Vitebsk and Polotsk, to Poland so as to be able to negotiate peace with Sweden together with the Rzeczpospolita. However, Matveev goes much too far when he explains Briukhovetsky's secession of 1668 by Ordin-Nashchokin's anti-Ukrainian attitude alone (ibid., 227). On concepts of foreign policy in Muscovy, see Zernack, "Die Expansion des Moskauer Reiches," 123ff.

74. Matveev, *Moskva i Malorossiia*, 235. Rumours of Ordin-Nashchokin's double-dealing were stirred up especially by the bishop of Mstsislavl, Metodii (see below), who wanted to harm Briukhovetsky. See V. O. Eingorn, "Ocherki iz istorii Malorossii v XVII veke," *Zhurnal Ministerstva Narodnogo Prosveshcheniia* (1899), 431.

75. Matveev, *Moskva i Malorossiia*, 238ff. Ordin-Nashchhokin made another mistake in February 1668, after the outbreak of the rebellion, because he did not know the individuals involved. Briukhovetsky thus obtained the letters directed against him (ibid., 239).

76. Ibid., 242ff.

77. The general quartermaster (*heneralnyi oboznyi*) P. Zabila, one of the main intriguers against Mnohohrishny, even suggested to the tsar that he appoint a

boiar as Hetman, "for if the Hetman is a Little Russian, nothing good will come of it." (AIuZR 9, no. 146). See also H. Schumann, "Der Hetmanstaat (1654–1764)," JGO 1 (1936):543ff.

78. B. Krupnyckyj, *Geschichte der Ukraine* (Leipzig, 1943), 131. Aleksei Mikhailovich and Nikon had made this suggestion for the first time after the conquest of Smolensk and Polotsk (Stupperich, "Der Anteil der Kirche," 81).

79. This was not accepted without resistance, as was shown by P. I. Petryk's rebellion against Mazepa in 1692. On the reduced significance of the "articles" as a treaty, see B. E. Nolde, "Essays in Russian State Law," *Annals of the Ukrainian Academy of Arts and Sciences in the U.S.* 4 (1955), 880.

80. D. Doroshenko, "Hetman Mazepa: Sein Leben und Wirken," ZOG 7 (1933):56.

81. The colonel of the Bila Tserkva regiment, Semen Palii, who led a rebellion against the Poles on the Right Bank from 1700 to 1703, wanted to place this part of the country under Mazepa's control, but was arrested by Mazepa on the tsar's orders. See O. Ohloblyn, *Hetman Ivan Mazepa ta ioho doba* (New York, 1960), 196ff.

82. Nolde, "Essays," 882ff. The whole process corresponded to the subordination of the Don Cossacks to the War College in 1721.

83. As a recent study shows, at the beginning of the 1580s there were hardly any Cossacks—about eight per cent—of Muscovite origin among the Zaporozhians. See S. Luber and P. Rostankowski, "Die Herkunft der im Jahre 1581 registrierten Zaporoger Kosaken," JGO 28 (1980):368ff.

84. Stökl, *Die Entstehung des Kosakentums*, 172.

85. Solovev, *Istoriia Rossii*, 5:643.

86. Novoselsky, *Pobegi krestian i khlopov i ikh sysk v Moskovskom gosudarstve vtoroi poloviny XVII veka* (Moscow 1926).

87. On the collective petitions and Assemblies of the Land, see Torke, *Die staatsbedingte Gesellschaft*, Chapters 3 and 4.

88. Smirnov, *Vosstanie Bolotnikova*, 124.

89. *Akty sobrannye v bibliotekakh i arkhivakh Rossiiskoi Imperii Arkheograficheskoiu ekspeditsieiu Imperatorskoi Akademii Nauk* (AAE) 4, no. 255, 1. After the rebellion had been crushed, Sofia explicitly prohibited such self-government on 8 October 1682 (ibid., no. 266).

90. PSZ, Series 1, v. 2, no. 978; SGGD 4, no. 158.

91. *Vossoedinenie*, 1, nos. 19, 107, 269.

92. I. P. Eremin, "K istorii russko-ukrainskikh literaturnykh sviazei v XVII v.," *Trudy Otdela drevnerusskoi literatury* 9 (1953), 291ff.; K. V. Kharlampovich, *Malorossiiskoe vliianie na velikorusskuiu tserkovnuiu zhizn*, v. 1 (Kazan, 1914).

93. In that year, the discharged bishop of Przemyśl, Isaiia Kopynsky, who later became Metropolitan (1631–3), asked Filaret for permission to immigrate to Muscovy because of the persecution of Orthodoxy (*Vossoedinenie*, 1, no. 15ff).

94. Ibid., no. 22. On the same point, cf. V. O. Eingorn, "O snosheniiakh Malorossiiskogo dukhovenstva s Moskovskim pravitelstvom v tsarstvovanie Alekseia Mikhailovicha," *Chteniia v Obshchestve istorii i drevnostei rossiiskikh* (1893),

1–2, IV.

95. Names in E. N. Medynsky, *Bratskie shkoly Ukrainy i Belorussii v XVI-XVII vv. i ikh rol v vossoedinenii Ukrainy s Rossiei* (Moscow, 1954), 111ff. Nikon had Kievans and even a Pole on his personal staff, and evidently had a soft spot for the West. See L. R. Lewitter, "Poland, the Ukraine and Russia in the 17th Century," *Slavonic and East European Review* 27 (1948–9):165ff.

96. Ibid., 425.

97. Schumann, "Der Hetmanstaat," 547.

98. D. Bantysh-Kamensky, *Istoria Maloi Rossii* (Moscow 1822), 222.

99. Matveev, *Moskva i Malorossiia*, 228. With respect to the treaty, it was of course the tsar's mood of the moment. For mistrust in the other direction—Khmelnytsky's of Aleksei Mikhailovich—see n. 30.

100. W. Philipp, "Altrussland bis zum Ende des 16. Jahrhunderts," *Propyläen-Weltgeschichte* (Berlin, 1963), 5:260.

Modern History

Marc Raeff

Ukraine and Imperial Russia: Intellectual and Political Encounters from the Seventeenth to the Nineteenth Century

Compared with the political and cultural relationships prevailing between dominant and subordinate nations in Eastern Europe, the relations obtaining between Ukraine and the Russia of Moscow and St. Petersburg appear, at first glance, paradoxical. One is struck by the fact that at the moment of its subordination to Muscovite Russia, it was Ukraine that enjoyed and exercised a clear cultural predominance; much later, in the nineteenth century, at the birth of modern national consciousness, Ukraine had the status of a peasant culture adjudged inferior and harshly repressed. The purpose of this paper is to explore the *how* of this development. I hope that, in so doing, I shall be able to raise meaningful questions and point to paths of investigation and terminological definitions that may yield satisfactory exploratory schemes. I approach the problem from the point of view of a Russian historian (in both senses of the adjective), for that is where my competence lies, but a partial (in the quantitative sense only) perspective should stimulate meaningful response and fruitful dialogue from the Ukrainian viewpoint as well.

It is superfluous in the present context to restate the significant contributions made by Ukraine, in particular by the ecclesiastical and educational institutions of Kiev, in transmitting and naturalizing Western ideas and intellectual techniques in the second half of the seventeenth century.[1] It may be useful, though, to recall that this contribution went far beyond the role played by the faculty and students of Peter Mohyla's Academy in implementing the religious policies of Moscow, in setting up the Greco-Slavonic-Latin academy in the capital, and in furnishing, in the person of Symeon Polotsky, an influential teacher of the tsar's children and, in the person of Teofan Prokopovych, the most effective ideological supporter and propagandist of the first emperor. For indeed it was not only the clergy who obtained access to Western ideas and works; the laity, too, especially the members of the elite, partook of this training, albeit in bowdlerized form. In this way the Ukrainian elite stood in sharp contrast to the widespread ignorance of secular learning prevalent among the Muscovite service nobility.[2] And it was precisely representatives of the educated lay elite from Ukraine who were drawn into the service of the tsar in ever greater numbers as the political integration of the Hetmanate and of Kiev progressed apace in the last decades of the seventeenth century.

The research of literary historians has recently documented a much wider knowledge and spread of Western works in Latin than had been assumed heretofore. This was particularly true of officials in the central bureaus of the Muscovite administration, especially the clerks of the *Posolskii prikaz*.[3] Of particular interest in the context of Russian political culture is the fact that in the second half of the seventeenth century quite a few treatises on rhetoric and logic (the basic intellectual tools of the period), as well as on politics and, naturally, theology, were circulated in manuscript form among the members of the Muscovite elite. This literature, too, had come to Moscow thanks to the mediation of Ukrainians and Belorussians who had direct links with Kiev and Poland, and indirect ones with Central and West European institutions of learning.[4]

To date the historiography has not stressed enough that, along with new literary forms and genres and more sophisticated homiletics, Ukraine also helped transmit to Muscovy the newly emerged European political culture of the late seventeenth century (although the particulars of the phenomenon remain to be investigated). To be sure, in this case, neither the Ukrainians nor those trained in Kiev were the only agents of transmission. The foreigners, mainly German, who came to serve the Muscovite tsar also conveyed the theoretical literature and practical instances of this culture. And toward the end of the century the Russians themselves were able to pick up the material at its source. But they hardly would have known where or what to turn to had the ground not been prepared by the Ukrainians. What then was this new political culture? Its philosophical underpinning was natural law and neo-stoicism, its intellectual foundation the rationalism of seventeenth-century natural philosophy, and its institutional implementation was to be found in the policies of absolute monarchies and territorial sovereignties. The rhetoric, logic and neo-scholastic metaphysics taught at the Kievan Academy served as indispensable mental preparation for the reception of the intellectual presuppositions of European political culture, while information on institutional practices was provided by foreign residents and Russian envoys abroad.[5]

The new European political culture may be denoted by the theories of cameralism and the practices of the well ordered police state. As I have tried to show elsewhere, it was a relatively coherent system of administrative practices based on a rationalist and voluntarist conception of man's relationship to the physical and social universe. The main purpose of this system was to reorient and discipline society in such a way as to maximize its productive potential in all realms so as to enhance the prestige of the sovereign and further the prosperity of his subjects. Once launched on this path, it was believed, men and society would progress indefinitely in making use of what nature provides. The practical realization of this political culture was to be the result of the leadership and direction of the sovereign power (usually the monarch), assisted by a body of officials (increasingly professionalized as a result of legal and cameralist studies), as well as by the co-optation of representatives of estates, corporations or other traditional sodalities. The well-ordered police state had an inbuilt drive to expand its area of concern and to reach out to regulate more and more public activities, a propensity that brought it into conflict with established local centres of power (which eventually succumbed).[6] But it is equally important to note that in addition to the conflicts between central authorities and local estates, much discussed in historical literature, there took place just as frequently a successful co-optation of local elites and corporate bodies. There was, therefore, no contradiction in principle, or even in practice, between the central power and autonomous local units, as long as the latter were willing to accept the state's political program in pursuit of the common goal of maximizing society's productive potential. In other words, the participation of regional estates and corporate bodies was one of the factors behind the success of the well-ordered police state. In this manner local autonomies and the influence of regional elites were preserved in ancien-régime Europe until the very end of the latter's existence at the end of the eighteenth and the beginning of the nineteenth centuries.[7]

The Muscovite state did not seriously try to import and adapt this European political culture, although under Tsar Theodore and the regency of Sophie it accumulated information about it. But the more energetic members of its elite, those who were thirsting for more dynamic and creative ways, felt attracted to the new culture from the West. Their most prominent representative, young Tsar Peter himself, taking advantage of the weakness and disarray of the traditional culture of Muscovy, found support when he decided to import and implement the European model at home, and he did so with a remarkable *esprit de suite* and willful energy. Yet Peter could not rely on corporate autonomous bodies, which were greatly underdeveloped in Russian society. He had to create an officialdom, a service class entirely subordinate to his will. In this connection two points need to be stressed, as they affect the general problem of Ukrainian-Russian relations.

In the first place, Peter had to "draft" all those capable of becoming members of an effective, relatively educated, and energetic administrative elite in order to put the country onto the path of material progress, military and political power, and cultural Europeanization. Of course he enlisted foreigners, whether residents of Russia or people especially hired for the purpose. He also endeavoured to attract to St. Petersburg members of the local elites from the newly acquired Baltic provinces, and naturally he was delighted to find that the Ukrainian educated elite, too, could serve his purposes. It is common knowledge that quite a few of his collaborators—especially in matters ecclesiastical and domestic—not only hailed from Ukraine but were also products of its educational institutions. As time went on, thanks to their better education and with the help of the client system, many more members of the Ukrainian nobility (*szlachta*) and Cossack officer stratum (*starshyna*) were drawn into the ranks of the empire's officialdom. A much needed task of historical scholarship is to describe how Ukrainians (and members of other non-Russian nationalities) penetrated the Russian administration in the reigns of Peter I and his immediate successors, to explain their role and assess their contribution in developing the imperial style of government.

The second point that should be mentioned in our context is that, in annexing and drawing into its orbit various "foreign" regions and territories, neither the Muscovite nor the Petrine state insisted on erasing local autonomies and traditions as long as they did not conflict with the imperial interests (this was the sticking point in the case of Ukraine, especially after Mazepa's so-called treason). This is not the place to go into the political and administrative relations between the Russian government and Ukraine; they were the consequence of important socio-economic developments, as has been demonstrated by Venedikt Miakotin and many others.[8] I only wish to point out that neither the acceptance of the notions and practices of the well-ordered police state nor the involvement of many Ukrainians in the St. Petersburg establishment signified the elimination of the special status, rights and privileges of Ukraine, even though there was much controversy as to the limits of autonomy and its institutional forms.[9] Nor was the relationship necessarily a one-way street. The representative of St. Petersburg was not only the executor of the ruler's will, even against the preferences and wishes of the local elite: he was also influenced by and learned from the latter. A case in point is the career of D. M. Golitsyn, who was for many years governor in Kiev; quite clearly he had in mind some of the political notions and experiences he acquired in Ukraine when, in 1730, he attempted unsuccessfully to limit the autocratic power of Empress Anne. That he was intellectually much influenced by Ukraine (and perhaps Poland) and its political culture can be deduced from his library and documented intellectual interests.[10] In brief, I am arguing that the "benevolent" and acquiescent attitude of the cameralist well-ordered police state toward regional autonomies and corporate traditions encouraged represen- tatives of the Ukrainian (and other) elites to enter the service of St. Petersburg. Acquainted with Western political culture, they fully accepted the long-range goal of maximizing productivity in order to increase the power and prosperity of the empire as a whole (in which they and their region would naturally share); they did not feel or believe that in so doing they were jeopardizing regional autonomy or their fellows' traditional rights and status.

It is not surprising that the members of the Ukrainian elite who joined the imperial establishment did quite well. Their better intellectual preparation and greater freedom of action as outsiders not bound by earlier traditions and prejudices made them particularly effective instruments of imperial policies. In addition, the clannishness that dominated the establishment favoured a self-de- fined and closely knit minority group.[11] Their usefulness was readily recognized by the authorities in St. Petersburg in deed as well as in word: in settling the

southern territories the Ukrainian service elites, quite naturally, received particularly desirable allotments and profitable inducements.[12] True, this did not
always lead to genuine prosperity in individual instances, partly because of
generally unfavourable economic, social and administrative conditions in the
empire and partly because the services expected in return proved too onerous.

As Ukraine was a border territory, it was also the staging area for the
numerous military campaigns the Russian Empire waged against Poland, the
Ottoman Empire, the Crimea, Persia, and the nomadic peoples of the south-
east. The military establishment stationed there was great, and because of its
strategic situation with respect to supplies, a large civilian administrative staff
was attached to it. The commanders-in-chief in Ukraine had broad civil as well
as military and diplomatic competence; they were most important and
influential personages not only locally but in St. Petersburg as well. They filled
their needs for administrative staff by turning to the graduates of local
educational establishments. Numerous members of the clergy, as well as
children of the *starshyna* trained at the ecclesiastical schools (or even the
Kievan Academy) entered the Russian state service on the staff of the governors and commanders-in-chief in Ukraine. The headquarters of N. V. Repnin
and P. A. Rumiantsev were filled with such young men who rapidly rose to
prominence thanks to their talents and good work, as well as the patronage of
their superiors, who frequently were their relatives as well. Many prominent
administrators and diplomats of the second half of the reign of Catherine II, and
in the reigns of Paul I and Alexander I as well, came from this group: I need
only mention the names of Bezborodko, Troshchynsky, Zavadovsky, and
Kochubei.[13]

Thus we see the significant involvement of Ukraine and its children in the
development of the imperial establishment and the expansion of the empire in
the eighteenth century (they were administrators of non-Russian areas as well).
They took on these roles because the education they received on the pattern of
seventeenth-century European intellectual style became an essential factor in
the creation of the Petrine imperial establishment. Moreover, their active
participation in imperial policy and administration did not, at first, force them
to renounce their regional allegiance, their commitment to the traditional and
separate ways of Ukraine. Only gradually did it become evident that their
involvement led automatically to greater control and uniformization of the
elites (mainly for cultural reasons, to which we shall turn later). And although
the central authorities did not always respect all the rights and privileges of the
newly incorporated regions (Ukraine, the Baltic region, later the Crimea and the
former Lithuanian lands), in the case of Ukraine and the Baltic provinces there
was no overt intention to eliminate their particular status.

True, traditional rights and privileges were eroded by social and cultural
integration, nibbled at and modified to suit imperial needs, but they were not
abrogated throughout the first three-quarters of the eighteenth century.[14] To the

extent that the local elites had become russified socially, economically and culturally—and this was mainly the case in the *slobodshchina* and the territories adjoining central Russia—their sense of regional autonomy was weakened. But it remained strong among those who considered themselves descendants and heirs of the seventeenth-century Cossacks.

This was clearly manifested at the Legislative Commission of 1767. All the instructions for the deputies from the *szlachta (shliakhetstvo*—significant preservation of seventeenth- and early eighteenth-century terminology) of "Little Russia" began with a strong expression of the wish to have their traditional rights and privileges, as they had been secured in the Treaty of Pereiaslav and in the legislation of Polish kings and Muscovite tsars, confirmed and restated in an unambiguous manner.[15] It is to be noted that the argument was historical and legal, as had been typical of regional estates in Western Europe in the early modern period. Treaties were contracts and had to be honored: practices, laws and rules that developed historically became traditions of unquestionable authority. Implicit in this argument was the notion that the treaty or contract was between equals, as further evidenced by the contributions of the Ukrainians to the furtherance of the empire's glory and prosperity. All this implied a recognition of the local liberties enjoyed by the elites, as well as their legal and economic privileges.

By contrast, the *nakazy* for the deputies of the nobility (and *nota bene*, in this instance the term *dvorianstvo*, not *shliakhetstvo*, is used) of the Slobidska and Chernihiv gubernias did not contain such references or, if they appeared at all, they were incidental and expressed in muted form.[16] As G. A. Maksimovich has established, the original drafts of several of the *nakazy* of these provinces did include a clear restatement of the rights and traditional privileges of the Cossacks. General Rumiantsev, however, through his agents (Bezborodko played a key role here, one that probably helped to launch him on his success-ful career in St. Petersburg), had these statements stricken and the deputies or marshals elected to bring them to the attention of the Legislative Commission forcibly removed.[17] Similar observations may be made about the *nakazy* from towns and cities of the region: they referred to the Magdeburg Law or the Lithuanian Statute, requesting that these be confirmed by Catherine and the Commission and included in the new code as the basis of their social, ad-ministrative and economic organization.[18]

The debates in the Legislative Commission itself, as they appear in the official minutes at any rate, clearly show that demands for the confirmation of regional autonomies and traditional rights—whether Ukrainian, Baltic or any other—went against the mainstream of opinion. Only differences in ways of life (nomadic, settled agricultural, etc.) were recognized as valid cause for administrative and legal differentiation—and this only in the expectation that, sooner or later, enlightenment and inescapable material progress would elimi-nate such distinctions as well. The government, prompted by the empress herself, stood firmly behind the Enlightenment notions of universally uniform development and progress. Supported by the Great Russian elite, which did not wish to see the nobilities of peripheral regions treated differently from itself, St. Petersburg displayed little interest in historical claims and was naturally opposed to special arrangements and status.[19] This was illustrated by the many complaints aired in the instructions to the deputies and in the debates in the Commission of 1767. A major criticism was the absence of rigid rules for automatic integration into the ranks of the ruling Russian elite, i.e., the lack of genuine equality of status between the Ukrainian elite and the Russian *dvorianstvo*.[20] The problem arose not only because of tensions with the Russian nobility with respect to access to the latter's ranks, but also because there were no clear definitions and rules governing the empire's favoured class.

Be that as it may, the legislation of Catherine II had two important consequences for the Ukrainian service elite: it made possible the expansion of serfdom into Ukraine, and by securing serf labour it enhanced the economic position of at least the upper ranges of Ukrainian society. The second consequence, which became manifest over a period of time, was the administrative integration of this elite into the Russian "establishment" as a result of the extension of the statute on the provinces (1775) and of the charters to the nobility and to the towns (1785). Many educated persons in Ukraine thus acquired an administrative function on the local level and, because of the intertwining of local and central establishments, their careers in the central apparatus were furthered as well. But here, too, further study would be necessary to determine the precise level of participation and integration on the basis of reliable statistical data. Naturally such a development encouraged the Ukrainian elite to acquire and share the values and social ways of its Great Russian colleagues. The integration was further stimulated, after the peace of Kuchuk Kainardji, by the opening up of the northern littoral of the Black Sea (*Novaia Rossiia*) to settlement and exploitation. Many Russians received lands and settled in Ukraine, intermingling with the local elite, and helped create a new type of russianized Ukrainian noble landowner and servitor.[21] The process was a slow one, and never quite completed, as witness Russian and Ukrainian belles lettres in the nineteenth century. It did, however, dilute the specific cultural traits and social character of the Ukrainian elite, which ceased to act as the "natural" cultural and political leader with respect to the common people, the peasantry.

Along with this slow process of social and cultural integration or uniformization (and down to the last quarter of the eighteenth century it was an open question whether the Russian or the Ukrainian linguistic, literary and intellectual traditions would prevail in Ukraine) there continued the more conscious, rapid and thorough process of admitting the Ukrainian servitors to the political, administrative leadership of the empire. The imperial bureaucracy was constantly expanding in the eighteeenth century, and the need for adequately prepared personnel was always acute. The educational traditions and institutions of Ukraine, imparting, as we have seen, the notions of cameralism, natural law and rigorous intellectual discipline, gave their products a head start. Ordinances or ukases required Ukrainian educational institutions (the Kievan Academy, the collegium at Kharkiv, as well as lesser ones) to send their graduates or students to the newly established University of Moscow for further training or to enroll them in various administrative offices particularly short of personnel. For example, we have evidence that the Kharkiv collegium helped staff the middle ranks of the imperial diplomatic service, especially specialists on the Ottoman Empire and surrounding territories.[22]

In conclusion on this topic, I want to make it clear, and cannot stress too strongly, that so far I have dealt only with the claims of regional autonomy and respect for traditional, historically and judicially defined, rights and privileges of the Ukrainian elites. While reference was naturally made to the Cossack Host and the agreement between Bohdan Khmelnytsky and Tsar Alexis on behalf of Ukraine, the sources do not speak of, or for, a Ukrainian nation. Their object of concern was a specific social organization, the status of a social class, while the means of preserving the identity of this territorial and social organization consisted in the confirmation of treaties, charters, and granted privileges. The distinction between Great Russian and Little Russian was defined in terms of differences in historical experience, not in terms of specific particularities of language, religion, cultural traits and the like. This is clearly illustrated in the case of the vocal spokesman for Ukrainian regional autonomy, H. A. Poletyka, in the middle of the eighteenth century.[23] I would call this ancien-régime autonomism or particularism (or, in German terminology, *Landespatriotismus*) for the benefit of the ruling strata, in which the common people had no place. Under conditions of a "pre-modern" world, where peasants thought only in exceedingly narrow local economic and social terms, this is not surprising.

New elements were brought into the picture by the intellectual and cultural developments that took place in the middle and second half of the eighteenth century, which, paradoxically, reinforced the trend toward uniformization (i.e., russification) while at the same time creating a basis for the rejection of the process. For members of the elite who wanted to make their careers in the imperial establishment in the latter part of the eighteenth century, the traditional seventeenth-century type of education was clearly no longer adequate. Technical subjects of practical value—e.g., geometry, fortification, and artillery for the military; foreign languages for diplomacy—moved to the centre of attention. The new trend had been introduced to Russia proper by Peter I and had resulted in the establishment of the Corps of Cadets and, later, in the founding of the university at Moscow, and still later in the pedagogical innovations brought about by I. Betskoi under the aegis of Catherine II. The Ukrainian schools, largely attended by children of the elite (*szlachta* and *starshyna*), followed suit, as did the private instruction given at home to the children of the more affluent. In this respect the history of the collegium at Kharkiv may be paradigmatic.[24] Established as an ecclesiatical school along seventeenth-century lines, it soon added the new disciplines to its curriculum to satisfy the needs of the children of the elite, who expected to pursue secular careers in the empire. In the last quarter of the eighteenth century the differences between the needs of the clerical and secular establishments had become so great that additional separate classes and courses were introduced at the collegium to meet the requirements of effective training for secular careers.[25]

The evolution just sketched was easy to make, for the original curriculum of the seventeenth century had already included such disciplines as philosophy and jurisprudence that provided the groundwork for cameralist studies. As had been the case in Central and Western Europe, too, the very foundations and elements of traditional cameralist instruction underwent a change in the course of the eighteenth century. The concepts of natural law were fully secularized; the principles of philosophical rationalism were extended to apply to the social realm. Finally, the notions of an expanding and limitless potential of productive resources, both human and natural, led to a belief in unlimited progress and the acceptance of the Enlightenment/*Aufklärung* as an ideology of freedom and rights and the satisfaction of needs to attain individual happiness. The same intellectual sources that had produced cameralist disciplines, literature and professors became the purveyors of Enlightenment/*Aufklärung* notions and programs.[26]

A reorientation in the intellectual premises and philosophical, moral, and even political consequences of the education received in Ukraine had to take place. The new cultural model became a type of individual who combined traditional religiosity with the moral pathos and optimism of the *Aufklärung*. This was the case of Hryhorii Skovoroda and, to a lesser extent, of A. Samborsky and A. Prokopovych-Antonsky, all products of the collegium at Kharkiv.[27] For our purposes it is also important to remember that both the *Aufklärung* and the Enlightenment differed from the intellectual modes prevailing earlier in that they assumed the uniformity of human nature and, consequently, the universality of the "laws" of social and cultural development and progress. Unlike cameralism, which recognized and made use of regional, cultural and historical diversities, the Enlightenment insisted that a basic uniformity underlay all diversities, so that the latter, being but external and accidental, would disappear with the triumph of enlightened notions and the reconstruction of society on their basis. In the course of the second half of the eighteenth century, elite education instilled ideas that led to a loss of interest in the preservation of diversified historical and legal traditions, but on the contrary advocated laws and principles that would result in a uniform society and culture throughout the empire. In this way the new curricula converged with the drive for institutional uniformity (i.e., russification) mentioned earlier. The more successful and dynamic Enlightenment culture, in direct contact with the world of European ideas, had its centre in Russia proper; the educational and cultural institutions of St. Petersburg (and to a lesser extent those of Moscow) set the tone and pace; it was they that now influenced the Ukrainians. All seemed to conspire to bring about the full integration of the Ukrainian elite and its culture into that of the empire, leading, in fact, to russification, since Russian political culture had achieved dominance and monopoly in the empire.

Paradoxically, at this very moment, events occurred and trends arose that had quite an opposite effect. First, with respect to the social policies of Catherine II: we have seen that the extension of the new provincial administration to Ukraine and the more energetic settlement of the southern steppe served to integrate still further the local elite of the empire into the pattern set by the Great Russians. It became desirable to accede to the new institutions and, to this end, to have one's elite status fully recognized and assimilated to the Russian (imperial) *dvorianstvo*. The threat of such a massive influx of new nobles did not sit well with either the established Russian nobility or the central government. Exacting proofs were required to prevent the poor and culturally unassimilated members of the local elite from joining the ranks of the imperial nobility.[28] It was precisely this policy that had two unexpected and paradoxical consequences. In the first place, it gave rise within the Ukrainian elite to a greater feeling of solidarity and of a sense of identity: not only did members of the Ukrainian elite have the same problems and needs, but their mutual testimonies were often used as proof to qualify for inscription on the rosters of the nobility. In the second place, proof and validation of noble status required submission of old charters, grants, diplomas, or testimony to the effect that ancestors had this or that position or owned a specific privileged domain. Naturally this resulted in a flood of forged genealogies and historical or legal documents. But it also stimulated a lively interest in history and furthered research and publication about the past to validate historical continuities and distinctiveness. Reinforced by the moral and emotional emphasis of the late *Aufklärung* (the "enlightenment of the heart"), this concern for the past paved the way for the quick and thorough reception of Romantic notions about folk, history and nation.

The opening of the university at Kharkiv (to replace the collegium), and the somewhat later creation of the Bezborodko lycée at Nizhyn, may serve as illustrations of the change in intellectual fashion. The story of these institutions is well known and I need not enter into it here.[29] Suffice it to recall that both owed their origins to the initiative of local personalities for the express purpose of providing an education that would prepare the students for state service and enhance the cultural identity of the local elite and population. To this end the students were to be taught the most modern aspects of all fields of knowledge, i.e., modern languages, natural sciences and the new disciplines of philology and history. Although the university at Kharkiv eventually was to be a creation of the state, it did embody the ideas and implement some of the goals that its main promoter, A. N. Karazyn, and his friends in the Kharkiv gubernia had advocated. Of even greater significance in our context was the fact that the university at Kharkiv served, as had the Kievan Academy in the seventeenth century (and, to a lesser degree, the collegium), to bring contemporary Western intellectual concerns and philosophical concepts to Ukraine, and then to transmit them to the capitals of the empire. It was a way station for professors and scholars hired in Western and Central Europe before they joined the universities of Moscow or St. Petersburg and the administrative offices of the central government. This was the case of such men as Balugiansky, Malinovsky, Schad, and Jacob.[30] In this manner a stream of *late Aufklärung* jurists and philosophers, as well as *early* representatives of philosophical idealism, was channelled through the university at Kharkiv to fertilize both Ukraine and the empire. Although the historical and philological studies at Kharkiv were given in Russian and were Russian-centred, they also led inevitably to an intense concern with specifically Ukrainian contributions and background. From the very beginning, both at Kharkiv and at Nizhyn, attention was paid to the special character of Ukrainian history and language, and the triumph of Romanticism extended this interest to the study of popular forms of linguistic, literary and artistic creation.

The efforts of the local elite to activate the cultural life of the region, as exemplified by the creation of the university and the lycée, are to be seen within the broader context of the formation of a civil society in the Russian Empire. Indeed, the first half of the reign of Alexander I witnessed the emergence of a civil society based on cultural activities and socio-political concerns. This can readily be illustrated by the appearance of numerous private societies and groups dedicated to a variety of cultural, philanthropic and educational purposes. The fashion was not limited to the capitals, or to Ukraine, but spread to other provinces and regions of the empire as well. In addition, they took up nationalistic, patriotic concerns during the wars against Napoleon, especially during the campaigns of 1812–15. After the war, European nationalism and liberalism imparted a new stimulus to Russian society to continue its efforts at playing a public role in cultural, social (i.e., philanthropic) enterprises. We cannot go into details here; besides, many aspects of this development are still inadequately investigated.[31] The government gave its categorical veto to these endeavors, driving the younger, more energetic and impatient generation into "dissidence" or the underground opposition that culminated in the Decembrist uprising.

In a sense, government suppression of civil society's velleities at securing a share in the public, cultural and social life of the empire tolled the death knell for the ancien-régime notion of regional autonomy as well. Indeed, the kind of civil society that had tried to constitute itself in the late eighteenth and the first quarter of the nineteenth centuries was a direct heir to the estate-based regional and corporate autonomies of the well-ordered police state and its cameralist philosophy. In the case of Western Europe, these autonomies had been a major element in the constitution of an *Öffentlichkeit* (i.e., public opinion), a counter-weight to centralized bureaucracy and absolutism.[32] And as an outcome of their "conversion" to the notion of Enlightenment and *Aufklärung*, these autonomous corporate bodies had fostered the ideologization of the concepts of unlimited progress and material prosperity of individuals and groups, as well as opposition to absolutism and enlightened despotism.

The Russian government's suppression of the first manifestations of civil society undercut the efforts of regional solidarities as well, for it turned the state against all forms of private initiative in public life, and in so doing stifled the attempts of the Ukrainian elite to constitute itself as a civil society and reactivate its regional identity. Most members of the elite, involved and in-tegrated as they were into the imperial establishment, acquiesced meekly and withdrew from the stage. From then on, the state viewed with suspicion and enmity all manifestations of regional and private initiative. It had totally inter-nalized the Enlightenment concept of uniformity and was unable and unwilling to accede to pleas for diversity and autonomy. The ruling establishment could not—did not want to—accept the juridical and historical arguments on which these pleas were based. It rejected the constraints of history, except to the limited extent that these could serve to validate its own position (and even there, it was very much divided in its own mind: witness the official polemics and censorship conflicts in the reign of Nicholas I over questions of Russian history).

The old regionalism was dead. A new nationalism, based on historicist an-thropology, philology and folk culture (or what was thought to be folk culture) was emerging under the influence of Romanticism, idealistic philosophy, and the government's complete refusal to grant civil society an active role. The new nationalism was not only very different in kind from the preceding sense of regional and historical identity, but was also in sharp opposition to the state, to the imperial establishment. The traditional elite of Ukraine, which had largely become russified, was only marginally involved in this new form and trend. The first and most energetic propagators of this new sense of national identity were the intellectuals (academics) who systematically developed its scholarly and philosophic justification.[33] They directed their efforts not at members of the elite but at those groups of society that had been denied, or had lost, the traditional regional privileges—the small landowners, the urban population, and eventually also the common people (peasantry). Because of harsh repression and persecution by the St. Petersburg government, such educational propaganda was carried out more easily from outside. This was to be the role of Galicia (Lviv). But this opens up another, altogether different chapter which is beyond the ken of my knowledge.

In conclusion I wish simply to restate some of the main points which, to my mind, emerge from the material that I have examined. The first point is that "nationalism" in our usual sense is a phenomenon that makes its appearance strictly in the nineteenth century (or at the earliest in the late eighteenth century, in some instances). It should be sharply distinguished from the claims of regional and estate autonomies of ancien-régime states and societies. It cannot be extrapolated backward into the earlier period. Not only did ancien-régime regionalism refer to specific historical and legal events to justify its claims to autonomy, if not outright independence, but its concern was not the "nation." It was only interested in the sense of identity and self-image of particular elites that were in existence at the moment the claims were raised. It was not an all-embracing psychological, political and cultural notion, but a limited pragmatic demand for the maintenance of traditional modes of public life. It is uncritical and anachronistic to project the concerns and basic assumptions of the new nationalism onto earlier forms of regional and social autonomy.

The second point that emerges from the material is this: the association of ancien-régime autonomism with the ideas of cameralism and the practices of the well-ordered police state produced an immanent developmental dynamic in both policy and thought. This consisted in the reception of the Enlightenment and of its notions of uniformity of human nature, set phases of cultural development, and belief in the universality of progress. The reception of these notions made for greater readiness to integrate into the larger unit—the empire. The pressures of material and social advantage, as well as the promises of cultural and political reward, led the Ukrainian elite to abandon its stand on regional autonomy and to acquiesce in its russification-both cultural (since it was universal) and social (since it preserved the elite's position and furthered its interests). The displacement of cameralism and well-ordered police state notions in favour of those of the Enlightenment in the political culture of imperial Russia, however, shifted the creative balance from Ukraine to St. Petersburg and Moscow. The modern Russian culture that was the outcome proved so dynamic as to become overwhelmingly attractive to the regional elites at the turn of the eighteenth century.

Thirdly, the ancien-régime autonomism had been capable of a compromise that both preserved regional identity and safeguarded imperial interests. But the new nationalism, rooted in the exclusivism and particularism of idealistic philosophy and Romantic historicism, was bound to clash with an establishment based on the drive toward uniformity and "rational constructivism" of the Enlightenment. The imperial government, acting on the basis of eighteenth-century conceptions and practice of cultural uniformity and universality of developmental laws, could neither understand nor accept national claims based on such totally different premises. The new nationalisms, on the other hand, saw in these claims the very basis of their existence and identity, and naturally could not compromise or surrender any of them.

Lastly, my analysis has shown the crucial roles of the educational establishments of Kiev and Kharkiv: Kiev for the transition from Muscovite to imperial political culture; Kharkiv for the intellectual transformation that fostered the russification of the elites on the one hand, but paved the way for their reception of idealism and Romanticism, which proved to be the necessary preconditions of modern nationalism, on the other. A great deal remains to be done to understand and clarify the mechanisms involved in these two transitional stages and periods. In particular, the role of Kharkiv in the chronology and character of the ideological and cultural transformation which proved so crucial to the destinies of both Ukraine and Russia remains to be studied in depth. But we cannot obtain reliable results unless we insist on the differences in contexts, concepts and trends, and stress the importance of chronological divides. Never forget Fustel de Coulanges' admonition: *en histoire, l'essentiel est le sens des mots.*

Notes

1. In addition to the general literature on the Kievan Academy see also K. V. Kharlampovich, *Zapadnorusskie pravoslavnye shkoly XVI i nachala XVII v.* (Kazan, 1898); idem, *Malo- rossiiskoe vliianie na Velikorusskuiu tserkovnuiu zhizn* (Kazan 1914); G. Florovsky, *Puti russkogo bogosloviia,* (reprint Paris, 1982); N. Petrov, "O slovesnykh naukakh i literaturnykh zaniatiiakh v Kievskoi akademii ot nachala i do preobrazovaniia v 1819 g.," *Trudy Kievskoi dukhovnoi Akademii,* 1866, 2: 305–30, 3: 343–88, 552–569; idem, "Iz istorii gomelitiki v staroi Kievskoi akademii," ibid., 1866, 1: 86–124.

2. Frank Sysyn, "The Problem of Nobilities in the Ukrainian Past: The Polish Period, 1569–1648," in I. L. Rudnytsky, ed., *Rethinking Ukrainian History* (Edmonton, 1981), 29–102.

3. A. M. Panchenko, *Russkaia stikhotvornaia kultura XVII veka* (Leningrad, 1973); A. V. Petrov, "Odin iz bibliofilov XVIII v. (Stefan Iavorskii i ego predsmertnoe proshchanie s knigami," *Russkii bibliofil,* 1914, no. 5; I. A. Shliapkin, *Dmitrii Rostovskii i ego vremia* (St. Petersburg, 1891); Io. Tatarskii, *Simeon Polotskii (ego zhizn i deiatelnost)*(Moscow, 1886).

4. G. Ia. Golenchenko, "Belorusy v russkom knigopechatanii," *Kniga—issledovaniia i materialy,* XIII (Moscow, 1966): 99–119 and I. M. Kudriavtsev, "Izdatelskaia deiatelnost Posolskogo Prikaza," ibid., VIII (Moscow, 1963): 179–244.

5. M. Raeff, "Transition from Muscovite to Imperial Culture" (Public Lecture delivered at the Metropolitan Museum of Art)" in Wolf Moskovich et al., eds. *Russian Literature and History—In Honour of Professor Ilya Serman* (Jerusalem, 1989), 170-77.

6. M. Raeff, *The Well-Ordered Police State: Social and Institutional Change through Law in the Germanies and Russia, 1600–1800* (New Haven, 1983).

7. Cf. in particular the studies of and in the circle of Dietrich Gerhard, *Alte und neue Welt in vergleichender Geschichts- betrachtung* (Göttingen, 1962) and D. Gerhard, ed., *Ständische Vertretung in Europa im 17. und 18. Jahrhundert* (Göttingen, 1969). Also Volker Press, Inaugural lecture, University of Tübingen, 1981.

8. V. A. Miakotin, *Ocherki sotsialnoi istorii Ukrainy v XVII-XVIII vv.*, 3 vols. (Prague, 1924–6); V. A. Diadychenko, *Narysy suspilno-politychnoho ustroiu livoberezhnoi Ukrainy* (Kiev, 1959).

9. Z. E. Kohut, "Problems in Studying the Post-Khmelnytsky Ukrainian Elite (1650s to 1830s)," in Rudnytsky, ed., *Rethinking Ukrainian History*, 103–19 and his *Russian Centralism and Ukrainian Autonomy—Imperial Absorption of the Hetmanate 1760s–1830s*, Harvard Ukrainian Research Institute Monograph Series (Cambridge, Mass., 1988).

10. On D. M. Golitsyn's reading, cf. N. V. Golitsyn, "Novye dannye o biblioteke kniazia D. M. Golitsyna," *Chteniia OIDR*, 195, 1900, bk. 4, sect. 4, pp. 1–16; B. A. Grabova, B. M. Kloss, V. I. Koretskii, "K istorii Arkhangelskoi biblioteki kn. D. M. Golitsyna," *Arkheograficheskii ezhegodnik za 1978 god* (Moscow, 1979): 238–53. Cf. also general studies of S. P. Luppov, *Kniga v Rossii v XVII veke* (Leningrad, 1970); M. I. Slukhovskii, *Bibliotechnoe delo v Rossii do XVIII veka* (Moscow, 1968); idem, *Russkaia biblioteka XVI-XVII vv.* (Moscow, 1973); I. de Madariaga, "Portrait of an Eighteenth Century Russian Statesman: Prince Dmitry Mikhailovich Golitsyn," *Slavonic and East European Review*, vol. 62, no. 1 (January 1984): 36–60.

11. D. E. Ransel, *The Politics of Catherinian Russia* (New Haven, 1975); John P. LeDonne, "Appointments to the Russian Senate 1762–1796," *Cahiers du monde russe et soviétique*, XVI-1 (janvier-mars 1975): 27–56.

12. Cf., for example, N. Polonska-Vasylenko, "The Settlement of the Southern Ukraine 1750–1775," *Annals of the Ukrainian Academy of Arts & Sciences in the U.S.*, IV-V, nos. 4(14)-1(15), 1955; H. Auerbach, *Die Besiedlung der Südukraine in den Jahren 1774–1787* (Wiesbaden, 1965); V. M. Kabuzan, *Zaselenie Novorossii v XVIII i pervoi polovine XIX veka* (Moscow, 1976); E. I. Druzhinina, *Severnoe prichernomore 1775–1800* (Moscow, 1959); idem, *Iuzhnaia Ukraina 1800–1825* (Moscow, 1970).

13. J. P. LeDonne, op. cit., and biographies of persons named. Cf. also D. Saunders, *The Ukrainian Impact on Russian Culture 1750–1850* (Edmonton, 1985).

14. Instructions of Catherine II to P. A. Rumiantsev in *Sbornik IRIO*, VII, (1871): 376–91.

15. *Sbornik IRIO*, 68 (1889): 127–248.

16. *Sbornik IRIO*, 68 (1889): 483–662.

17. G. A. Maksimovich, *Vybory i nakazy Malorossii v Zakono- datelnuiu Komissiiu 1767 g.* (Nizhyn, 1917).

18. *Sbornik IRIO*, 144 (1914): 3–135.

19. M. Raeff, "Uniformity, Diversity and the Imperial Administration in the Reign of Catherine II," *Osteuropa in Geschichte und Gegenwart (Festschrift für Günther*

Stökl) (Köln, 1977), 97–113. Cf. also, for another area, A. Kappeler, *Russlands erste Nationalitäten. Das Zarenreich und die Völker der Mittleren Wolga vom 16. bis 19. Jahrhundert* (Köln and Vienna, 1982).

20. "Proshenie malorossiiskogo shliakhetstva...," *Kievskaia starina*, no. 6 (1883): 317–45; *Sbornik IRIO*, 32 (1881): 573–85 and 36 (1882): addendum doc. #33, 332–39.

21. Druzhinina, op. cit.; M. Raeff, "In the Imperial Manner," in *Catherine II: A Profile* (New York, 1977): 197–245.

22. Saunders, op. cit.

23. H. A. Poletyka's speech to the Commission of 1767 in *Sbornik IRIO*, 36 (1882), 340–56; N. Vasylenko, "Zbirka materiialiv do istorii Livoberezhnoi Ukrainy...," *Ukrainskyi arkheohrafichnyi zbirnyk*, I (1926): 142–61; S. D. Nos, "Blagodarstvennoe pismo G. A. Poletiki...," *Kievskaia starina*, no. 11 (1890): 334–35; cf. also F. E. Sysyn, "Ukrainian-Polish Relations in the Seventeenth Century: The Role of National Consciousness and National Conflict in the Khmelnytsky Movement" in P. J. Potichnyj, ed., *Poland and Ukraine: Past and Present* (Edmonton and Toronto, 1980), 58–82; D. Miller, "Prevrashchenie kazatskoi starshyny...," *Kievskaia starina*, 56–7 (January-April 1897); L. Okynshevych, "Znachne viiskove tovarystvo v Ukraini-Hetmanshchyni XVII-XVIII st.," *Zapysky Naukovoho tovarystva im. Shevchenka*, vol. 157 (Munich 1948); O. Ohloblyn, "Ukrainian Autonomists of the 1780s and 1790s and Count P. A. Rumiantsev-Zadunaisky," *Annals of the Ukrainian Academy of Arts and Sciences in the U.S.* VI, nos. 3, 4 (21–2), 1958, 1313–26.

24. D. I. Bagalei, *Opyt istorii Kharkovskogo universiteta* (Kharkiv, 1893–8, 1904); A. Ia. Efimenko, *Istoriia ukrainskogo naroda*, vyp. I-II, (St. Petersburg, 1906); A. S. Lebedev, "Kharkovskii kollegium kak prosvetitelnyi tsentr Slobodskoi Ukrainy...," *Chteniia OIDR,* 1885, bk. 4, sect. 1, pp. 1–103; Saunders, op. cit.

25. Bagalei, op. cit., 41–2; Lebedev, op. cit.; also D. Bagalei, "Dva kulturnykh deiatelia iz sredy kharkovskogo dukhovenstva..." in his *Ocherki iz russkoi istorii* (Kharkiv, 1918), 1: 18–53.

26. On the distinction between Enlightenment and *Aufklärung*, cf. M. Raeff, "Les Slaves, les Allemands et les Lumières," *Revue Canadienne d'études slaves*, 1–4 (1967): 521–51; also F. Valjavec, *Geschichte der abendländischen Aufklärung* (Vienna and Munich, 1961).

27. On these personages, cf. *Russkii biograficheskii slovar.* The special literature on Skovoroda is extensive; for preliminary orientation see J. T. Fuhrmann, "The First Russian Philosopher's Search for the Kingdom of God" in L. B. Blair, ed., *Essays on Russian Intellectual History* (Walter Prescott Memorial Lectures, V) (Austin and London, 1971), 33–72 and *Skovoroda—Philosophe ukrainien* (Paris, 1976).

28. Efimenko, op. cit.; Kohut, op. cit.

29. Cf. J. T. Flynn, *The University Reform of Tsar Alexander I, 1802–1835* (Washington: Catholic University of America Press, 1988). G. A. Kushelev-Bezborodko, *Litsei kniazia Bezborodka* (St. Petersburg, 1859); N. A. Lavrovskii, "Gimnaziia vysshykh nauk kn. Bezborodko v Nezhine 1820–1823," *Izvestiia istorichesko-filologicheskogo instituta kn. Bezborodko v Nezhine*, III (1879),

sect. 2, pp. 102–258 and the material to be found in *Sbornik istoriko-filologicheskogo obshchestva, Nezhin*, vols. 1–8, 1896–1912/13. Also cf. Orest Pelech, "Towards a Historical Sociology of Ukrainian Ideologies in the Russian Empire of the 1830s and 1840s," unpubl. Ph.D. diss., Princeton University, 1976.

30. Bagalei, *Opyt istorii Kharkovskogo universiteta* and Saunders, op. cit., and biographies of personalities mentioned.

31. M. Iu. Lotman, "Dekabristy v povsednevnoi zhizni (Bytovoe povedenie kak istoriko-psikhologicheskaia kategoriia)" in V. G. Bazanov and V. E. Vatsura, eds., *Literaturnoe nasledstvo dekabristov* (Leningrad, 1975), 25–74.

32. R. Kosellek, *Kritik und Krise* (Munich, 1959); J. Habermas, *Strukturwandel der Öffentlichkeit* (Neuwied, 1965).

33. M. Hroch, *Die Vorkämpfer der nationalen Bewegung bei den kleinen Völkern Europas* (Prague, 1968) (Acta universitatis Carolinae Philosophica et historica—Monographia XXIV).

Edgar Hösch

Paul I and Ukraine

The processes underlying domestic policy during the reign of Paul I (1796–1801) have not always received due attention in historical research. Most historians of Russia still seem to doubt that in this confusing period between the glorious reigns of Catherine II and Alexander I, in this "stormy passage between two major seas,"[1] the tsarist empire saw the introduction of policies that pointed to the future and were important for the "modernization" of inherited social and economic structures. To be sure, V. O. Kliuchevsky criticized the "rather widespread disregard of the significance of this short-lived government" in the famous series of lectures on Russian history that he delivered toward the end of the last century, rejecting the view of this period as "a kind of accidental episode in Russian history."[2] Nevertheless, little has been done so far in specialized research to correct this one-sided picture and to attempt a more balanced interpretation of the reign. Preliminary research presented in 1916 by M. V. Klochkov,[3] whose institutional focus appears "old-fashioned" today,[4] has been taken up very hesitantly by later historians.

Only recently have there been indications that at least some aspects of the domestic and foreign policies of Paul I are being better elucidated in the light of new sources. In 1979 Hugh Ragsdale published a number of relevant studies in a collection that gives a good insight into the present state of research in Western (Anglo-Saxon) countries.[5] Not long ago, in an essay on the imperial regime during the reign of Paul I that appeared in *Vestnik Leningradskogo universiteta*, the Soviet scholar S. M. Kazantsev enjoined his Marxist coleagues not to limit themselves to a general condemnation of Paul's reactionary administration. If the tsar's frequently cited "liberal" concessions are to be comprehended and placed into their proper context, a more discriminating treatment is required.[6]

"Modern scholars tend towards sympathy with Paul," notes Roderick McGrew, not without a critical undertone, regarding these partial attempts at rehabilitation. He rightly points out the devastating effects of Paul's despotic ruthlessness and his lack of understanding of the political process and human relations. For objective reasons, Paul did not lend himself to depiction as a misunderstood Romantic hero, but came to be regarded as a tyrant and a political incompetent.[7] This negative overall judgement is quite legitimate, but should not obscure the fact that many legislative and administrative measures introduced by Paul I and his advisors and aides were rational in conception, and that their diplomatic initiatives and military-strategic undertakings were well-founded.[8] Perhaps the tsar's policy toward Ukraine can serve as an instructive example of this thesis.

*

In the context of Russo-Ukrainian relations in recent centuries, from the incorporation of Left-Bank Ukraine into the tsarist empire after 1654 until the fall of the Russian autocracy, the reign of Paul I certainly does not mark any breakthrough with far-reaching consequences for the co-existence of the two neighbouring peoples. Nor can it boast spectacular events such as those of the preceding period, when Catherine II profited from the partitions of Poland to unite almost all areas of Ukrainian settlement under the sceptre of the Russian tsars. The reign of Paul I cannot compare with the subsequent glorious period of Alexander I, whose progressive constitutional ideas and experiments pointed to innovative methods, especially in the integration of the western borderlands of the empire, with their diverse customs, legal traditions and institutions. The Ukrainian areas, which were divided into a number of guberniias, are treated here only as a territorial frame of reference in order to bring the domestic reforms of Paul I, together with their specific causes and consequences, into sharper focus, as well as to elucidate the intentions of the tsar and his advisors and the general topic of continuity and change in Russian nationality policy.

This article does not open up any new, hitherto unknown sources on the domestic policy of Paul I. Only those materials published in the official collection of laws of the Russian Empire are used and analyzed with respect to areas of Ukrainian settlement.[9] In regard to the territory of partitioned Poland, the comprehensive study by P. Zhukovich provides valuable preliminary findings and will frequently be used as a reference.[10]

It is well known that legal texts reflect actual administrative practice only in the rarest cases—certainly not in Russia at the end of the eighteenth century. Only more or less substantiated conjectures can be made about the concrete effects of particular measures taken by the central government. The frequent repetition of the same decrees indicates that legislation was slow to affect everyday life. As sources relevant to this problem are not yet available in quantity, historical interpretation can deal only with the intentions and avowed goals of the legislators.

In the period under consideration, Ukrainians did not, of course, appear as a national unit of reference affected by legislative measures. Legislative acts referred primarily to a whole region or to individual guberniias and the social groups inhabiting them; there were no particular measures restricted to Ukrainian territory. Generally speaking, these laws were conceived as means of implementing state policy in border areas within a multi-ethnic environment. They aimed primarily at stronger integration and centralization, the maintenance of law and order, and the effective suppression of dangerous revolutionary stirrings. According to the Senate ukase of 16 November 1797,[11] all the peoples that had come under Russia's sceptre should, "like the limbs of a body and children of one father," enjoy the same rights and lead an equally happy life.

On a broader scale, the Ukrainian population was most probably first affected by measures dealing with the peasantry. No special "national" component can be discerned in this policy, but one must have emerged as a result of Paul's restoration of the aristocratic Polish character of local administration and justice in this south-western border area of the empire.[12] The donation of land to deserving nobles is of secondary importance in this context, and there is no indication of a conscious policy of Russification. It seems that Paul followed his mother's example in the generous distribution of land, but his opportunities were considerably limited in the south-west because of a land shortage. Russian peasants were most affected by this policy.[13] Those who benefited from it were primarily Polish nobles, to whom properties confiscated by Catherine II were returned, as well as individual privileged groups of peasants who still claimed inherited property rights.[14]

Significant changes in the social structure of the southern guberniias (Katerynoslav, Voznesensk, the Caucasus, and the province of Tavriia) were brought about by the repeal of the peasants' freedom of movement, which was ordained on 12 December 1796.[15] The measure was justified by the need to restore order and to secure property rights in perpetuity, but in practice it was equivalent to a further extension of serfdom. It put an end to the migration of dissatisfied peasants, which had functioned as a kind of regulatory measure to counteract the all too blatant intensification of demands on the lower strata of the population by landlords and by the state. The mitigation or remission of burdensome obligations (e.g., tax reduction, abolition of the grain tax[16] and pasture tax,[17] the deregulation of the salt trade,[18] etc.), as well as the tsar's appeal to limit peasant labour obligations to three days per week,[19] were only makeshift corrective measures intended to blunt the growing potential for unrest. The frequent disturbances in the western and south-western regions, which provided the government with repeated opportunities for intervention, serve to indicate the very considerable problems of integration in the former Polish territories of Ukraine.

It would appear that another aspect of Paul's policy toward Ukraine consisted of numerous direct measures intended to foster the active economic development of the southern region by opening up new resources and strengthening entrepreneurial initiative. This policy, with its material incentives for promising economic enterprises, was tailored more to the "foreigners" (Greeks, Armenians, Jews) living in South Russia than to eager social climbers from the local peasantry.[20] The land surveys and cartography projects commissioned by the authorities were an essential element of this long-term economic policy, whose consequences the Ukrainian peasants did not always consider beneficial.[21]

In many respects, the government of Paul I carried on the plans and initiatives of Catherine II. Even more than his ill-regarded predecessor, Paul I emphasized the consolidation of state finances in order to "place the empire's future economy on such a firm basis that our revenue will suffice to cover necessary expenses."[22] He hoped to achieve this lofty goal by means of strict accounting, reduction of government spending by trimming the bureaucracy, and a more balanced distribution of burdens among his subjects. Compared with Catherine II, Paul I sounded new accents from the very beginning: a stronger emphasis on the idea of legitimacy and legal security; guarantees of hereditary privilege and prescriptive rights. The new ruler was at pains to counterpose this approach to the ruthless proceedings of his mother, both in international relations and in domestic policy.

As a successor to the throne, Paul I had already distanced himself from the practice of unscrupulous power politics vis-à-vis his weak Polish neighbour and had deplored the violent encroachments on the right of autonomy carried out by Catherine II in the western borderlands of the empire as part of the unification of Russia's administrative system.[23] Paul's teacher, Nikita Ivanovich Panin, had strengthened his will to change policy, to "eradicate the Potemkin spirit,"[24] and had sharpened his eye for the evident abuses caused by legislative arbitrariness and favouritism. Paul's written proclamations of this period make apparent his determination to bring about a moral and institutional renewal of the Russian autocracy in the spirit of the eighteenth-century Enlightenment by means of policies opposed to those followed during the hated regime of his mother.[25]

From a purely quantitative point of view, Paul undoubtedly ranks far ahead of Catherine II as a legislator; his pathological addiction to regulations drove him to pay ever greater attention to detail—indeed, "he was obsessed with details."[26] But he was also firmly opposed to previous administrative practice. Paul's demonstrative release of imprisoned Polish patriots immediately following his accession to the throne was already an indication of his declared intent to make reparations and a promise to adhere to ethical norms of behaviour in international relations. The rejection of his mother's policies was continued in the partial abolition of her administrative reforms in the western border areas, which, in the words of Marc Raeff, had been the first phase of a "consistent and conscious policy of eliminating traditional, historically conditioned administrative units in favor of a pyramidal structure of identical subdivisions," and had been intended to pave the way for integration and "uniformity, first administrative and economic, then institutional and social, and finally cultural."[27]

The establishment of new guberniia boundaries in the Russian Empire, enacted on 12 December 1796, a few weeks after the change of administration, ended the first period of restoration.[28] It saw the re-establishment of old legal privileges and a restitution of traditional institutions by means of a series of uniform decrees for the "privileged" provinces of Little Russia, Latvia, Estonia,

Vyborg, Courland, Lithuania, Minsk, Belorussia, Volhynia, Podolia and Kiev.[29] When the Little Russian guberniia was created out of the three former governorships on the Left Bank, with a new administrative centre at Chernihiv, it was explicitly declared on 30 November 1796 that the administrative and legal constitution was to be re-established "as it had formerly existed according to local laws and traditional customs," and that the selection of judges should be carried out "with the strictest regard for Little Russian law."[30] At the same time important decisions had already been taken concerning the future administrative structure of Ukrainian territory. Specifically, the formation of a separate Kiev guberniia on the Right Bank out of formerly Polish areas was announced.[31] The revision of the empire's administrative boundaries was to include the re-establishment of the so-called Slobodian Ukraine (Kharkiv guberniia) within the frontiers of 1765, the formation of a guberniia of New Russia in the south out of Voznesensk province and the Tavriian region, and the partition of the south-western lands acquired from Poland into the guberniias of Volhynia and Podolia.[32]

It would certainly be unwarranted to conclude from the execution of these decrees that there had been a return to previous conditions and a restoration of former rights of autonomy in the western border guberniias. Despite his emphatically legalistic attitude, the new emperor was hardly inclined to give up the effective instruments of unified decision-making authority that had been acquired by the central government as a result of Catherine's reforms. State supervision was in fact strengthened in the newly acquired western provinces by establishing the new office of inspector (*fiskal*).[33] The governor remained an omnipotent plenipotentiary of the central government, with his bureaucracy and the fullness of his authority, as did the financial administration, which overrode the guberniia officials. Military recruitment had already been taken out of the hands of local administrators.[34]

Despite his far-reaching concessions to social forms that had evolved historically in the western border areas, Paul I did not want to legitimize his rule by means of a rigid, reactionary policy. Rather, it is characteristic of the domestic policies for which he was responsible that legalistic adherence to principle was combined with surprisingly far-reaching pragmatism in matters of detail. Considering the negative consequences that made themselves apparent in the later years of his reign, it is clear—as McGrew correctly stresses[35]—that there was a striking discrepancy between the sublime principles borrowed from the political philosophy of enlightened European absolutism and the "actual political behavior" of the emperor. From the outset there was ample discretion for ad hoc decisions to clarify dubious facts or settle competing demands.

In determining the precise borders of the new guberniias, the governors were granted a full measure of regulatory discretion according to local conditions and requirements. It is obvious that when this decision was made considerations of practicality took precedence over all too anxious considerations having to do with possible historical or even ethnographic associations.[36] For example, the governor of Slobodian Ukraine, Privy Councillor Teplov, demanded authority over Great Russian villages in order to avoid the dismemberment of his guberniia, indicating in a petition to the Senate that this would ensure better administration and division of territory. At the same time he offered to relinquish authority over scattered Ukrainian settlements that had been administered from Slobodian Ukraine before 1765, but had meanwhile been attached to neighbouring guberniias.[37] During the implementation of the imperial decree on efficient partition of territory, procedures regarding the subdivision of individual guberniias were applied rather schematically at times. For practical reasons, the dissolution of old administrative centres and the upgrading of certain rapidly developing settlements to county seats could scarcely have been avoided in any case.[38] Moreover, it would hardly have been possible to formulate binding regulations for the restoration of previous conditions in an area whose administrative division had been changed several times in the course of the eighteenth century, especially since the Polish partitions.

In the numerous disputed cases that awaited definitive resolution, the central administration generally did not close its mind to well-founded arguments presented by local authorities. Not infrequently, workable regulations were applied in neighbouring guberniias. To take a typical example, the newly established Kiev guberniia had been given a peculiarly hybrid character by its unification with Right-Bank territory. It is true that during the entire reign of Paul I the traditional associations with the Left Bank were maintained by successive military governors of Kiev, who were in charge of the Little Russian government,[39] but the territorial reorientation toward the west inevitably brought Kiev closer to the bordering guberniias of Podolia, Volhynia and Minsk in everyday administrative and judicial practice. In order to regularize the administration of justice, it was necessary not only to reorganize the court system in Kiev so as to establish an appeal procedure and determine jurisdictional authority, but also to bring about a more comprehensive integration of routine procedure and to co-ordinate the applicable legal norms.[40] These norms were based on different traditions—Lithuanian, Polish, Ukrainian, Russian, and German. Despite the continuing paramount significance of the Lithuanian Statute, it had proved impossible to establish binding legal norms during the eighteenth century.[41] Pragmatic solutions were now sought by the Senate, which had been asked to serve as an arbitrator. The Senate applied its remedies on the vexed questions of the language to be used in court and the deadline for appeals in judicial cases to the neighbouring Ukrainian guberniias. In both cases an impossible situation had been created in the attempt to carry out the imperial decree of 30 November 1796, which required the re-establishment in Little Russia of the traditional cort system according to previous law and custom.

Regarding the question of appeal deadlines, the local authorities pointed out in a memorandum that the Little Russian nobility adhered to the Lithuanian Statute, "in which no period of time is established for appeal of a decision, but it is simply stated: Where these statutes do not apply, other Christian laws are to be obeyed; accordingly, in 1756, the Senate followed the book of civil jurisprudence, according to which only citizens can be tried, and in which a period of six weeks is prescribed for filing an appeal in Little Russia, and a period of eighteen weeks is prescribed for an appeal to the Senate against the hetman's decision, since at that time there was no fixed appeal period in Russia either. However, since Your Imperial Majesty has been pleased to ordain by decrees of 17 August and 13 September 1797 a period of one year for appeals in Great Russia and Poland, the Director of the Little Russian Guberniia, Field Marshal and Knight Count Saltykov, asks the Senate: in Little Russia, should one observe the former period of eighteen weeks, or the period of one year?"[42] In its verdict the Senate decided on a procedure that attempted to do justice to local usage as well as to state interest by means of a legal combination: "Having compared all the conditions heretofore described, the Senate is of the following opinion: in order to ensure the uniform observance of the said period in the guberniias of Little Russia and Kiev, in consideration of their great distance from St. Petersburg and of the fact that both Poles and Little Russians are under their jurisdiction, to extend to one year the period of appeal against superior court decisions to the Senate, with due regard for the provisions of the Ukase of 17 August concerning the court's power to delay the execution of judgments, but to retain the former period of six weeks within the guberniia."[43]

Pragmatic considerations also served to justify deviations from previous practice concerning the language question in order to secure overriding imperial interests. The Polish language was only to be used in the lower—assize and local—courts for all matters. In superior courts, bilingualism was established as the norm, because here, according to instructions,[44] it was not only elected representatives of the local nobility who participated, but also secretaries and crown councillors. Moreover, the guberniia administration served as an organ of control, and the Senate was involved in its capacity as court of appeal. Correspondence of the superior court with authorities who used the Polish language in their internal affairs was also to be conducted in the Russian language.[45] In a basic instruction of 25 December 1799 it was made clear that the restitution of former rights and privileges in Little Russia and the other guberniias had not altered the "general political principles" of guberniia administration and financial management. Accordingly, those residing in the privileged guberniias would also have to observe standard government regulations in their dealings with the central and guberniia authorities.[46]

Nor did the administration of Paul I allow itself to be handicapped unnecessarily by zealously proclaimed principles of a "new" policy in other areas. When it came to matters essential to the stability of the empire—restoring government finances, securing tax revenue, recruiting competent bureaucrats—existing provincial rights of autonomy were abolished without regard for legal scruple. The nobility, as a source of support for the monarchy, appears to have been confirmed in its hereditary rights, but at the same time it was put under strict obligation to serve the state, regardless of the privileges granted by Catherine II. The nobles were subjected to the principle of equality before the law and made to bear their share of obligations to the state—experiences that could at times be painful. Involvement in the administration of justice, which again became a right of the nobility of the "privileged" provinces, meant the assumption of a considerable financial burden when the costs of maintaining guberniia courts and police were abruptly shifted to the nobility. In order to ensure the equal distribution of these costs among the noble estates, a ukase of 18 December 1798 required that each guberniia make an annual lump sum payment to the treasury.[47] A total of 1,640,000 rubles was collected as follows: 35,000 from Slobodian Ukraine; 80,000 from Little Russia; 30,000 from New Russia; 63,000 from Volhynia; 65,000 from Podolia; 72,000 from Kiev; and 16,000 rubles from the Slobodian landlords in the Don Cossack region. This was justified by pointing out the nobility's privileged position: "As noted above, We have limited the guberniia budget to the absolute necessities: whereas the greater part of it is used to ensure the administration of justice, the maintenance of public order and the safeguarding of general security—all offices held by members of the nobility; and whereas, in addition, this first estate of the empire has been treated preferentially as an object of Our sovereign favour, and has again received a new proof of Our solicitude through the establishment of an assistance bank for its benefit in order to maintain noble families in full possession of their property, We consider it equitable that they provide for the general welfare out of their own means..."[48]

Because of the increasing militarization of the administrative apparatus and the growth of state supervision in every important sphere of activity, local nobilities continually lost power during the reign of Paul I. This trend proved irreversible, culminating with the displacement of elected noble representatives by state appointees who were not always chosen from the local aristocracy,[49] as well as with a further increase in the power and decision-making authority of the governor as agent of the central authorities.

The interests of the state were protected with casuistic subtlety against all-too-excessive claims of hereditary rights and privileges, and the satisfaction of egregious demands was avoided. With a ukase of 16 September 1797 Paul I confirmed the traditional privileges of the citizens of Kiev, as he had already done for the Greeks of Nizhyn.[50] The ukase decreed that "the citizens of this old residence of Our forefathers, who rest with God, are hereby guaranteed inviolable possession of all their rights, liberties, privileges, city revenues and benefits by the Autocrat of all the Rusians, just as these have been granted to the said city by the patents and privileges of Our ancestors, which we renew and confirm by the present decree."[51] Soon afterward the citizens of Kiev presented a patent granted by Tsar Aleksei Mikhailovich in 1654 that exempted the townspeople from military service. They asked for the remission of recruitment obligations, especially the payments imposed on merchants in lieu of recruitment. The Senate, which dealt with this issue, at first objected to recognizing the applicability of the privilege to contemporaries because of the changes that had occurred in the composition of the Kiev citizenry and the undeniable territorial changes that had taken place. When Paul I insisted that comprehensive restoration of the old privileges be applied literally, i.e., limited to the same number of merchants and citizens who had been granted the privilege in 1654, the Senate was obliged to conduct a laborious historical investigation. Reliable figures on the composition of the Kiev citizenry in 1654 were no longer to be found in the archives, according to the Senate, because the great fire of 1718 had destroyed all the documents. Approximate figures, calculated on the basis of the revisions of 1782 or 1795, therefore had to be used to determine the size of the group of established citizens who would be granted the privileges of 1654.[52]

In other cases in which the tsar saw the principle of equality jeopardized or humane ideals endangered by putative loyalty to tradition, he did not hesitate to change outdated practices. On 16 October 1798 he brusquely refused assent to a Senate report, giving no further reason for his decision, and prohibited the sale of Little Russian peasants, even those without land.[53] In the absence of legal ordinances, and given the equalization in the status of Little Russian and Great Russian peasants, the regional high court had declared it permissible to apply the practices usual among landlords dealing with Great Russian serfs. Notwithstanding the strictly formal arguments presented by experts, the governor had had misgivings and requested a ruling by the Senate, which agreed with the opinion of the high court, but was unable to convince the tsar of the correctness of its interpretation.

Sharp conflicts over church policy repeatedly presented the administration with opportunities to attempt pragmatic solutions.[54] Obviously, a domestic policy favourable to Polish Catholic noble landowners called for particular discretion. Paul's understanding of and somewhat open sympathy for the interests of the Catholic Church, his attitude to the Jesuits[55] and the Papal Curia,[56] as well as his role in the Maltese question, repeatedly gave rise to broad speculation and misunderstanding, which must have greatly complicated the competitive co-existence of hostile church organizations, especially at the local level. The Orthodox Church was expected to reorganize itself extensively in all parts of the country in order to adjust the borders of bishoprics to new administrative boundaries and to bring about a standardization of nomenclature. [57] Despite the open support given to efforts to bring the Uniates into a common Russian church organization, Orthodox zealots were kept in check in the western regions. Despite the cardinal importance ascribed to religion as a defence against the revolutionary *Zeitgeist* and a bulwark of the monarchic idea, it was stringently forbidden to impose a hasty, one-sided choice favouring one of the established churches in areas of mixed denomination. This state of affairs explains the vacillation of the authorities, who only reacted in extreme cases. The central government inclined toward the idea of religious tolerance, distancing itself from excesses and forced conversions.[58] It assisted both the Roman Catholic and the Uniate churches in reorganizing themselves.[59] From an Orthodox—i.e., Ukrainian—viewpoint, such a policy of equal treatment and mediation between the hostile ecclesiastical groups undoubtedly warranted a negative assessment, and there was no lack of critical and angry commentary from contemporaries.[60]

The search for pragmatic solutions also influenced—and handicapped—policy on the Jewish question during the era of Paul I.[61] The most recent research by John Doyle Klier shows convincingly that in the 1790s the contradictory and incoherent policies of Catherine II, which attempted to combine greater integration of Jews into existing forms of social and economic activity with continued discriminatory restrictions, were superseded by the vigorous promotion of legal equality for Jewish citizens, which had been promised them earlier. In practice, however, authorities seem to have contented themselves with partial solutions whenever influential social groups put up resistance. Klier considers the attempt "to gain adequate knowledge of Jewish life" [62] a positive feature of Paul's reign.

*

If one attempts to strike a balance and evaluate the particular policies of Paul's reign discussed in this article, both with reference to the emperor's personality and to the government programme for which he was responsible, then Kliuchevsky's impressionistic overall judgment does not always prove to be a helpful point of departure. In Kliuchevsky's view, this tsar's reign was organically linked with the past as a protest and with the future as a first unsuccessful attempt at a new policy, a lesson for Paul's successor.[63] The tsar's policy toward Ukraine shows particularly that as a reformer—which he undoubtedly wanted to be, and was, though often with inadequate means and insufficient results—he was more closely linked with his predecessor than he himself was willing to admit with his demonstrative attitude of protest. He was no more successful than Catherine II in dealing with the principal defects of the Russian administration: poor information and inadequately qualified bureaucrats, corruption and obstruction. To some extent, Paul I had to avail himself of the same aides and councillors as Catherine II. Out of profound inner conviction and, more particularly, because of the bitter experience of revolutionary upheaval in France, Paul shared his mother's conviction that only an autocratic regime could offer a form of government adequate to the vast expanses of the Russian Empire.[64] One of his most influential councillors,

Count Aleksandr A. Bezborodko (died 6 April 1799), a descendant of the Ukrainian Cossack nobility whose political career had begun during the reign of Catherine II, expressly confirmed the tsar in this opinion in his famous memorandum of 1799, but also strongly urged him to adhere to his self-imposed rules and norms.[65]

Law and order was the slogan with which Paul I sought to distance himself from his mother and launch a renewal of the monarchic idea in Russia. The example of Ukrainian territory, which has been the focus of attention in this article, clearly shows that Paul's reforming activity found expression in laws and decrees primarily during the early years of his reign.[66] They best exemplify the implementation of well-prepared and carefully considered ideas of reform, a "trend toward rationalization, centralization, and administrative efficiency."[67] The "madness" so often referred to; the incoherent rage of a suspicious and pathologically moody despot; the "course of arbitrariness and despotism"[68]— these images, which have so obscured the Emperor Paul both for contemporaries and for posterity, belong only to the second half of his short reign.

The heightened attention that Paul I initially devoted to the historically conditioned diversity of his multi-ethnic empire led in local administration to an abrupt departure from Catherine's more rigorous policies of unification. When it came to the implementation of particular decrees, however, violent interventions from the outside were only half-heartedly countered. Because of his elitist conception of government, Paul was not interested in a reassessment of political regionalism in the border regions, let alone any promotion of separatist tendencies. Bureaucratization and centralization, which he consistently favoured in the supposed interest of the empire, would ultimately render meaningless all the concessions he was temporarily inclined to grant the local noble associations. The fate of Ukraine during the reign of Paul I provides an instructive example of the hopelessness of tsarist nationality policy. The various social groups could not resist the growing pressure for uniformity that necessarily proceeded from the central administration of an autocratic regime. Only an early renunciation of a one-sided policy that favoured the nobility and a far-reaching federalization of the multi-ethnic Russian state could have created the necessary basis for trust and smoothed the way toward lasting reconciliation. The gradual reduction of the emperor's unlimited privileges would have been a necessary second prerequisite. Paul showed remarkable initiative in regard to the first point, which would ultimately cost him the throne, but for various reasons neither he nor his successors would accept the second condition.

Translated by Gisela Forchner
and Myroslav Yurkevich

Notes

1. Roderick E. McGrew, "A Political Portrait of Paul I from the Austrian and English Diplomatic Archives" in *Jahrbücher für Geschichte Osteuropas* N.F. (1971):503–29. Quotation on 528.

2. V. O. Kliuchevsky, *Sochineniia* (Moscow, 1971), 5:189.

3. M. V. Klochkov, *Ocherki pravitelstvuiushchei deiatelnosti vremeni Pavla I* (Petrograd, 1916).

4. John L. H. Keep, "Paul I and the Militarization of Government" in Hugh Ragsdale, ed., *Paul I: A Reassessment of His Life and Reign* (Pittsburgh, 1979), 91–103. Quotation on 91.

5. Cf. n. 3 above. Partial reprint from *Canadian-American Slavic Studies* 7 (1973).

6. S. M. Kazantsev, "O politicheskom rezhime Rossiiskoi imperii v 1796–1801 gg.," *Vestnik Leningradskogo universiteta. No. 5. Ekonomika, filosofiia, pravo*, vyp. 1 (1980):99–106.

7. R. McGrew, "Some Thoughts on Paul I," *Study Group on Eighteenth-Century Russia. Newsletter* 8 (1980):35–7. Reference on 37. (Review of Hugh Ragsdale's book.)

8. Edgar Hösch, "Zar Paul I (1796–1801) und die russische Mittelmeerpolitik am Ausgang des 18. Jahrhunderts," *Saeculum* 18 (1967):294–315. Cf. Norman E. Saul, "The Objectives of Paul's Italian Policy" in *Paul I: A Reassessment of His Life and Reign*, 31–43. Reference on 41: "Paul's Italian policy demonstrates that a rational foreign policy that complemented a reactionary ideological outlook was pursued," and Ole Feldbaek, "The Foreign Policy of Tsar Paul I, 1800–1801: An Interpretation," *Jahrbücher für Geschichte Osteuropas* 30 (1982): 16–36 with the concluding remark: "In 1800 and 1801 Paul I defined and developed a rational and consistent overall foreign policy" (36).

9. *Polnoe sobranie zakonov Rossiiskoi imperii* (henceforth PSZ). *Sobranie 1-e*, v. 24–6.

10. P. Zhukovich, "Zapadnaia Rossiia v tsarstvovanie imperatora Pavla," *Zhurnal Ministerstva Narodnago Prosveshcheniia*, (1916): v. 63, 183–226; v. 64, 207–63; v. 65, 186–275.

11. PSZ no. 18 248.

12. Zhukovich, v. 63, 201ff.

13. Ibid., v. 64, 213ff, gives individual examples.

14. Ibid., 229.

15. PSZ no. 17 638, cf. no. 17 734, 17 872.

16. I. e., conversion of grain delivery obligations to cash payments beginning in 1797. Grain stored in state granaries was offered for sale to the peasants.

17. PSZ no. 18 009 (in the province of Tavriia).

18. PSZ no. 17 802 (in Slobodian Ukraine).

19. PSZ no. 17 909 (5 April 1797); cf. Klochkov, 559ff.

20. E.g., the question of extending the cultivation of silkworms to the newly acquired

Ukrainian territories (PSZ no. 18 240, with special reference to the Greeks, Armenians, and colonists residing there); cf. PSZ no. 18 009, 18 093, 18 325, 19 290, as well as the various measures intended to promote Black Sea commerce (cf., e. g., PSZ no. 17 919, 17 939, 17 941, 18 373).

21. PSZ no. 18 670 (Kiev guberniia), no. 18 475 (Western regions), no. 18 707 (New Russia); cf. Zhukovich, v. 64, 230.

22. PSZ no. 18 278 (18 December 1797).

23. McGrew, *Political Portrait,* 508.

24. K. Stählin, *Geschichte Russlands von den Anfängen bis zur Gegenwart* (Königsberg and Berlin, 1935), 3:17.

25. Claus Scharf, "Staatsauffassung und Regierungsprogramm eines aufgeklärten Selbstherrschers: Die Instruktion des Grossfürsten Paul von 1788" in E. Schulin, ed., *Gedenkschrift Martin Göhring. Studien zur europäischen Geschichte* (Wiesbaden, 1963), 91–106. Reference on 104. Cf. David L. Ransel, "An Ambivalent Legacy: The Education of Grand Duke Paul," in *Paul I: A Reassessment,* which provides interesting new documentation on Paul's personal development.

26. McGrew, 510.

27. Marc Raeff, "Uniformity, Diversity, and the Imperial Administration of the Reign of Catherine II," *Osteuropa in Geschichte und Gegenwart. Festschrift für Günther Stökl zum 60. Geburtstag* (Cologne and Vienna, 1977), 97–113. Quotations on 105–12.

28. PSZ no. 17 634; cf. Zhukovich, v. 63, 192 ff.

29. PSZ no. 17 584 (28 November 1796, Estonia and Livonia); no. 17 594 (30 November 1796, Little Russia); no. 17 637 (12 December 1796, Vyborg); no. 17 681 (24 December 1796, Courland; cf. no. 17 785).

30. PSZ no. 17 594, Par. 3. For the important changes that were nevertheless made to the earlier Polish-Lithuanian legal system, see Zhukovich, v. 63, 205–7.

31. Ibid., Par. 7. Cf. Zhukovich, v. 63, 194ff.

32. PSZ no. 17 634, Par. 2, 4 and 6.

33. PSZ no. 18 826 and 19 218. Cf. also the supervision established by the Senate, PSZ no. 19 139, 19 211 and 19 212.

34. Zhukovich, v. 64, 244.

35. McGrew, *A Political Portrait,* 528.

36. PSZ no. 18 166, 18 117.

37. PSZ no. 17 948. Cf. the proposals to include the scattered Ukrainian and Russian settlements in Voronezh guberniia in a single administrative unit (PSZ no. 18 116).

38. PSZ no. 18 317 (transfer of the administrative centre from Katerynopil to Zvenyhorodka in Kiev guberniia), PSZ no. 18 166 and 18 242 (transfer of the registry office for real estate transactions—the so-called *kontrakty*—from Dubno to Kiev.

39. Zhukovich, v. 63, 197.

40. Cf. PSZ 18 135, 18 563, 18 670, 18 850. Zhukovich, v. 63, 207ff.
41. V. Kubijovyč, ed., *Ukraine: A Concise Encyclopaedia* (Toronto, 1963–71), 2:38b. Cf. *Istoriia Ukrainskoi RSR* (Kiev, 1977—9), 2:253–3.
42. PSZ no. 18 252.
43. Ibid. Cf. PSZ no. 18 147 (for Minsk, Podillia and Volhynia) and no. 18 828.
44. PSZ no. 18 135 or 18 850.
45. Ibid. Cf. Zhukovich, v. 63, 207ff.
46. PSZ no. 19 230.
47. PSZ no. 18 278.
48. Ibid. Cf. Klochkov, 488ff.
49. Zhukovich, v. 63, 203. Cf. the regulations on noble voting assemblies, PSZ no. 17 789, 17 790, 19 154.
50. PSZ no. 18 071. Cf. patents of privilege for Armenians, PSZ no. 19 166, 19 167, 19 168, 19 169; also the establishment of a city council in Odessa, intended primarily for resident aliens (Greeks, Albanians, Moldavians, Bulgarians) and modelled on the councils of the Baltic cities of Riga and Reval, PSZ no. 17 967, 18 346, cf. no. 18 355.
51. PSZ no. 18 142.
52. PSZ no. 18 336 and 19 214. Cf. Zhukovich, v. 64, 250ff.
53. PSZ no. 18 706.
54. For details, see Zhukovich, v. 65, 225–75.
55. William A. James, "Paul I and the Jesuits in Russia," Ph.D. dissertation, University of Washington, 1977.
56. *Paul I: A Reassessment*, 33ff. and R. E. McGrew, *Paul I and the Knights of Malta*, 44–75.
57. PSZ no. 19 156 (16 October 1799).
58. It also protected the Orthodox Church from efforts to win over its faithful on the part of Roman Catholics (PSZ no. 18 818) and Uniates (PSZ no. 19 263).
59. PSZ no. 18 734 and 18 504.
60. Zhukovich, v. 65, 232ff, shares this opinion.
61. Zhukovich, v. 64, 251ff.
62. John Doyle Klier, "The Origins of the Jewish Minority Problem in Russia, 1772–1812," Ph.D. dissertation. University of Illinois (Urbana), 1975, 166–228. Quotation on 167.
63. Kliuchevsky, ibid.
64. Scharf, 96ff.
65. Marc Raeff, *Plans for Political Reform in Imperial Russia, 1730–1905.* Englewood Cliffs, N.J., 1966), 69ff.
66. Cf. McGrew, 511f.
67. McGrew, 503, summarizing Klochkov's views. Cf. Erik Amburger, *Ingermanland. Eine junge Provinz Russlands im Wirkungsbereich der Residenz und Weltstadt St. Petersburg-Leningrad* (Cologne and Vienna, 1980), 1:177: "In

November 1796, when Paul succeeded his mother as head of state, he undertook
to rescind or at least thoroughly modify her administrative reforms on a scale not
previously encountered in such undertakings." Everything he did was motivated
by resentment of his mother and hatred of her councillors and favourites. Since
the tsar took over an administration that was by no means well-ordered, but half-
completed and full of contradictions, some of his innovations had a thoroughly
positive character that contributed to valuable reforms..."

68. Marc Raeff, *Michael Speransky, Statesman of Imperial Russia, 1772–1839.* 2d
rev. ed. (The Hague, 1969), 32.

Martha Bohachevsky-Chomiak

Ukrainian and Russian Women: Co-operation and Conflict

A look at the participation of women in the community and political life of their societies can shed as much new light on the societies as on the women. This study focuses on some of the distinct characteristics of Ukrainian women, looks briefly at the women's organizations in Ukraine at the turn of this century, and discusses the interludes of co-operation between Russian and Ukrainian women. In conventional terms, both women and Ukrainians are considered "minorities," although in Ukraine neither of the two groups is a real minority. Students of women in the Russian Empire or in the Soviet Union largely ignore the nationality implications, while studies of the non-Russian nationalities tend not to focus on women's issues.[1] A focus upon feminism is itself not useful, since in Eastern Europe feminism continues to be a rather odious term. Although feminism is simply an extension of human rights to the female half of the population, nations where few human rights and a low standard of living exist are often blind to the specifically sexual aspect of discrimination. Articulated feminism is a product of an educated and leisured class, usually associated with political liberalism. The feminist perspective in Eastern Europe is more diffuse, and it is necessary to look at various women's activities to obtain an adequate picture.

No Ukrainian and very few Russian women considered the "woman question" central to their interests. The Russians, however, specifically debated some aspects of it. The Ukrainians in the Russian Empire discussed it only marginally. Some Russian women participated in movements that can be labelled feminist. Ukrainian women involved in such movements avoided the designation.

Leftist political groups welcomed the participation of women, usually under the tutelage of the more experienced males. Middle-of-the-road liberals also admitted some participation of women in public life, provided, as the Ukrainian Mykhailo Drahomanov phrased it in one of his letters to the socialist Ivan Franko, that someone took care of the children. Women's participation in Ukrainian organizations was taken for granted by Ukrainian community activists, since those involved in social and political causes were of leftist orientation. This predisposed them, in theory at least, to accept the principle of women's equality while essentially keeping within the parameters of conventional sex-role divisions.

Ukrainian women and Russian radical women were frequently drawn into public activity by males, who persuaded them of the irrelevance of feminist striving to genuine social and political concerns as they defined them. Writing about the woman issue in Russia and Ukraine, generally confined to this tendency, led activists to overlook the special characteristics of women as a whole and to ignore the importance of a "women's perspective." The few contemporaries who wrote about the early stages of Ukrainian women's movements and the equally few historians who even mentioned women in their works implicitly or explicitly stressed the similarities between the experiences of Russian and Ukrainian women.[2]

In fact, the differences are more important. When studying the historical development of Ukrainian women and their organizations, one is struck by the features that distinguish them from Russian women, not by the similarities. Hence the anomaly: the Ukrainian perception and presentation of the development of the women's movement is at variance with what actually happened, to the detriment of the Ukrainians themselves.

One explanation of this anomaly is that those who wrote about the women's movement in the Russian Empire, as well as the first women activists themselves, were members of the intelligentsia. They suffered from its disregard of historicity and historical thinking. By the end of the nineteenth century, the Ukrainian intelligentsia often received its philosophical, social, political and economic ideas through Russian channels. It considered reactionary tsarism its prime enemy and was attracted to ideologies that did not lead it to study its own past. Later commentators based their research on published accounts of activities in the capital cities, overlooking local developments. The Ukrainian intelligentsia in particular, which failed to see its organic connection with the Ukrainian countryside, was always surprised by the surge of support (*stykhiia*) emanating from that source. Influenced by the Russian intelligentsia, from which it took over many of its ideas and rhetorical devices, the Ukrainian intelligentsia failed to grasp its own potential strength. The police analysts, on the other hand, who kept better records of local events than did the activists themselves, feared precisely the link-up of the villages with the democratic leaders. They expected that such an alliance would most probably take shape in Ukraine. This emerges clearly from a perusal of the *Okhrana* documents dealing with political and community organizations in Ukraine between 1880 and 1914.

There was a connection between the study of minorities and interest in women. A number of historians attracted to the study of Ukrainian history within the Russian Empire (a history of a minority in such a formulation) were also drawn to the study of women and social history.[3] The linking of Ukrainian historiography to that of the oppressed masses and the Russification of Ukrainian upper classes also influenced the manner in which the history of Ukrainian women was perceived.

Since the eleventh and twelfth centuries, the legal rights of women in the Kievan state, especially among the upper classes, have been commensurate with those of men in certain circumstances.[4] Women inherited property, managed it, participated in court cases and could initiate divorce proceedings. According to the historian Nataliia Polonska-Vasylenko, they married on the basis of equality. The old marriage vows were the same for both partners: "I take you as my helper." Upon Ukraine's incorporation into Russia in the seventeenth century, this phrase was replaced by the more familiar "be faithful and obey" for the women, a result of the tsarist government's direct interference in Ukrainian social mores and ecclesiastical customs.[5] The rights of women to their property, however, theoretically remained intact throughout the formation and expansion of the Russian Empire.

The Tatar invasion did not change Ukrainian social mores: the seclusion of upper–class women and their subordination to men, which had occurred in the north, in Russia, did not take place on Ukrainian territory. In contrast to the subordinate and passive Russian women, Ukrainian women appear to have been as free and resolute as any frontier women. The constant struggle with the Tatars and Turks provided the raw material for sagas and songs, some of them written by women. These carried the spark of female activism and independence even into modern times.[6] Subsequent Polish encroachment on Ukrainian and Orthodox privileges strengthened the resolve of the Ukrainians to create institutions for their defence. Women participated along with men in building churches and financing schools. If necessary, women ran local affairs in the absence of their husbands.[7]

Russian presence in Ukraine manifested itself as a series of encroachments by a colonizing and centralizing government. The tsarist government re-introduced serfdom in Ukraine in its Western variant of *panshchyna* (a specific number of days devoted to working exclusively for a landlord) rather than the Russian *obrok* (payment of a part of the harvested crop to the landlord). Both Russian and Ukrainian peasants were also subjected to state taxation. Because the serf system was different in Ukraine and Russia, it prevented the development of peasant homogeneity. Ukrainian customs remained more humane than those of the Russians. Even after the incorporation of Ukraine into the Empire and the granting of noble status to the Ukrainian Cossack officers, direct contact with the Russians was limited. This prevented the adoption of the vestigial subordination of women that was the norm for the pre-Petrine Russian upper classes. Ukrainian upper-class women, like their peasant counterparts in a more circumscribed sphere, remained autonomous within marriage. Life changed less for the Ukrainian woman on the *khutir* (the individual homestead in the steppe areas of Ukraine) than for her husband, who was drawn into civilian or military imperial service.[8]

The differences between Ukrainian and Russian women were recognized by women who relied on their own experience and avoided either formal schooling or informal socialization by the intelligentsia. Larysa Kosach Kvitka, better known under the literary pseudonym "Lesia Ukrainka," was the most famous child of Olha Drahomanov Kosach, the Ukrainian woman activist, writer and publisher whose pseudonym was Olena Pchilka. The mother educated her children outside the Russian school system according to a "great books" method that she herself developed. Lesia Ukrainka contrasted the seclusion and supervision of Russian women with the dignity and independence of Ukrainian women. In a drama written in 1910 (*Boiarynia*), she recreated the shock experienced by a Ukrainian woman who moved into upper-class Russian society in the seventeenth century.

More than half a century earlier, Mariia Vilinska Markovych Zhuchenko, whose literary reputation as Marko Vovchok was enhanced by her being the first prose writer in the Russian Empire to focus upon the fate of female serfs, had grasped the brutalizing aspects in the modernization of the Empire. In one of her short stories, "Instytutka," Vovchok contrasted the savage high-handedness of a "progressively educated" young lady from St. Petersburg with the humane casualness that pervaded an old Ukrainian household.

The differences in the historical experiences of Ukrainian and Russian women were also clear to Hanna Chykalenko Keller. the daughter of a rich Ukrainian activist. She was brought up in Ukraine and educated in Western Europe. In an unpublished memorandum about Ukrainian women that Keller prepared for the International Women's League of Peace and Freedom, which met in Geneva in June 1920, she wrote:

> It is probably in the [fifteenth through the seventeenth] centuries that we must look for the origins of the relative independence of Ukrainian women in the following epochs. The upper classes of the Ukrainian population as well as the common Cossacks led a warlike existence defending the frontiers against foreign invasion. Women were often obliged to follow their husbands in their expeditions, even to take part in battle. Fighting at the side of the men for the defence of their country, the Ukrainian woman of this time displayed great energy and great strength of character. In her husband's absence, she was accustomed to rely on herself, on her own initiative. She took part in political life, in the Diets and public assemblies; she was admitted to law courts. The religious movements of the time found passionate partisans among Ukrainian women, who studied religious doctrines, founded monasteries, schools, hostels, actively collaborated in the spread of instruction and benevolence, and took part in ecclesiastical communities that played so great a role in the struggle for national independence in Ukraine.[9]

Legal measures intended to limit the growth of absolutism failed in both Ukraine and Russia. In Ukraine this also resulted in a blurring of national identity. Women, less exposed to modernization and less prone to ideological thinking, were able to preserve their identities longer than men. For them, the line of what was Russian, what was imperial, and what was Ukrainian, was not so much muted as overlapping. In other words, some women did not see the two identities as being mutually exclusive, although they also did not conflate the two completely. Just as one lived in the city and in the country, so some of the women considered themselves Russian subjects but of Ukrainian coloration. For instance, one of the families in which the serf-poet and bard of the Ukrainian national renaissance, Taras Shevchenko, found not only friendship and support, but love, were the Russian Volkonskys. Their property in the heart of Ukraine—in Poltava—belonged to the granddaughter of the last Hetman of Ukraine. The son of the Decembrist Volkonsky, whose mother, abandoning him, had been the first Decembrist wife to follow her husband into exile, was raised in Poltava by his paternal uncle. The gentry which visited the household knew Ukrainian songs and memorized Shevchenko's poetry.[10] Nikolai Gogol's mother supplied him with the raw material of Ukrainian legend that he transformed into Russian short stories. Many families treasured elaborate peasant costumes of the region in which they lived. Gentry families in Ukraine were often run by the woman, since the husband, in military or civil service of the Empire, spent little time on the estates. With the spread of education and travel to the capitals Russian women in Ukraine, who viewed Ukrainian national reawakening as a charming manifestation of regionalism, were as astonished as the men by the Ukrainian national-liberation struggle, which coincided with the revolution.[11]

The mother of the last Hetman of Ukraine was a Ukrainian peasant woman who built her own village house as Natalka Rozumykha in 1742, and an elaborate church in Kozeltsi in 1745 as Countess Nataliia Rozumovska.[12] Her grandson, exemplifying the integration of the family into the imperial structure, rose in the Russian bureaucracy. But her great-great-grand-daughter, Sofia Perovskaia, was one of the five persons who in 1881 finally succeeded in assassinating the Russian tsar. To students of Russian history, Perovskaia was the epitome of the selfless, dedicated Russian woman. Her Ukrainian contemporaries, exemplifying an historical memory not yet eroded by later ideologies, however, remembered her ties to the old Rozumykha.

The woman issue emerged in the Empire in the 1860s. As in the United States, where it had been connected with slavery, the woman question in the Russian Empire was tied to serfdom. In the Ukrainian provinces it became part of the broad spectrum of national issues. The commonality of experience of Russian and Ukrainian women described by some modern writers was the commonality of the progressive intelligentsia. The struggle against autocratic tsarism for human and political rights was its common bond, but the definition of these terms provided the material for discord. It seems that the first woman of the intelligentsia to publish a political appeal was a Ukrainian, Khrystyna D. Alchevska, noted for her pioneering work in literacy schools for adults. In Herzen's London-based *Kolokol* of 8 March 1863, she entreated the women of Russia to come to the aid of the Poles, who had raised their last armed revolt against the tsarist government. She signed the appeal, couched in terms of imperial loyalty and universal enlightenment, "Ukrainka,"[13] illustrating that at the time the idea of a Ukrainian identity did not exclude adherence to a heterogeneous Empire as far as the non-Russians were concerned.

There is no way to distinguish Russian and Ukrainian female participants in the two great revolutionary currents of the nineteenth century, populism and Marxism. Psychologically, socially and intellectually the motivation and type of activity pursued by the women were the same. There were women in all camps. Neither Russian nor Ukrainian women produced notable theoreticians or ideologists. Both produced workers for the revolution, its martyrs and its saints. Neither among the Russian nor the Ukrainian women were there any double agents: we do not know whether this should be attributed to female virtue or to an oversight on the part of the *Okhrana*. More Russian women revolutionaries played significant symbolic revolutionary roles than did their Ukrainian counterparts. Although women participated even in the leadership of all specifically Ukrainian parties and organizations, in none did they achieve power. An argument could be made that the Ukrainian national movement was essentially liberal, not radical, and that liberals were wary of female emancipation—this despite the fact that the Ukrainians considered themselves radicals.

The revolution of 1905 was actually a prolonged series of crises and expectations, interspersed with promises, pogroms, the formation of legal parties and the convocation of a representative assembly. Systematization of the parties, their subordination to party discipline, and the development of party structures and programmes resulted in a decline in political participation by Russian and Ukrainian women alike.

In 1900, Ukrainian students had organized the Revolutionary Ukrainian Party (RUP), in which Marxist-oriented youth was active. Early in 1905, Ukrainian Marxists from the RUP formed a separate Ukrainian Social Democratic Labour Party. In an attempt to undermine the Ukrainians and diminish their significance in the all-Russian Marxist movement, a group of Marxists in Ukraine, at Lenin's behest, founded the Ukrainian branch of the Russian Social Democratic Labour Party (RSDLP). They called it *Spilka*—Union—and it was meant to be autonomous but subordinate to the Russian centre. Unlike other Marxist groups in the Russian Empire, this one began to enjoy grass-roots support, and its propaganda was effective in the countryside. Despite its national heterogeneity, the *Spilka* was acquiring a pro-Ukrainian orientation. Both the *Okhrana* and the RSDLP feared this development. The RSDLP tried to dilute it by decreeing that the *Spilka* should work with all peasants in the Empire. When this manoeuvre failed to contain Ukrainian influence, the RSDLP dissolved the *Spilka*.

Many women had been attracted to the *Spilka*. Liudmyla Drahomanova was considered a candidate for one of its posts, as were Lesia Ukrainka and her sister, Olha (Kryvyniuk). The participation of Jewish women was significant:

Maria Notelevna Michels joined it when she was barely nineteen. Gaia-Leia Moiseevna Kirnos, a midwife, offered the use of her address for mail, while Gilda Vulfovna Vulfson served as a liaison between Kiev and Chernihiv.[14]

The Marxists were the only political party to take an official stand on women's liberation and to organize activities and demonstrations centering on women. (The Constitutional Democrats voiced some support for woman suffrage.) In this fashion they mobilized women as a group and contributed to the raising of women's consciousness. But there was no specific attempt to associate women's liberation with nationalism. Women most active in the Marxist movement in Ukraine, such as Evgeniia Bosh and Rozaliia Zalkind, known as Zemliachka, showed no interest whatever in the nationality question.

The differences between Russian and Ukrainian women emerge more sharply in cultural activity and in work among the peasants. Russian women's work among the peasants concentrated on revolutionary consciousness-raising or some form of education, while Ukrainian women stressed the gathering of ethnographic material. This type of work was easy for women, who were closer to the village than men. Moreover, ethnographic materials were frequently the creations of village women. Compared to Ukrainian women, few Russian women engaged in gathering peasant artifacts and folklore. The compilation of songs, stories, artifacts and handicrafts of the peasants, pioneered by Olena Pchilka, brought Ukrainian women closer to the peasants and prevented the alienation which so painfully plagued the Russian intelligentsia.[15] Symbolically, Pchilka's book on folk ornaments in Ukraine was published in 1876, the year in which Ukrainian publishing was banned by the notorious Ems Ukase. It was as if the mute symbols of the peasant women were articulating the existence of a people who were banned from speaking out.

While the young Ukrainian woman might go to the villages and come back with material that could be considered of immediate relevance to the national cause, her Russian conterpart would more likely come to grips with sexual discrimination. The Ukrainian woman, on the other hand, generally encountered national discrimination first.

For Ukrainians, even the most conventional forms of public activity—literature, collection of ethnographic material, and theatre—were more hazardous politically than were similar activities for Russian women. For example, when Russian women went into the theatre, they took up a profession connected with an urban existence. Ukrainian theatre troupes, short of funds and hounded by the police from town to town and village to village, became vehicles for the expression of national sentiment. Mariia Zankovetska, the most popular Ukrainian actress, who turned down a lucrative position in St. Petersburg, was characterized by a younger contemporary as "the incarnation of Ukraine."[16] The celebration of the twenty-fifth anniversary of her career in Kiev on 15 January 1908 became a demonstration of Ukrainian national solidarity.[17]

There was a double standard in the treatment of Ukrainians and Russians. Publishing in Ukrainian presented the same insurmountable difficulties for Ukrainian men as for Ukrainian women; it was much easier for Russians, and in Russia. Ukrainians were given harsher punishments than Russians for similar political activities. Ukrainian women fared badly in the police annals. They were frequently portrayed as more violent revolutionaries than their husbands. Indeed, if one were to base oneself solely upon police activities, even taking into consideration the predictable overstatement inherent in any report written for superiors, it would seem that the families of all conscious Ukrainians were rabid revolutionaries. "Ukrainophilism" was tantamount to revolution, and an oblique hint at it was enough to destroy chances for advancement in Ukrainian, though not necessarily Russian, cities.

It was much more difficult for Ukrainian women, or for women whom the *Okhrana* suspected of being involved in the Ukrainian cultural renaissance, to organize than it was for Russian women. Women in Kiev, for instance, were not able to gain permission to hold women's university-level courses until 1879, ten years after similar courses had been organized in Moscow. The *Okhrana* had seen them as part of the cultural "Ukrainophile" movement.

Since women were barred from a university education, the higher women's courses, taught by a university faculty outside the state-run universities, were an avenue used by moderates to circumvent government opposition to women's education. At the same time, the liberals hoped that higher education would prevent women from engaging in clandestine political activity. In Kiev, the initiative for the women's courses came from middle-aged liberal women whose secure positions in society were determined by class and marriage. The wife of Professor S. S. Gogotsky, an esteemed faculty member at St. Vladimir University, was the moving force behind the effort. She was accused of Ukrainophile and revolutionary tendencies. The fact that the Lysenko Choir, singing Shevchenko's poetry set to music, performed at fund-raising concerts, and that Ukrainian activists in the *Hromada*, an old boys' club of Ukrainian liberals (who barred women from membership), also supported the courses, made the *Okhrana* wary of the whole undertaking. When the courses were finally opened in 1879, women flocked to them. Three years later the government suspended them in the wake of the tsar's assassination. The suspension, lasting some five years, led to the formation—without official sanction—of the first Ukrainian women's organization in the Russian Empire, the Study Circle led by Olena Dobrohaeva. When the courses were reestablished, the *Okhrana* went out of its way to make participation difficult.[18]

Ukrainian women activists either lived similar lives or were forced into them. Throughout Ukraine, complained a woman who married into a Ukrainian family, "all these provincial families, scattered throughout the various homesteads, were related either by blood or by marriage. They formed a closed world to which an outsider could not readily adjust."[19] Activist Ukrainian families banded together in the cities and were subjected to the same type of discrimination.[20] Women rendered mutual assistance, encouraged one another and sheltered those in need. They did the work necessary for the cause, including smuggling of publications and even some arms, but did not give up legal work. This manifested itself in such uncharacteristic gestures as the embroidering of a decorative cloth that would be used to greet Alexander II when he passed through Poltava.[21] For the most part, however, Ukrainian women were forced into a revolutionary role by the government's adamant identification of Ukrainianism with anti-government activity.

Sofiia Lindfors Rusova, an educator and author of popular textbooks who had a winning way with young people, was particularly distrusted by the *Okhrana*, which characterized her as "hopeless, incapable of reforming herself, and definitely a terrorist who encourages in youth the most extreme views."[22] Since, together with her husband, she published an uncensored version of Shevchenko's *Kobzar* in Prague in 1876, the *Okhrana* mistrusted everything she did. Rusova, however, was as far removed from terrorism as she could be: her interest was the education of youth. She particularly enjoyed trying out her primers on village children.

Lack of contact among Russian and Ukrainian women, as well as rumours about the revolutionary proclivities of Ukrainian women, fed the popular image of the valiant Ukrainian revolutionary woman: one who smuggled guns in her elaborately coiffed hairdo and hid illegal leaflets in diapers. The fears of the male *Okhrana* on the one hand, and the hopes of the Ukrainian male intelligentsia on the other, helped to fix that image.

It was also more difficult for women in Kiev to organize a Women's Club not associated with the conservative Philanthropic Society than it was for women in other cities to organize similar societies. In May 1895, Kievan women petitioned the government "to permit the ladies (*damy*) to meet on a regularly scheduled basis, to spend free time in comfort, pleasure and usefulness, taking care of women's material and spiritual needs." The government saw no objections, but the police refused to grant permission simply because Liudmyla A. Taranovska, whose name headed the petition signed by fourteen women, was associated with the so-called Ukrainophile group. The women did not get a formal answer for five years, at which time student unrest made legalization of the new Kiev organization unlikely. It was only in 1910, when the initiative to establish the club was renewed by the Countess Adelaide K. Plater, that permission was finally granted. By that time Ukrainian and progressive Russian women had developed other forms of activity, and the Kievan Women's Club provided little but fellowship for its members.[23]

What led the Russian women to feminist awareness or outright political activity led their Ukrainian counterparts to the realization of their subordinate status as Ukrainians. Few Ukrainian women in the Russian Empire produced feminist writings. On the contrary, among the most actively engaged women we find the predictable negation of feminist concerns, in good social-democratic tradition. Lesia Ukrainka, for instance, argued that the woman issue was a non-issue. At the same time she canned jam, cooked for her younger siblings, and embroidered blouses—tasks never expected of her brother. For women who thought as she did, the goal was universal liberation. Self-sacrifice, not self-assertion, was the order of the day.

But Ukrainian women were aware of feminist concerns. The major similarities between Russian and Ukrainian female activists at the turn of the century were that both desired some political rights and both were involved in helping the poor. Ukrainian women, even in organized women's groups, tended to be more democratic than Russian women. There were not enough Ukrainian women to form philanthropic societies for the support of Ukrainian causes. Russian philanthropic societies were composed of extremely conservative women to whom Ukrainian causes were anathema. Only individual Ukrainian women of some means could fund Ukrainian needs. One such person was Ielysaveta Skoropadska Myloradovych, the benefactress of the Shevchenko Scientific Society in Lviv. Because such societies were banned in Eastern Ukraine, she could not fund one in Poltava, where she lived. Nor were the Ukrainian women as involved as the Russians in eradicating prostitution. The primary work of the Ukrainian women was directed at relief efforts, literature and literacy.

Feminist organizations became popular in the Russian Empire between 1901 and 1908. During this time, membership in women's organizations peaked, and feminist concerns offered an opportunity for confrontation and co-operation among the nationalities making up the empire. Russian feminists—though not those who study them—became aware of the nationality question.

Russian and Ukrainian women co-operated in the Kiev branch of the Society for the Protection of Women. Unlike the Russian chapters, whose membership was made up of titled upper-class women, the Kiev branch was composed of women of the intelligentsia. The Kiev branch tried to develop positive ways of helping the poor. Women students who belonged to it worked side by side with older women. Women of different nationalities—Ukrainian, Russian, Jewish and Polish—co-operated with each other.[24]

For years the Kiev branch was run by Dr. V. G. Kliachkina, a Russian whose daughter became a Ukrainian patriot as a result of living and working among Ukrainians. Its leadership included women of different nationalities and classes, among them Rozaliia Isakovna Margolina, Sofiia Aleksandrovna Sats, Mariia Aleksandrovna Kostetska, Zinaida Vasylivna Mirna and Anna Kharitonovna Gołęba. It maintained a cheap dormitory, a subsidized cafeteria, an employment office, a literacy school for adults and a free legal clinic. It ran a sewing school whose profits were used to offset the expenses of its other ventures. It held various cultural activities for adults. It tried to attract Russian, Jewish and Ukrainian working women, but was successful only with the latter.

Most Jewish women, despite special efforts made to reach out to them, avoided organizations with an implicitly Ukrainian coloration and preferred, if any, women's societies with a Russian orientation.[25]

An important aspect of the Revolution of 1905 was the spontaneous growth of local organizations. In the Ukrainian areas the most significant of these were the Prosvita (Enlightenment) societies. These community organizations for the promotion of literacy and dissemination of knowledge were patterned upon those founded three generations earlier among Western Slavs, including the Galician Ukrainians. Ukrainian women were very active in Prosvita in Eastern Ukraine and in the dynamic co-operative movement that survived well into the 1920s.[26]

Another aspect of the Revolution of 1905 was the growth of specifically feminist societies that sought to exert political influence. The attempt to create a Women's Progressive Party failed, but the All-Russian Union for the Equality of Women, established in Moscow in 1905, struck a responsive chord among women in the urban centres of the Empire.[27]

Most of the Union's members were women of liberal convictions. Branches sprang up in Kiev, Odessa, Poltava and Kharkiv. The membership increased steadily between 1905 and 1908, when the women were agitating for the vote.[28]

Non-Russian women joined the Union, using it to raise the nationality issue. Russian feminists, unused to open public debate, were more responsive to issues raised by non-Russian women than were their male counterparts, who were inured to political discussions.

At the first Congress of Women, held from 6 to 9 May 1905 in Moscow, the element of surprise came from the Ukrainian, Jewish, Polish and Belorussian women. They insisted, in return for joining the Union, on its acknowledgement of the principle of national and organizational autonomy and the right of all nationalities in the Russian Empire to cultural self-determination. According to the minutes, which were later published and whose rough draft reflected the intensity of the debate:

> these statements brought forth a very heated exchange of views. The supporters of a general program argued...that [the inclusion of the nationality issue] would weaken the unity of the masses and necessitate the inclusion of a debate on the agrarian and the workers' issue [which the women tried to avoid.]

But the debate proved, in the words of the minutes, beyond doubt that "for the oppressed nationalities the issue of national freedom was the most pressing one." After accepting the principle that the Union and its program were political and not philanthropic organizations, the congress, with only four abstentions, "acknowledged the right of the different nationalities which are part of Russia to political autonomy and national self-determination."[29]

The influx of new members meant that at each major gathering the nationality issue had to be discussed anew. At the Third Congress of the Union, held from 8 to 12 October 1905, "there were political resolutions from Lithuanian, Polish and Ukrainian women demanding a federative structure for Russia," which resulted in the ratification of

> a statement to the effect that the liberation of women is inseparably tied to the achievement of autonomy for their native land (*rodnoi krai*) and its liberation from the yoke of Russification.[30]

Some Russian women, smarting under the snubs they received from their male liberal colleagues who would not commit themselves to woman suffrage, used their responsiveness to the nationality issue as proof of their political sophistication. "This question had barely emerged in Russian society, and our association was one of the first to solve it in a positive fashion," boasted Chekhova.[31]

Ukrainian women particitated in all aspects of the work and in all women's congresses, but had no illusions either about the strength of liberalism in the Russian Empire or about the impact the feminist organization could make. Among the Ukrainian women, Olena Pchilka, Liubov Ianovska and Anna Dmitriieva were the most active. It was Pchilka, one of the editors of the first Ukrainian women's almanac in 1887, who mustered public support for Ukrainian women at the congress.[32]

It was also Pchilka who forced the Poltava branch of the Union to come out openly with a pro-Ukrainian statement. That brought about a split in the branch, for the Russian women would not agree to the following addition to the program:

> Ukrainian women, in addition to the bitter and painful aspects of the women's issue in general, are also in large measure influenced by the difficult circumstances which stem from the oppression of the Ukrainian nation. The woman of Ukraine, who belongs to a nation of many millions that is deprived of political rights and has been forced to subject itself to a centralized government for generations, could not help but experience all the consequences of the nation's spiritual subjection. Since the Treaty of Pereiaslav, when Ukraine lost its political independence [1654], language, the sole means of expressing [one's] thoughts, could be developed only by individuals. Their works could not be published in their native land. Elementary schools, which used to be of high quality in Ukraine, were slowly reduced to such a level that they lost all their national and community characteristics (*natsionalno-hromadski prykmety*). The denationalization of Ukrainian women who have gone through the Russian school was the inevitable consequence of the political system, which had as its aim the separation of the cultured part of society from the whole of the nation. Such a situation greatly harmed the national communal cause—the upbringing of the younger generations. The Ukrainian women consider it their prime duty to take a stand on this matter (*obstaty za tse dilo*).
>
> Ukrainian women add their own demands to the platform—that an autonomous federative structure be introduced into government, based upon the ethnic territorial principle, and that decentralization in the administrative structure of the

government also be implemented; that elections be held on the basis of universal suffrage, with no distinction of sex or nationality; that the vote be direct, equal and secret. Moreover, all persons residing in Ukraine, without regard to sex or nationality, must enjoy the same equal rights that guarantee all the usual freedoms.[33]

Pchilka and Ianovska prepared papers for one of the congresses held in 1908. Pchilka's was on "the tasks of Ukrainian women."[34] Neither historians nor memoirists noted this work of the Ukrainian feminists. This early demand for Ukrainian political autonomy has been overlooked for so long that it is impossible to identify all the women who were involved.[35]

Pchilka wanted to create a central Ukrainian women's organization in the Russian Empire. She was opposed by Ukrainian activists, male and female, who maintained that this would be an unnecessary dissipation of Ukrainian strength. In the journal she published, Pchilka continued to report on women's affairs, specifically on difficulties experienced by women lawyers, the struggle against prostitution, progress of women's higher education, and the like. But she was more perturbed by the growth of reaction than by feminist concerns. None of the Russian liberals came to the aid of the Kiev Prosvita when the government harassed the society in which so many women participated.[36]

As the women gained in educational and occupational opportunities, and as the likelihood of effective liberalization of Russia under tsarism decreased, the feminist movement lost most of its supporters. The years immediately preceding the outbreak of the First World War were marked in Ukraine by the growth of national consciousness among Ukrainians and by an increased opposition to it among Russians. Women in Kiev and Kharkiv tried to continue co-operation among the nationalities. They were able to stave off a formal break until 1917.

During the First World War, women working in the Tatiana Committees, in the *zemgor* and in the hospitals did so in order to help the needy, not out of feminist considerations. Many Galician Ukrainians were among the refugees, political prisoners and prisoners of war. It was under the aegis of the "Society to Aid the Population of South Russia that Suffered from the War," composed of both men and women, that Liudmyla Starytska- Cherniakhivska was able to visit the Galician Ukrainians exiled and imprisoned in Eastern Ukraine and somewhat alleviate the conditions under which they were being kept.[37]

The war strengthened the patriotism of the Russian feminists. Co-operation between moderate women of both nationalities was as doomed as that between men. The formal break with the Russian women in Kiev came after a massive Ukrainian demonstration held on 19 March/1 April 1917. Russian women of Kiev, especially Russified Jewish women, objected so strenuously to Ukrainian participation in the women's organization that centralized all Kievan women's organizations during the war that the Ukrainian women had to resign.[38] This marked the day of national revolution for the Ukrainian feminists—if they had thought of themselves in those terms.

No Ukrainian woman played a determining role in the establishment of Soviet power in Ukraine. No woman identifying herself primarily with the Ukrainian cause was prominent in the leadership of the Bolshevik party, even in its initial Ukrainian variants. Evgeniia Bosh, a Jewish woman from Odessa who was among the leaders of the Ukrainian Soviet Republic and is duly recognized as such, was primarily interested in a unified party, in the international proletariat, and in preserving the unity of the former lands of the Russian Empire. That was also the case with the women who helped establish Soviet influence in Ukraine through the *zhinviddily* (women's chapters organized by the Communist Party).

Information on the Ukrainian *zhinviddily* is sketchy, incomplete and contradictory. Western scholars consider that they were run by Aleksandra Kollontai, and after 1926 by Olga Pilatskaia. Both women represented the centralizing tendencies of the Bolshevik party; neither had any contacts with the specifically Ukrainian wing or with Ukrainian communists, who in turn did not consider the women's issue to be their primary interest. In reality, Kollontai had little direct control over the Ukrainian *zhinviddily* between 1924 and 1926. At this time, when the party was oriented toward Ukrainization and the influence of the so-called "national communists" had reached its height, women's work was co-ordinated by the head of the *zhinviddily* at the Central Committee of the Communist Party (Bolshevik) of Ukraine by Marusia O. Levkovych, a school teacher from Kharkiv who joined the party in 1919 and who seems to have vanished in the maelstrom of the 1930s.

Soviet female activists in Ukraine complained that there was a tremendous amount of opposition to the work of the *zhinviddily*, especially in the villages. The major problem was that the *zhinviddily* reflected the aspirations of the Muscovite centre, not that of the specific locality. Russian-speaking women were used to disseminate propaganda in Ukrainian villages, and the Ukrainians banded together against the Russians. Another problem was that the women spouted Bolshevik rhetoric, helped in grain requisitions and proposed the expropriation of even small private farms to which the Ukrainians were attached. Ukrainian Marxist women, in turn, specifically denied any possibility of international co-operation among women on any grounds other than Marxist. In their overviews of "women's movements in the capitalist states" they did not mention Ukrainian women outside the Soviet Union, nor even their interest in Soviet Ukraine.

By 1926, when Olga Pilatskaia (1884–1937) took over the Ukrainian *zhinviddily*, Ukraine claimed to have organized one and one-half million women in party organizations. About seventy thousand activists had gone through various stages of party training. Pilatskaia, a dedicated communist of Russian nationality, trudged on foot from village to village trying to overcome the hostility with which she was met. But she stressed that she was working for the economic progress of the USSR and of Russia, and the fact that she worked for Ukraine had no direct relevance to her.[39] That contributed to her lack of popularity.

Communists created obstacles for Ukrainian women activists whose previous work in women's organizations and in Prosvita now led officialdom to consider them bourgeois nationalists. Women activists, such as Liudmyla Starytska-Cherniakhivska, became defendants in trials and were given harsh sentences. Olena Pchilka, who spoke out against the anti-Ukrainian policies of the new government, was saved from repression only by her association with Lesia Ukrainka, by then deceased, yet sanctified by her death.

The only genuine co-operation among Ukrainian and Russian women on an organized, not individual, scale had been within the liberal feminist movement between 1905 and 1910. Russian women, disenfranchised and painfully experiencing their own inequality, agreed to other women's demands for national equality. Free of political and ideological ballast, the Russian feminists had recognized the logic of the minorities' demands. Russian and Ukrainian liberal men, however, were impervious to the justice of women's demands. In time, the women succumbed to socialization by the men. The Russians, with their stress upon the unity of the empire and the primacy of the struggle against autocracy, disregarded their own feminists, who in turn dropped the stress on autonomy in an attempt to imitate the men. Ukrainian men simply ignored Ukrainian women, treating feminism as untimely in much the same manner as Russian liberals treated the striving for national autonomy. Ukrainian women, socialized into service for a cause, did not consider it proper to stress any of their independent achievements.

The focus upon women's organizations points out the importance of local history in recreating the fuller story of the past. In that story the role of Russian and Ukrainian women has often been overlooked, which is understandable. What is less understandable is the way in which many Ukrainians have both failed to note Ukrainian women's activities or to discern the differences between Russian and Ukrainian women. Additional study of Russian and Ukrainian women in their social contexts may illustrate more points of contact between women of the dominant nationality and other women. Although the Ukrainian women did not see eye to eye with the Russians, there were some opportunities for joint work. The study of women's organizations and women's participation in community activities thus opens yet another perspective on Russians and Ukrainians that draws us away from ideologically defined groups.

Notes

1. Considerations of space prevent a discussion of aspects of the woman question or
   of feminism. For the purposes of this article I have dealt with women activists in
   general, without differentiation of the various types of involvement in national,
   community or revolutionary activities. Although education was an important
   factor in women's issues, and although Ukrainian women were involved in all its
   aspects (there even seems to have been stronger pressure in the Ukrainian
   provinces for the education of peasant women than in the Russian ones),
   considerations of space prevent me from even touching upon the subject.

   I have placed greater stress on Ukrainian than on Russian women, since
   materials on the latter are much more readily available than on the former. (A
   convenient introduction to Russian women is Richard Stites, *The Women's
   Liberation Movement in Russia* [Princeton, 1978], although the information in it
   on the Union for the Equality of Women is incomplete and therefore slanted.)

   I would like to thank some of the persons and institutions facilitating my
   research: the American Association of University Women, which enabled me to
   take a year for the completion of the research; IREX, which made research in the
   archives and university libraries of Kiev, Lviv and Moscow possible; a Fulbright
   Faculty scholarship, which made possible invaluable research in Poland; the
   Harvard Ukrainian Research Institute, which provided a forum for testing ideas on
   the subject; and the Ukrainian National Women's League of America and the
   World Federation of Ukrainian Women for initiating and supporting the project.
   My special thanks go to Yaryna Turko Bodrock of Widener Library, Liubov
   Abramiuk Volynec and Svitliana Lutska Andrushkiv of the New York Public
   Library, and to Basil Nadraga of the Library of Congress for help in locating
   elusive publications.

2. For instance, Pavlo Hrabovsky, a progressive Ukrainian activist and writer, wrote
   in the Galician Ukrainian newspaper *Narod* in 1884, the year in which the
   Galician Ukrainian women convened their first public rally: "The Ukrainian
   woman walked alongside the Muscovite woman, for history had tied them
   together so that we do not see any difference between one and the other." Writing
   as Pavlo Hrab, "Deshcho v spravi zhinochykh typiv," *Narod* (Lviv), 1 and 15
   April 1884, quotation from p. 108.

   Zinaida Mirna, an undisputed Ukrainian patriot and women's activist, as well
   as a member of the Central Rada, the government that unsuccessfully fought the
   Bolsheviks, expressed similar views as late as 1937. She wrote from Prague,
   where she had emigrated: "The women's movement in Ukraine cannot be separated from the whole Russian women's movement, since for more than two hundred
   years Ukraine, conquered under Muscovite rule, had to live a common life with
   Russia, and all events of a political, economic and cultural character [in the
   Russian Empire] were reflected in the life of Ukraine." "Zhinochyi rukh na
   Velykii Ukraini do Revoliutsii," *Zhinka* (Lviv), no. 4, 1937.

3. Oleksandra Ia. Efimenko, the first woman in the Empire to receive a doctorate in
   history (in Kharkiv in 1910), was drawn by personal and professional
   considerations not only to Ukrainian and social history, but also to the Ukrainian

cause. Mykola Kostomarov, after his political and scholarly activity on behalf of Ukrainians, gravitated toward the study of the social history of Russian women. Danylo Mordovtsev, whose best-selling books popularized the Cossack period, also wrote a book on women.

There are very few works dealing with Ukrainian women. Nataliia Polonska-Vasylenko, in a long-awaited slim volume on outstanding Ukrainian women, complained that many of them had been "completely forgotten by their descendants." *Vydatni zhinky Ukrainy* (Winnipeg, 1969), 101. The book was part of an unfinished project initiated by Milena Rudnytska to prepare a collective work on the history of Ukrainian women. The project never got off the ground, owing partly to lack of funds and partly to lack of access to primary sources. Correspondence to that effect in the papers of Milena Rudnytska in the Archives of the Ukrainian Academy of Arts and Sciences in the U.S. (*UVAN*). Also see Natalka Levenets Kohuska, *Chvert stolittia na hromadskii nyvi, 1926–1951: Istoriia Soiuzu Ukrainok Kanady* (Winnipeg, 1952), supported by interview with Anna Kobrynska in New York on 21 March 1981. Oleksander Luhovy (Oleksander Vasyl Ovrutsky-Shvabe), *Vyznachne zhinotstvo Ukrainy* (Toronto, 1942), is a mixture of fact, fiction and conjecture.

4. One of the first articles on the history of Ukrainian women was published, appropriately, in the first women's periodical, *Meta* (Goal), in Lviv on 1 June 1908. Its author, Ivan Krypiakevych, later became a leading scholar of Ukrainian history. In the article he pointed to an early matriarchal system on the territory of Ukraine, but argued that the role of woman in primitive Slavdom was one of complete subjection to the male. Ivan Krypiakevych, "Zhinka v istorii Ukrainy," *Meta*, no. 7, 1 June 1908, 4–5.

5. Polonska-Vasylenko, 78–9.

6. For instance, Marusia Churai, the half-legendary author of a series of popular songs in the seventeenth century, continues to inspire contemporary Ukrainians. Lina Kostenko's *Marusia Churai: Istorychnyi roman u virshakh* (Kiev, 1979) was a best-seller. Churai's songs continue to be sung.

7. Ihor Losky, "Ukrainska zhinka v kozatsku dobu," *Zhinka*, no. 15–16 (August 1935), stressed the active role of all Ukrainian women. The role of upper-class women in the establishment of the Kiev Mohyla Academy emerges in Z. I. Khyzhniak, *Kyievo-Mohylianska Akademiia* (Kiev, 1970). Poles also stressed that the precariousness of life in the steppes drew Ukrainian women into the fray and enabled them to choose and divorce husbands at will. The less sensational parts of Dr. Antoni [Rolle], *Niewiasty kresowe* (Warsaw, 1883), were reprinted that year in vol. VI of *Kievskaia starina*, 268–309.

8. G. S. Vinsky, a hot-headed soldier from Ukraine's lower elite, served in the Russian army under Catherine II. He was exiled to Siberia as a result of a financial scandal at the time of the destruction of the *Sich*, the Cossack stronghold. In his memoirs, *Moe vremia: Zapiski* (new edition in Oriental Research Partners Memoir Series, vol. 11), which probably idealizes his childhood, he stressed the differences between Russian and Ukrainian women. He also wrote that "at this time, the Little-Russians lived only among themselves; except for Greeks and Poles, foreigners were unknown to them; even with the Great

Russians they hardly had any contact," 23.

9. This is from numbered page "1a" of a mimeographed and edited typescript, with errors corrected, in the Hanna Chykalenko Keller papers in the Archives of UVAN, uncatalogued. An unpublished autobiography of Keller is also in the file, as well as some correspondence with her father.

10. Pavlo Zaitsev, *Zhyttia Tarasa Shevchenka* (Paris, 1955), 98–9; also quoted in Polonska-Vasylenko, 105.

11. See especially Dmytro Doroshenko, *Moi spomyny pro nedavnie-mynule (1914–1920)* (Munich, 1969), 484, as well as the memoirs of Mariia Livytska, *Na hrani dvokh epokh* (New York, 1972). Even in the correspondence of the totally russified N. A. Belozerskaia, the attraction of Poltava is evident. A younger relative wrote to her in Ukrainian at the beginning of the century, Tsentralnyi Gosudarstvennyi Arkhiv Literatury i Iskusstva, f. 58, op. 1, ed. khr. 21, p. 2; also see letter from I. A. Gen, ibid., ed. khr. 26, p. 4. The Russian émigré memoir literature is too large to quote here.

   A few examples must suffice to illustrate the complex family relation- ships resulting from political and national disagreements. Oleksandra Oleksiivna Vynohradova broke her engagement to Symon Petliura for ideological reasons. An ardent populist, she could not abide his Marxist orientation. Eventually she married a Prosvita activist, Kopeliovych, who was of Jewish origin. Her sisters, Olena, a sculptor, and Varvara, a pianist, refused to speak Ukrainian, and all the brothers opted for the Russian side. This information from Oleksander Zhorliakevych, a Galician Ukrainian serving in the Sichovi Striltsi in Kiev in 1918/19, whom Lidiia Vinogradova, a doctor, sent away from Kiev to her family in Kharkiv when he developed pneumonia, letter of 10 June 1978, pp. 3–4. Arnold Margolin's elder daughter, who grew up before the lawyer became consciously pro-Ukrainian, is a Zionist uninterested in the Ukrainian national movement with which her younger sister, Liubov M. Hansen, identified herself.

12. Luhovy, *Vyznachne zhinotstvo Ukrainy*, 127.

13. Recent Soviet scholars, among them O. R. Mazurkevych and T. M. Riznychenko, have attributed the proclamation to Alchevska. Fuller discussion in M. I. Mukhin, *Pedahohichni pohliady i osvitnia diialnist Kh. D. Alchevskoi* (Kiev, 1979). Al- chevska wanted to name her literacy school for adults in honour of Shevchenko, and was the first to put up a monument to the poet. She also pioneered in the didactic patriotic celebrations commemorating various occasions, as well as in the public wearing of peasant costume by educated women. But tsarist government regulations forced her to stop teaching in Ukrainian and use Russian, which was less effective among the Ukrainian-speaking peasants who constituted the bulk of the proletariat that settled in Kharkiv. Tsentralnyi Derzhavnyi Istorychnyi Arkhiv (Kiev), f. 2052, op. 1, spr. 96, 97ff. contains much of Alchevska's corres- pondence.

14. *Okhrana* file on the *Spilka* in Tsentralnyi Gosudarstvennyi Istoricheskii Arkhiv, Moscow, f. 102, D. P. VII No. 8468 (25 VIII, 1906–29 I, 1913) po nabliudeniiu za formalnym doznaniem o deiatelnosti Kievskoi revoliutsionnoi organizatsii *Spilka*, 121: "It was the major disseminator of revolutionary propaganda in the villages, and the centre of the activities of [the revolutionaries]." The police

considered it a seedbed of Ukrainian unrest, and were perturbed by the quantity of materials in the "Galician dialect" that the *Spilka* used. Soviet works, on the other hand, stress that the goal of the *Spilka* was to prevent the formation of a separatist Ukrainian revolutionary organization and to encourage Ukraine's proletariat to join the all-Russian revolutionary organization rather than the Ukrainian ones, which, by implication, were having greater success in recruiting workers and peasants. See, e.g., *Kotsiubynskyi iak hromadskyi diiach* (Kiev, 1968), using as evidence other *Okhrana* information found in Tsentralnyi Derzhavnyi Istorychnyi Arkhiv, Kiev, f. 274, No. 1215, p. 54. Additional information on *Spilka* in TsDIA, Kiev, f. 274, op. 4, od. zb. 301. Ukrainian authors abroad see the *Spilka* as an attempt to limit the influence of the Ukrainian Marxist intelligentsia, e.g., Ivan Maistrenko, *Istoriia Komunistychnoi Partii Ukraiiny* (n.p., 1979), 13–15, basing himself upon Panas Fedenko, *Ukrainskyi hromadskyi rukh u XX st.* (Poděbrady, 1934).

15. The alienated heroines emerged in Volodymyr Vynnychenko's portrayals of life in the urban centres of Ukraine, just as they did in Mikhail Bulgakov's descriptions of life in Kiev.

16. Oleksander Lototsky, *Storinky mynuloho* (Warsaw, 1932), 2: 213.

17. Tsentralnyi Derzhavnyi Istorychnyi Arkhiv, Kiev, f. 102, op. 100, ed. khr. 28 g 3, 1908, p. 26; also *Russkie vedomosti*, 17 January 1908; and *Ridnyi krai*, 15 January 1908. The latter journal was edited by Olena Pchilka.

18. The two major sources on the Kiev Higher Courses for Women are a booklet of thirty-five pages published in Kiev by the University Press in 1884 entitled *Istoricheskaia zapiska i otchet o kievskikh vysshikh zhenskikh kursakh za pervoe chetyrekhletie 1878–1882* in Tsentralnyi Derzhavnyi Istorychnyi Arkhiv URSR (Kiev), f. 707, op. 151, sprv. 30; and a series of documents and correspondence about the courses dated from 12 September 1878 to 16 June 1879, ibid., f. 442, op. 828, od.zb. 146. The apprehension of the lower administration and the *Okhrana* concerning the whole "Ukrainophile" movement emerges clearly in these documents.

19. Mariia Tkachenko Livytska, born into a middle-class but upwardly mobile Russified Ukrainian family, married the man who would become the president-in-exile of the Ukrainian National Republic. Quotation from *Na hrani dvokh epokh*, 92.

20. The Starytskys, the Kosaches, and the Lysenkos lived in neighbouring houses. Like the Rusovs and the Kovalevskys, they had extreme difficulty in travelling in the Russian Empire and abroad. See, for example, Tsentralnyi Gosudarstvennyi Istoricheskii Arkhiv, D.D. Politsii 102, O.O. No. 438, 1899, p. 2. The police stressed that Rusov had contacts with the Old Hromada, as well as with liberals who moved from Ukraine, among them the Petrunkevich brothers and Countess Panina.

21. Rusov, "Kak ia stal chlenom Gromady," *Ukrainskaia zhizn*, no. 10 (1913): 40–49.

22. Tsentralnyi Gosudarstvennyi Istoricheskii Arkhiv, f. 102, O.O. Delo Dept. Politsii, no. 438, 1899, p. 4. After the Revolution, the Bolsheviks offered Rusova a chair in pedagogy at Kamianets-Podilsky. She escaped to Galicia after two

years. Her most radical activity was the denunciation of the Soviet Union's destruction of its own population before the International Women's League for Peace and Freedom in 1934.

23. Tsentralnyi Derzhavnyi Istorychnyi Arkhiv, Kiev, f. 442, op. 625, spr. 273, pp. 1–9. The revolutionary activity of the Plater family in the 1863 Polish uprising was apparently forgotten.

24. The Russian Society for the Protection of Women, founded in 1900, was affiliated with the central office in London.

25. Information on the Kievan branch in Tsentralnyi Derzhavnyi Istorychnyi Arkhiv, Kiev, fond 442, op. 643; *Otchet za 1912 god*, ibid., spr. 48, pp. 36 and 15, on attempts to reach out to Jewish working women. Polish women had their own organizations throughout Ukraine, in addition to working in central ones. Jews in Ukraine also developed a network of self-help organizations; for full listings see M. V. Dovnar-Zapolsky and A. I. Iaroshevich, eds., *Ves Iugo-Zapadnyi Krai: Spravochnaia i adresnaia kniga* (Kiev, 1913).

26. The analysts in the Special Section of the *Okhrana* reported that even legally sanctioned Ukrainian organizations were engaged in revolutionary activity, connected with both the Social Revolutionary and the Social Democratic parties. To top it all off, they had ties with the Galician Ukrainians, who, in the terminology used by the police, followed in Mazepa's footsteps in trying to break the tie with Russia; Tsentralnyi Gosudarstvennyi Istoricheskii Arkhiv, f. 102, op. 13, ed. khr. 163 m 15 ch 5/1911, pp. 1–4. Ukrainian organizations were among the first to fall victim to the reaction that followed the liberalization of 1905.

27. The Women's Progressive Party, after the requisite preamble on the rights of women and men, proclaimed that "all Russian citizens, regardless of differences in sex, religion and nationality, are equal before the law." While not actually coming to grips with the terminology it was using, the stillborn party also proclaimed "the unification (*obedinenie*) of all the nationalities (*narodnosti*) inhabiting Russia in the name of all human ideals. All-Russian (*russkie*) nationalities shall enjoy full freedom in the use of their language in print, in the courts, in education and in public agencies. The language of the state will be Russian." Tsentralnyi Gosudarstvennyi Istoricheskii Arkhiv, f. 516, ed. khr. 17, p. 31. The Publications Commission planned a booklet on "The Woman Question and Autonomy of Nationalities," ibid., ed. khr. 6, p. 4, but this was dropped from the list in the published version of the programme, ibid., ed. khr. 14, p. 56. In St. Petersburg, the Women's Club, reflecting some interest in the nationality issue, invited A. A. Stakhovich to speak on the controversial Kholm area. They also sponsored a round-table discussion on "The Meaning of the Ukrainian Question," and asked V. M. Speransky, a philosopher, to speak on Maria Bashkirtseff, the Ukrainian painter who lived her brief life in France and left a frank diary; TsGIA, f. 516, ed. khr. 15, pp. 32, 44 and 60.

28. In Kharkiv, one of the first points raised was that the Union should join the International Council of Women, the oldest international women's organization; TsGIA, f. 516, ed. khr. 12, p. 11 and 16–17. The moving force behind the Union in Moscow was Mariia A. Chekhova, wife of the educator. She worried not only

about the long-range plans of the Union but also how the women who were not used to speaking would manage to run the meetings and congresses; TsGIA, f. 516, ed. khr. 14, esp. pp. 147–57.

29. TsGIA, f. 516, ed. khr. 28, p. 28. The programme demanded equality for women as a matter of course, and specifically stressed the need for Russia to convene a constituent, not only a representative, assembly, ibid., ed. khr. 1, p. 4.

30. TsGIA, f. 516, ed. khr. 5, p. 37 for the latter quotation, p. 68 for the former. Chekhova received letters from many non-Russian women that reiterated the demands for autonomy, TsGIA, f. 516, ed. khr. 18, 24–8 and ed. khr. 7.

31. *Ibid.*, ed. khr. 5, p. 71. Some Russian feminists were hurt by the failure of the liberals to come out openly for woman suffrage. Shakhmatova complained that the Constitutional Liberal Party would give the vote "to all the Samoeds, Chukchi, Tungus and Iakuts, but deny it to women," ibid., ed. khr. 1, p. 50.

32. Olha Kosach Kryvyniuk, ed., *Lesia Ukrainka: Khronolohiia zhyttia i tvorchosty* (New York, 1970), especially 767; Pchilka, "Ukrainky i ikh pratsia na Zhinochomu Zizdi v Sanktpeterburgu," *Ridnyi krai*, no. 8 (1909): 8–10; also "Zhinochyi zizd," *Ridnyi krai*, no. 39 (9 December 1908): 2 and no. 9 (1909): 12–13, news items. The flexible statute of the Union of Equality enabled the establishment of ethnic branches. In Kamianets-Podilskyi, Polish women under the leadership of the wife of the governor (Dunin-Borkowski) organized a society affiliated with the Union but Polish in membership. *Soiuz zhenshchin*, no. 3 (October 1907): 14; also TsGIA, f. 516, ed. khr. 7. Individual branches of the Union stressed the need for autonomy, see report of delegate Zelenskaia (no first name given) from Kiev at the Congress of 21 May 1906, TsGIA, f. 516, ed. khr. 5, pp. 94–96.

33. Quoted in a news item on the women in *Nova hromada: Literaturno-naukovyi misiachnyk*, no. 1 (1906): 131–2; also see TsGIA, f. 516, ed. khr. 5, p. 66.

34. Report of the October 1908 Congress in *Soiuz zhenshchin*, no. 12 (December 1908): 12, mentions the work of Pchilka. I have been unable to locate it. It may be in the Pchlika Archive at the Institute of Literature, Academy of Sciences in Kiev. I have been unable to work in that archive.

35. One reason was the association of the feminists with the liberals. The Ukrainian progressives were more at home in the radical camp, at least as far as rhetoric was concerned. The few Ukrainians writing brief informative sketches on the history of the women's movements in Ukraine had limited access even to published sources. Hence, Pchilka is sometimes credited with the actual establishment of a central Ukrainian women's organization that "issued a manifesto demanding autonomy for Ukraine." Iryna Pavlykovska, *Na hromadskyi shliakh: Z nahody 70–littia ukrainskoho zhinochoho rukhu* (Philadelphia, 1956), 72.

36. A particularly strong article in *Ridnyi krai*, no. 25 (1909): 9–12.

37. Some Galician Ukrainians, among them the educator Konstantyna Malytska, were exiled by the Russian military command in a futile attempt to eradicate Ukrainianism. Others, of whom Metropolitan Andrei Sheptytsky was the most prominent, were taken hostage. Among the prisoners of war was the young Olena Stepaniv, the first woman to volunteer to serve in the Austrian Imperial Army

after the outbreak of war. A number of Russophile Galician families answered the lure of the White Tsar, some of them encouraged by the more tangible lure of the ruble. A few were romantic maidens who thought they were being rescued from provincial Galicia, only to be abandoned by their rescuers.

38. Zinaida Mirna, "Zhinky v Ukrainskii Tsentralnii Radi," *Almanakh Zhinochoi doli* (Kolomyia, 1929), 14.

39. N. V. Akhmatova and E. N. Tsellurius, *Tovarishch Olga* (Moscow, 1969), 122–3; Stites, *The Women's Liberation Movement in Russia,* passim and *Zhinocha volia: Chytanka* (Kharkiv, n.d. [probably 1925]), and *Ukrainska Radianska Entsyklopedia* II, 1925. Stites views the Ukrainian *zhinviddily* as a provincial phenomenon and completely overlooks national communism.

POLITICS

John A. Armstrong

Myth and History in the Evolution of Ukrainian Consciousness

Approaches centering on myth and symbol set the pattern for social-science investigation during the 1980s much as group theory prevailed during the 1950s, structural functionalism in the 1960s, and "policy studies" in the 1970s. A small but revealing sign is the devotion of a whole series of panels, at the 1982 Rio de Janeiro convention of the International Political Science Association, to "Symbols and Myths." Like all trends in intellectual affairs, the new emphasis is part of a long-range cycle, for which the revival of the work of the German phenomenologist Ernst Cassirer is sufficient indication. But it is equally true that contemporary concerns for myth and symbol contain impressive new conceptual elements derived, especially, from anthropology. I believe that the new approach, combining elements from the philosophical idealism which constituted the starting point for nationalist historical thinking with the critical stance of the phenomenologist and the anthropologist, is especially suitable for explorations of national evolution such as the early stages of Ukrainian development.

In my view, therefore, the approach stressing myth and symbol will in a sense supersede critical approaches to Ukrainian national identity which prevailed in the decades following World War II. Let me hasten to add that this sweeping judgement is directed as much at my own writings as others'.[1] Moreover, the term "supersede" is intended only in the sense of conceptual analysis, not in terms of substantive results. Myth, symbol and related concepts constitute an illuminating way of looking at data and even at generalizations, not a requirement for entirely new materials. Moreover, the older critical approaches have provided indispensible preparation for the new departure. One may hope that they will ultimately combine with the new approach to form a new synthesis.

What were these older critical approaches? The earliest, like the myth-symbol model, emphasized the role of ideas. As developed by Friedrich Meinecke, Hans Kohn and Carlton Hayes, nationalism as a branch of the history of ideas treated the phenomenon as the spread, from one elite to others, of a doctrine originating in Western Europe during the Enlightenment, the French Revolution and Romanticism.[2] This doctrine represented something new under the sun—the notion that each group with sharply distinguishable cultural characteristics ought to constitute an independent—or at least autonomous—

polity. Focus on the idea of nationalism encouraged concern for the effects of historical traditions, acceptance of an established state, religious conflict, and popular practice; in practice, though, the dominant group characteristic was perceived to be linguistic. Generally, all these elements, but especially language, were regarded as "primordial," not necessarily in the sense of having existed from time immemorial, but as elements taken as given for the historical period which the students of nationalism regarded as decisive.[3] Their investigation, accordingly, was primarily if not solely concerned with how and why such elements became incorporated in national ideology. To put the matter another way, assuming that diffusion of the idea of nationalism was the issue, the approach implicitly rejected concern for the *longue durée*, that is, for the possibility that identity has been a highly persistent phenomenon, but one that has been characterized by shifting, heterogeneous attributes.

For obvious reasons, the history of ideas approach had a special appeal for scholars dealing with what were called "ahistorical nations," including the Ukrainians. In the short-range historical perspective the appearance of nationalism among such "unconscious" groups could be atttributed to diffusion. The rapid heightening of nationalist intensity could be traced to successive ideological influences, such as that of the Action Française. Unquestionably such interpretations have considerable validity, apart from their utility in providing a preliminary framework which makes the longer-range perspective afforded by myth and symbol comprehensible. Without awareness of the derivative nature of much Ukrainian thinking during the inter-war period, efforts to apply myth analysis to earlier phases of Ukrainian identity can be very misleading. For example, it would be quite wrong to regard Ukraine as an "ahistorical nation." Like all other examples of ethnic consciousness, Ukrainian consciousness arose through the efforts of elites composed of nobles, clergy, bourgeois, i. e., of "clerks" in the old, broad sense of the term. What is needed, therefore, is a long prespective in which the activities of these bearers of high culture can be placed.

Hayes, Kohn and Meinecke concentrated almost entirely on ideas. The bearers of these ideas were traced almost exclusively in biographical terms. After World War II, scholars who applied the idea of nationalism approach to the Ukrainian experience were, on the other hand, highly sensitive to the complexities of social structure. These scholars endeavoured to apply sociological methods to the study of the transmission of nationalist notions, especially in Soviet Ukraine. Iwan Koropeckyj's analysis of "Demographic Change among Russians and Ukrainians" is an excellent example of the genre. Earlier works include, notably, Boris Lewytzkyj's *Die Sowjetukraine* and books by Yaroslav Bilinsky, Robert Sullivant and Jurij Borys.[4] Methods such as cohort analysis are especially pertinent for recent Ukrainian history, with its intense generational conflict and the salience of such categories as sons of Ukrainian Catholic priests and children of "de-kulakized" peasants. Like the history of ideas, the sociological approach has constituted an essential step in preparing for better understanding of identity. Sociological quantification will continue to supplement the study of Ukrainian evolution, even, when feasible, for chronologically remote periods. Elsewhere I have expressed, with due awareness of the practical limitations of quantification, the view that every social generalization ultimately is quantitative in nature and should be made so in fact to the degree our knowledge and resources permit.[5] At times Ukrainian scholars have expressed fear that concern for the "hard data" of career patterns, demographic distribution, cohort characteristics and the like leads to "materialism," or, still worse, to Marxist materialism. To me such concerns have always appeared groundless. In fact, many of the conceptual underpinnings of sociological approaches, notably Parsonian structural functionalism, derive from quasi-idealist philosophies such as Max Weber's. More significant is the circumstance that the methods and approaches derived from sociology do not themselves provide the conceptual tools for handling a long-range development such as national identity. The foremost Parsonian political scientist, Gabriel Almond, makes the point in another context when he urges his colleagues to "take the historical cure."[6] The question, then, is what models are most appropriate for providing that longitudinal dimension *for our subject*?

Among the sociological approaches (especially those emphasizing quantification), potentially the most relevant for investigation of the *longue durée* is Karl Deutsch's model in *Nationalism and Social Communication*.[7] Appearing in 1953, this innovative book elevated to a methodologically sophisticated level the concern for "channels for communication" that some of us had begun to perceive as critical to the diffusion of nationalism in a huge, partially unstructured region such as Eastern Ukraine. The significance of cities for identity diffusion, the options inherent in the availability of several linguistic codes, and, above all, the distinction between latent and overt identity are all spelled out by Deutsch. His concern for processes of modernization, on the other hand, produced a chronologically truncated model mainly applicable (like the idea of nationalism approach) to nineteenth- and twentieth-century phenomena. Although his earliest pioneering work had recognized the importance of the symbolic *content* of communications, *Nationalism and Social Communication* emphasized overt, physical networks. Restoring concern for the symbolic content would, I think, make the book's model highly useful for investigations of the *longue durée*. Like the religious symbols discussed by Clifford Geertz, symbols of ethnic identity constitute "stored meanings" which sum up what group members know of the world and their place in it.[8] To understand their impact, one must also examine the communications networks by which they are transmitted synchronically in space and the mythic structures by which the symbols are integrated and transmitted diachronically from generation to generation.

The Myth and the Ukrainians

My brief presentation cannot be an application, even in outline form, of the new approach combining myth, symbol and communication to Ukrainian identity. All I intend to do is suggest some ways in which an application might proceed and certain problems it would encounter. The peculiar brevity of *overt* Ukrainian national experience made shorter-range approaches attractive a generation ago. This brevity makes application of the myth approach correspondingly difficult. In my own explorations, a step-by-step comparative approach (perhaps "groping" would better express my proceeding) has been most satisfying. Initial attention to the extraordinary persistence of diaspora ethnic identity, embracing as many millennia, at the overt level, as an "ahistoric" nation extends to centuries, impressed me with the appropriateness of the myth-symbol interpretation. Properly modified, such an approach is just as applicable to Ukrainian identity. Moreover, because it raises issues that are not so obvious as they are for Armenians or Jews, the approach may be even more revealing for Ukrainians.

Anyone even moderately familiar with Ukrainian thinking may immediately object that concern for the distant past, for the *longue durée*, has not only been present throughout the past century, but has been the core of the nationalist argument. Far from rejecting such a critique, I must defend myself by recalling that nearly thirty years ago, when the conventional attribution of "father of Ukrainian nationalism" would have been to Mykola Kostomarov or Taras Shevchenko, I explicitly used this phrase to refer to Mykhailo Hrushevsky.[9] The *Istoriia Ukrainy-Rusy* occupies a central place on my shelves, for it is as striking a monument to nineteenth-century exhaustive documentation as one can find.[10] I am utterly incompetent to judge whether the version of Kiev and its successors that Hrushevsky presented is "truer" than other versions. The basic insight provided by the anthropological approach is that such questions are irrelevant for identity except insofar as they affect a constitutive myth. Claude Lévi-Strauss forcefully expresses this position: "Our method thus eliminates a problem which has, so far, been one of the main obstacles to the progress of mythological studies, namely, the quest for the *true* version, or the *earlier* one. On the contrary, we define the myth as consisting of all its versions, or, to put it otherwise, a myth remains the same as long as it is felt as such.[11] In another work Lévi-Strauss relates this theoretical position, which may at first reading appear cavalier, to a specific and highly charged political context: "Under what conditions is the myth of the French Revolution possible?" He replies that it is a matter of context, that if "we place ourselves outside it—as the man of science is bound to do—what appeared as an experienced truth first becomes confused and finally disappears altogether."[12]

If one accepts Lévi-Strauss's anthropological analysis, the *purely scientific* effect of a work like Hrushevsky's is myth-dissolving rather than myth-constituting. Indeed, one may doubt that Hrushevsky converted many people, even intellectuals, to Ukrainian nationalism. Let me be blunt: how many educated Ukrainians have really read his ten volumes and compared them carefully to, say, V. O. Kliuchevsky's five-volume history of Russia? How, then, can I consider Hrushevsky to have played an indispensable role in the evolution of the Ukrainian identity myth? The answer, which I could not have formulated in the 1950s, begins with the assumption that scientific history itself had become a part of the supranational intellectual myth of the nineteenth century. By the late nineteenth or earlier twentieth century, a national ideology had to provide, superficially, scientific historic validation for its myth, but in reality had to dissolve competing myths by scientific critiques. The great competitor for the Ukrainian myth was the potent version of "primordial" East Slavic evolution which Muscovy had been developing for centuries and which nineteenth-century historians such as Kliuchevsky apparently validated.[13] Hrushevsky's work, by effectively neutralizing the Russian historians' version, permitted the active development of the Ukrainian myth to proceed according to the formula which Eric Dardel [14] advances: "The myth past cannot be dated, it is a past 'before time,' or, better, outside time. Primordial actions are lost in the night of time... [the myth narrator] draws the audience of the story away, but only to make them set themselves at the desired distance"—which, for Ukrainian nationalists, was a distance sufficient to permit confident action. Of course, Hrushevsky, a man of many talents, took his turn at this action, but I consider his fundamental contribution to have been his superb intellectual legitimization of the national myth.

The special relationship of scientific scholarship and Ukrainian national identity is clarified by a brief look at the linguistic question, which has usually played such a critical role in the evolution of nationalism. In my observation, the most neglected work on the history of Ukraine is Antoine Martel's "La langue polonaise dans les pays ruthènes." [15] As far as my inexpert appraisal goes, the conclusions of this French scholar—who died a half-century ago—stand up well in the light of subsequent specialized studies. His basic point is that, as late as the seventeenth century, a vast area of the Dnieper Valley was inhabited by Eastern Slavs still indistinguishable in national identity. Inhabitants remote from one another did use considerably different *patois*, but the most sharply differentiated speeches were separated by innumerable transitional dialects shading off into one another rather than by sharp linguistic boundaries. Such was especially the case between the groups known today as "Ukrainians" and "Belorussians." Only gradually, under the centrifugal influences of cultural centers in Kiev and Lviv on the one hand, and Vilnius on the other, did distinctive languages emerge. Even today the Polissian linguistic boundary can be delineated only by resort to arbitrary isoglossic definitions. The situation in certain regions such as Smolensk adjoining present-day "Russian-language" regions was not then very different. Moreover, *all* these Dnieper Slavs retained a diffuse memory of their descent from Kievan Rus' as well as a sharper sense of their common Orthodoxy.

Antoine Martel believed that the linguistic allegiance and ethnic identity of the area still (in the seventeenth century) presented various options. The evolution of a common East Slavic literary language in Poland-Lithuania was one; acculturation to the prestigious Polish literary speech was another; a third was eventual ascendance of the evolving Muscovite literary language. The option ultimately taken up would depend in large measure on political pressures. In evaluating this analysis, I am impressed by the parallel with "Greater Romania" along the north-western coasts of the Mediterranean. In both cases the apparently natural evolution of a broadly based literary language in the central linguistic zone was thwarted by the intrusion of peripheral languages backed by political power—Polish and Muscovite Russian in the Dnieper region, Castilian, Tuscan and the *langue d'oïl* in the Mediterranean area.[16] What is clear is that subsequent linguistic studies which disregard the impact of political power and the myths of identity which such power upholds cannot fully explain the outcomes.

The brief references just presented suggest that what is at stake in the evolution of national identity is neither demographic nor linguistic continuity, as historiography or philology may determine them, but the acceptance of mythic versions more or less deliberately manipulated. If this is true, the pertinent question becomes not "Did the core population of Kievan Rus' remain in what is now Ukraine?" or "Whose speech more closely resembles a putative undivided East Slavic?" but "Whose myth can relate most satisfyingly to the myth of the great period of early East Slavic development?" It is trite to remark that the myth of the Polish-Lithuanian polity, which even as late as the seventeenth century appeared to possess many advantages, foundered on the question of religion. From our present perspective, the pressures of the Counter-Reformation on the Orthodox Eastern Slavs appear—not least to Roman Catholics—to have been an inexcusable blunder. It is hardly surprising that even Soviet Russians, therefore, have treated the rebellion of Bohdan Khmelnytsky and his "choice" in the Treaty of Pereiaslav of the Orthodox Tsar as the central drama of the "ingathering" of the Rus' legacy.[17] By the seventeenth century, however, as Jaroslaw Pelenski has demonstrated, the Muscovite Russian imperial myth had absorbed highly variegated elements. In particular, the temptation for the princes of Muscovy to claim and gradually to absorb the heritage of the steppe empires erected a formidable barrier to their subsequent adoption of the Kievan myth, which derived from a polity fundamentally different from the autocratic Eurasian empires. In the plain-speaking Stalinist historiography, the issue was clear: "The most important result of the unification [at Pereiaslav] with Russia was the circumstance that Ukraine was incorporated into a centralized state. Political centralism was the mighty instigator of economic and cultural progress."[18] The most striking aspect of centralization under Peter I (and his successors, who really began to incorporate the Zaporozhian Ukraine) was the subordination of the Orthodox Church to Caesaropapism. It is highly significant that Peter resorted to Lutheran theories exalting the ruler's power in order to legitimize the subordination. Like the other pressures for centralization which Marc Raeff so trenchantly analyzes, church subordination, therefore, was as much the result of Western European influences as of Russian tradition. Later (during the eighteenth and the first half of the nineteenth century) cameralistic and Enlightenment absolutism exerted similar pressures toward centralization. From this standpoint, heightened Russian autocracy was one aspect of a general European movement toward absolutist rule in multi-ethnic polities—what Austrian bureaucrats termed the "Good Enlightenment." But it is important to point out that the impact of such Western ideas, together with the process of bureaucratic centralization which they legitimized, reached Russia nearly a century later than they did Western and Central Europe.

Since the strongest external manifestation of the myth of Orthodox unity (which had attracted Khmelnytsky) has been the presence, for many centuries, of the Orthodox ecclesiastical head in Moscow, the negative effect of the tension between centralizing and archaicizing elements in the later Muscovite Russian myth is evident. More positively, strains arising from the inconsistent sources of this myth afforded an opportunity for the counter-myth, which was to form the basis for Ukrainian identity, to arise. Whatever the demographic or linguistic connections may have been, it is obvious that the Eastern Slavs of Kievan Rus' did not *call* themselves "Ukrainians." The heart of the Kievan commonwealth itself was near the steppe "border." As Russian no less than Ukrainian historiography recognizes, Kiev was, therefore, a frontier society, engaged in perennial conflict with successive nomadic agglomerations. Until the Mongol invasion such conflict was compatible with a high degree of decentralization, sometimes verging on communal democracy. Like many other "borderers," Kievans (as far as one can perceive their mentality) retained a significant element of individual or clan independence in their identity consciousness. The overwhelming Mongol victory disrupted this spirit of independence, although (I am indebted for this suggestion to Jaroslaw Pelenski) the Halych region may have retained a more open type of society. By mimesis of the steppe empires, autocratic centralism slowly developed in most effective defensive reaction to the extreme pressures of Mongol-Tatar rule, which otherwise might have become genocidal. Given the limitations of the period in resources and control mechanisms, centralization was necessarily accompanied by quasi-independent, indeed anarchic warrior outposts on the edge of the steppe—the numerous little "Okrains" or "Ukraines" that Günther Stökl has graphically described.[19] These Cossack warriors were neither ideologically self-sufficient (because viable legitimizing myths are nearly always produced by a "great tradition" elaborated in cities and religious centres) nor technologically autonomous (the cannon that defeated the steppe raiders had to be cast in a large, stable polity). From the sixteenth-century Oka frontier down to the eighteenth-century conquest of Azov, the tsars gradually dominated and domesticated the south-eastern Cossacks most dependent on Moscow for these urban artifacts. Possibly the south-western Cossacks were somewhat less dependent on Polish cities. In any case, as noted earlier, the Dnieper Cossacks' legitimizing ideology was ultimately incompatible with the Counter-Reformation myth of the Polish elite.

The physical impact of Khmelnytsky's rebellion inculcated among Orthodox clergy and peasantry of the middle Dnieper valley an enduring myth of a saviour from the frontier. This myth, more than distinctive language or the memory of Kievan Rus', constituted the foundation of an embryonic "Ukrainian" identity. However, the myth components of individual heroism, unconstrained movement, and local independence do appear to have been more compatible with the diffuse memory of Kiev than was the Russian centralizing autocratic myth. It is worth noting that similar mythic elements appeared elsewhere along a very long frontier between Islam and Christendom.[20] Many of these *Antemurale* mythic elements were incorporated into the constitutive myths of nearby Christian polities—the Castilian monarchy, the Habsburg Empire, Poland, Russia. But the frontier experience had its own momentum, occasionally facilitating the preservation or emergence of separate identity myths. As in Ukraine, some of these could be used by nineteenth-century nationalists as starting points for their ideologies.

Problems of Symbolic Identification for Ukrainians

The sketch just presented merely suggests directions a more competent, detailed analysis might take. Awareness of such directions is a necessary preliminary for suggesting ways in which the myth-symbol approach can identify problems that both Ukrainian nationalist intellectuals and outside students of their movement must encounter.

A familiar problem is the extreme difficulty any nationalist myth encounters when the customary foci of high culture, the cities, are almost entirely dominated by alien cultures. The only feasible alternative for myth elaboration, a non-urban high culture centering on royal court and gentry lifestyles (as in Poland and Hungary), was also unavailable to Ukrainians. Leading families from the Cossacks, like the Skoropadskys, rapidly identified with either the Russian service nobility or the Polish gentry, since status ascent was associated with assimilation to a high culture. As accelerated urban growth belatedly reached Ukraine, lower-status Ukrainians moving to the cities frequently assimilated in accordance with the pattern Karl Deutsch has analyzed. Further investigation of the sociological factors involved may explain why certain intellectuals persisted in their Ukrainian identity or reidentified themselves as

Ukrainians in the late nineteenth-century urban environment of "Little Russia." Likewise, while it is apparent that chance and opportunism affected the larger group which re-identified itself as Ukrainian after the February Revolution, closer investigation may be rewarding. Certainly one influence was the latent availability of the Cossack myth version.

It seems clear, though, that this myth, with its strong Orthodox overtones and explicit associations (negative as well as positive) with Russian hegemony was less significant for the one sociological group—sons of Ukrainian Catholic priests—which can be clearly identified as fervent, articulate adherents of the Ukrainian cause prior to World War I. The presence in Galicia of a distinctive religious subdivision provided (as for numerous other nineteenth-century national awakenings) the principal basis for reidentification. The marginal position of priests' sons in a semi-feudal society which provided no special niche for *Catholic* clerical *families* constituted an obvious social-psychological incentive for asserting separate ethnic identity. It is significant that this group hesitated for decades between re-identification with Russia (where Orthodox clerical families did have special status) and development of a Ukrainian identity. What role did the Cossack myth play in this process of choice? Was it irrelevant, or did it present an obstacle to re-identification as Russians? Did the myth ultimately provide an epiphany of national assertiveness? How did this process effect the continuing tension between the Eastern and Western Ukrainian versions of nationalism? What is needed is study of these questions, not so much as an exercise in the overt expression of ideas, but in terms of shifting symbolic attachment.

I have pointed out that the myth is the integrating phenomenon through which symbols of national identity acquire a coherent meaning. It is, nevertheless, possible to perceive the broad outlines of a national constitutive myth without being able to specify most of its symbols. This aspect of myth-symbol interrelation has recently been explored most penetratingly by the French historian Maurice Agulhon in *Marianne au combat: L'imagerie et la symbolique républicaines*.[21] As the earlier quotations from Lévi-Strauss indicate, the way in which the Left-Right division in the French body politic has been intensified and perpetuated by myths of the Revolution is a commonplace. But how these competing myths were communicated to potential adherents, especially through successive generations, is not so well understood. By concentrating on the feminine symbol of the Republic as reflected in the visual arts, especially in public statuary, Agulhon provides a striking demonstration of the importance of non-verbal communication.

Secular art and architecture of the type Agulhon discusses has been used by established polities for centuries to symbolize identity. Such symbolism, usually associated with urban centres or royal courts, was unavailable to Ukrainians. For certain similarly deprived ethnic groups (e. g., the Irish and the nineteenth-century Poles) ecclesiastical symbolism provided a potent alternative. Cults of patron saints (Patrick, Stanislaus), the rich symbolism of pilgrimage centres, dedicatory liturgies and mythic linkage to remote national rulers were virtually denied to Ukrainians as such. St. Vladimir, as his monument in Kiev still testifies, had been incorporated into Russian imperial symbolism. The Pecherska Lavra was and is a general East Slavic pilgrimage center, although both Nazi violence and Soviet actions indicate that the occupying powers feared that the monastery may become a Ukrainian symbol. But competition for these and other religious identity symbols, such as the Kremianets monastery, deserve closer scrutiny than Friedrich Heyer or I realized should be devoted to them.[22]

Deprived of most public symbols of identity, cultivators of the Ukrainian myth were obliged to revive almost forgotten symbols (the *tryzub*) or elevate such popular customs as the peasant chorus, the *bandura*, and distinctive peasant dress to the level of symbols. Apart from the difficulty of standardizing customs (such as dress) peculiar to numerous specific localities, the latter procedure encounters two major obstacles. One is the difficulty, emphasized by the French ethnologist André Varagnac, of institutionalizing any popular customs once the age of mass consumption and communication has arrived. Varagnac points out that the Catholic Church, with all its resources, failed to institutionalize "St. Joan of Arc Fires" during the early twentieth century.[23] Soviet sociologists occasionally come close to admitting that the regime cannot institutionalize new *byty*, especially rites of passage.[24] It is hardly surprising, therefore, that Ukrainian nationalists have sought other types of symbols. For some, emphasis on tangible differences between Russian house styles and Ukrainian forms have appeared promising as symbols of identity. At one time I shared this position, and I continue to suspect that certain Soviet Ukrainian writers emphasize distinctive house styles in order to hint at ethnic differences. The most authoritative investigations of European experience indicate, however, that such popular artifacts as house styles, furnishings and village layouts usually transcend ethnic boundaries, and are readily diffused for instrumental reasons without exercising perceptible influence on identity.[25]

Distinctive natural landscapes may have a higher potential for symbolizing identity, as David E. Sopher suggests: "The phenomenological view may be especially valuable for the recognition of landscape symbols that are taken as ethnic markers, if care is taken to apprehend images of very different scale; the cultural geographer may ask how these are related to different ecological circumstances. Landmarks which may endure for long periods, as cultural markers of ethnicity go, can become, through their shared symbolic value, an especially powerful means of ethnic identification."[26] The great German medievalist, Karl Vossler, once expressed his astonishment that so little scholarly attention had been devoted to the symbolic effect of place names.[27] Anyone who has traveled to central Russia and to the mid-Dnieper region observes the striking contrast between the vast, mysterious birch forests so beloved of Russian writers and the gentle, open *lesostep*. Reflections of such differences seem to appear in such Soviet works as *Istoriia mist i sil Ukrainskoi RSR*[28] and possibly even in party secretary P. E. Shelest's last venture into publishing. Close scrutiny, perhaps involving statistical content analysis, of differential use of images in Soviet Russian and Soviet Ukrainian political speeches and literary productions might be rewarding. One ought to recognize, though, that one can expect too much from landscape symbolism. After all, both Russia and Ukraine are highly varied. With a few exceptions such as the birch forest and the broad Dnieper River, specific landscape symbols that resonate throughout the length of either cultural area while clearly distinguishing it from the other are rare.

Anthropological surveys, if permitted, might uncover more direct evidence of the strength of landscape symbolism; it is significant, however, that most of the data so far available are derived from literary or rhetorical works. In other words, the impact of Ukrainian visual symbols cannot be apprehended directly, but only through verbal reflections. Verbal expression is itself highly symbolic. Indeed, the normal "border guards" distinguishing one ethnic group from another have been linguistic, like the ancient Hebrew shibboleths or the special vocabulary adopted by medieval German-speaking Jews.[29] Unfortunately for the development of corresponding Ukrainian linguistic border guards, the perpetuation of Church Slavonic into the modern period inhibited the growth of a common East Slavic linguistic vehicle (apart from the Muscovite version). As Polish authorities noted, the lack of a linguistic vehicle suitable for expressing precisely the common body of East Slavic legal principles inhibited the autonomous development of the Dnieper Slavs.[30]

From the mid-nineteenth century on, concern for a Ukrainian literary language distinct from Russian has sometimes even taken an exaggerated turn. Questions of language have received enormous attention from scholars within and outside the Ukrainian S.S.R. These writings exibit a strong implicit awareness of the symbolic significance of language, as contrasted to its purely instrumental aspects. Even within the limitations imposed on Soviet expression, such awareness surfaces in criticism of the mixture of Russian locutions in nominally Ukrainian speech and writing. Nevertheless, it seems to me, there is a certain disjuncture between the artificial linguistic "border guard" solutions usually advanced and the fundamental relationship between myth and symbol in the evolution of Ukrainian identity. The linguistic purism of Ukrainian intellectuals is derived from Central European models for national symbolism in which the nineteenth-century vogue of scientific philology played an inordinate role comparable to the position of scientific history in contemporary intellectual circles. For late twentieth-century Ukrainian identity, such models appear not merely somewhat anachronistic, but geographically and cultural peripheral.

It is easier for an outsider inexpert in the specific disciplines involved to criticize the relationship between recent Ukrainian purism and the development of more appropriate symbols than it is to suggest solutions or even lines of investigation that might lead to solutions. Contemporary sociolinguistics, notably those branches which consider language as code rather than instrumental communication, may have a good deal to contribute, however. A personal observation may be illustrative. On my first brief visit to Ukraine in 1956, Intourist guides dispatched from Moscow occasionally asked me to translate public notices in Ukrainian. While visiting a collective farm some eighty kilometers south of Kiev, I overheard two of these guides commenting to each other that they could not understand what the *kolkhozniks* were saying. At two distinct levels, therefore, Soviet Russians recognize that Ukrainian constitutes a distinctive language. At the purely official level, Ukrainian notices appear everywhere; but Russians and many urban Ukrainians, hardened to the hypocrisy of official Soviet symbolic tokenism, expect all important discussion to take place in the "all-union" language. At the rural level, the Russians expect Ukrainian to remain what the sociolinguist terms a "restrictive code," suitable only for semiliterate discourse. Because reliance on restricted code is always a badge of status inferiority, ordinary Ukrainians try to acquire Russian—as witness the great increase shown in recent censuses of Ukrainians using Russian habitually or as their second language. The tendency to abandon Ukrainian is overwhelming, in fact, for Ukrainians outside the Ukrainian Republic. Yet the fact that many such persons continue to identify themselves as Ukrainians means that at least in the short run maintenance of linguistic border guards is not essential to identity. Such identity depends, instead, on the constitutive myth of a freer, less centralized Ukrainian ethnic society, accompanied by, perhaps, greater appreciation for military traditions and individual heroism.[31] To express the matter differently, there is a sharp dichotomy within the Soviet Union between the Ukrainian language as a set of trivialized official symbols, evidently regarded as expendable by many Ukrainians, and the humiliating reality of popular Ukrainian as a low-status restrictive code. Over several generations the efforts of devoted intellectuals personally concerned with verbal communication have established the language as an adequate literary vehicle, but (in Eastern Ukraine) such efforts have not bridged the gap between the two truncated symbolic versions of the language in general Soviet usage.

Sociolinguists, primarily concerned with Third-World nations, suggest a variety of strategies to cope with such situations. Some strategies implicitly treat bilingualism as a transitory stage in the adoption of a dominant linguistic code, but others suggest preservation of separate spheres of language use in which the general, dominant language takes over expression of purely instrumental significance (technology, etc.), whereas intercourse with a high affect content remains in the native speech.[32] What the latter strategy implies is the strengthening of the symbolic relationship between the native language and the ethnic constitutive myth. There are great obstacles to such an undertaking under Soviet conditions. It would appear, nevertheless, that such has been the purport, perhaps unconscious, of many Ukrainian-language publications which have incurred official disfavor. Close investigation, in symbolic and socio-linguistic terms, of the messages conveyed by these publications and their Soviet official critics could be very rewarding. Such investigation might even suggest new strategies for relating myth to symbol in Ukrainian identity.

As I pointed out at the start of this article, the social-science emphasis on myth and symbol implies new ways of looking at familiar data rather than discovery of fresh bodies of evidence. Neither the old themes nor even the old conceptual devices are expendable, especially since the phenomenological aspects of the myth-symbol approach involve complex problems which can only be resolved by protracted application of the tools of the sociology of knowledge. In the meantime, if old concepts should be discarded—as sometimes happens in over-enthusiastic adoption of new theories—more will have been lost than one can hope to gain. All the same, fresh ways of looking at familiar themes can be revealing. The new approach points to some older investigations that have moved into blind alleys, whereas some paths hitherto rejected as too stony might be developed into broad highways. At the very least, utilization of new models—*not* ten or twenty years after they have passed in the general community, but while they still represent the cutting edge of scholarly discourse—can move Ukrainian studies toward the dynamic centre of Western social science.

Notes

1. John A. Armstrong, *Ukrainian Nationalism,* 2d ed. (New York: Columbia University Press, 1963) 3rd ed. (Englewood: Ukrainian Academic Press, 1990); and "Collaborationism in World War II: The Integral Nationalist Variant in Eastern Europe," *Journal of Modern History* XL (1968): 396–410.

2. Friedrich Meinecke, *Cosmopolitanism and the National State* (Princeton, 1970); Carlton J. H. Hayes, *Essays on Nationalism* (New York, 1933).

3. The tendency to accept ethnic (primarily linguistic) identity as "primordial" continues to influence such major analyses as Arend Lijphart, *Democracy in Plural Societies* (New Haven, 1977), 17ff.

4. Boris Lewytzkyj, *Die Sowjetukraine, 1944–1963* (Cologne, 1964); Yaroslav Bilinsky, *The Second Soviet Republic* (New Brunswick, N.J., 1964); Jurij Borys, *The Russian Communist Party and the Sovietization of Ukraine* (Stockholm, 1960), revised ed., *The Sovietization of Ukraine 1917–1923* (Edmonton, 1980).

5. John A. Armstrong, *The European Administrative Elite* (Princeton, 1973), 43.

6. See my remarks in "Development Theory: Taking the Historical Cure," *Studies in Comparative Communism* VII (1974): 217ff.

7. Karl W. Deutsch, *Nationalism and Social Communication* (Cambridge, 1963).

8. Clifford Geertz, *The Interpretation of Cultures* (New York, 1973), 127.

9. *Ukrainian Nationalism*, 7. Neither at the time this book was first published nor at present have I contended that Hrushevsky's writing had a greater impact on Ukrainians than did the works of Shevchenko. What I do contend is that Hrushevsky's systematic argument was essential, in the nineteenth-century intellectual context, for legitimizing the Ukrainian identity myth (especially the Khmelnytsky component) as a national constitutive myth capable of contending with other contemporary national myths.

10. Mykhailo Hrushevsky, *Istoriia Ukrainy-Rusy*, 10 vols. (New York, 1954–8).

11. Claude Lévi-Strauss, *Structural Anthropology* (New York, 1963), 216–17.

12. Claude Lévi-Strauss, *The Savage Mind* (Chicago, 1966), 254.

13. V. O. Kliuchevsky, *A History of Russia*, 5 vols. (New York, 1911–31).

14. Eric Dardel, "The Mythic: According to the Ethnological Works of Maurice Leenhardt," *Diogenes*, no. 7 (1954): 38.

15. *Travaux et Mémoires de l'Université de Lille*, Nouvelle Série, Droit et Lettres, no. 20, 1938.

16. This analogy is elaborated in my book, *Nations before Nationalism* (Chapel Hill, 1982), Chapter 8.

17. See especially Andrij Moskalenko, *Khmelnytskyi and the Treaty of Pereyaslav in Soviet Historiography* (New York, 1955, mimeo.)

18. A. Baraboi, "K voprosu o prichinakh prisoedineniia Ukrainy k Rossii v 1654 godu," *Marksist-Leninist* II (1939): 87–111.

19. Günther Stökl, *Die Entstehung des Kosakentums* (Munich, 1953).

20. I treat the subject at length in *Nations before Nationalism*, Chapter 3.

21. Paris, 1979.

22. *Ukrainian Nationalism*, Chapter 8; Friedrich Heyer, *Die orthodoxe Kirche in der Ukraine von 1917 bis 1945* (Cologne, 1953).

23. André Varagnac, *Civilisation traditionelle et genres de vie* (Paris, 1948), 57.

24. A. I. Kholmogorov, *Internatsionalnye cherty sovetskikh natsii* (Moscow, 1970), 64ff.

25. Bruno Schier, *Hauslandschaften und Kulturbewegungen im östlichen Mitteleuropa* (Göttingen, 1966).

26. David E. Sopher, "Place and Location," Louis Schneider and Charles M. Gonjean, ed., *The Idea of Culture in the Social Sciences* (Cambridge, 1973), 107–8.

27. Karl Vossler, *Aus der romanischen Welt* (Karlsruhe, 1948), 88.

28. 26 vols., Kiev, 1968–74.

29. Max Weinrich, "The Reality of Jewishness versus the Ghetto Myth: The Sociolinguistic Roots of Yiddish," in *To Honor Roman Jakobson*, III (The Hague, 1967), 2199ff.

30. Martel, 45.

31. See the interesting observations (based on recent interviews) in S. Enders Wimbush and Alex Alexiev, *The Ethnic Factor in the Soviet Armed Forces:*

Preliminary Findings (Santa Monica, 1980), 24–5.

32. W. P. Robinson, "Restricted Codes in Socio-Linguistics and the Sociology of Education," in W. H. Whiteley, ed., *Language Use and Social Change* (Oxford, 1971), 90ff.

John S. Reshetar, Jr.

Ukrainian and Russian Perceptions of the Ukrainian Revolution

The sudden onset of any revolution usually finds its principal actors unaware and unprepared. The complete breakdown of established relationships and prevailing values necessitates a basic reorientation in outlook and attitudes that is difficult to accomplish and that usually requires time. The total dissolution of old bonds and forms that results from the revolutionary situation requires a restructuring of relationships, institutions and patterns of political authority. In its most extreme form in a fully consummated revolution, the first are last and the last become first in a total reversal of roles.

However, revolutions also result in chaotic conditions and in outcomes that may not be clear and complete for some time. A revolution may lead to profound changes and may release new social and political forces without bringing about a complete reversal of roles between oppressor and oppressed. Thus the Ukrainian Revolution did not achieve the goal of independent statehood for Ukraine, although a species of surrogate statehood was achieved in the form of the Ukrainian Soviet Republic. A fully consummated revolution does not permit restoration of the old order and, instead, presumably establishes totally new attitudes and relationships. However, the forces of restoration in the Russian Revolution assumed various forms and sought to nullify the Ukrainian Revolution and to restore as far as possible the status quo ante in the Ukrainian-Russian relationship. The Ukrainian Revolution did not result in a basic reordering of the relationship between Ukrainians and Russians, although certain changes can be said to have occurred.

A total restructuring of the relationship would have required Russian abandonment of imperial claims and a willingness to relinquish hegemony. It would have meant giving up political centralism and the implied invidious distinction between "greater" and "lesser" peoples. Such a restructuring would also have required a more intense and more sustained commitment on the part of a larger portion of the Ukrainian population.

Ukrainian perceptions of the revolution changed with relative rapidity as a result of changing circumstances. As the Russian response to the Ukrainian Revolution became clearer, the goals of the revolution changed. In general, Ukrainian perceptions must be understood in terms of the conditions in which the national movement developed and the policies of imperial Russia that nourished it and enabled it to gain appeal. More than two and a half centuries of Russian influence (initially) and subsequent direct rule over Eastern Ukraine had a demoralizing effect on the Ukrainians as well as providing a basis for mass rejection of Russian rule. The entire train of events since the Treaty of Pereiaslav (1654) provided the grievances that led to the Revolution: the increased presence of arrogant Russian officials and the violation of Ukrainian rights under the treaty; the Moscow Patriarch's arrogation of the rights of the Ukrainian Orthodox Church in 1686 (which church had enjoyed de facto autocephaly with nominal ties to the Ecumenical Patriarchate of Constantinople); the Battle of Poltava (1709) and the defeat of Hetman Ivan Mazepa; the introduction of serfdom into Ukraine by Catherine II; the dissolution of the Zaporozhian Sich in 1775; the Valuev decree and the Ems ukase, which placed severe limitations on the use of the Ukrainian language and sought to prevent its development as a literary language and as a medium of public communication.

The repressive conditions imposed upon Ukrainians by the tsarist regime during World War I led to an inevitable reaction with the regime's collapse. In 1914 publications in the Ukrainian language were banned, including the Kiev daily, *Rada* (despite its support of the Russian war effort); the editor of *Ukrainska khata*, Pavlo Bohatsky, was exiled to Siberia; and Olena Pchilka's Poltava weekly, *Ridnyi krai,* was also banned. The Prosvita societies were banned. Professor Mykhailo Hrushevsky was arrested and exiled from Ukraine. The Russian military occupation of Lviv and Chernivtsi led to the arrest and exile of Metropolitan Andrei Sheptytsky and many other prominent Galician Ukrainians and the banning of numerous Ukrainian-language publications, including the Shevchenko Scientific Society's *Literaturno-naukovyi vistnyk.* Thus not a single Ukrainian-language newspaper remained on Ukrainian territory.[1] The wartime situation gave the reactionary Russian Black Hundreds the opportunity to disseminate the crudest kind of Ukrainophobia, which not only found an audience among unthinking Russians but also made many Ukrainians more nationally conscious and aware of their country's plight and the need to oppose such calumny.

Ukrainian Perceptions

Initially, in the heady and euphoric atmosphere that ensued from the collapse of the Russian monarchy and the Empire, Ukrainians could only perceive their own revolution as an integral part of the Russian Revolution. Thus they sought an accommodation with the Russian Provisional Government which had emerged from the Duma. The Ukrainian community in Petrograd, led by the Society of Ukrainian Progressives (*Tovarystvo ukrainskykh postupovtsiv,* TUP) branch in the Russian capital, addressed an aide-mémoire to the Provisional Government in which it requested the latter to: appoint Ukrainians to official posts in Ukraine; establish the post of commissar for Ukrainian affairs in the

Provisional Government; introduce the use of the Ukrainian language in the courts and schools; establish Ukrainian studies courses in colleges and universities; authorize use of the Ukrainian language in the Orthodox Church in sermons and other matters; and rescind the Russian Orthodox Church administration that had been imposed on the Ukrainian Catholics in Eastern Galicia during the war.[2] The release of incarcerated Galician and Bukovynian Ukrainians was also demanded. These were very modest demands that did result in initial concessions and in the release of Professor Hrushevsky, Metropolitan Sheptytsky and others.

The emergence of the Ukrainian Central Rada (Council) in Kiev, under the presidency of Professor Hrushevsky, meant the establishment of a de facto Ukrainian government with the formation of the Rada's General Secretariat. However, disagreement soon developed as the Rada sought to broaden Ukrainian autonomy and the Provisional Government sought to limit it.[3] The leaders of the Rada evinced both hesitancy and determination according to circumstances. Thus they assumed the initiative and issued the Rada's First Universal of 10 (23) June 1917 in which they reaffirmed the demand for autonomy and protested the Provisional Government's refusal to accept accreditation of a commissar for Ukrainian affairs to represent the Rada in Petrograd, as well as its unwillingness to provide treasury funds to the Rada for "national-cultural needs" and to designate a single official of the Provisional Government as its sole representative in Ukraine (who was to be chosen by the Rada).

The Rada's decision to form the General Secretariat resulted from the Provisional Government's intransigence, its unwillingness to take any positive action, and its deferring all important questions to the All-Russian Constituent Assembly. However, the Provisional Government did accept the Rada's Second Universal, adopted on 3 (16) July 1917, but then sought to reduce its effect by issuing its own so-called "Instruction" of 4 (17) August 1917 that attempted to limit the Rada's jurisdiction and authority. Although the Rada, whose membership was now more than 800 with the inclusion of non-Ukrainian members, officially accepted the "Instruction," the tensions between Kiev and Petrograd increased.

If the Rada manifested a degree of moderation during the summer of 1917, it was due to the fact that at the time it lacked the necessary financial and military support. Thus it did not have the power to tax and had to rely on contributions. Although it was able to organize some military units in a rapidly deteriorating military situation, the Russian forces in the Kiev garrison supported the Provisional Government. Thus if the Rada had proclaimed Ukrainian independence, instead of autonomy, in the First or Second Universal, such an act would probably have precipitated a crisis involving the use of armed force and dissolution of the Rada. The Rada's self-restraint was also prompted by the presence of non-Ukrainian members who constituted approximately one-quarter of the membership and were not supportive of Ukrainian independence.[4]

While accepting an autonomous status for Ukraine that was ill-defined, the Rada even in its First Universal held out the prospect of ultimate independence: "Ukrainian People! Your fate lies in your own hands. In this difficult time of universal disorder and ruin, prove by your unity and your statesmanship that you, a nation of workers, a nation of tillers of the soil, can proudly and with dignity take your place beside any organized nation-state, as an equal among equals."[5] Thus there was implied, in the above statement and in the assertion "we shall build our life," a commitment to popular sovereignty and national equality including independence.

Yet the hesitancy to sever the tie with revolutionary Russia is evident even in the Rada's Third and Fourth Universals. The Third Universal of 7 (20) November 1917 was prompted by the collapse of the Provisional Government and proclaimed the establishment of the Ukrainian People's Republic (*Ukrainska Narodnia Respublika*, UNR). However, it also asserted: "Without separating ourselves from the Russian Republic and maintaining its unity, we shall stand firmly on our soil, in order that our strength may aid all of Russia, so that the whole Russian Republic may become a federation of equal and free peoples."[6] The Third Universal foresaw both Ukrainian and All-Russian Constituent Assemblies and the "great fraternal construction of new governmental forms which will grant the great and weakened Republic of Russia health, strength and a new future." Even the Fourth Universal of 9 (22) January 1918, which proclaimed Ukrainian independence, did not rule out the possibility of "federative ties with the people's republics of the former Russian state."[7]

The Rada's reluctance to sever the tie with revolutionary Russia until Lenin's seizure of power can be attributed to the general belief in "Russian democracy," i.e., in the liberal and democratic forces that were thought to be present in Russia. It was hoped that these forces would actually reverse the pattern of national discrimination and inequality that had characterized the Russian Empire. This faith in the emergence of a new Russia remained unfulfilled and was to be dissipated in the painful and bitter experience of Ukrainians as a result of the "new" forms that Russian political life was assuming. The blind urge to re-establish the tie with Russia was seen in the conduct of two diametrically opposed Ukrainian political leaders of the revolutionary period—Hetman Pavlo Skoropadsky and the head of the Directory, Volodymyr Vynnychenko.

Skoropadsky proclaimed a federation of the Ukrainian State with Russia on 14 November 1918 as his German-sponsored regime faced collapse at the close of World War I. Although this act may have been designed to win support from the Entente powers, it only served to discredit Skoropadsky and fuel the fires of the nationalist Ukrainian revolt that was being organized in Bila Tserkva by the Directory of the restored Ukrainian People's Republic.

Vynnychenko, always more the literary author moved by emotion than the tested political leader, saw in Russian Bolshevism a potential ally that, in theory at least, "employed coercion and inequality in order to establish equality and destroy all coercion."[8] Indeed, he came to the remarkable conclusion that the armed conflict between Lenin's Soviet Russian government and the Ukrainian People's Republic in December 1917 and January 1918 arose as a result of the latter's failings and incorrect policies.[9] When the Hetmanate of General Skoropadsky was being overthrown in November 1918, Vynnychenko, as head of the Directory, entered into an agreement with Lenin's emissaries in Kiev (Christian Rakovsky and Dmytro Manuilsky) to coordinate efforts in the uprising and also promised to have the Directory legalize the Communist Party in Ukraine.[10] Vynnychenko also spent the summer of 1920 in Moscow and visited the then Soviet Ukrainian capital of Kharkiv twice in a vain attempt to come to terms with Lenin and the Ukrainian communist regime.[11]

Others abandoned their faith in "Russian democracy" much earlier. For Professor Hrushevsky, writing near Sarny on 4 February 1918 during the evacuation from Kiev, the "old Muscovite centralism" had re-emerged "under the mask of Bolshevism."[12] Hrushevsky noted that the "orientation on Muscovy, on Russia" had ceased to exist, having been "burned in my study" —a reference to the deliberate and wanton shelling of Hrushevsky's home in Kiev and the burning of his study by Soviet Russian forces that invaded Ukraine under the command of Muravev in January 1918.[13] In a historiosophical statement Hrushevsky observed:

> Great causes are born amidst great pain. All the current strivings of the leading Ukrainian politicians—that the birth of the new life would occur without pain, without acute disruptions, without bloody conflicts—were in vain. Our Ukrainian Revolution unfortunately did not develop independently but had always to march with the convulsive movements and the casting about of the Russian Revolution, chaotic and frightening. The Russian Revolution drew us through blood, through ruin and through fire.[14]

Yet Hrushevsky, while depicting the Russian invasion of Ukraine as a fratricidal act, also expressed the view that Ukraine was not only for Ukrainians but included other peoples who wished to contribute to its well-being.

Of the various Ukrainian leaders, Symon Petliura probably had fewer illusions regarding the Russians, for he had resided in Moscow, where he edited the Russian-language journal, *Ukrainskaia zhizn* (Ukrainian Life), that was designed to inform the Russian public of Ukrainian conditions and also acquaint it with Ukrainian aspirations. Viewing the revolution in retrospect, Petliura (in a letter written to General Mykola Udovychenko in 1922) offered the following statement:

> I observed that the Ukrainian parties possess revolutionary force, some of them disruptive, but do not possess creative organizational strength. I observed that

they did not perceive what was *most important*: whether Ukraine as an independent state should in its foreign policy orient itself on Europe or on Moscow-Asia. It became clear that the Asiatic heritage among us is still too strong: the SRs, part of the SDs (Vynnychenko) gave pre-eminence to Moscow, not to Europe. It was necessary to base ourselves on Europe, which, as a matter of fact, did not know us and did not understand us, while at the same time it was necessary to develop our own strength. The sooner the sense of independence from Moscow crystallizes itself among our people, the sooner we will have an independent Ukraine.[15]

For Petliura independent Ukrainian statehood was the paramount value, and it is not surprising that among the Ukrainian leaders it was he who persisted steadfastly in waging the armed struggle in the face of unfavourable odds. Petliura can be likened to Marshal Józef Piłsudski, who placed Poland's national independence above his commitment to socialism. Although Petliura was at least nominally a social democrat, he might also be compared with the Finnish social democrat Vaïno Tanner, for whom, it has been said, "nothing good ever came out of Russia, except for the chaotic conditions of 1917, which made Finland's independence possible."[16] Yet one cannot find any overt expressions of Russophobia in Petliura's writings, whether in Ukraine or as an émigré, although for him the enemy was "Moscow" or "Bolshevism" or simply an unnamed "enemy." In contrast to Petliura, other prominent Ukrainian leaders withdrew from the armed struggle and went into exile.[17]

The disagreements among the Ukrainian leaders occurred in conditions that would have severely tested the mettle of more experienced men. Left alone by its neighbors and permitted to develop its own future, the Ukrainian People's Republic would probably have emerged as a viable political entity despite the differing views of its leaders. However, the Central Rada and the idea of Ukrainian independent statehood were opposed by the Russians in Kiev, who initially supported the Provisional Government. With the collapse of the Provisional Government, the Bolsheviks and the Kiev Soviet challenged the Rada by means of a general strike which was precipitated by the Rada's disarming of pro-Bolshevik military units.[18] However, the Bolshevik strategy was to combine an uprising in the Ukrainian capital with an armed invasion from the north. Although the Rada's forces did suppress the uprising in Kiev, they were unable to cope with the four military groups of the Bolshevik invasion force, which had 30,000 troops, 60 pieces of artillery and ten armoured trains.[19]

The relatively brief Bolshevik occupation of Kiev in 1918 established the pattern of resolving the issues of the revolution by force of arms, with propaganda appeals playing a secondary, though very important, role. The Ukrainian leaders were at a disadvantage in having to move from what was essentially an apolitical cultural nationalism to positions of autonomy and federalism and, finally, independent statehood in a matter of one year. The need for such a rapid reorientation inevitably produced some uncertainty and disagreement.

Among the basic cleavages that defined the various Ukrainian perceptions of the revolution was the desire to be "socialist" —though in varying degrees—and the fear of some that they were not sufficiently "socialist." Thus Professor Hrushevsky thought it advisable to join the youthful Ukrainian Socialist Revolutionaries, although he was far removed from them in age, experience, temperament and outlook. Yet the most fundamental cleavage in perception of the revolution was probably best illustrated in the respective positions of Vynnychenko and Petliura. Vynnychenko became increasingly radical and doctrinaire as the revolution progressed. In December 1918 and January 1919 he moved closer to a national-communist position in advocating the establishment of a soviet (*radianska*) system in Ukraine. Vynnychenko reasoned that his strategy would nullify the effectiveness of the "social slogans" being used by the Bolsheviks and would compel the latter to confront the Directory Government "only as Russian nationalists" offering Ukrainians *Russian* soviet rule, which supposedly would be rejected in favour of Ukrainian soviet rule. Vynnychenko, in subsequently justifying his position, contended that "it should have been clear to any more or less far-sighted politician that the logical development of the movement will lead to Bolshevism and that in the interests of Ukrainian statehood it was necessary not to release the initiative from one's hands and to assure in advance the Ukrainian character of that [Bolshevik] regime (*vlada*) which must inevitably come."[20]

When this position proved unacceptable to the Ukrainian military leaders (who argued that workers' soviets or councils would assure the dominance of the non-Ukrainian urban elements), Vynnychenko proposed a system of toilers' councils (*systema trudovykh rad*) that would have given dominant representation to the Ukrainian peasantry. For Vynnychenko, who advocated a "multifaceted liberation," the struggle against the bourgeoisie, which was largely non-Ukrainian, took precedence over the achievement of national statehood or would in the end, if given precedence, actually assure national statehood.[21]

Vynnychenko's Marxism and atheism contrasted with Petliura's advocacy of parliamentarism and commitment to more traditional Ukrainian values. Thus Vynnychenko disliked the Orthodox clergy and objected to their participation in public exercises under the Rada and the Directory, while Petliura advocated an autocephalous Ukrainian Orthodox Church with its own patriarch in Kiev.[22] Although Petliura was also a social democrat and supported the various social and economic goals of the revolution, he gave primacy to the goal of independent national statehood. For Vynnychenko, all goals were to be pursued simultaneously and with the achievement of the socio-economic revolution national independence would presumably be assured.

The major Ukrainian parties of the revolutionary period had difficulty overcoming their past, because in the pre-revolutionary period they were "for the most part copies or simply affiliates of the Russian parties."[23] Fearing accusations of "chauvinism" initially and believing in the "magnanimity of Russian democracy," the parties imposed restraints upon themselves that in the end were detrimental to the national cause.[24] The most popular party was that of the Ukrainian Socialist Revolutionaries, who attracted subsequent peasant support by recognizing individual farming despite their advocacy of socialization of the land. The Ukrainian SRs, together with the Social Democrats, obtained a clear majority of the vote in Ukraine in the elections to the All-Russian Constituent Assembly in November 1917, pre-empting the claims of the Russian SRs and demonstrating that there was a popular (largely peasant) ethnic base for the Ukrainian Revolution.[25]

The Social Democrats had more articulate intellectuals in their leadership, while the SRs had closer ties to the Ukrainian peasantry. Efforts at establishing a viable coalition of the two parties proved unsuccessful. The SRs, who had dominated the Central Rada, tended to lose support as a result of their being associated with the arrival of Austrian and German occupation forces in February 1918. Both parties were in agreement in their opposition to the Hetmanate of General Skoropadsky, but the Directory Government that succeeded it was led by the Social Democrats.

The disagreements that existed between the Ukrainian parties —as well as their quarrels with the communists (both Russian and Ukrainian)—issued from the question of the extent to which the Ukrainian Revolution was a part of the Russian Revolution. Thus such issues as the class struggle, the agrarian problem (the peasant hunger for land), the growing anarchy, and the nature of the (non) Ukrainian city with its frequently inimical or indifferent alien elements, served to distract the Ukrainian parties from fully consummating the achievement of national statehood. The fact that Ukraine in 1919 was invaded by Russian Bolshevik forces and by General Denikin's Russian (White Guard) Volunteer Army and was also the object of an ineffective French military intervention—in addition to the invasion of Eastern Galicia by Polish forces— could only complicate perception of the revolution and the effort to answer such questions as: who is a friend and who is a foe and who might be a worthy ally and a source of external support.

These circumstances produced divisions in both major Ukrainian parties as left wings developed and sought an accommodation with Ukrainian communism. Thus left Social Democrats formed the independent Ukrainian Communist Party (UKP) and attempted to pursue a national-communist course while left SRs (the *Borotbisty*) were ultimately to accept absorption (and worse) into the Russian-sponsored Communist Party (Bolshevik) of Ukraine. The splintering and resultant diffusion of the revolutionary cause inevitably led to mutual recriminations.

There was the frequently expressed charge that the Rada as well as the Directory was tardy in addressing socio-economic issues, especially that of land reform.[26] The disagreement prompted by Vynnychenko's attempts at a fellow-traveller role in conjunction with his "mission to Moscow" resulted in his employing bitter personal attacks on Petliura, to which the latter did not respond in kind.

The Galician Ukrainians, who had proclaimed a Western Ukrainian Republic and were defending themselves against an invasion by Polish forces seeking to annex Western Ukraine, sought aid from the Directory and could not participate initially in its military efforts against the Russian Bolsheviks.* Following the Polish military occupation of Eastern Galicia and the retreat of the West Ukrainian Army across the Zbruch River into Central Ukraine, the Galician forces concluded an agreement with Denikin's army in November 1919 after experiencing untold suffering and deprivation in the "quadrangle of death."†

The Western Ukrainian Republic had entered into an act of union with the Directory and the Ukrainian People's Republic in January 1919. Apart from the ideal and principle of *sobornist*, for the Galician Ukrainians this union was prompted by the practical consideration of obtaining such weapons and supplies as the Directory could make available. Yet the Western Ukrainian leadership was uneasy regarding the union with the Eastern Ukrainian doctrinaire socialist intelligentsia that formed the Directory Government.[27] The more disciplined and orderly Galician Ukrainians, having been trained in Austrian parliamentarism and accustomed to a constitutional order, rejected socialist panaceas. They feared being drawn into the maelstrom of the social revolution and were concerned lest the disorders that were so prevalent in Central and Eastern Ukraine spill over into Western Ukraine. The principal Western Ukrainian negotiator with the Directory and the principal author of the text of the Act of Union, Dr. Lonhyn Tsehelsky, was shocked by the excesses of the rabble (*holota*) that occurred following the overthrow of the Hetmanate. He was also shocked by the arbitrariness and lack of discipline that characterized the *otamanshchyna*—rule by insubordinate local military commanders or chieftains.[28] In his view the Directory, in appealing for the overthrow of the Hetmanate, fostered the conditions that led to its own defeat and resulted in the sovietization of Ukraine. Thus the leaders of the two Ukrainian republics viewed the revolution very differently.

---

* The Sich Sharpshooter units, consisting of Galician Ukrainians, played an important role in overthrowing Hetman Skoropadsky and were among the Directory's most reliable military units.

† When the Western Ukrainian Army, as a result of desperation and disease, concluded its accommodation with Denikin's Army, Petliura regarded it as an act of betrayal. Similarly, when Petliura concluded the treaty of 21 April 1920 with Poland, recognizing the Polish acquisition of Eastern Galicia, the Western Ukrainian leaders regarded it as a betrayal of their cause.

The issue of the class struggle, as advocated by the socialists, versus the struggle for national liberation not only served to distinguish perceptions but also dissipated the energies and efforts of the various Ukrainian leaders and parties. Yet whatever the disagreements, there was a consensus among them regarding the need to restore Ukrainian national rights and to assert Ukrainian ethnic distinctiveness and a separate identity. Irrespective of their differences, all sought to obtain recognition and equality for the Ukrainian language and to assure education at all levels in their language. It was this shared perception of the revolution and the consensus regarding recognition of national rights that in the end proved to have the greatest impact on subsequent events.

Russian Perceptions

Most Russians perceived the Ukrainian Revolution either as something unreal, without substance or meaning, or as an undesirable temporary consequence of the Russian Revolution. Accustomed, as a result of the imperial system, to regarding Ukraine as "Little Russia," the "South," "South Russia" or the "Southwestern Region," Russians were now compelled to cope with the growing claims of a national movement that they had traditionally ignored or ruthlessly suppressed whenever it manifested itself in quasi-political forms.

Ukrainophobia was not common to all Russians. Thus the recognition of Ukrainian as a language separate from Russian by the Imperial Academy of Sciences was, to a significant degree, due to the efforts of Fedor Korsh and Aleksei Shakhmatov.[29] Yet such quasi-official recognition in the aftermath of the 1905 Revolution, with its limited freedom of the press, could not rectify the effects of the policy of discrimination that had persisted for so many decades. There was also the effort of Bishop Nikon Bezsonov (himself a Russian and auxiliary bishop of Volhynia) as a deputy in the Fourth Duma to introduce the Ukrainian language into the schools of Ukraine. In response, Russian ecclesiastical authorities transferred the bishop to Krasnoiarsk in Siberia in order to hamper his role as a deputy.[30]

Official policy encouraged the popular stereotypical view of the Ukrainian language as a dialect (*narechie*) and of Ukrainian culture as rustic and peasant-bound. Ukrainophilism, cultural in nature, was ridiculed and regarded as doomed. Any interest in restoring Ukrainian political rights—lost as a result of Russian violations of the terms of the Treaty of Pereiaslav—or in seeking any aid from abroad for the defence of cultural rights (including aid from Western Ukraine under Austrian rule) was branded as *Mazepinstvo* and equated with treason. The figure of Hetman Ivan Mazepa was used to symbolize and condemn "separatism" and secession of Ukraine from Russia. The Russian Orthodox Church, which professed to minister to the spiritual needs of Ukrainians, anathematized Mazepa annually on the first Sunday of the Great Lent in a ceremony rendered ironic by the fact that Mazepa, as a philanthropist, had built a number of Ukrainian Baroque churches.

The figure of Taras Shevchenko, whose poetry symbolized the perseverance and enrichment of the Ukrainian language as well as antipathy to Russian rule, was regarded with disdain in official circles and with an apparent fear that bordered on the pathological.[31] For it is only in such terms that one can explain the February 1914 ban by the Russian ministry of the interior on public observances commemorating the centenary of Shevchenko's birth.[32]

Although such Russian critics as Chernyshevsky and Herzen recognized Shevchenko's talent, the prevalence of the official view reflected a desire to suppress the Ukrainian language, culture and the press and to regard such a situation as "normal." The policy of systematically denigrating everything Ukrainian as allegedly "inferior" to what was Russian was rationalized in terms of a cultural Darwinism that justified the struggle of two cultures in which the supposedly less worthy culture and language should be expected to perish. In the eyes of the advocates of this policy, suppression of Ukrainian culture provided "proof" that what was being suppressed did not really exist nor could it exist.

It was with the burden of such a past that the Russian Provisional Government perceived the Ukrainian Revolution. Although the Provisional Government offered the Poles an independent state on 16 (29) March 1917—subject to approval by the All-Russian Constituent Assembly—it apparently regarded Ukrainian claims as being of secondary or tertiary importance at best or as a nuisance or annoyance that would likely go away if ignored or neglected. Indicative of the Provisional Government's general attitude was its refusal to grant Finland independence and its decision to dissolve the Finnish parliament when the latter asserted its authority in July 1917 and claimed sovereignty in all matters other than foreign policy and military legislation and administration. The Provisional Government contended that it alone had acquired the powers of the defunct Russian monarchy, while the Finnish Social Democrats, who constituted a majority in the dissolved parliament, contended that the Finnish legislature had rightfully assumed authority.[33]

When a similar conflict developed between the Provisional Government and the Ukrainian Central Rada, the former contended that only the All-Russian Constituent Assembly could determine the extent and nature of Ukrainian autonomy.[34] Although the supposed supreme authority of the yet to be elected All-Russian Constituent Assembly was a convenient device for justifying delay and for rationalizing the status quo, the impelling nature of revolutionary developments made such a policy increasingly untenable. The Provisional Government's refusal to recognize the right of national self-determination (except for the Poles) and its reliance on the Constituent Assembly posed the basic question of what kind of veto the Assembly would have over Ukrainian rights. If the membership of the Constituent Assembly were to reflect the ethnic composition of the Empire, the Russians would themselves be a minority in that body.

From the Ukrainian point of view the basic question was: who shall have the moral, legal and political authority to decide the future of the Ukrainian people? Between July and September 1917 the Rada was demanding convocation of a Ukrainian Constituent Assembly. For the Russians this raised the question of the respective jurisdictions of the two constituent assemblies and the issue of whether the All-Russian Constituent Assembly would have a veto over the actions of the Ukrainian Constituent Assembly. However, the issue could not be resolved because time was running out on the Provisional Government. It is indicative of that government's lack of foresight and its inability to define priorities that in the last days of its existence it ordered Vynnychenko and two other members of the Rada's General Secretariat to Petrograd "for personal explanations with regard to reports on agitation in Ukraine in favour of convoking a sovereign Constituent Assembly."[35] Thus what the Russians permitted themselves—a sovereign constituent assembly—they were unwilling to permit the Ukrainians. When Vynnychenko and his colleagues arrived in Petrograd the Provisional Government was no longer in existence. A Russian Provisional Government that was incapable of defending itself against its Russian opponents was nevertheless prepared to pursue a firm policy against the Rada.

For the Russians the very existence of the Rada brought the specter of Ukrainian "separatism" too close to realization and posed a threat to the notion of a "Russia" that was "one and indivisible." The suspiciousness and intransigence of the Provisional Government and its successors reflected a complex of attitudes, prejudices and claims regarding Ukraine that Russians had acquired as a result of their dominant position in the imperial system. Only some of the more salient components of this Russian mind-set can be discussed within the confines of this article.

The teaching of history in terms that justified the imperial system and the subjugation of other peoples by the Russians had resulted in what can only be termed an obsession with Kiev and a claim to the Kievan Rus' state. By arrogating to themselves the Kievan heritage rather than being content with the very respectable and contemporaneous Novgorod heritage, Russians asserted a claim to Ukraine which they were then unwilling to abandon. For the imperial syndrome—which transcended the tsarist order—Ukraine came to be regarded as a pivotal region rivalled only by Siberia or Central Asia as the Empire's most valuable possession. Ukraine's strategic value enabled Russia to exert pressure on Poland, Hungary and the Danubian Basin, and the Balkans and also provided access to the Crimea. Thus Russia's claim to empire would be significantly reduced without Ukraine.

By claiming the Ukrainians as "Little Russians" or by insisting on the cultural closeness of Ukrainians to Russians, Russians were able to give themselves (actually the Eastern Slavs) a substantial majority of the empire's (Soviet

Union's) population. Thus the Ukrainians have played a crucial, though substantially involuntary, role in the demographic basis for Russia's claim to empire. The alleged cultural closeness of Ukrainians to Russians was based on the Russian refusal to recognize the Ukrainian language as more than a "dialect" or "variant" of the Russian language. Russians would also point to their claim to such historical figures as Bortniansky, Gogol and Feofan Prokopovych in support of their arguments regarding cultural (historical) ties.

Russians readily developed affection and attachment to Ukraine, for it is always expedient to "love" what you covet. Russians were attracted to the Ukrainian landscape, southern warmth and agricultural abundance and were charmed by Gogol's *Evenings on a Farm near Dikanka*. Having developed an attachment to Ukraine, they could not readily divest themselves of it.

The fact that the majority of Ukrainians were of the Orthodox faith, as were the Russians, contributed to the Russians' taking Ukrainians for granted. Since this superficial common identity was promoted by the use of the Church Slavonic language for liturgical purposes, it is evident why Russians opposed the introduction of contemporary language, whether Russian or Ukrainian, into the liturgy. For example, Bishop Parfenii Levytsky of Podillia, who preached in Ukrainian and encouraged priests to do so, was transferred to Tula, and other Ukrainian bishops who advocated the use of the Ukrainian language were punished by what Oleksander Lototsky termed the Russian "synodal-police system."[36] Russians tended to ignore or minimize the unique traditional Ukrainian Orthodox religious practices or to eliminate them and impose conformity with Russian practices.[37]

The Russian attitude toward Ukraine was also affected by the phenomenon of *Malorosiistvo* ("Little Russianism"), which preserved some of the distinctiveness of the Ukrainian way of life as well as the language, but acquiesced in Russian domination of Ukraine and viewed negatively or with indifference Ukrainian efforts to achieve independent statehood (even historically).[38] *Malorosiistvo* cultivated provincialism instead of nationalism and was a consequence of Russian rule and a desire to serve and gain personal advantage within the imperial system. It was based on the implicit precept "to be lesser is better" and represented a willingness to settle for a subordinate status in the perpetual shadow of Russia. While nationally conscious Ukrainians condemned the *Maloros* as a renegade (*pereverten*), Russians usually saw them as "proof" that Ukrainians were ultimately vulnerable to Russification or could at least be confined to perpetual subservience. Influenced by the corrupting nature of *Malorosiistvo*, Russians could ask why more Ukrainians did not emulate the notorious Ukrainophobe A. I. Savenko, who proposed that the domes of Kiev's churches be rebuilt in the Russian onion-shaped style.[39] Such figures as M. V. Rodzianko, president of the State Duma and M. I. Tereshchenko, the Provisional Government's finance minister and minister of foreign affairs, were regarded by Russians as model "Ukrainians" (actually Little Russians). Thus the burden of "Little Russianism" weighed heavily on the Ukrainians, but also misled the Russians in the matter of how the mass of Ukrainians really perceived them.

Many Russians apparently believed the myth that the Ukrainian national movement was a "German-Austrian creation" designed to "destroy" or at least "dismember" Russia. A related myth was that the Ukrainian national movement was the work of a limited number of alienated intellectuals who were "enemy agents." That such myths were widespread in Russian society is evident in the fact that prior to the revolution the editors of the Russian-language journal *Ukrainskaia zhizn* published three editions of a work entitled *Ukrainskii vopros* (The Ukrainian Question) which was designed to respond to the false charges that *Ukrainstvo* (Ukrainianism) represented "nihilism," "socialism," "separatism," "Austrophilism," or Polish or German intrigue.[40] The superficial and undiscriminating Russian observer could seize upon the following isolated facts in support of these preposterous allegations: Professor Hrushevsky spent the years from 1894 to 1913 in Galicia as professor of history at the University of Lviv and also headed the Shevchenko Scientific Society and established the *Literaturno-naukovyi vistnyk*;[41] Petliura spent the year 1905 in Lviv as a member of the Revolutionary Ukrainian Party; Ukrainian-language publications, including political pamphlets, were printed in Galicia and smuggled into Eastern Ukraine. The Union for the Liberation of Ukraine (*Soiuz vyzvolennia Ukrainy*), which was established by Eastern Ukrainian émigrés in Lviv, had its headquarters in Vienna (it moved to Berlin in 1915) and conducted political education programs among Ukrainian prisoners of war held in Germany; it also openly sought the downfall of the Russian autocracy.[42] Subsequent events such as the recognition of Ukraine by the Central Powers in the Treaty of Brest-Litovsk and the German approval of the Hetmanate were also regarded as "proof" of "Austro-German intrigue."

The Russians who accepted this canard ignored the fact that Eastern Ukrainian intellectuals were attracted to Galicia largely because of the relatively free conditions that prevailed there under Austrian rule in contrast to the repressive measures employed by the tsarist regime against Ukrainians. If Professor Hrushevsky could have taught Ukrainian history at the universities of Kiev or Kharkiv he would probably not have accepted the position in Lviv. Indeed, the question of foreign aid raises parallels: the Muscovite state emerged as a result of collaboration with foreign interests (the Mongols), and Bolshevism would also qualify as a "German creation," because the Bolsheviks received financial aid from Germany during World War I.[43] If one were to apply the logic of Russian Ukrainophobes to Finland, that country would also qualify as a "German creation" because of the aid that the Finns received from Germany in their struggle for independence in 1918.

Oleksander Lototsky argued that the "German issue" amounted to a calculated attempt by Russian chauvinists to "strangulate Ukrainianism" and compromise it, as well as to provide a rationalization for taking measures against any Ukrainian bookstore, club or the language itself. According to Lototsky, even Ukrainian sausage shops irritated the Russian Black Hundreds (the Union of the Russian People).[44] The practice of denigrating everything Ukrainian was presumably calculated to reduce or even destroy Ukrainian self-confidence, but it also reflected the arrogance, obtuseness, insensitivity and self-aggrandizement that characterized much of the Russian minority living in Ukraine. Most members of this minority refused to learn the Ukrainian language and were unwilling to accept any changes in their privileged status and in the Ukrainian-Russian relationship. Their dominant position in the Ukrainian cities had led them to believe that they had a veto over Ukrainian developments. Like the Bourbons, they sought neither to learn anything nor to forget anything.

From the vantage point of the Russian capital, the Central Rada represented a threat that went far beyond the potential loss of Ukraine. The Rada saw itself as leading the other non-Russian nationalities in the demand for a federal democratic order. To this end it organized a Congress of Nationalities which met in Kiev from 8–15 (21–28) September 1917 and was attended by 92 delegates representing Belorussians, Georgians, Jews, Estonians, Latvians, Lithuanians, Tatars, Romanians (Moldavians), Buriats and Cossacks. The Congress adopted resolutions in support of national-personal autonomy, the equality of languages (with no special advantages to the Russian language in schools, courts and religious institutions), the right of each nationality to have its own constituent assembly, and non-Russian representation at the peace conference to be convened at the end of the war. The decision to establish a Council of Nationalities, with Hrushevsky as president and its seat in Kiev, reflected the hopes of the other non-Russian nationalities that the Rada would lead the way to a better future.[45]

Federalism as a solution to the nationalities problem was not supported by any of the Russian political parties or movements during the revolution. This fact, together with the vague promises of autonomy that emanated from the Provisional Govenment, confined the positions of the various Russian parties and political orientations to a narrow spectrum. The most representative positions on this spectrum were those of the Socialist Revolutionaries, the Constitutional Democrats or Kadets (Party of People's Freedom), the Denikinite Volunteer Army (White Guards), and the Social Democrats.

The badly divided but temporarily popular Russian Socialist Revolutionary (SR) Party was generally as vague and ineffective as its programme in its position on Ukraine and the claims of the other non-Russian nationalities. Although the SRs paid lip service to limited national self-determination, many were anti-federalist and favoured a centralized republic. Although they were willing to grant independence to Poland, they were adamant in opposing Finnish independence. At the Third SR Congress in July 1917, Mark Vishniak appeared to favour a broad federation and granting Ukraine separate coinage, its own postal system and national military units, but not the right to impose tariffs.[46] Yet the Congress, while approving Vishniak's theses "in general," is said to have reflected "an undercurrent of feeling indubitably hostile to the dissolution of the imperial entity."[47] The Russian SRs rejected demands for separate constituent assemblies for each non-Russian nationality and, instead, insisted on the authority of the All-Russian Constituent Assembly. Under the circumstances, the emergence of a separate Ukrainian Socialist Revolutionary Party was hardly surprising.

The Kadets (Constitutional Democrats) supposedly represented the "liberal" position, which could be defined as such only in comparison with that of the Russian Octobrists, who had opposed Ukrainian autonomy or any concessions favoring the development of Ukrainian culture or language equality. The Kadets were willing to permit the use of non-Russian languages in the elementary schools, favouring autonomy only for Poland, and constantly opposed federalism and advocated the "unity of the Russian State."[48] Although Professor Pavel Miliukov opposed the ban on the Shevchenko centenary observances in 1914, he also opposed Ukrainian autonomy (as well as Finnish independence) in 1917. When the Provisional Government recognized a very limited autonomy for Ukraine, six Kadet ministers resigned. When the Rada adopted the Third Universal, the Kadet member of the Mala Rada, S. Krupnov, resigned in protest.[49]

The most extreme "liberal" position on Ukraine was held by the Kadet Petr Struve, whose intolerant views were ultimately rejected even by the Kadet leadership. Struve, a former socialist of Baltic German origin, contended in 1911 that the existence of a separate Ukrainian culture was a threat to the emergence of an "all-Russian culture." He seriously contended that the multinational empire was actually a "national empire." In 1915 Struve visited Russian-occupied Galicia and advocated that it be Russified, but his view was rejected by the Kadet leadership. While denigrating Ukrainian culture, Struve unwittingly paid the Ukrainians a compliment in contending that the successful development of their culture would result in an "unprecedented schism of the Russian nation" and, implicitly, the demise of Russia as a great power.[50] Significantly, Struve along with the Kadets became a supporter of General Denikin and Baron Wrangel.

The so-called White Movement of Russian generals together with its Kadet advisors was hostile to the Ukrainian nation and to Ukrainian statehood. General Alekseev, the founder of the White Movement, in a letter dated 21 November 1917, expressed hostility toward the Rada, referring to it as an "intelligent, serious opponent, skillfully led and subsidized from outside [*sic*]" and advising that it be discredited.[51] General Anton Denikin, who assumed command of the Russian Volunteer Army, was the son of a Russian army captain and a Polish mother who apparently sought to prove his loyalty to

Russia by advocating its alleged unity and indivisibility.[52] Denikin rejected a federal solution and was supported in this by the various Kadet Party politicians who were attracted to him. He refused to have any dealings with General Skoropadsky's Hetmanate even after the latter advocated federation.

The Volunteer Army also refused to have any contacts with the Directory Government. Ukrainian leaders were depicted as "Austro-German agents" under the Rada, and the Directory was equated with the Bolsheviks.[53] As Denikin's prospects improved temporarily in April 1919, his programme called for territorial and not ethnic autonomy and proposed the division of Ukraine into three territorial units. Among Denikin's advisers was Vasilii V. Shulgin, a notorious anti-Semite, monarchist and Ukrainophobe: Shulgin told the French Colonel Freydenberg that as between the Directory, headed by Petliura, and the Bolsheviks, the latter were the "lesser evil."[54] Denikin's military successes were short-lived, and Ukraine contributed to his defeat in 1919. He insisted upon taking Kiev rather than concentrating all his forces on the taking of Moscow. In the areas of Eastern Ukraine occupied by Denikin's army, Ukrainian schools were closed and denied any public funds, and the Russian language was imposed: such policies led to widespread rebellion behind Denikin's lines. Whether prompted by cynicism, ignorance or bigotry, Denikin's anti-Ukrainian policies contributed significantly to his defeat.

Although the Russian "liberals" who gravitated to Denikin endorsed his policies, one of their number, the Provisional Government's ambassador to France, Vasilii A. Maklakov, advocated an understanding with the non-Russian nationalities, recognizing that the anti-Bolshevik White Movement could not succeed in isolation.[55] This advice was rejected even though Maklakov attempted to render it acceptable with the following argument: "The centralized structure was not the strength but the weakness of Russia: as soon as Russia is reborn—liberal and democratic and not tsarist—the non-Russian nationalities will comprehend the advantage of being united with her."[56]

The belief that the non-Russian peoples would inevitably be drawn to union with Russia, once the great Russian regeneration occurred, was not unique to Maklakov. The Russian Social Democrats held a similar view that the nationalities would lose interest in being separated from a socialist Russia. Thus the Ukrainian Revolution was seen as destructive of "class solidarity."

The Bolshevik view of the Ukrainian Revolution, as expressed by Lenin, underwent several changes. Initially Lenin defended the Central Rada in its disagreements with the Provisional Government. He also likened Ukraine to Finland, Poland and Norway—in terms of the latter's separation from Sweden. Once the Rada proclaimed the UNR and Ukraine's independence, Lenin adopted a hostile policy and declared war. The first Soviet invasion of Ukraine in January 1918 was openly hostile to everything Ukrainian: the language was regarded as "counter-revolutionary," bookstores and print shops were closed, and portraits of Shevchenko were trampled underfoot.[57] The Ukrainian Soviet government, which was established in Kharkiv, initially referred to itself as the UNR, although it was largely non-Ukrainian in composition. Its defeat and retreat to Moscow, where the Communist Party of Ukraine held its first congress in July 1918, posed the question of the relationship of Ukrainian communism to the Russian Communist Party. The fact that the ethnically Ukrainian Communists were in a minority meant that the Russian-dominated Katerynoslav faction (led by Emmanuil Kviring) demanded that the Communist Party of Ukraine be an integral part of the Russian Communist Party, which under the circumstances meant forfeiture of Ukrainian support.

The Russians who dominated the Communist Party leadership in Ukraine refused to reckon with Ukrainian nationalism or to learn the language, and this contributed to the second Soviet defeat in Ukraine (in 1919). Lenin's appointment of the unqualified Christian Rakovsky as the leading Soviet official in Ukraine was indicative of his ignorance of Ukrainian conditions. Lenin had been warned to abandon support of the Ukrainophobe Katerynoslav Group in the remarkable work written by Serhii Mazlakh and Vasyl Shakhrai, *Do khvyli,* which was published in Ukrainian in Saratov in 1919.[58] The authors of this forthright statement of Ukrainian national communism asked Lenin how his version of "self-determination" differed from that of Woodrow Wilson, who favoured the restoration of the "one and indivisible" Russian Empire. Lenin did not reply directly, but the second Bolshevik defeat in Ukraine did result in Lenin's "Letter to the Workers and Peasants of Ukraine" (28 December 1919), in which he stated that Ukrainian independence was recognized. However, Lenin also made the usual demand for an international alliance (*soiuz*) of workers and their international fraternity. While calling for "*voluntary* union of nations—a union that would not permit coercion of one nation by another," Lenin conceded that it would take time to overcome the lack of confidence in the Ukrainian-Russian relationship.[59]

Lenin was the sole Russian leader to at least pay lip service to Ukrainian independence and to recognize that Ukrainians, as an oppressed people, had legitimate grievances against the Russians. Yet his view of the relationship assumed that the Russian "proletariat" would undergo a quasi-miraculous metaphorphosis under Bolshevik tutelage, purging itself of Russian chauvinism and imperialism, and would become the bearer of liberation and a new internationalism. For Lenin the Entente Powers replaced Germany as the embodiment of imperialism. Yet he ignored, with respect to Russia, that most important test of imperial and colonial rule, namely the (Russian) belief that certain peoples must be "protected," are incapable of being left alone, cannot govern themselves and cannot be entrusted with determining what is in their own interest. Thus Lenin also apparently suffered from the presumptuousness of those Russians who believed that such allegedly independent peoples can only gain deliverance through union with Russia.

Three years after addressing the letter to the Ukrainian workers and peasants, Lenin was to express serious doubts regarding the expected changes that were to occur in the Russians whom he had armed with the new dispensation of Marxism-Leninism. In what can be regarded as his "testament" on the nationalities problem, Lenin at the end of December 1922 warned against "that truly Russian type, the Great Russian chauvinist, essentially a scoundrel and an oppressor, which is the typical Russian bureaucrat." He expressed concern that the Soviet regime was being taken over by "chauvinistic Great Russian riffraff (*shval*)." [60]

Thus a basic difference in perception by Ukrainians and Russians lay in the fact that the Russians were not seeking deliverance or independence from foreign rule, as Ukrainians were. Russians were not seeking the end of discrimination against their language and culture, as Ukrainians were. The Russian forces of restoration (and reaction) were unwilling to be content with an ethnic Russia. They were unwilling to permit Ukrainians to seek their own destiny and develop indigenous solutions to their problems. Unable to discard their old mind-set regarding Ukraine, Russians could not abandon their image of a "Russia" that was supposedly "one and indivisible" and, instead, retained old messianic pretensions, although in a new Soviet Marxist-Leninist form. In branding nationally conscious Ukrainians with what was regarded as a pejorative term, "Petliurite," many Russians sought to demean if not nullify the Ukrainian Revolution and grant only a species of token recognition and grudging acceptance of a separate Ukrainian nation in the form of the Ukrainian Soviet Socialist Republic.

Russians and Ukrainians misperceived each other's purpose at critical junctures. Ukrainians could not perceive themselves as entirely free agents and as shapers of their own destiny. Too many Ukrainians cultivated and cherished the illusion of a new Russia that could be trusted to respect Ukrainian rights. Too many Ukrainians failed to separate the national struggle from the socio-economic revolution and give the former priority.

The revolutionary period provided an opportunity for a basic reordering of the Ukrainian-Russian relationship. However, that opportunity was lost because of the misperceptions that characterized both sides. Instead of a basic change in the relationship, the Ukrainian-Russian contest of will was merely transferred to a different plane and assumed somewhat different forms, but the substance of the contest remained essentially unchanged.

The Russian attitude toward Ukraine and the lost opportunity served to confirm the significance of the basic thesis of a volume of essays published in 1907 by Mykhailo Hrushevsky and entitled *The Liberation of Russia and the Ukrainian Question*. In Hrushevsky's view, the future of Russia was related to and even dependent upon the resolution of the Ukrainian problem. In 1917–1920 the Russians had a choice but failed to take the opportunity of embarking upon a totally new and different course in their relations with the

Ukrainians. Russian reluctance to come to terms fully with the Ukrainian problem meant that the option of abandoning Russia's authoritarian and expansionist past was forfeited. This forfeiture was to leave a profound imprint on the subsequent development of Ukraine and Russia.

Notes

1. Oleksander Lototsky, *Storinky mynuloho* (Warsaw, 1934) 3: 270–71.

2. Ibid., 340–42.

3. The disagreement centred on the number of quasi-ministerial posts to be included in the General Secretariat and the number of Ukrainian provinces (*gubernii*) to be included in its jurisdiction. The Provisional Government opposed the establishment of such Ukrainian government departments as Supply, Post and Telegraph, Justice, Transport and Military Affairs and sought to limit the number of Ukrainian portfolios to nine. The Provisional Government was also unwilling to recognize the Rada's claim to the provinces of Kharkiv, Kherson, Tavriia, Katerynoslav and Bessarabia. On the deteriorating relationship between the Rada and the Russian Provisional Government see Wolodymyr Stojko, "Ukrainian National Aspirations and the Russian Provisional Government" in Taras Hunczak, ed., *The Ukraine, 1917–1921: A Study in Revolution* (Cambridge, Mass., 1977), 4–32 and Oleh S. Pidhainy, *The Formation of the Ukrainian Republic* (Toronto, 1966). See also John S. Reshetar, Jr., *The Ukrainian Revolution, 1917–1920: A Study in Nationalism* (Princeton, 1952), Chapter 2.

4. Borys Martos, "Pershyi Universal Ukrainskoi Tsentral'noi Rady", *Zoloti rokovyny: Do 50–richchia velykoi ukrainskoi natsionalnoi revoliutsii ta vidnovlennia ukrainskoi derzhavnosty* (Jersey City, 1967), 20–21.

5. Hunczak, 385. For the texts of all four Universals see the appendix in Hunczak, 382–95.

6. Ibid., 388.

7. Ibid., 395.

8. Volodymyr Vynnychenko, *Vidrodzhennia natsii* (Kiev and Vienna, 1920), 2: 188.

9. Ibid., 136.

10. Ibid., 3: 158–9.

11. Vynnychenko's view of the Russians is expressed in his diary and represents a curious combination of revolutionary idealism and the harsh reality of observed Russian conduct. Initially Vynnychenko was both attracted to and repelled by the Russian Bolsheviks. Occasionally he referred to Russia as *Katsapiia* and to "*katsap* communists" who were said to be prepared to sacrifice "world socialism" for their own imperialism. Nevertheless Vynnychenko and his wife journeyed to Moscow in May 1920 on a Czechoslovak diplomatic passport (under the assumed names of Josef and Natalie Simon). They were accompanied by the Czech social democrat Jaromir Nečas and by Vynnychenko's secretary, Oleksander Badan.

Vynnychenko's diary indicates that he had serious doubts regarding the "mission to Moscow" and saw it as a "road to Calvary." Much of the time in Moscow, between May and September 1920, Vynnychenko spent waiting. Although he held talks with Chicherin, Radek, Kamenev, Zinoviev and Trotsky, he was not received by either Lenin or Stalin. In Lenin's Moscow Vynnychenko sensed the dominance of the Russian "elemental force" (*stikhiia*) that rejected the idea of communism and genuine federation. When Chicherin was more interested in the disposition of the Donets Basin and the Kuban, it was evident to Vynnychenko that the concern was "for Russia, for *themselves* as a nation" and not for communism. By 11 June, less than three weeks after arriving in Moscow, Vynnychenko concluded that his journey was "absolutely unnecessary, idealistic, the journey of a sentimental youth, a gymnasium student" and that "nothing has changed, they [the Russians] have learned nothing." See Volodymyr Vynnychenko, *Shchodennyk, Tom I, 1911–1920* (Edmonton and New York, 1980), 287, 336, 412–13, 415, 430–32, 437–8. Vynnychenko's dislike and distrust of the Russian Bolsheviks was usually tempered by his contempt for the bourgeoisie and its hatred of the Bolsheviks. Thus he feared becoming an unwitting ally of the class enemy and this fear apparently made it impossible for him to reconcile the national and social revolutions in Ukraine.

12. Mykhailo Hrushevsky, "Ochyshchennia ohnem," in *Zoloti rokovyny*, 72.

13. Mykhailo Hrushevsky, "Kinets moskovskoi oriientatsii," *Zoloti rokovyny*, 74.

14. Ibid., 73–4. Hrushevsky's statements were originally published in 1918 in a volume entitled *Na porozi novoi Ukrainy, Hadky i mrii* and are also reprinted in *Vyvid prav Ukrainy*, ed. Bohdan Kravtsiv (Krawciw) (New York, 1964), 208–29.

15. Symon Petliura, *Statti, lysty, dokumenty* (New York, 1979), 2: 516.

16. Marvin Rintala, *Four Finns* (Berkeley and Los Angeles, 1969), 57.

17. Vynnychenko left the leadership twice—first early in 1918 and again early in 1919; in the former instance the Socialist Revolutionaries replaced the Social Democrats and in the latter instance he resigned because he was not acceptable to the Entente and questioned that orientation. Hrushevsky retired from active political life with the overthrow of the Rada; he took up residence in Vienna, where he founded the Ukrainian Free University and the Ukrainian Sociological Institute and also published the newspaper, *Boritesia, poborete*.

18. Iakiv Zozulia, ed., *Velyka Ukrainska Revoliutsiia, Kalendar istorychnykh podii* (New York, 1967), 37–8.

19. Ibid., 44. The Bolshevik force that succeeded in taking Kiev (with the aid of Russian elements within the city) consisted of approximately 6,000 troops. See Dmytro Doroshenko, *Istoriia Ukrainy, 1917–1923* (Uzhhorod, 1930; reprint edition, New York, 1954), 1: 284.

20. Vynnychenko, *Vidrodzhennia natsii*, 3: 140. Although this statement may have been calculated in view of Vynnychenko's efforts in the summer of 1920 to come to terms with the Russian Bolsheviks, it nevertheless reflects the extent of his commitment to Ukrainian national bolshevism.

21. Ibid., 3: 135–6, 141–2, 167–76. While residing in Austria in 1919 Vynnychenko was attacted to the Foreign Group of the Ukrainian Communist Party, which was

formed in Vienna in September 1919 and commenced publication of *Nova doba* in March 1920. Vynnychenko regarded the Ukrainian Directory as serving the interests of the Entente Powers and was of the opinion that Petliura should be opposed by a Ukrainian revolutionary leader and not by the foreign communist Christian Rakovsky, whom Lenin had placed at the head of the Ukrainian Soviet Republic. Rakovsky's presence, in Vynnychenko's view, transformed the social war into a national war, whereas Vynnychenko's presence in the Ukrainian Soviet government would supposedly have weakened the UNR and Petliura's forces, which he branded as "the Ukrainian counter-revolution." Vynnychenko believed that "If the revolution is victorious, the national cause will prevail. If reaction is victorious, the national cause will perish." This rationale behind Vynnychenko's unsuccessful journey to Moscow and Kharkiv in 1920 was based on his search for harmony between the national and social goals of the revolution and his fear of choosing between them. Yet Vynnychenko was also haunted by the fear that he might betray the Ukrainian nation and that in joining the Russian Bolsheviks he would "strangle with one's own hands one's nation and oneself," while if he joined the Directory and Petliura he would be "strangling the revolution . . . and that which I regard as good for all humankind." While in Moscow Vynnychenko was apparently offered the post of deputy head of the Soviet Ukrainian Council of Commissars; Trotsky also offered him the military commissariat, but it was clear that this was to be a figurehead post, as there was not to be any separate Ukrainian army. Vynnychenko states that his demand for a seat on the Politburo was refused. Thus he concluded that he was being offered a purely "decorative" role and that if he were prepared to join the Russians in what they were doing in Ukraine they would not question his credentials as a communist. He concluded that in order to be in Ukraine, on the terms offered him in Moscow, he would have to cease being a Ukrainian.

Vynnychenko sought from Moscow an end to "maltreatment and mockery" in Ukraine, state independence for Ukraine, an independent and truly Ukrainian government, use of the Ukrainian language in all institutions and schools, and an independent Ukrainian army. Yet he also advocated a "military and economic alliance" and the "closest mutual aid" and a (joint?) struggle for Galicia. Vynnychenko objected to Ukraine's being denied separate membership in the Comintern. He was disturbed by what he regarded as Soviet "lies, hypocrisy and deception." On his second visit to Kharkiv, in August 1920, he noted that the *Ukapisty* (Ukrainian Communist Party members) were being "terrorized by the russificators" and that even if he were to accept Moscow's unattractive terms "one cannot be certain that some Russian Black-Hundred [reactionary] who now calls himself a communist will not denounce you [to the authorities] and that you will not find yourself in the hands of the Cheka [the security police] or somewhere more distant." While in Kharkiv, Vynnychenko sensed that Soviet rule in Ukraine was an occupation regime based on "the ration, punishment and shooting" and was depressed by the general fatigue and apathy of the population. He noted that "Communist Moscow's" rule reflected "the old Russian national trait of hypocrisy, brutality, unpardonable coercion, the old habit of belief in the providential role of Russia . . ." Vynnychenko could not accept Dmytro Manuilsky's repeated assurances that the Communist Party of Ukraine was committed to Ukrainization; he regarded his remaining in Ukraine as a "Golgotha"—a road to Calvary. Vynnychenko left Soviet Russia on 23 September 1920, bound for European exile, disillusioned with the Russian betrayal of the revolution but still guided by what he regarded as the "highest law": "to be of value to others and to be true to yourself." See Volodymyr Vynnychenko, *Shchodennyk,* 1: 396–7, 409, 432–4, 438, 441, 445, 454–5, 464, 467–8, 475, 479, 481.

Vynnychenko's bargaining position in Moscow was undoubtedly weakened as a result of the Soviet military successes in Ukraine in the summer of 1920. If Petliura's and Pilsudski's forces had been able to retain control of Kiev in June 1920 it is possible that Vynnychenko's position in the negotiations with the Russian Bolsheviks would have been strengthened.

For a critical appraisal of Vynnychenko's views as utopian and naive see Ivan L. Rudnytsky, "Volodymyr Vynnychenko's Ideas in the Light of His Political Writings," *Essays in Modern Ukrainian History,* ed. Peter L. Rudnytsky (Edmonton, 1987), 417–36.

22. Vynnychenko opposed "priests, *Te Deums,* church bells with all the Petliurite accessories." *Vidrodzhennia natsii,* 3: 166–7. Cf. Petliura, *Statti, lysty, dokumenty,* 1: 400–03.

23. Lototsky, 3: 325.

24. Ibid. For a more detailed discussion of the origins and differences between the various Ukrainian political parties see Jurij Borys, *The Sovietization of Ukraine, 1917–1923,* revised edition (Edmonton, 1980), Chapter 3.

25. For an analysis of the results of the Constituent Assembly elections in Ukraine see Steven L. Guthier, "The Popular Base of Ukrainian Nationalism in 1917," *Slavic Review* 38 (March 1979): 30–47.

26. On the role of peasant rebellion in the Ukrainian Revolution see Arthur E. Adams, "The Great Ukrainian Jacquerie," in Hunczak, *The Ukraine, 1917–1921,* 247–70 and the chapter on Nestor Makhno by Frank Sysyn in the same volume. See also Michael Palij, *The Anarchism of Nestor Makhno, 1918–1921: An Aspect of the Ukrainian Revolution* (Seattle, 1976).

27. Lonhyn Tsehelsky, *Vid legend do pravdy* (New York, 1960), 76–7 and 80–82.

28. Ibid., 91, 123–4, 132–9 and 154–61.

29. See Imperatorskaia Akademiia Nauk, *Ob otmene stesnenii malorusskago pechatnogo slova* (St. Petersburg, 1905); see also *Peterburska Akademiia Nauk v spravi znesenia zaborony ukrainskoho slova* (Lviv, 1905).

30. Lototsky, 3: 104 and 292.

31. The Russian antipathy to Shevchenko was expressed by the literary critic Vissarion Belinsky, who regarded the Ukrainian languge as doomed and unworthy of literature. See Victor Swoboda, "Shevchenko and Belinsky" in George S. N. Luckyj, ed., *Shevchenko and the Critics, 1861–1980* (Toronto, 1980), 303–23. Cf. Mykola Hudzii's contribution to the same volume.

32. Lototsky, 3: 121–2.

33. Robert P. Browder and Alexander F. Kerensky, eds., *The Russian Provisional*

Government, 1917 (Stanford, 1961), 1: 344–5, 351–2; cf. 319–21.

34. Ibid., 1: 376–7, 385–6 and 396.

35. Ibid., 1: 401. Elections to the Ukrainian Constituent Assembly were not authorized until 16 (29) November 1917. It was to have 301 members and elections were not held until 9 January 1918, when 171 members were elected in parts of Ukraine not occupied by the Bolsheviks. See Zozulia, 36 and 45. Vynnychenko claimed that the Provisional Government was planning to arrest the members of the Rada's delegation that went to Petrograd. See Vynnychenko, *Vidrodzhennia natsii*, 2: 59–60. See also Doroshenko, 157.

36. Lototsky, 3: 220–21.

37. See N. Polonska-Vasylenko, *Istorychni pidvalyny Ukrainskoi Avtokefalnoi Pravoslavnoi Tserkvy* (Munich, 1964), as well as her article "Osoblyvosti Ukrainskoi Pravoslavnoi Tserkvy" in *Ukrainskyi zbirnyk* 14 (Munich, 1958), 59–95.

38. "Malorosiistvo" in *Entsyklopediia ukrainoznavstva, Slovnykova chastyna*, 4: 1451.

39. Lototsky, 3: 271.

40. Ibid., 189–90.

41. See Lubomyr Wynar, *Mykhailo Hrushevsky i Naukove Tovararystvo im. Tarasa Shevchenka* (Munich, 1970).

42. On the Union for the Liberation of Ukraine see Oleh S. Fedyshyn, *Germany's Drive to the East and the Ukrainian Revolution, 1917–1918* (New Brunswick, N.J., 1971), 30–48, as well as his chapter, "The Germans and the Union for the Liberation of the Ukraine, 1914–1917," in Hunczak, 305–22.

43. On German aid to the Bolsheviks, see Z.A.B. Zeman, ed., *Germany and the Revolution in Russia, 1915–1918: Documents from the Archives of the German Foreign Ministry* (London and New York, 1958). Evidence in the Austrian State Archives indicates that initially the Union for the Liberation of Ukraine did channel some funds to Lenin; see Stefan T. Possony, *Lenin: The Compulsive Revolutionary* (Chicago, 1964), 169–70.

44. Lototsky, 3: 277–9.

45. Pavlo Khrystiuk, *Zamitky i materiialy do istorii ukrainskoi revoliutsii, 1917–1920* (Vienna, 1921), 2: 21–3 and Doroshenko, 153–4.

46. Oliver H. Radkey, *The Agrarian Foes of Bolshevism* (New York, 1958), 216–17.

47. Ibid., 219.

48. Browder and Kerensky, 317.

49. Zozulia, 35.

50. See Richard Pipes, *Struve, Liberal on the Right, 1905–1944* (Cambridge, 1980), 210–19, especially 211 and 213. On the inflexibility and lack of realism of Kadet policies, see William G. Rosenberg, *Liberals in the Russian Revolution: The Constitutional Democratic Party, 1917–1921* (Princeton, 1974).

51. Anna Procyk, "Nationality Policy of the White Movement: Relations between the Volunteer Army and the Ukraine" (Ph.D. dissertation, Department of History, Columbia University, 1973), 43. It should be noted that some of the Russian

generals adopted a more realistic position. Thus General Dukhonin, the Russian Supreme Commander, recognized the Rada on 9 (11) November 1917, but was murdered at Staff Headquarters on the following day. See Zozulia, 35. General Kornilov in his proposed political programme in early 1918 equated Ukraine with Poland and Finland and stated that their "strivings toward state regeneration" should be supported. Miliukov opposed this position. (Procyk, 54).

52. Procyk, 90 and 95–6.

53. Ibid., 226–7 and 235.

54. Ibid., 211–14. It is revealing that in his final years Shulgin took up residence in Soviet Russia, where the authorities published his views in what was apparently an affront to Ukrainians and Jews.

55. Ibid., 180–93.

56. Ibid., 188–9. This statement is from a letter to V. A. Stepanov, dated 30 April 1919, in the Wrangel Military Archives at the Hoover Institution.

57. Vynnychenko, *Vidrodzhennia natsii*, 2: 271–2.

58. See Serhii Mazlakh and Vasyl Shakhrai, *On the Current Situation in the Ukraine*, ed. Peter J. Potichnyj (Ann Arbor, 1970), Chapter 20. On the failure of the second Bolshevik invasion of Ukraine see Arthur E. Adams, *Bolsheviks in the Ukraine: The Second Campaign, 1918–1919* (New Haven, 1963).

59. V. I. Lenin, *Polnoe sobranie sochinenii*, 5th ed. (Moscow, 1963), 40: 42–4. The Eighth Conference of the All-Russian Communist Party (of Bolsheviks) in early December 1919 approved a Central Committee resolution of 29 November 1919 "Concerning Soviet Power in Ukraine" which supposedly recognized Ukrainian independence but defined the relationship between the Ukrainian and Russian republics as a "federal" relationship. It supposedly committed the Russian Party to "eliminate all barriers to the free development of the Ukrainian language and culture" and to "transform the Ukrainian language into an instrument of communist enlightenment of the toiling masses." See *KPSS v rezoliutsiiakh i resheniiakh sezdov, konferentsii i plenumov TsK,* 8th ed. (Moscow, 1979), 2: 124–6. Vynnychenko's "mission to Moscow" in 1920 was designed to determine the exact meaning of these professed commitments and whether this resolution or the old "one and indivisible" Russia was the policy of Lenin's Central Committee. However, Vynnychenko suspected that the idea of communism and a "federation of equal and independent [sic] members" was unacceptable to the Russian *stikhiia*. Vynnychenko, *Shchodennyk, Tom I, 1911–1920*, 435.

60. Lenin, 45: 357.

Yaroslav Bilinsky

Political Relations between Russians and Ukrainians in the USSR: The 1970s and Beyond

To the memory of ANATOLY P. BEKLEMISHEV (1890–1959):
Scion of an old Russian family, citizen of Kiev, patriot of Ukraine.

Political relations between Russians and Ukrainians reach back into the Middle Ages, and, as every schoolboy in Ukraine knows, they have been rather close in the last 327 years* except in the case of one region, the relatively smaller Western Ukraine. To be linked with another people for eleven generations is a serious matter. My intuition tells me, however, that the twelfth generation since the Treaty of Pereiaslav, i.e., the Ukrainians living from about 1981 to 2010, may well turn out the decisive one: it will determine the *modus vivendi* with the Russians for a great many years, possibly forever. The question for the two peoples is whether the traditional close, actually stifling relationship is to be continued or whether it can be replaced with one that is more free, more like that between equal nations and states. I believe it would be a great mistake to assume that the problem concerns only the smaller nation— the 42.3 million Ukrainians compared with the 137.4 million Russians.[1] The further development of the Russians as a free people hinges on their abandonment of a totalitarian empire, and since Ukraine is by far the most populous and richest non-Russian republic,[2] the growth of the Russian nation will be determined by its finding a solution to the Ukrainian question.

After a brief survey of official policies this article will concentrate on the relations between Russian and Ukrainian dissenters. In the third part, I shall ask some political questions which are very important for the two peoples in the long run, whether or not they have already been raised in the dissident literature.

---

* In his article for this volume, "The Unloved Alliance: Political Relations between Muscovy and Ukraine during the Seventeenth Century," Hans-Joachim Torke brings out that **effective** political union between Ukraine and Muscovy was not established immediately in 1654. For the sake of convenience I shall use that date, however, pleading the liberty of a non-historian.

Official Policy

Soviet nationality policy in the last decade has been one of aggressive denationalizing, with a heavy emphasis on the predominance of the Russians and with a notable lack of candor. For a relatively clear statement of Leonid Brezhnev's approach we have to go back to his keynote address at the celebration of the fiftieth anniversary of the establishment of the Soviet Union on 21 December 1972.

Brezhnev asserted at the ceremony that the nationality question in the USSR, which had been inherited from the Russian monarchy, "had been solved completely, definitely and irrevocably."[3] He warmly praised the Russian people for making "huge efforts and, to put it plainly, sacrifices" to help overcome the backwardness of the "national," non-Russian periphery (*natsionalnykh okrain*).[4] Brezhnev had been even more outspoken in his praise "of the great Russian people, above all," when at the 24th Party Congress in 1971 he had said:

> Its revolutionary energy, selflessness, diligence, and profound inter- nationalism have rightly brought it the sincere respect of all the peoples of our Socialist Fatherland.[5]

At the anniversary celebration almost two years later Brezhnev was genuinely pleased with the increased significance of Russian: it had become the language of mutual communication of all the nations and ethnic groups of the Soviet Union and had, moreover, emerged as a universally recognized world language. [6] In the USSR there had become "firmly established, had become a true reality (*realnoi deistvitelnostiu*) *a new historical community of men—the Soviet people (sovetskii narod)*." [Emphasis in original.][7] He warned the non-Russian nationalities:

> The further rapprochement of nations and ethnic groups of our country constitutes an objective process. The Party is against the artificial forcing of [this process]—there is no need for this whatsoever, this process is being dictated by the entire course of our Soviet life. At the same time the Party considers inadmissible any efforts whatsoever to delay the process of the rapprochement of nations, to create obstacles to it under this or that pretext, artificially to reinforce national isolation, for this would contradict the general direction of the development of our community, the internationalist ideas and ideology of the communists, the interests of the building of communism.[8]

There is more to Brezhnev's almost lyrical references to the Russian and the new Soviet people than meets the eye. First of all, without any explanation whatever, the 1972 celebration was held not on the true date (30 December) but on Stalin's birthday. Stalin was discreetly praised as one of the noteworthy Party leaders (*vidnye deiateli partii*) who had, under Lenin's leadership, to be sure, participated in the development of Soviet nationality policy: Stalin's name was inserted after those of M. I. Kalinin, F. E. Dzerzhinsky and

Ia. M. Sverdlov. But Stalin's name was omitted when Brezhnev quickly glossed over Lenin's critique of the mistaken view of some comrades with respect to "autonomization" (in truth, Stalin had been the champion of those views).[9] Brezhnev's speech of 21 December 1972 thus had not only a distinctly pro-Russian but also a transparently pro-Stalinist hue. Secondly, by and large, the First Secretaries of the non-Russian republics did *not* support the assimilationist idea of the "new historical community, the Soviet people."[10]

At the 26th Party Congress in February-March 1981, Brezhnev repeated many of his themes of 1972, but in somewhat muted form. No longer did he boldly claim that the nationality problem had been solved. After two positive assertions—

Without faltering (*neuklonno*) there has been strengthened the fraternal friendship of all the peoples of our multinational Fatherland.

Today the unity of the Soviet nations is solid as it never has been before. [*Continuing applause.*] [Emphasis in original.][11]

Brezhnev admitted:

This does not mean, of course, that all questions in the sphere of nationality relations have already been solved.[12]

Seemingly with an even hand Brezhnev denounced both [Russian] "chauvinism" and [non-Russian] "nationalism," both "anti-Semitism [and] Zionism." His reference to the Soviet people in 1981 was also much less strident than in 1972.[13]

Between Brezhnev's aggressive keynote speech at the fiftieth anniversary of the establishment of the USSR and his almost subdued statement to the 26th Party Congress there have been the adoption of the new Soviet Constitution in 1977 and the decision, in late 1978 and early 1979, to press for an especially intensive Russification of the non-Russian peoples. The 1977 Constitution did not abolish the Union Republics, nor did it deprive them of the formal right of secession. But apart from those two concessions to the sentiments of the non-Russian peoples it was a move backward. It provided for a more centralized government, and on closer legal analysis its paragraphs appear more compatible with the outright abolition of the Union Republics than even with traditional Soviet pseudo-federalism.[14]

The intensive Russification policy of 1978–9 was carried out in two stages. In the first stage, the USSR Council of Ministers on 13 October 1978 passed a still unpublished decree "Concerning Measures for the Further Improvement of the Study and Teaching of Russian in the Union Republics." Essentially, the decree appears to have called for starting the teaching of Russian from the *first* semester of the *first* grade in non-Russian elementary schools. For whatever reason, this decree has been surrounded with extraordinary secrecy. According to a private communication received by a Baltic-American scholar, the decree was apparently delivered to Republic educational officials by special couriers, to be read and memorized in a special room, without making written notes; the copy of the original decree was then returned to the courier. In their turn, the Republic Communist Party Central Committee Bureaus issued detailed confidential decrees on implementation.[15] If this be true—and I have no reason to doubt the veracity of my sources—this would make Russian the first *lingua franca* of a multinational state to be introduced in the stealth of night, by secret courier!

The Tashkent Conference of 22–4 May 1979 basically called upon the appropriate authorities to intensify the teaching of Russian at the *kindergarten* level, in elementary and secondary schools, in vocational schools and in institutions of higher learning. To that end, more and better teachers of Russian were to be trained in a great hurry. Similar efforts were made to keep the advance draft recommendations of the Tashkent Conference, which had been circulated to republic officials in March 1979, secret from the people, but those efforts failed.[16]

I would regard the Soviet nationality policy of the 1970s as lacking in candor for the following main reason. Given the upsurge of Russian nationalism in the Soviet Union, given the top priority officially accorded to the development of the resources of the RSFSR (the rich West Siberian oilfields, but also the poor non-black-soil zone in northern and central Russia), given the ever–increasing animosity between the Russians and other Slavs on the one hand and Soviet citizens from Central Asia and Transcaucasia on the other—I find it hard to believe that the present leaders of the Soviet Union are really serious about creating a single Soviet people out of some hundred nationalities in the long run and, in the short and intermediate run, teaching every single Uzbek village boy and girl fluent Russian. The "growing together of all Soviet peoples" may really be an ideologically acceptable smokescreen for a more limited operative policy with two variants. The maximal variant would be the linguistic and eventual identificational assimilation of the peoples in the European part of the USSR: the Belorussians and the Ukrainians, the three Baltic peoples, the Moldavians, and assorted other peoples such as the Mordvinians. The minimal operative variant, however, would be to completely assimilate the Belorussians and the Ukrainians, creating in the process a kind of East Slavic empire.[17]

Linguistic, though not indentificational, assimilation has proceeded rather far in Belorussia.[18] It is certainly not a secret that linguistic Russification also presents a danger to the more numerous Ukrainians, though not to the same degree as for Belorussians.[19] This is not the place to go into operative details, however.

Let me conclude this quick survey of official policies by suggesting that a more candid—but also less politic—summary of recent Soviet nationality policy would read: We say that we want to form a single Soviet people composed of all fraternal Soviet nations, but we really mean that we want the Russians to be on top of a thoroughly Russified East Slavic trinity—the Russians, the Belorussians and the Ukrainians—and we will also be satisfied with a larger unit, including the Estonians, Latvians and Lithuanians; the Moldavians; and also some of the "internal" (i.e., "republic-locked") non-European peoples of the RSFSR.

Russian Dissenters and the Ukrainian Question

Taking my cue from the late Andrei Amalrik's "wheel of ideologies," I would like to start my survey with liberal Marxism.[20] Neither the late Russian writer Aleksei Kosterin nor the late Major-General Petro Hryhorenko [Petr Grigorenko] in his first period of dissent (roughly from 1961 to 1976), both genuine Marxist–Leninists, said anything on the Ukrainian question directly. Judging, however, from their sympathetic attitude toward the plight of the Crimean Tatars,[21] it could be assumed that their feelings toward the autonomist or perhaps even separatist Ukrainians would have been equally sensitive. Hryhorenko, who was, of course, an ethnic Ukrainian, became a leading charter member of the Ukrainian Helsinki Group in 1976 and gradually evolved into a moderate Ukrainian nationalist.

Another publicist who is frequently cited among the liberal Marxist dissenters is the historian Roy A. Medvedev.[22] One bona fide defender of Soviet human rights, in a conversation with this writer, indignantly questioned Roy Medvedev's dissident status. He pictured Medvedev as a hidden conformist, with good access to Western media and enjoying—for a Soviet dissident—the very best of duplicating facilities. This may be a somewhat negative view of the brother of the genuine, expelled dissident Zhores Medvedev. At most, Roy Medvedev has tried to play the role of a very cautious, very responsible critic of the regime, so cautious, in fact, that he is known to have shown his writings to Soviet officials before circulating them in *samizdat*.[23]

The nationality question does not apparently play a major part in the voluminous writings of Roy Medvedev, unlike in the work of Kosterin and Hryhorenko. To the extent, however, that Medvedev's position on the Ukrainian question can be ascertained it appears, on balance, hostile. On the whole, Medvedev endorses the allegedly natural linguistic and identificational assimilation of Ukrainians to Russians, which sometimes—not very precisely—has been dubbed Russification. According to Medvedev, Ukrainians in Ukraine should be allowed to maintain their culture, but upon leaving the boundaries of the Ukrainian SSR they should be assimilated to Russians. For example, he specifically opposes the demand made by Ivan Dziuba[24] that Ukrainians outside Ukraine should be taught in Ukrainian.[25] Medvedev accepts as "progressive"[26] or, at least, "inevitable"[27] and hence morally unobjectionable the mixing of

nationalities and the consequent linguistic-cultural Russification. In his book
On Socialist Democracy, for example, he writes:

> Certain demographic processes have ... made national problems more acute ...
> In certain regions and cities of the Ukraine, Ukrainians have become a
> minority.[28]
>
> One cannot ignore the process of *natural* Russification taking place in many
> republics, particularly with regard to language (and often the culture as a
> whole) ... In Kiev today, there are just a few Ukrainian schools left, and they
> have been able to maintain their enrollment only by introducing English [!] as the
> medium of instruction in several subjects.[29]

Medvedev would also like questions about nationality to be eliminated from
Soviet personnel questionnaires and from internal passports in order to facilitate
identificational assimilation to the Russians.[30] Later Medvedev criticizes
Solzhenitsyn's Russian nationalism and isolationism, but then states: " ... it is a
fact that the national life of Russians is hampered to a far greater degree than
that of, say, Armenians, Georgians, and the Uzbek peoples." He immediately
continues: "Thus, for example, the villages and hamlets of basically Russian
districts are in an immeasurably more neglected condition than the villages of
Ukraine, Moldavia, the Transcaucasus and the Baltic." [Emphasis added][31]

Medvedev's territorial ideal is the status quo. He says: "All of the USSR's
republics must take part in the development of Siberia's riches and use them in
their own economies."[32] As if to deliberately becloud the issue of national self-
determination, in his treatise *On Socialist Democracy* Medvedev offers the
ingenious proposal of *compulsory periodic* referenda on secession. He writes:

> The best way to guarantee this right [of secession] would be to institute a
> compulsory referendum in every republic at least once every ten years. Obviously
> this presupposes absolutely free discussion of all national problems, as well as the
> inevitable appearance of groups and movements in favour of secession. The
> referendum should be conducted by secret ballot under the supervision of special
> commissions composed of representatives from the other Union Republics. The
> Supreme Soviet of each Union Republic should also have the right to hold a
> referendum in exceptional circumstances before the expiration of ten years, but
> not within one year of the next regularly scheduled referendum. Certainly a vast
> majority in all the Union Republics would vote to remain in the USSR. But if a
> republic were to secede, there should be a further compulsory referendum after
> ten years on the question of whether or not to rejoin the Union. It could be held
> earlier if the population demanded it.[33]

Given the long history of political pressures to maintain and strengthen the
USSR, Medvedev's proposals appear to have been designed to help advocates
of the pseudo-federal, *de-facto* unitary status quo (note, in particular, the
provision for a compulsory follow-up referendum on "whether or not to rejoin
the Union").

The most important personality in the liberal–democratic centre is indubitably Academician Andrei D. Sakharov. Unlike those of Roy Medvedev, Sakharov's views on the nationality question have undergone several changes. In his 10,000–word treatise on *Progress, Coexistence, and Intellectual Freedom* of June 1968 we find passing references to Stalinist and current anti-Semitism, to the disgraceful treatment of the Crimean Tatars, but also to Stalin's Ukrainophobia.[34] This shows that from the beginning Sakharov has been sensitive to violations of human rights of members of different non-Russian nationalities, Ukrainians included. At the same time it would appear that at first Sakharov did not think that the Ukrainian problem, for instance, was sufficiently important to merit analysis. In his first appeal to Brezhnev and other Soviet leaders of 19 March 1970, which was co-signed by physicist Valentin F. Turchin and by Roy Medvedev, Sakharov explicitly demanded the restoration of all rights to nations that had been forcibly resettled by Stalin. Interestingly enough, possibly under the influence of Roy Medvedev, he also called for the abolition of the registration of nationality in internal passports and for the deletion of the question pertaining to nationality from personnel questionnaires.[35]

It is not until 1971–2 that Sakhararov raises the question of nationality more systematically, that he truly grapples with it. In his memorandum of 5 March 1971 he writes: "One must point out the increasingly acute nationalities problem." (In his postscript of June 1972 he even accuses the Soviet government of a "deliberate aggravation of nationalities problems.")[36] Besides calling for the repatriation of the Tatars and for allowing the emigration of Jews ("urgent problem" no. 3) and besides protesting against national discrimination in the allotment of jobs, Sakharov makes an interesting new suggestion that the right of secession of the non-Russian Union Republics be legally clarified and that citizens not be prosecuted for raising that problem, but that open discussion of the issue be allowed. He writes:

> In my opinion, a juridical settlement of the problem and the passing of a law guaranteeing the right to secession would be of great internal and international significance as a confirmation of the anti-imperialist and anti-chauvinist nature of our policies. *The number of republics tending toward secession is, to all appearances, very small, and these tendencies would doubtless become even weaker with time as a result of the future democratization of the USSR.* [Emphasis added][37]

He also assures his readers that even if any republic seceded peacefully from the USSR it "would maintain intact its ties with the socialist commonwealth of nations."[38]

Implicitly, Sakharov shows a certain coolness toward the prospect of secession. He evidently hopes that the "future democratization of the USSR" would obviate the need for such a break-up of the Soviet empire. At the same

time it should be stressed that Sakharov would emphatically defend the human
rights of non-Russians who were being unjustly persecuted by the regime, even
if the victims did not share Sakharov's liberal-democratic, centrist views. For
instance, repeatedly Sakharov defended the Ukrainian nationalist Valentyn
Moroz, who stood somewhat right of centre.[39]

More recently, writing from exile, Sakharov expressed his profound distrust
of nationalism, even in its mildest, "dissident" form. He wrote on 4 May 1980
that the idea of national superiority was the third "simple-minded idea" of "the
ideology of the Soviet bourgeois," which he considered "rather typical, alas, of
workers and peasants and wide [circles of the] intelligentsia as well." He
continued:

> [That idea] assumes heavy, hysterical and "pogromist" forms in some Russians,
> but not only among them. How often we happen to (*prikhoditsia*) hear: we are
> spending [our resources] on those black (or yellow) apes, keep feeding those
> drones. Or: it is all the fault of those Jews (or Russians, Georgians, *chuchmeki*—
> i.e., inhabitants of Central Asia). Those are very frightening symptoms after 60
> years of the declared "friendship of peoples." Officially, the Communist ideology
> is an internationalist one, but quietly [the regime] is manipulating nationalist
> prejudices (at first, with some caution, and I hope that those forces will never be
> untied—as if after class hatred we were in need of a racial one!). I have become
> convinced that nationalist ideology is dangerous and destructive even in—at first
> sight—its most humane dissident forms.[40]

Does Sakharov's outburst against Russian and non-Russian nationalisms
even in their "most humane dissident forms" mean a deliberate revision of his
1971 demands to put the secession provisions of the Soviet constitution to a
test? I do not know—it may just be an emotional reaction of a great man
embittered by undeserved exile and the harassment of his family. In any case,
actions speak louder than words. History will not forget the smooth and effective co-operation between the Ukrainian Helsinki Group and the older Moscow
Helsinki Group, which latter strongly overlapped with the Sakharov circle.

Sakharov was offered the chairmanship of the Moscow Public Group to
Further the Implementation of the Helsinki Accords by its de-facto organizer,
Iurii Orlov, but he declined. Nevertheless, Sakharov's wife—Elena Bonner
—did formally join the group, and Sakharov himself "approved its establishment and helped it as much as he could."[41] Among the charter members of the
Moscow Group was also the Ukrainian Major–General Petro Hryhorenko. The
formation of the Moscow Helsinki Group was publicly announced on 12 May
1976.

Half a year later, on 9 November 1976, a Ukrainian Helsinki Group was set
up in Kiev. Its head was the writer, poet, and former high Party official Mykola
Rudenko. Why was the Ukrainian Group formed at all? The Moscow Group
was certainly not insensitive to the plight of the Ukrainian dissidents. Far from
it—its memoranda widely publicized the persecution of Ukrainians.[42] The

Moscow Group was also generous in supplying its Ukrainian fellow-dissidents with technical facilities. In the words of Lyudmilla Alexeyeva, who served as unofficial secretary and assistant to Orlov in the first eight months: "At first the Ukrainian and Lithuanian Helsinki Groups relied on the assistance of the Moscow Group, which introduced them through foreign correspondents to the public abroad."[43] A Ukrainian-American sympathizer confirmed this, but also emphasized that eventually the Ukrainian Group established its own direct contacts abroad. It is best to let Rudenko himself answer the question why he established the Group, for which he, an invalid since World War II, was eventually sentenced to seven years' labour camp plus five years' exile:

> It is incorrect [to say] that our Group is a section of the one in Moscow. We collaborate with the Muscovites; they are actively supporting us, for they are genuine democrats. But from the [very] beginning we have decided not to enter into a relationship of *subordination*, because we have that which is not understood by every Russian. [Emphasis added][44]

What were the Ukrainians to struggle for by themselves? We can assume that the Ukrainian cultural renaissance or, to put it negatively, resistance to the Russification of schools of all kinds, of the press and of book publishing, was best carried out by the Ukrainians.[45] Secondly, only Ukrainians could fully appreciate the shock felt at their republic's exclusion from participation in the Helsinki Conference and from the signing of the Helsinki Final Act, while a number of European mini- and micro-states such as Liechtenstein and San Marino were fully represented.[46] In general, it would seem that discussions about Ukrainian political self-determination, about the exact present and future political status of Ukraine might eventually have led to differences of opinion had the Ukrainian dissidents tried to work within the Moscow Helsinki Group exclusively and had they not set up a group of their own almost from the beginning.

Acting within the Soviet constitution and according to their interpretation of the Helsinki Accords, the members of the Moscow Group did not formally even touch upon the sensitive question of an eventual secession of individual republics—the suppression of individual and of some group rights (the rights of believers, the right of citizens to emigrate, and the right of Crimean Tatars to repatriation) was deemed controversial enough. It also seems that the existence of independent but less experienced national Helsinki Groups served the better–established Moscow Group as a kind of buffer against the authorities: any unreasonably radical statement originating in Kiev or in Tiflis could be plausibly disowned. On the other hand, it would also appear that informally members of the Moscow Group—with the obvious exception of General Hryhorenko—tended to be less positive and more reserved on the question of eventual independence for Ukraine than on the question of the independence of Lithuania and the other two Baltic countries. It appears to one student that in the Moscow Group it was tacitly taken for granted that the Balts would opt out of the USSR at the very first opportunity, whereas one could not be so sure about the Ukrainians. One tended, therefore, to evade the problem by saying that it was one to be solved by the Ukrainians themselves. This ambivalence about the political future of Ukraine within the majority of the Moscow Group was another good reason for establishing a separate Helsinki Group in Kiev.[47]

Lyudmilla Alexeyeva has explained the attitude of the Moscow Helsinki Group to Ukrainian political aspirations as follows:

> The Moscow Helsinki Group, being an organization engaged in the defence of rights, unconditionally defends the constitutional right of every Union republic to determine what its status as a state should be, and Ukraine, obviously, is no exception. We have defended and will continue to defend the right of everyone to express himself and act in accordance with those constitutional guarantees. Not being a political organization, the Moscow Helsinki Group did not express an opinion, nor should it have, either for or against Ukraine's secession, and not only Ukraine's but that of any one of the Union republics as well. We feel that the determination of the statehood status of any given republic is the sovereign right of its people. Ukrainians and only Ukrainians, and no one else, should decide the fate of Ukraine. We feel that interference from Moscow in resolving that problem—not only on the government level but on the public level as well—would be tactless.[48]

In my judgment at least, this does not refute our finding about the ambivalence that a majority of the Moscow Group had about the possibility of an independent Ukraine.

But as in the case of Academician Sakharov, reservations about the political future of Ukraine did not prevent the Moscow Helsinki Group as a whole or its individual members from vigorously defending Ukrainian activists who were being persecuted by the regime, irrespective of their ideologies. Thus, for instance, on 14 September 1979 the Moscow Group issued, over the signatures of Elena Bonner, Sofia Kalistratova, Malva Landa, Viktor Nekipelov, Tatiana Osipova, and Iurii Iarym-Agaev, its Document no. 102 entitled "The Events in Ukraine: Criminal Terror [Unleashed] Against the Human Rights Movement (*pravozashchitnogo dvizheniia*)." Comparing the present repressions with the arrests of young Ukrainian intellectuals in 1965 and 1972, the document reads:

> It seems as if the year 1979–80 is turning into the very same squall of total repression. It appears that the authorities have set themselves the goal of total suppression of *national* and legal free thinking (*svobodomysliia*) in Ukraine. [Emphasis added][49]

In November 1979 the indefatigable Malva Landa fired off as many as three protests defending three Ukrainian dissenters: Halyna Tomivna Didyk, Iurii Badzio, and Mykola Horbal.[50] Whereas Badzio and Horbal belong to the new liberal generation of dissenters, the late Ms. Didyk (then sixty-seven years old) had been a high officer of the Ukrainian Insurgent Army (UPA), which had once been linked to the extreme nationalist Organization of Ukrainian Nationalists (OUN). Since their human rights were being attacked, Landa came to the defence of all of them, without regard to ideology, as Sakharov had once defended Valentyn Moroz.

To sum up, co-operation between the Moscow and the Ukrainian Helsinki Groups was limited. The main reason for this was that the regime promptly arrested or exiled the leading members of both groups. Playing the devil's advocate, however, I would say that there would have been limitations on their mutual ties even without arrests: the differences on political questions—specifically those relating to the status of Ukraine—would have surfaced sooner or later. Nevertheless, there existed a truly amazing amount of co-operation in defending both the "national" (cultural?) and individual (or civil) rights of persecuted Ukrainians. This furnishes a solid base for wider political co-operation in the future.

Also in the liberal–democratic centre we find as early as 1969 the remarkable "Programme of the Democratic Movement of the Soviet Union," which had been anonymously signed by "The Democrats of Russia, Ukraine, and the Baltic States" (*Pribaltiki*). The nationality question (Section 3) occupies four pages out of a total of thirty-nine. The "Democrats" boldly state their two premises:

1. The Soviet Union is a *forcible* union of peoples around the Great Russian national core.
2. The present authority of the Russian state over the peoples and their lands has been acquired during 500 years of external expansion, beginning at the end of the fifteenth century [the rule of Ivan III].[51]

In their extensive analysis they touch upon such subjects as the persecution of Balts and Ukrainians for "nationalism,"[52] economic exploitation of the economically developed republics (Ukraine, Belorussia, the Baltic states) for the benefit of the underdeveloped areas of Siberia, the Far North, the Far East, etc.;[53] the artificially induced immigation of outsiders ("into the non-Russian republics there is being poured a large percentage of outsiders [*prishlogo naseleniia*], i.e., in fact there is being introduced a foreign garrison composed of civilians [*inorodnyi grazhdanskii garnizon*];"[54] and the compact ethnic minorities living outside their republics (for instance, Ukrainians living outside the Ukrainian SSR) who have no schools in their own language.[55] The two most important broad aims of the "Democrats" in the field of inter-ethnic relations are:

3. The Russian progressive intelligentsia understand and take account of [the fact] that without freedom of nations there cannot be individual freedom or full democratization of society.
4. The national-liberation movement of the peoples of the USSR shall [*dolzhno*]

act in full solidarity with and complement the Russian [movement] for political freedoms, for the democratization of society.[56]

K. Volny (a pseudonym) put it even more clearly:

Nationalist movements among the peoples of the USSR are natural and valuable allies of the democrats, for democracy is the best condition for genuine self-determination and the basis of the free organization of one's own national way of life. Hence the internationalism of the movement.[57]

Very noteworthy also are the seven detailed goals of the "Democratic Movement" on the nationality question, as follows:

5. The political self-determination of nations by means of an all-national balloting [referendum] with the participation of a supervisory commission of the UN.
6. The offer of cultural or economic autonomy to nations that have chosen not to secede from the Union of Democratic Republics.
7. The solution of territorial questions only with the help of an arbitration commission of the UN.
8. The restitution of all moral, cultural, territorial, and material losses of the nationalities incurred under great-power hegemony.
9. The right of each small people to restrict the number of foreigners according to a norm acceptable for its ethnic existence.
10. Non-interference of the Union of Democratic Republics in the domestic affairs of the nations that have seceded.
11. Friendship, co-operation and mutual respect of the seceded nations and the Union of Democratic Republics within the framework of the UN.[58]

This interesting programme had, alas, one serious drawback: its authors refused to go public, and thus it was at first impossible to tell how many people and of what calibre were behind the "Democratic Movement of the Soviet Union." (Volny's claim that the Movement comprised 270,000 members, including 20,000 active leaders, should be taken with more than a grain of salt.)[59] According to Dr. Albert Boiter, formerly of Radio Liberty, the KGB succeeded in arresting the core group of Democratic Movement activists in December 1974—January 1975. They turned out to be five: Sergei Soldatov, Kaliu Myattick, Matti Kiirend, Arvo Varato, and Artem Iuskevych. "[Although] of different ethnic origins, all five were born in Estonia in the [1930s], all were from the technical intelligentsia (four engineers and a medical doctor), and all resided in Tallinn," writes Boiter.[60] To add to the confusion, all five regarded themselves simultaneously as members of the Estonian Democratic Movement. Soldatov, an engineer, was a Russian; Iuskevych (or, as sometimes spelled, Iushkevych), who died in Tallinn on 28 January 1982, was a Ukrainian;[61] the other three were probably Estonians. In any case, Iuskevych was not well known among among Ukrainian dissidents. It is true, however, that, while in exile in 1977, the late Vasyl Stus, a leading Ukrainian poet and literary scholar, did support the imprisoned Soldatov's claim to become the "ideological secretary" of the Estonian Democratic Movement.[62] To sum up, the ideas of the Democratic Movement are interesting, but the Movement itself may consist of a relatively narrow circle of dissidents, with Iuskevych and Stus being its only clearly identifiable links to Ukraine.

It was also in 1969 that two remarkable treatises were published by two Russian dissidents who appear to straddle the liberal and (Russian) nationalist social philosophies (or super-ideologies): the late Andrei Amalrik and an intellectual writing under the pseudonym of V. Gorsky. Both predict the inevitable break-up of the Soviet empire. As far as I can tell, Amalrik's essay *Will the Soviet Union Survive Until 1984?*, which had been written between April and June 1969, preceded that of Gorsky, "Russian Messianism and the New National Consciousness." Amalrik predicts that the Soviet Union will drift into a long-drawn-out war with the People's Republic of China. Under prolonged stress, first the East European communist countries will break loose, then some of the Union Republics (the Baltic, the Caucasus, and Ukraine will experience intensified anti-Russian nationalism, then Central Asia and the regions along the Volga).[63] Most likely, according to Amalrik, "the unavoidable 'de–imperialization' will take place in an extremely painful way," with power passing into the hands of extremist elements.[64] But Amalrik does not rule out a peaceful transition (as desired by "The Democratic Movement of the Soviet Union").

Gorsky's vision is more general; he even refuses to speculate on precisely what might touch off the disintegrative process:

> The communist regime, which attained external unity by means of military-political intervention and terror, only aggravated the old sins. In so doing, it predestined the inevitability of catastrophe for Russia. For the processes of national consciousness and the national movement for independence, squeezed by the grip of Soviet imperialism and chased into the underground, are those active centrifugal forces which, *when freed*, will inevitably lead to the collapse of the Soviet empire. Not only the satellite nations but the Baltic countries, Ukraine, the Caucasus, and the peoples of Central Asia will, without fail, demand their right to break away and depart from the notorious "indissoluble union" . . . [Emphasis added] [65]

The importance of both Amalrik's and Gorsky's works for our topic is that two leading Russian intellectuals envisaged a possible secession of Ukraine as early as 1969. But with Amalrik having suffered an untimely death and Gorsky not having revealed his true identity, any more concrete follow-up questions from the Russian as well as the Ukrainian side, alas, have to wait.

Turning now to representatives of what Amalrik called the social-religious and neo-Slavophile ideologies, both of them essentially under the social philosophy of Russian nationalism, whom Roman Szporluk, in turn, has called the "culturalists"[66] and John B. Dunlop—*vozrozhdentsy*,[67] I would like to make a few general and possibly controversial comments. The various kinds of Russian nationalists—I am not using the term in a pejorative sense, which is common, paradoxically, to both Soviet official and American popular sources—are exceedingly important in that they appear to have deep roots in Soviet society, among the masses as well as the educated elite. Their roots may reach even deeper than those of the liberal humanitarian and democrat Academician Sakharov. Furthermore, at least some of the tenets of Russian nationalism were favoured by Brezhnev's communist regime. At the same time, by and large, on the Ukrainian question, the Russian nationalists tend to be very conservative. They will make concessions only to cultural aspirations, but remain somewhat insensitive to Ukrainian political goals and interests. I sincerely hope that ultimately Aleksandr Isaevich Solzhenitsyn will prove a glorious exception to that rule. A union between Russian nationalism and political, especially imperial, conservatism was perhaps to be expected, but in the long run such a tie may be a tragedy as much—if not even more—for the Russian nation itself than for the Ukrainians.

Stated briefly, in chronological order, members of the All-Russian Social Christian Union for the Liberation of the People, of 1964–7, claimed to speak on behalf of all nationalities of Great Russia [*Velikoi Rossii*]. If the monarchist Evgenii A. Vagin accurately represents the Union leaders, his group was "categorically against breaking up the union of Russia, Belorussia and Ukraine."[68] At the same time, Vagin "might be willing to grant self-determination" to formerly Polish, Catholic Western Ukraine, and he also seems to be agreeable to giving Eastern Ukraine "full autonomy, including independence in conducting [its] foreign affairs [*sic*]."[69]

The position of the All-Russian Social Christian Union on the Ukrainian question may have influenced the concepts of such former Union members as Vladimir Osipov and even such non-members as Solzhenitsyn. Osipov considers Ukrainians and Belorussians to be Russian. Although, in general, Osipov appears fairly liberal (the non-Russians in the Russian-led multi-national state might be allowed cultural autonomy), the question should be asked whether this would apply to the Ukrainians.[70]

Next in chronological, though perhaps not in rational order, we find the anonymous "*Slovo natsii*" of 1970 [The Nation Speaks or A Manifesto to the Nation—both these translations make sense]. The "Russian Patriots," in whose name the pamphlet was written, evidently attack "The Programme of the Democratic Movement of the Soviet Union," particularly the latter's section on the nationality question. "Russia is one and indivisible" is the "Russian Patriots'" forthright battle-cry.[71] Their particular ire is reserved for the Belorussians and, above all, the Ukrainians. The latter have allegedly won a disproportionate influence in all-Union Party politics. At one time the Ukrainians had been considered only as part of the Russian people. Now they fancy themselves a separate people, and their vociferous nationalists even shout about separation from Russia. Such an attempt is declared to be doomed to failure because it is utterly absurd. "Within the territory of Ukraine there live seven million Russians and probably an equal number of Russified Ukrainians, so that it would have been more correct to transfer entire provinces to Russia."[72]

The following paragraph is reproduced *in toto*, both as a counterweight to the text from the Programme of the Democratic Movement and in order to convey the stridently self-confident tone of the Russian Patriots' Manifesto:

> As you know, there exists in Ukraine a strong nationalist movement. But the aims it sets itself are utterly unreal. Were the question of Ukraine's independent exist-ence really to arise, there would inevitably have to be a review of its boundaries. Ukraine would have to concede: (a) the Crimea; (b) the *oblasti* of Kharkov, Donetsk, Lugansk and Zaporozhe, which have a predominantly Russian population; (c) the *oblasti* of Odessa, Nikolaevsk, Kherson, Dnepropetrovsk, and Sumi, whose population has become Russified to a considerable extent and which were opened up during the course of history by the efforts of the Russian state. What could the remaining part count upon without an outlet to the sea and with-out the basic industrial areas? Let the Ukrainians themselves reflect on that. Let them think also of the claims the Poles might lay to the western regions (*oblasti*), the population of which is of pro-Polish disposition. We suggest that the result could only be the return of the prodigal son. And as for Ukrainian pretensions to the Kuban and the *oblasti* at the centre of the Chernozem [Black Soil] belt, they are nothing short of ridiculous and we disregard them entirely, as we do the appetite displayed by foreigners for our territories (by which we mean the so-called "Bessarabian question").[73]

Incidentally, a reference to *Slovo natsii* in no. 17 of the *Chronicle of Current Events*, a *samizdat* journal published by a Russian group that is close to, but not identical with, the Sakharov circle, provoked what, to my knowledge, is the only recorded polemic between liberal–democratic Ukrainian and Russian dissenters. Complained the editors of no. 5 of the *Ukrainian Herald*, a sister publication of the *Chronicle:*

> The Ukrainian reader has welcomed the appearance of the *Chronicle*. It is notable for its objectivity, extensive coverage, and relative accuracy of information, providing a rounded picture of the political trials unknown to the majority of people in the USSR.
>
> However, some have raised their voices to point out, without denying the im-portance of the *Chronicle*, that it has rather unilaterally and pretentiously assumed the stance of a supranational or all-Union journal, when in fact it is the product of Russian (and possibly, in part, Jewish) circles. It has also been noted that the sparse informational reports from the republics are worked in as though they were supplementary to the quite extensive description of events in Russia, mostly Moscow—this in and of itself creating a false impression of the situation in the USSR.

It is very hard to obtain information on the attitude toward the national question held by the various underground groups, organizations, and "parties" that have arisen in recent years in Russia... The impression obtained is that the participants in these groups, while aiming at very radical changes in many spheres of social life, wished—to one degree or another—to preserve the status quo on the national question.

Along with organizations and groups that raise the question of democratic transformations in the USSR, others have appeared that criticize the government and the "liberals" from reactionary, openly chauvinist positions, seeking even a formal liquidation of the USSR and the creation of a military-democratic unitary state "of all the Russias." Let us quote the brief description of one such document of Russian samizdat given by the *Chronicle* in its issue no. 17, "Message to the Nation."[74]

The criticism of the *Ukrainian Herald* was exaggerated; its reference to the "in part, Jewish" circles was inappropriate; and, in any case, the last word rested with the Moscow *Chronicle*. Exhibiting a superb sense of historical responsibility it reprinted in its no. 22 the polemical editorial from no. 5 of the *Ukrainian Herald* and thereby saved it from oblivion (no legible copies of that particular issue reached the West, the only issue known to be lost).

In 1971, within one year of the publication in *samizdat* of *Slovo natsii*, there appeared the Russian nationalist journal *Veche*, which was edited, except for the last issue, by Osipov. *Veche* did not take an explicit stand on the Ukrainian question, but it published a highly laudatory article on the tsarist Russian General Skobelev, who had conquered Central Asia,[75] and also serialized a glorification of the Slavophiles by Russian architect M. Antonov.[76] Antonov is an admirer of Tsar Nicholas I; he also happens to be a close associate of fellow-architect A. Fetisov, who venerates both Stalin and Hitler and who considers that Siniavsky and Daniel should have been shot.[77]

This brings me to the older writings of Solzhenitsyn in which the world-famous Russian author has obliquely touched upon the Ukrainian question: his "Letter to the Soviet Leaders" of September 1973;[78] his follow-up essay "Repentance and Self-- Limitation in the Life of Nations" of November 1973;[79] and his rebuttal to Sakharov's critique of the "Letter," which was published in *Kontinent*.[80] Solzhenitsyn's position on Ukrainian political aspirations appears to have remained unchanged, but the degree of his disclosure of that position has slightly, but importantly, varied.

Solzhenitsyn's footnote at the very end of his section on the "Russian North-East" in the "Letter" is well known:

Such a relocation [of the centre of state attention and state activity to the North-East] would oblige us [*dolzhno*], sooner or later, to withdraw our protective surveillance of Eastern Europe. Nor can there be any question of any peripheral nation being forcibly kept within the bounds of our country.[81]

Not so well known is the fact that in an earlier version of the "Letter," possibly in the original version submitted to Brezhnev, Solzhenitsyn had been a bit more concrete and more positive from the viewpoint of non-Russian nations—*but with the exception of Ukrainians.* He had written:

> Of course, such a shift must mean, sooner or later, lifting our trusteeship from Eastern Europe, the *Baltic republics, Transcaucasia, Central Asia, and possibly even from parts of present-day Ukraine.* Nor can there be any question of our forcibly keeping any peripheral nation within the borders of our country. [Emphasis added][82]

Whoever is familiar with the ideas of Vagin, of the All–Russian Social Christian Union for the Liberation of the People, and with *Slovo natsii* cannot help noticing that in his first version Solzhenitsyn is apparently considering detaching some "Russian" or "Russified" parts of today's Ukrainian SSR and adding them to the RSFSR. Paradoxically, the second, more general version appears to allow for the possibility of leaving the territories of all seceding republics intact. Has Solzhenitsyn changed his view on the proper territory of a Ukrainian state, or has he merely drawn the veil of generalities over a premature disclosure of concrete territorial plans? I believe the latter is the case, and Roy Medvedev was not too far off the mark when he bluntly criticized Solzhenitsyn:

> The fate of other nationalities of the Soviet Union does not worry Solzhenitsyn much. As may be noted from one of his comments, he would think it desirable to separate the "border nations" from the USSR, *with the exception of* Ukraine and Belorussia. [Emphasis added][83]

A reading of the "Letter" (in its final version) shows two fairly sympathetic references to the Ukraine, but from his essay on repentance and his reply to Sakharov's critique it would appear that Solzhenitsyn does not draw a sharp distinction between the Russian and Ukrainian peoples and that he regards the history of Ukraine as history of Russia.[84] He frequently refers to the suffering of both the Russian and the Ukrainian peoples.[85] There is a very simple explanation for this: Solzhenitsyn is a Russian whose maternal grandfather was a Ukrainian and whose maternal grandmother was "almost entirely of Ukrainian origin."[86] There is also in Solzhenitsyn a tendency toward all-embracing, almost mystical constructs. But whatever the explanation, at least so far, Solzhenitsyn has not been able to disentangle the different political aspirations of the Ukrainians from those of the Russians.

This is not to say that in his writings Solzhenitsyn is irrevocably hostile toward Ukrainians as such. On the contrary, his innate feelings of sympathy or, even more, his blood ties, will probably lead him to be tolerant of Ukrainian *cultural* aspirations. It is also true that repeatedly Solzhenitsyn has proved his sympathies toward Ukrainians by having the Solzhenitsyn Fund—officially known as the Russian Common Fund—support Soviet prisoners of conscience of many nationalities, including many Ukrainians. One hopes that this will lead

Solzhenitsyn to revise the political conception that he still seems to share with Vagin and others, viz., that of Great Russia, of Belorussians and Ukrainians being fundamentally only parts of one big Russian people.

To sum up our rapid survey of dissenters' attitudes on Russo-Ukrainian collaboration: there appears to be much hope in that such a cooperation has become a reality within the Helsinki movement, which in turn is linked with the liberal–democratic Sakharov circle. But much has still to be accomplished. Not unexpectedly, a political dialogue with conservative Russian nationalism has just begun. So far, it has stressed differences rather than such similarities as the common strong hostility of many Russian and Ukrainian nationalists to the communist regime, with its anti-religious campaigns and its terrible agricultural policies.

A safer and possibly wiser course—does not the Hegelian owl always fly after the day is over?—would have been to break off here, with a sharp look into the past and an expression of somewhat hazy but pious hopes for the future. But instead of playing it safe, I have promised to touch on important and sensitive questions that may or may not have been explored by the dissenters. For reasons of space, I propose to do this without overly elaborate documentation. These are meant to be points for discussion, not chapters in a treatise on Russo-Ukrainian relations! A participant in the conference has called the last section "futuristic"—so be it. I shall also try to combine brevity with a lack of dogmatism—the two go together often—but it is not up to me to judge my success.

Questions for the 1980s and Beyond: Both Old and New

Basic premise of right to independence

It would appear to me that in order to be fruitful any dialogue between Russians and Ukrainians should start from the basic premise that both the Russian and the Ukrainian peoples have the right to independence, not just to somewhat vague "self-determination." [87]

A strong argument can be made that the Ukrainian people determined their fate in 1917 and that the establishment of a formally independent Ukrainian SSR in December 1917 constitutes Lenin's recognition of that fact, as does the retention of the secession clause in all three constitutions of the USSR, including the latest of 1977, and in all the constitutions of the Ukrainian SSR. The efforts of Stalin, Khrushchev, and Brezhnev effectively to undermine the formal sovereignty (autonomy, really) of Ukraine by extreme centralization have created unnecessary tensions. Those tensions have harmed the Ukrainians, but also the Russians, by making the latter partners in an enterprise of dubious political wisdom, namely, the restoration of the Russian Empire more than two generations after its fall.

It seems to me that political prudence would dictate that, at a minimum, Ukrainians should retain all the rights promised them in the Soviet constitution and should be allowed to become the dominant nation within the boundaries of today's Ukrainian SSR. Any attempt to restrict Ukraine to a tiny enclave of so-called genuinely Ukrainian provinces—the Kiev-Poltava rump state—cannot serve as basis for discussion between Russians and Ukrainians.

Besides territorial integrity of the Ukrainian republic, the premise of political independence would also imply that the modalities in which the Ukrainians would exercise their national will not be spelled out in excessively restrictive detail, as has, for instance, been done in the "Programme of the Democratic Movement of the USSR," or in Medvedev's *On Socialist Democracy.* Should the communist regime continue in force in the last two decades of this century and beyond—the critical twelfth generation of Ukrainians since the Pereiaslav Treaty with Russia—the Ukrainian Party leaders will have their hands full merely to limit the damage brought about by the dismissals of Ukrainians from high Party posts—the Secretariat and the Politburo—from 1965 to 1977,[88] by the relative neglect of Ukrainian economic interests, by the heavy-handed Russification drive, and, last but not least, by the costly policy of expansionism abroad. The modality of politics will then be more of the same: limited public demands for more investment, jockeying for better positions, and lobbying behind the scenes in the Party and government offices in the Kremlin. Possibly the Ukrainians could strike a deal with those Russian leaders who are not enamoured of the prospect of building up Siberia at the cost of neglecting the industry of European Russia.

On the other hand, in any kind of major crisis, which might be set off by a spreading war in the Middle East, or, more likely, one over control of Europe, a provisional Ukrainian republican government—probably supported by sections of the Soviet armed forces—will have to make quick decisions on whether to continue to work together with Russia in the role of junior partner on the same basis as previously (strict subordination) or on the East European, possibly even the Polish model (that is, ranging from dependence in foreign affairs but genuine autonomy in internal policy-making—the model of present-day Hungary—all the way to loosening foreign ties and insubordination in internal policy—the Polish model prior to the imposition of martial law on 13 December 1981). Or the provisional Ukrainian government may opt for complete and immediate independence. It is, of course, possible that Russian nationalists, especially if they be guided by the advice of so-called Russian Patriots of *Slovo natsii*, would make it their immediate task to try to crush the Ukrainian "insurrection" by a military campaign against Kiev, which would necessitate the immediate establishment of an efficient and formidable, really a Stalinist dictatorship in Moscow. I do not believe that they would succeed, at least not so easily as they did in 1917–20. Nor do I believe that the Russian people would welcome another Stalin, even though he be dressed in the uniform of Nicholas II and able to speak Russian without an accent.

It is devoutly to be wished that eventually, after due deliberation, the quick decision of the provisional Ukrainian government be either endorsed or rejected by the people of Ukraine, who will express their will freely. For that reason the development of the democratic human–rights movement in Ukraine and its co-operation with Russian democrats is of capital importance: for the first time since the early twentieth century Russian and Ukrainian liberals have worked together as political partners rather than enemies. However, for the sake of long-term Russo-Ukrainian political co-operation—within an East Slavic confederation or, more likely, as independent countries—Russian liberals such as the authors of the Programme of the Democratic Movement and implicitly Sakharov, too, ought not to insist on the technical device of a plebiscite.

First of all, the very question of who should vote in such a plebiscite is bound to engender very acrimonious disputes (Should recent Russian immigrants to Ukraine vote? What about those Ukrainians who, in one way or another, have been compelled to leave Ukraine and express a desire to return to their homeland? What about Ukrainian soldiers, many of whom are stationed in the Soviet Far East? What about the Crimean Tatars, who definitely should be allowed to return to the Crimea and to settle down before a plebiscite is held?). Secondly, for similar reasons, since World War II plebiscites have been pretty much discredited in theory and practice.[89] The last plebiscite involving an entire European people was held on 13 August 1905, when Norway broke the old dynastic union with Sweden and became an independent state. The populations involved were relatively small, and the plebiscite seems merely to have confirmed the well-known desire of the Norwegian people to become independent and to have served as a face-saving device for Sweden.[90] But how would one conduct a plebiscite in a hotly disputed territory the size of France, with a population of some fifty million?*

What the people of Ukraine ultimately decide is a matter of passionately held beliefs and difficult rational judgment. A union that has lasted for eleven generations should not be rejected lightly, as if out of hand. But when 325 years after Pereiaslav a trained Ukrainian philologist has to set about writing a 1,400–page manuscript presenting reasons why his nation has "The Right to Live," and when his work is "stolen" during a secret search of his apartment and destroyed before publication, when he himself is later sentenced to seven years of strict-regime labour camp and five years of exile—i.e., to twelve years of legal punishment after six years of self-inflicted punishment for writing out (in longhand!) such a monstrously long plea for national autonomy, not even independence—then a rational conclusion might perhaps be that the marriage

---

* In his comments, Professor John A. Armstrong agreed with the writer that holding a plebiscite in Ukraine would be inappropriate.

concluded at Pereiaslav has not worked out and that a divorce or, at least, a temporary separation would be indicated for the welfare of both parties.[91]

Separation and divorce would also seem the only rational way out when a Russian nationalist painter who has been painting Pope John XXIII, Nicholas II, Solzhenitsyn, and Stalin—Ilia Glazunov—at the price of withholding some of his most controversial works, which, however, remain intact and are well known through *samizdat* reproductions—can go from exhibition to exhibition (Moscow, Leningrad, West Berlin—three times in West Berlin!), can collect rapturous comments from hundreds of thousands of patriotic Russian visitors, and reap one official honour after another ("People's Artist of the RSFSR," 1979; "People's Artist of the Soviet Union," 1980), while a group of four Ukrainian artists who in 1964 produced an unorthodox stained glass window depicting an angry Taras Shevchenko had their work smashed and were viciously persecuted (two, Liudmyla Semykina and Halyna Sevriuk, were expelled from the Artists' Union of Ukraine; the third, Panas Zalyvakha, was arrested in 1965 and sentenced to five years of strict–regime camps; the fourth, Alla Horska, was first expelled from the Artists' Union and then, on 28 November 1970, killed under mysterious circumstances).[92]

Restriction on Russian immigration into Ukraine and on Ukrainian outmigration from that republic

In principle, free movement of persons is a human right which ought to be zealously defended. But when much of the movement is deliberately manipulated to help strengthen one nationality over another, perhaps the time has come for the stronger group to practice self-limitation and to curb its politically destabilizing *Wanderlust*. Taking only very rough indicators, we notice that from 1959 to 1979 the number of self-declared Ukrainians in the Ukrainian SSR increased from 32.2 million in 1959 to 36.5 million in 1979, i.e., by 4.3 million or 13.5 per cent overall, whereas self-declared Russians in Ukraine increased from 7.1 million in 1959 to 10.5 million in 1979 (3.3 million or 47.7 per cent).[93] Closer analysis would also show that Russians in Ukraine are more urbanized and better educated than the Ukrainians, and curiously enough it also shows that Ukrainians in Russia are more urbanized and better educated than Ukrainians in Ukraine.[94] Has by any chance the officially inspired exchange of cadres anything to do with channelling educated Russians into Ukraine and educated Ukrainians out of Ukraine? How much of the extraordinarily high growth of Russians in Ukraine (while from 1959–79 the Russian minority in Ukraine grew by 47.7 per cent, Russians in the USSR as a whole increased only by 20.4 per cent) is due to the natural increase of long-time Russian residents in Ukraine, how much to migration, and how much to possible assimilation of Ukrainians to Russians (part of which may be due to assimilation of children of mixed Russo-Ukrainian marriages)?[95] Whatever objective figures the demographers can and will come up with, the political fact is that Ukrainian dissidents do suspect that deliberate encouragement of population exchange between Russia and Ukraine does take place, which cannot but embitter Russo-Ukrainian relations.[96] Such a population exchange makes sense only if it is believed that it is possible to disperse and simultaneously Russify a sufficient number of Ukrainians to break their will to resist. This is a dangerous assumption, given the fact that officially self-declared Ukrainians in the Soviet Union number as many as 42.3 million and latent and imperfectly Russified Ukrainians may number several million more.

Russification of Ukrainians within and outside Ukraine

The natural spread of the knowledge of Russian, the *lingua franca* of the empire, is one thing, but the insistent introduction of Russian into Ukrainian kindergartens and the first grades of Ukrainian elementary schools is something altogether different. At a time when Ukrainians living in Russia are not allowed to obtain their elementary and secondary education in Ukrainian, even though the Ukrainian emigrants might be living in a compact mass, Russians living in Ukraine attend numerous Russian-language schools that tend, moreover, to be better equipped and staffed; they have Russian theatres, newspapers, and similar privileges.[97] There are Ukrainians, of course, who prefer to give a Russian-language education to their offspring in order to help them make careers in the increasingly Russian-dominated Party and governmental apparatuses. The point nevertheless stands that the official pressure to learn Russian in the last two decades has been so heavy-handed as to provoke Ukrainian opposition and probably discredit for a long time the natural, as opposed to the forcible, spread of the Russian language. Since about 1978 the Russification policy has not only been heavy-handed, but has become positively ludicrous, for instance, in its attempt to train "kindergarten linguists" in Ukraine.[98]

Moreover, so tense and so foul is the officially supported climate of Russification in Ukraine that a Ukrainian intellectual and writer fluent in ten languages is not permitted to address a shopgirl in Ukrainian in Kiev, the capital of the Ukrainian republic! Another customer who spoke Russian angrily reprimanded him:

> There, listen to him talking! You, fellow, are not in Lvov to be speaking *that* language![99]

If a Russian from Kiev allowed himself such an outburst, it would be bad enough; if it had been a Russified Ukrainian, this would have been ten times worse. I think that even without citing the usual statistics on Ukrainian-language schools in Ukraine—insofar as they are not state secrets—and data on Ukrainian-language books, etc., I have proved the point that such official policies as teaching kindergarteners the differences between Russian and Ukrainian grammar and vocabulary and such attitudes as calling for Russian only in the capital of Ukraine are a disgrace to the great Russian language and culture and a serious impediment to Russo-Ukrainian cooperation. I am delighted that the declaration of democratic Russian and Ukrainian émigrés of 30 September 1979 recognized Russification as a danger to the Ukrainian people and pledged every effort to fight it.[100] I think, however, that the declaration did not go far enough: such brutal policies may or may not help to denationalize the Ukrainians, but they certainly corrupt the Russians themselves.

Economic interests, mutual and competitive

It would seem to me that once such major obstacles to Russo-Ukrainian cooperation as non-recognition of the Ukrainians' right to independence, population exchanges designed to undercut the strength of Ukrainians in their republic, and Russification at any cost were removed, the Ukrainian and Russian political leaders would be able to sit down together and discuss those economic interests which unite them as well as those which are divisive. For instance, Ukraine of whatever political status—semi-autonomous, autonomous, or independent—would be able to produce more food and sell it to European Russia and some East European countries, and the Russians would not have to invest major sums in the economically marginal lands of the Russian non-black-earth zone. Furthermore, with many investments it might still be possible to extract substantial coal and some natural gas in Ukraine instead of sinking huge sums into Western Siberial oil fields with their tremendous overhead expenses. In the fuel sector, Ukrainian interests might be wholly compatible with those of European Russia, though, of course, they will clash sharply with those proposed by the "Siberia first, at any price" school. In foreign policy and international economic relations Ukraine might serve both as a buffer and also, when necessary, as a bridge between Russia and Poland. But first those three major impediments must be removed. Secondly, Russo-Ukrainian relations will be much more harmonious if the autonomous or independent Ukrainian republic is wise in its internal policy. Here the shoe will be, so to speak, on the other foot.

Necessity of wise internal policy toward Russian, Jewish, and Crimean Tatar national minorities on the part of the Ukrainian government

In the twentieth century, a Ukraine only for ethnic Ukrainians would not be in the best interests of the country. The Russian minority in Ukraine is simply too large for expulsion. Some—though not all—of those Russians would be able to trace their arrival in Ukraine back to the eighteenth and nineteenth centuries, if not even earlier. Ukraine has also contained a sizeable Jewish minority (it was 634,000 in 1979). The exact number of Crimean Tatars is impossible to ascertain (the official numbers according to the 1979 census— 132,272—appears small).[101]

As I see it, the Ukrainian government will be morally compelled to reach an agreement with the Crimean Tatars on their repatriation to and settlement in their ancient homeland, as well as on their political status within the Ukrainian republic. Such an agreement is in the vital interests of Ukraine, for no politically sensitive person will ever contemplate yielding the Crimea to Russia, whether or not this be to the liking of the Russian Patriots from *Slovo natsii*, and in order to keep the Crimea Ukraine must strike an honest bargain with the Crimean Tatars. The Crimean Tatars will probably insist on cultural autonomy as a bare minimum, and they may also demand the reconstruction of Tatar cultural monuments that were brutally razed *immediately* after the war, when the Crimea was part of the RSFSR. In that case the bill ought to be negotiated with Moscow.*

With the Ukrainian Jews relations have considerably improved from what they used to be before World War I and in the chaos of the struggle for independence in 1917–20.

The really difficult problem would be relations with the numerous Russian minority, some of whom may be politically loyal to Ukraine and some of whom regard themselves as defenders of the ancient lands of "Great Russia" (*Velikoi Rossii*) against the pretensions of "upstart Ukrainian nationalists." Some of the Russians, both loyalists and anti-Ukrainian chauvinists, may also have been living in Ukraine for generations, if not centuries, and may always have considered that they have been living at home. It would seem to me that Ukrainians would be extremely ill–advised to lump all the Russians in Ukraine together and declare them national enemies, for many of them may be friends who will be urgently needed for the political and economic reconstruction of the country. Fortunately, two members of the Ukrainian Helsinki Group do represent two major national minorities: Dr. Vladimir Malinkovich, a physician and medical researcher by profession, considers himself a Russian, and Yosyf Zisels, a television engineer, considers himself a Jew.

What is needed—and this may, at first sight, seem inconsistent with the vociferous Ukrainian protests against Russification, but actually is not—is to abandon the somewhat restrictive identification of Ukrainian nationality with the Ukrainian language and to think in broader, territorial terms.[102] The fact that many ethnic Ukrainians and almost all ethnic Russians in the cities speak Russian rather than Ukrainian is not yet a cause for despair as long as they

---

* In his comments, Professor John A. Armstrong disagreed with the writer that the Crimea should remain a part of a restructured Ukraine.

consider themselves Ukrainians (in the territorial sense) and act in the interests of the Ukrainian republic rather than those of the RSFSR, a new Great Russia, or whatever. Conversely, stories abound among Ukrainian émigrés in Canada and the United States that some of the best Ukrainian in Ukraine is spoken by agents of the KGB out to entrap Ukrainian tourists from the West who are depressed over the decline of the Ukrainian language.[103]

In short, Ukrainians should learn to think more in political-territorial and less in linguistic-ethnographic terms and be more tolerant of Russians and Jews who are really Ukrainian patriots but still prefer to speak Russian. As controversial as it may sound, the Russians who stay in Ukraine and who opt for Ukrainian citizenship should be given extensive cultural autonomy and guaranteed equal access (non-discrimination) in employment, possibly including the highest decision-making posts. The same would apply to the Jews, the Crimean Tatars, and any other national minority. Possibly Russian will even be used by the republican authorities temporarily as an unofficial second language, with Yiddish or Hebrew, if requested, as a third, Tatar as a fourth, etc. All this will require a major psychological adjustment, for many Ukrainians—by no means all—still identify Ukrainian nationality with the Ukrainian language and are instinctive and, above all, indiscriminate Russophobes.

Conclusion

There is cause for both hope and alarm in the history of contemporary Russo-Ukrainian relations and in our bird's-eye view of outstanding future problems. There is cause for hope in that some kind of dialogue and common political action has begun in the liberal–democratic circles of dissenters in the Soviet Union and among the third wave of the Russian emigration abroad.* There is cause for alarm in that most Russian nationalists, even among the dissenters, with, I fervently hope, the exception of Aleksandr Solzhenitsyn, appear as much concerned about the restoration of the Russian Empire, which minimally should include Ukraine and Belorussia as strictly subordinate peoples, as they appear to be eager to change the communist regime. Goodness alone knows what the ultimate fate of the Russian and Ukrainian nations will be, but now is the time to talk the issues over and to act on them as much as possible. The Ukrainians have independence to gain; the Russians may have to lose an empire if they want to become free. Gorsky may be right when he asserts:

> The collapse of the Soviet empire will not be humiliating or unnatural for Russia.

---

* In his comments, Roman Szporluk mentioned the existence of a Russian identity crisis. He argued that the Russians themselves should work out a number of problems with regard to what they consider their national territory as a prerequisite to their developing a conception of Russo-Ukrainian relations.

Deprived of her colonies Russia will not lose its political importance. Freed from the yearnings for occupation and coercion, it will confront its true problems: the building of a free democratic society, religious renaissance, and the creation of a national culture.[104]

Gorsky may sound like an optimist, but he is quite far-sighted.

Postscript: March 1990

The contribution was written in 1981–82, before the accession of Gorbachev to power in March 1985. The author believes that the situation has remained essentially unchanged, with the possible exception of the "Law of the Ukrainian Soviet Socialist Republic on Language in the Ukrainian RSR." The law was passed 28 October 1989 and entered into force 1 January 1990. The full consequences of that act are not yet clear at the time of writing.

Notes

1. Figures are from the 1979 census. See "Vsesoiuznaia perepis naseleniia," *Vestnik statistiki*, no. 2 (1980): 24.

2. The key position of Ukraine in the Soviet empire is stressed by Seweryn Bialer, *Stalin's Successors: Leadership, Stability and Change in the Soviet Union* (New York, 1980), 222ff. and Table 25. Our conclusions, however, differ somewhat from Bialer's.

3. L.I. Brezhnev, "O piatidesiatiletii Soiuza Sovetskikh Sotsialisticheskikh Respublik," *Pravda*, 22 December 1972, 2.

4. Ibid., 2.

5. *Izvestiia*, 31 March 1971, 7.

6. Brezhnev, "O piatidesiatiletii...," 3.

7. Ibid., 3. See also Y. Bilinsky, "The Concept of the Soviet People and its Implications for Soviet Nationality Policy," *The Annals of the Ukrainian Academy of Arts and Sciences in the U.S.* 14, no. 37–38 (1978–1980): 95ff.

8. "O piatidesiatiletii...," 3.

9. Ibid., 2.

10. For documentation see Michael Rywkin, "Code Words and Catchwords of Brezhnev's Nationality Policy," *Survey* 24, no. 3 (Summer 1979): 84ff. and Bilinsky, "The Concept of the Soviet People . . . "

11. *Pravda*, 24 February 1981, 7.

12. Ibid., 7, immediately following second quotation.

13. He said: "There are going on (*proiskhodiat*) the flourishing and mutual enrichment of national cultures, the formation of the culture of the Soviet people—the new social and international community," ibid., 7. Brezhnev's

reference to the Soviet people was not emphasized, and the entire paragraph, in which the quoted sentence was the third from the end, merited only simple applause.

14. In the early 1960s, when most of the work on the amendment of the constitution was done, many of the legal drafting commissions dropped the republics' right of secession and changed the related clauses accordingly. Suddenly, in 1977 word came to restore that right, which was done, without, however, readjusting the now logically incompatible provisions. See A. Shtromas, "The Legal Position of the Soviet Nationalities and Their Territorial Units According to the 1977 Constitution of the USSR," *Russian Review* 37, no. 3 (July 1978): 267ff. See also Bilinsky, "The Concept of the Soviet People...," note 7. Shtromas, a former Soviet Lithuanian lawyer, was a member of several legal research institutes that participated in the drafting of the new Soviet constitution in the 1960s.

15. One such confidential follow-up decree, that of the Estonian Party Bureau (Minutes no. 105, para. 1 of 19 December 1978) was leaked to the West in *Eesti Paüevaleht* (Sweden), 15 November 1980. See Romuald Misiunas and Rein Taagepera, *The Baltic States: Years of Dependence 1940–1980* (London and Berkeley, 1982). See also the title and brief summary of the decree in the editorial "Sovershenstvovat izuchenie i prepodavanie russkogo iazyka," *Russkii iazyk v natsionalnoi shkole*, no. 1, (1979): 2–5. See also Y. Bilinsky, "Expanding the Use of Russian or Russification? Some Critical Thoughts on Russian as a Lingua Franca and the 'Language of Friendship and Cooperation of the Peoples of the USSR,'" *Russian Review* 40, no. 3 (July 1981): 323ff.

16. Bilinsky, "Expanding the Use of Russian...," 320ff.

17. The recent Soviet emphasis on the East Slavic peoples related by blood has been noted by Bialer, *Stalin's Successors*, 224 and 224n.; by Roman Solchanyk, "The Politics of Hematology and Contemporary Soviet Nationality Policy," RL 107/79 (*Radio Liberty Research Bulletin* or *RLRB*) (30 March 1979); and by S. Enders Wimbush, "The Russian Nationalist Backlash," *Survey* 24, no. 3 (Summer 1979): 43. Reference should also be made to the classic analysis of the "younger brothers" by John A. Armstrong, "The Ethnic Scene in the Soviet Union: The View of the Dictatorship," in Erich Goldhagen, ed., *Ethnic Minorities in the Soviet Union* (New York, 1968), 14–20.

18. According to the 1979 census, 74.2 per cent of Belorussians gave Belorussian as their "native" language, compared with 80.6 per cent in 1970 (see note 1 above). In 1972–3, with ethnic Russians constituting approximately one–tenth of the total population, 51.4 per cent of all the pupils in the Belorussian SSR attended Russian-language schools, but in the Belo- russian cities and towns as many as 97.6 per cent of the children did so (see K. Kh. Khanazarov, *Reshenie natsionalno iazykovoi problemy v SSSR* [Moscow, 1977], 137—source courtesy of Professor Bohdan Bociurkiw). See, however, Jan Zaprudnik on Belorussian resistance to Russification ("Belorussia and the Belorussians," in Zev Katz et al., eds., *Handbook of Major Soviet Nationalities* [New York, 1975], 67ff.).

19. The proportion of self-declared Ukrainians who gave Ukrainian as their "native" language decreased from 85.7 per cent in 1970 to 82.8 per cent in 1979. See *Vestnik statistiki*, no. 2 (1980): 24. For related documentation see Y. Bilinsky,

"Expanding the Use of Russian...," 320, 326, 327n.

20. Andrei Amalrik, "Ideologies in Soviet Societies," in Andrei Amalrik, *Will the Soviet Union Survive Until 1984?* (New York, 1981), 179. Originally the essay was published in *Survey*, no. 199 (1976).

21. On the less well known Kosterin, see Y. Bilinsky, "Russian Dissenters and the Nationality Question," in Ihor Kamenetsky, ed., *Nationalism and Human Rights: Processes of Modernization in the USSR* (Littleton, Colo., 1977), 79.

22. Among others, by Amalrik, 182.

23. See his portrait by David K. Shipler, "A Wary Soviet Dissident Irritates Friend and Foe," *New York Times*, 23 February 1979 (source courtesy of Ms. Linda Verba).

24. On 9 November 1973, or eight months after having been sentenced to five years' imprisonment, Ivan Dziuba publicly repudiated his 1965 treatise *Internationalism or Russification?* See M. I. Holubenko's introduction to Ivan Dzyuba, *Internationalism or Russification? A Study in the Soviet Nationalities Problem* (New York, 1974), xxii.

25. See Roy Medvedev, "Blizhnevostochnyi konflikt i evreiskii vopros v SSSR," May 1970, *Arkhiv samizdata* (henceforth: AS) 496, p. 29, in *Sobranie dokumentov samizdata* (henceforth: *SDS*), vol. 7 (Munich, n.d.). A long excerpt has been translated as "*Samizdat*: Jews in the USSR: Document: Soviet Union," *Survey* 17, no. 2 (Spring 1971)—see p. 196 for citation. Henceforth I will give double references to the document.

26. Ibid., 28/195, 196. See also the vigorously worded article by Alexander J. Motyl, "Roy Medvedev: Dissident or Conformist?," *Survey* 25, no. 3 (Summer 1980): 80.

27. See Roy Medvedev, *On Soviet Dissent: Interviews with Piero Ostellino* (New York, 1980), 47; also Motyl, 84.

28. Roy A. Medvedev, *On Socialist Democracy* (New York, 1975), 85.

29. Ibid., 85, 87. See also Motyl, 79. Emphasis added.

30. See Medvedev, "Blizhnevostochnyi konflikt...," 30–31/197–8. For more detailed discussion and documentation see also Bilinsky, "Russian Dissenters...," 79–80.

31. Roy Medvedev, "What Awaits Us in the Future? (Regarding A.I. Solzhenitsyn's Letter [to the Soviet Leaders]), in Michael Meerson Aksenov and Boris Shragin, eds., *The Political, Social and Religious Thought of Russian "Samizdat"—An Anthology* (Belmont, Mass., 1977), 77. See also Medvedev's critique of Russian nationalism in *On Socialist Democracy*, 87–90.

32. Ibid., 80. If anything, Medvedev appears to champion the European Russian centre and north-west (79ff.).

33. Medvedev, *On Socialist Democracy*, 280; see also Motyl, 83.

34. Andrei D. Sakharov, *Progress, Coexistence and Intellectual Freedom* (New York, 1968), 54, 65–6.

35. See Andrei D. Sakharov, "Manifesto II," in Andrei D. Sakharov, *Sakharov Speaks* (New York, 1974), 128–9.

36. See his "Memorandum" of 5 March 1971, ibid., 135–50, and "Postcript to

Memorandum" of June 1972, ibid., 151–8. 1971 quotation on p. 142, 1972 quotation on p. 155.

37. Ibid., 149.

38. Ibid.

39. See, for instance, Andrei D. Sakharov, *My Country and the World* (New York, 1975), 97. This writer himself listened to Sakharov's tape-recorded appeal, transmitted by telephone to the First World Congress for Soviet and East European Studies in Banff in September 1974, to work for the release of Valentyn Moroz and the Crimean Tatar leader Mustafa Dzhemilev. Moroz was also mentioned among seventeen Soviet political prisoners in Sakharov's letter to President Carter of 21 January 1977. See Andrei D. Sakharov (ed. Efrem Yankelevich and Alfred Friendly, Jr.), *Alarm and Hope* (New York, 1978), 47. Also, in his Nobel Prize speech, Sakharov mentioned, without extensive comment, the names of 113 Soviet political prisoners. Thirty-two of those, including Moroz, can clearly be identified as Ukrainians. See *Alarm and Hope*, 16.

40. Andrei D. Sakharov, "Trevozhnoe vremia," 4 May 1980, AS no. 4,000, p. 11, in *Materialy samizdata* [henceforth: *MS*], no. 23/80 (20 June 1980).

41. Liudmila [Lyudmilla] Alekseeva [Alexeyeva], "Iurii Orlov—rukovoditel Moskovskoi Gelsinskoi Gruppy," *Kontinent*, no. 21 (1979): 191.

42. "More than 30 of [the approximately 200 documents up to the present time]in one way or another refer to the situation in Ukraine." See Lyudmilla Alexeyeva, "On the Fifth Anniversary of the Ukrainian Helsinki Group," *Smoloskyp* 3, no. 13 (Fall 1981): 10.

43. Lyudmilla Alexeyeva, "The Human Rights Movement in the USSR," *Survey* 23, no. 105 (Autumn 1977–8): 75. This writer has treated the establishment of the Ukrainian Helsinki Group at length in Y. Bilinsky and Tönu Parming, "Helsinki Watch Committees in the Soviet Republics: Implications for the Soviet Nationality Question" (unpublished research report prepared for the National Council for Soviet and East European Research under contract 621–9, March 1980), 5–17 to 5–41. See also condensation in Bilinsky and Parming, "Helsinki Watch Committees in the Soviet Republics: Implications for Soviet Nationality Policy," *Nationalities Papers* 9, no. 1 (Spring 1981): 4–7.

44. Mykola Rudenko in a letter to Dr. Andrew Zwarun and Bohdan Yasen, President and Secretary of the Helsinki Guarantees for Ukraine Committee of Washington, D.C., of 1 January 1977. See also Bilinsky and Parming, "Helsinki Watch Committees . . . ," 5.

45. From the viewpoint of the Moscow Helsinki Group this has been later confirmed by Lyudmilla Alexeyeva (see her "On the Fifth Anniversary . . . ," 10:

> There evolved, without prior arrangements, a certain division of labor between the Moscow and Ukrainian groups. The Ukrainian Helsinki Group was comprised mainly of participants in the Ukrainian national movement. They knew the essence of the Ukrainian national problem very well—their lives were devoted to it. The pathos in the work of the Ukrainian Helsinki Group consisted of defending the national dignity of Ukraine, its culture and rights to independent development. All the documents of the Ukrainian

Group in one way or another are connected with this. Naturally, the Moscow Helsinki Group, while it was in complete solidarity with its Ukrainian colleagues, did not specifically deal with this problem.

She adds the interesting sidelight that representatives of the non-Ukrainian population of Ukraine such as Crimean Tatars and Ukrainian Jews continued to deal with the Moscow Group directly.

46. This comes out most distinctly in the Ukrainian Group's *Memorandum no. 2*, reproduced in Bilinsky and Parming, *"Helsinki Watch Committees ...,"* A-39 to A-43.

47. This writer's inferences from four interviews with charter members of the Helsinki Group and with an American diplomat who at one time had been in Moscow.

48. Alexeyeva, "On the Fifth Anniversary ...," 10.

49. 6 chlenov Mosk. OGS (E. Bonner i dr.). *Dokument no. 102.* "K sobytiiam na Ukraine. Ugolovnyi terror protiv pravozashchitnogo dvizheniia" (Moskva)/ 14.9.1979, AS no. 3894, in *MS* no. 11/80 (21 March 1980).

50. Malva Landa: (1) "K arestu Iuriia Badzo (K istorii rukopisi 'Pravo zhit')," 6 pp., AS no. 3839, in *MS*, no. 4/80 (4 February 1980); (2) "K arestu Mykoly Gorbalia," AS no. 3852, 7 pp. in *MS*, no. 6/80 (18 February 1980); and (3) "O neprekrashchaiushchikhsia presledovaniiakh Didyk Galiny Tomovny", 2 pp., in *MS*, no. 12/80 (12 March 1980).

51. "Programma Demokraticheskogo Dvizheniia Sovetskogo Soiuza" (SSSR, 1969 god), *SDS*, vol. 5, AS no. 340, 24.

52. Ibid., 27 (point 13).

53. Ibid., (point 14).

54. Ibid., 27–8 (point 15).

55. Ibid., 28 (point 16).

56. Ibid., 28.

57. "Ocherk K. Volnogo, 'Intelligentsiia i demokraticheskoe dvizhenie'," *SDS*, vol. 8, AS no. 607, 35; transl. in *Survey* 17, no. 3 (Summer 1971): 185.

58. "Programma Demokraticheskogo Dvizheniia...," 28–9.

59. "Ocherk K. Volnogo ...," 36; or in *Survey*, 185.

60. Samisdat-Archiv, e.V. (Albert Boiter, comp.), *SDS*, vol. 30: Khelsinskii samizdat iz SSSR (Munich, 1978), 219.

61. Sakharov, *Alarm and Hope*, 16. See also "Pomer Artem Iuzkevych," *Svoboda* (Jersey City, N. J.), 9 February 1982, 1.

62. *SDS*, vol. 30, 224. (According to Soldatov, who reported Stus's support, the latter represented the Ukrainian national-democratic movement in Kiev. For Stus's biography, see Helsinki Guarantees for Ukraine Committee, *The Human Rights Movement in Ukraine: Documents of the Ukrainian Helsinki Group 1976–1980* (Baltimore, 1980), 263–4.

63. Andrei Amalrik, *Will the Soviet Union Survive Until 1984?* (New York, 1970),

63.

64. Ibid., 64. Two years before his death, at a conference on "The Future of the Soviet Union," 13–15 September 1978, Amalrik seemingly abandoned his prediction of a break-up of the empire. Writing about the "gap between the multinational character of society and the centralized character of the state," he noted: "The efforts of the central powers to replace minority customs and languages by common Soviet, that is, Russian equivalents become ever stronger." He also seemingly held out the possibility that centralization and Russification would be intensified, "gradually proceeding to the abolition of the Union Republics and the establishment of a formally unitary state." See Andrei Amalrik, "The Soviet Union—Approaching 1984," in Robert Wesson, ed., *The Soviet Union: Looking to the 1980s* (Stanford, 1980), 254. But as I read him, Amalrik remained skeptical about the success of such a centralizing policy, given the growing national self-awareness of the non-Russian peoples (especially that of the second generation) and the demographic balance, which is turning against the Russians. His conclusion, especially the last three sentences, remains as pessimistic as ever (see p. 260).

65. V. Gorskii, "Russian Messianism and the New National Consciousness," in *The Political, Social and Religious Thought of Russian "Samizdat,"* 392.

66. Roman Szporluk, "History and Russian Nationalism," *Survey* 24, no. 3 (Summer 1979): 2.

67. John B. Dunlop, "The Russian Nationalist Spectrum Today: Trends and Movements" (Paper presented at the 13th National Convention of the AAASS, 20–23 September 1981), 11. See also Dunlop's excellent earlier article, "The Many Faces of Contemporary Russian Nationalism," *Survey* 24, no. 3 (Summer 1979): 18–35.

68. John B. Dunlop, *The New Russian Revolutionaries* (Belmont, Ma. 1976), 214. See also Szporluk, 9ff.

69. Dunlop, *The New Russian Revolutionaries*, 215.

70. Szporluk, 10n.

71. "Slovo natsii," in *SDS*, vol. 8, AS no. 590, 18. See also the excellent analysis of that document by Dmitry Pospielovsky, "The Resurgence of Russian Nationalism in *Samizdat*," *Survey* 19, no. 1 (Winter 1973): 59–63.

72. "Slovo natsii," 16.

73. Ibid., 16–17. Translation from "A Word to the Nation," *Survey* 17, no. 3 (Summer 1971): 196–7. N.B.: According to the 1970 census the Russians did *not* constitute the absolute majority in any Ukrainian oblast, except in the Crimea. See *Radianska Ukraina*, 25 April 1971, 2.

74. See "Ukrainian Journal Evaluates Russian Dissidents," in George Saunders, ed., *Samizdat: Voices of the Soviet Opposition* (New York, 1974), 424–5.

75. "General M.D. Skobelev kak polkovodets i gosudarstvennyi deiatel," *Veche*, no. 2 (19 May 1971), in *SDS*, vol. 21, AS no. 1020, 48–66.

76. M. Antonov, "Uchenie slavianofilov—vysshii vzlet narodnogo samosoznaniia Rosii v doleninskii period," *Veche*, no. 1 (Jan. 1971) and no. 2, in *SDS*, vol. 21;

AS no. 1013, 13–14 and AS 1020, 4–27.

77. Pospielovsky, 65 and 65n.

78. Aleksandr Solzhenitsyn, *Pismo vozhdiam Sovetskogo Soiuza* (Paris, 1974), as reprinted in *SDS*, vol. 28, AS no. 1,600.

79. Alexander Solzhenitsyn, "Repentance and Self-Limitation in the Life of Nations," in Alexander Solzhenitsyn et al., *From Under the Rubble* (Boston, 1975), 105–43.

80. Alexander Solzhenitsyn, "Sakharov and the Criticism of 'A Letter to the Soviet Leaders,'"in *Kontinent* (Garden City, N.Y., 1976), 14–23.

81. Solzhenitsyn, *Pismo* . . . , 15 n.

82. As cited by Theodore Shabad, "Solzhenitsyn Asks Kremlin to Abandon Communism and Split Up Soviet Union," *New York Times*, 3 March 1974, 26.

83. Medvedev, "What Awaits Us in the Future? . . . ," 77. Dunlop is more diplomatic in saying: "As for relations between Great Russians, Ukrainians and Belorussians, Solzhenitsyn seems to favour some kind of federalism." (Dunlop, "Solzhenitsyn in Exile," *Survey* 21, no. 3, 139).

84. The clearest reference is in Solzhenitsyn's attack on Poland "for energetically annexing *our* territory and oppressing *us*" in Solzhenitsyn, "Repentance . . . ," 131. Altogether, on this and the following two pages (i.e., 131–3), Ukraine, its provinces and its leaders are mentioned twelve times, those of Belorussia—three times, and those of ethnic Russia—five times.

85. For instance, see Solzhenitsyn, "Sakharov . . . ," 21.

86. Dunlop, "Solzhenitsyn in Exile," 139–40n.

87. This was recognized in the "Russian-Ukrainian Declaration" of 30 September 1979. See *Kontinent*, no. 24 (1980): 4 and *Ukrainski visti* (Detroit), 13 August 1980, 1.

88. Removed from the Secretariat were: Vitalii Titov in April 1965 and Podgorny in December 1965. From the Politburo: Shelest in April 1973 and Podgorny in May 1977.

89. It is not a coincidence that there is no article on "plebiscite" in the *International Encyclopedia of the Social Sciences* (IESS) (New York, 1968). Using the index I have found a brief—and negative—reference in Dankwart A. Rustow's article on "The Nation": "As a practical expedient . . . plebiscites can determine national boundaries *only in marginal situations* [emphasis added] and even then the choice needs to be defined, and the result enforced, either by the common consent of pre-existing neighboring states or else by a predominant concert of outside powers. As Sir Ivor Jennings has written, 'On the surface it seemed reasonable: let the people decide. It was in fact ridiculous because the people cannot decide until somebody decides who are the people' . . . " (IESS, 2: 11). Guenther Jaenicke in "Plebiszit," *Handwörterbuch der Sozialwissenschaften* (Stuttgart, 1964), vol. 8, also tends to be rather skeptical: "In view of the contemporary practice [of states] the principle that changes in the sovereignty of a territory [*staatliche Zugehörigkeit*] can only be undertaken on the basis of a plebiscite cannot as yet be regarded as having universal validity..." (347).

Compare this with the period between the wars. See (1) Sarah Wambaugh's "Plebiscite" in *Encyclopedia of the Social Sciences* (New York, 1934), 12: 163–6; (2) her *Monograph on Plebiscites with a Collection of Official Documents* (New York, 1920); (3) her *Plebiscites since the World War with a Collection of Official Documents*, 2 vols. (Washington, 1933), and (4) her *The Saar Plebiscite with a Collection of Official Documents* (Cambridge, Mass., 1940).

90. With a total population of 2.2 million in 1900 in Norway and a total population of 5.1 million (1900) in Sweden (see United Nations, Department of Social Affairs Population Division, ..., *Demographic Yearbook 1949–50*, 2d issue [New York, 1950], 93 + 94 for figures), the plebiscite was held only in Norway. 435,376 persons were entitled to vote, 371,911 or 85.4 per cent actualy voted, 368,208 voted for separation, 184 voted against, and 3,519 ballots were declared invalid (see official report of the Norwegian Department of Justice in Sarah Wambaugh, *Monograph on Plebiscites* [1920], 1070ff.). For background see Wambaugh, ibid., 165–9; also Johannes Mattern, *The Employment of the Plebiscite in the Determination of Sovereignty* (Baltimore, 1920), 112–14.

91. Obviously I am referring to the sad case of Iurii Badzio. See (1) Malva Landa's plea, note 50 above; (2) Badzio's own protest or open letter to the Presidium of the USSR Supreme Soviet, in which he reconstructs the argument of the manuscript from memory, "Govorit Iurii Badzio: 'Pravo zhit,'" AS no. 3840, in *MS*, no. 4/80 (4 Feb. 1980), 9 pp.; and (3) information on his fate in Marco Carynnyk, ed., *Ukraine and the Helsinki Accords: Soviet Violations of Human Rights, 1975–1980* (Toronto and New York, 1980), 260.

92. On Glazunov see: (1) Edmund Stevens, "Slavophiles Blame All Soviet Ills on Karl Marx," (London) *Times*, 16 November 1979; (2) Bondarenko's interview with I. Glazunov on Radio Liberty—*MORS*, 460 OJ, 17 August 1979; (3) David Willis, "Soviet Censors Try New Track," *Christian Science Monitor*, 24 September 1979; (4) Radio Moscow 2, 27 September 1979, at 16:00 + 20:15, *MORS* 5542 22, 27 September 1979; (5) Radio Moscow 1, 4 July 1980, 20:15 in *MORS* 357 04, 5 July 1980; (6) Craig R. Whitney, "Leninist Ideology Gripped by Crisis," *New York Times*, 13 October 1980; and (7) TASS English service 30 1981 (all these sources courtesy of Roman Solchanyk, Radio Liberty). Also on Glazunov see Dunlop, "The Many Faces of Contemporary Russian Nationalism," 29ff., and his "The Russian Nationalist Spectrum Today...," 5–6 got a nice sample of rapturous comments (from *Khudozhnik i Rossiia*, Düsseldorf, 1980). On the Ukrainian Group see: *Ukrainian Herald, Issue IV* (Munich, 1974), 7–30; also Kenneth C. Farmer, "Politics and Culture in the Ukraine in the Post-Stalin Era," *Annals of the Ukrainian Academy of Arts and Sciences in the US* 14, no. 37–8 (1978–80): 200–01.

93. Most of the figures from Roman Solchanyk, "The Ukraine and Ukrainians in the USSR: Nationality and Language Aspects of the Census in 1979," in collection RFE-RL *Radio Liberty Research Bulletin*: The All-Union Census of 1979 in the USSR (Munich, 1980), RL 100/80 (11 March 1980).

94. Point made briefly, with figures, in Myroslav Prokop, "Violations of Political and National Rights in Ukraine, 1975–80," in Carynnyk, ed., 50. For more extended discussion see Robert A. Lewis, Richard H. Rowland, and Ralph S. Clem, "The

Growth and Redistribution of the Ukrainian Population of Russia and the USSR:
1897–1970," in Peter J. Potichnyj, ed., *Ukraine in the Seventies* (Oakville, 1975),
151–63, and same authors, *Nationality and Population Change in Russia and the
USSR: An Evaluation of Census Data, 1897–1970* (New York, 1976), 141–63 and
202–21.

95. The Soviet demographer S.I. Bruk, ["Ethnographic Processes in the USSR (Using
Materials from the Postwar Population Censuses)"], *Istoriia SSSR,* no. 5
(September-October 1980): 24–47, as abstracted in the *Current Digest of the
Soviet Press* 32, no. 50, 10, suggests that part of the increase in Ukraine's Russian
population may be due to Ukrainians who earlier had given Russian as their
native language (2+ million in 1959) and now in 1979 changed their nationality.
This would not be incompatible with the extremely valuable findings of Lubomyr
Hajda, "Nationality and Age in Soviet Population Change," *Soviet Studies* 32,
no. 4 (October 1980): 475–99, who found that between 1960 and 1970 Ukrainians
had relatively more small children than the Russians.

96. See, for instance, the complaints by Vitalii Kalynychenko of August 1977, cited
in Prokop, 49, and an even sharper protest in "Demographic Statistics Exposing
the Colonial Policy of Moscow's Occupation Forces in Ukraine," *The Ukrainian
Herald Issue 7–8: Ethnocide of Ukrainians in the USSR, Spring 1974* (Baltimore,
1976), 66ff.

97. For documentation see especially *The Ukrainian Herald Issue 6: Dissent in
Ukraine* (Baltimore, 1977).

98. See Bilinsky, "Expanding the Use of Russian . . . ," 322–3.

99. Ibid., 328.

100. "Russko-ukrainskoe zaiavlenie," 4.

101. See Table in Ann Sheehy, "Ethnic Muslims Account for Half of Soviet
Population Increase," Radio Liberty, *Report on the USSR,* volume 2, number 3
(January 19, 1990), p. 17. The semi-secret data from the 1989 census shows as
many as 268,739 Crimean Tatars, an increase of 103.2 per cent.

102. In this I would agree with the thoughtful article of Roman Szporluk, "Russians in
Ukraine and Problems of Ukrainian Identity in the USSR," in Potichnyj, ed., 213.

103. Many Ukrainians can speak Russian but greatly resent being forced to do so.

104. Gorskii, "Russian Messianism . . . ," 393.

CULTURE AND RELIGION

James Cracraft

The Mask of Culture: Baroque Art in Russia and Ukraine, 1600–1750

These observations concerning Russian and Ukrainian cultural developments between roughly 1600 and 1750 turn on the terms "Baroque", "art" (meaning fine art), and "mask," the last serving here as a metaphor in various senses. My purpose is to say something about the phenomenon of cultural Europeanization (preferred to "Westernization") in early modern Russia and Ukraine and, given the overall theme of this collection, something also about the relationship between these two historical processes. For it is agreed, I think, that in some degree "Russia" and "Ukraine" denote not only methodologically separate, but actually distinct, historical entities; and that however much they may be related, therefore, major historical developments in the one will have been different in their origins, course, and consequences from apparently similar developments in the other. The Renaissance in Italy was different from the Renaissance in France; the career of the Baroque in Ukraine should have been different from its career in Russia. Indeed, my investigations of the problem to date strongly suggest that this was so.

It might be noted that such a perception has not been readily available to the disinterested inquirer. If one reads the relevant (and extensive) passages of the monumental history of "Russian" art compiled by Grabar and others (1909), one finds that the story begins in Ukraine—the "Ukrainian Baroque"—continues in Moscow—the "Moscow Baroque"—and culminates in St. Petersburg, particularly in the architecture of Rastrelli, the supreme representative of the "St. Petersburg Baroque" and the first artist of any kind (Grabar tells us) to have been known in Russia beyond the confines of the court. The St. Petersburg Baroque, also entitled the "Russian Baroque" proper, then swept all before it—in the Ukrainian parts of the Empire as well (as witness, most obviously, Rastrelli's St. Andrew's church in Kiev). And this remains, in essence, the view from afar (e.g., Hamilton, 1975). There is in fact little Western writing on the Baroque in either Russia or Ukraine that incorporates more recent research.

II

The literature on the Baroque in Europe now fairly rivals, in quantity if not perhaps in quality, that devoted to the Renaissance or to Classical antiquity itself. Moreover, general historians, building on the work of their colleagues in architecture, painting, sculpture, and literature, have applied the term to a whole civilization, one which is said to have flourished in Europe between about 1600 and 1750, whence it spread to Latin America and colonial Asia, there also to flourish until well into the nineteenth century (Braudel, 1972). The Baroque's historiographical rise is itself a curious topic, signifying as it does a more tolerant, more catholic and/or relativist outlook in recent historical scholarship, among other things (a decline, conversely, of "Enlightenment" or "Neo-classical" biases). Yet as a historiographical term "Baroque" lacks precision, the result, in part, of applying it to broad ranges of often quite discrepant phenomena (and of describing its attributes, too often, in rather windy prose). The remark made some thirty years ago by a German authority still stands: "Baroque remains a nominalistic term with a heuristic value and not an ab-solute one" (von Faber du Faur, 1958).

At any rate, it is clear that the term "Baroque" is used properly first with regard to certain buildings erected in Rome between the 1620s and the 1660s; next, to imitative buildings erected later in the seventeenth and then in the eighteenth century in Rome, northern Italy, Switzerland, Austria, Bavaria, and beyond; then, to the works of painting and sculpture that are so much a part of these buildings' decorative plan and, from there, to any painting, engraving, or carved object of the period which resembles these works. But the term is also applied to the overall plan and/or decorative details of gardens, parks, and even whole townscapes that are seen to embody principles of Baroque art more narrowly so called (Białostocki [1977] reminds us that the period itself pro-duced no theory of Baroque art); to the contemporary musicals, theatricals, and ceremonials that are seen as somehow embodying these principles; and, finally, to literature. "Baroque" has been used to describe works in Latin or in the vernaculars classifiable as of poetry, drama, oratory or even of philosophy and theology (Leibniz, Neoscholasticism) whose forms and themes exhibit features more or less strongly reminiscent of the salient characteristics of Baroque architecture, painting, and sculpture (cf. Tomassoni, 1963).

What these principles and salient characteristics are, concretely, technically, I will not attempt to say. Suffice it to refer to the significant departures from the norms of Renaissance-classical architecture to be observed in the works of Bernini, Borromini, Pietro da Cortona and their immediate followers: to the fluid or open ground plans of these buildings; their highly ornate, often quite inventive decoration; and their multimedial optical illusions. The rest is "Baroque" by extension.

III

Baroque works of art, it becomes increasingly clear, were also produced in the Slavic lands (Angyal, 1961, is the first general study; see also Rogov and others, 1979). In some Slavic centres, of course, the production was considerble. One thinks immediately of the Baroque architecture of Prague, Cracow, Lviv, or St. Petersburg, and of literary developments in Poland and Bohemia (Hernas, 1973; Součková, 1980). Yet in so saying I would stress that for most of the period in question most of the Slavic world subsisted as yet either on or beyond the borders of Europe, "Europe" understood as the homeland of a particular cultural synthesis or rather succession of cultural syntheses dating back to the early Middle Ages. I would stress that in its primary historical manifestation the Baroque was a central and, more particularly, a southern European phenomenon; one that was Latin and Mediterranean in origin, Roman Catholic and especially Jesuit in dissemination, and aristocratic if not royal, indeed papal, by patronage. In fact, the advance of the Baroque in Europe and beyond provides a textbook case of the theory of cultural diffusion, with Rome as the "centre of spread." Where the Catholic church was not strong, or not even tolerated; where the Jesuits (or the Franciscans, the Dominicans, the Carmelites) could not work; where sympathetic princes did not rule: there the Baroque appeared late, and then sporadically, when at all. The obstacles to be overcome by the advancing Baroque in, say, Holland, England, or Russia were political and religious more than aesthetic or geographical. Ignorance or misconstruction of these fundamental points—of the very nature of Baroque art—has obscured its history in both Russia and Ukraine while giving rise, especially in Soviet scholarship, to quite remarkable distortions.

The earliest comprehensive application of the term "Baroque" to works of Ukrainian and Russian architecture, painting, and sculpture of the seventeenth and eighteenth centuries is to be found in that monumental history of "Russian" art by Grabar and others referred to above (1909). Their formulations engendered debate in succeeding years over the nature and limits of the Baroque as applied to local art, debate which at times reflected the advance of Baroque scholarship in the West (Lukomsky, 1911; Nekrasov and others, 1926; Shmit and others, 1929; Zalozieckyj, 1929). The initiatives of Grabar and associates, not surprisingly, were found in need of refinement and further exploration. They were also criticized, rightly, for having conferred so to speak the Baroque dignity on rustic phenomena lacking any demonstrable connection with contemporary European art. But Soviet ultranationalism and ideological simplisticism soon supervened. It was asserted in effect that as an inherently reactionary art, at once Catholic and "feudal," the Baroque could have had little impact on Russian and, more surprisingly still, Ukrainian cultural history. One hesitates to embarrass our Soviet colleagues in such matters, but the reformulations regarding Russian architectural developments of the first half of the eighteenth century published by Grabar and others in 1954 are a case in point. Lately, to be sure, there are signs that a more sophisticated and in part positive picture of the Baroque and its influence is emerging there (Vipper, 1978). Indeed, the editor of one Soviet collection goes so far as to identify a whole "Baroque age" (*epokha barokko*) in Russian art history. For if, as she says, the term "does not define all aspects of the many-sided artistic activity of the first half of the eighteenth century" in Russia, it was the "leading tendency"; moreover, "in significant measure it was precisely in Baroque forms that the classical tradition of West European art was adopted, which in turn made possible the transition from Old-Russian to modern [Russian] art" (Alekseeva and others, 1977). Things had come a long way from the deprecations of the Baroque habitual to an entire generation or more of Soviet scholars.

Unhappily, it cannot be reported that any such realignment distinguishes Soviet Ukrainian art scholarship. There the flowering of Baroque art on Ukrainian territory is still treated, in neo-populist fashion, as a largely if not wholly indigenous development. Biletsky's survey (1981) is a welcome if only partial exception to this rule. For in general the interdependence and eventual convergence of seventeenth- and eighteenth-century Ukrainian and Russian art continue to be stressed in Soviet scholarship at the expense of the former's European and especially Polish sources, a feat that is accomplished, in part, by simply ignoring western Ukraine. While this goes on, of course, the early modern cultural history of both Russia and Ukraine cannot be properly understood.

The term "Baroque" was first applied to the work of a Russian writer in the 1930s, in an article showing the German influences on Trediakovsky (Pumpiansky, 1937). Eremin used the term in his studies of Simeon Polotsky published in 1948 and 1953. Yet by 1962 the situation was still such that Morozov could complain, in the journal *Russkaia literatura*, of a certain "hush-up" (*zamalchivanie*) in Soviet literary scholarship concerning the "problem of the Baroque." Drawing on his researches as a biographer of Lomonosov, Morozov proposed so broad an applicaton of the term in Russian literary history as to provoke a long and excruciating rebuttal by Academician Likhachev (1968; 1969). The ensuing polemics, conducted in succeeding issues of *Russkaia literatura* and elsewhere, reveal elements of the nationalistic and ideological biases mentioned above in connection with Soviet art scholarship. The polemics also suggest that the Soviet literary establishment was finally coaxed into a begrudging acceptance of the Baroque as a valid historical and critical category by the work of Polish, Czech, and East German specialists in "Russian" as well as their own, respective literary histories.

Abroad, meanwhile, Dmytro Chyzhevsky almost single–handedly established a full Baroque period in the history of Ukrainian and then of Russian literature. His depiction of a Ukrainian literary Baroque has been criticized, however, for being at once static and isolated from its wider, especially Polish connections: as reflecting, to quote Milosz, "the sky of ideas" (Grabowicz, 1977); while in their enthusiasm to promote the supposed independence and maturity of seventeenth- and eighteenth-century "Russian" letters, it may be feared, Soviet scholars will play loose with the Baroque in its primary, and essential, European significance (cf. Segel, 1973; 1974). Another Western student proposes the term "Russo-Ukrainian scholasticism" to cover literary developments in Russia between roughly 1650 and 1750, with only "Baroque influences" appearing in both verse and prose (Drage, 1978). A basic problem, as Professor Segel says (1974), is that "there is so little *Russian* literature that lends itself to consideration as Baroque." Nor is the material base much improved when we turn to the Ukrainian literature of the period, particularly if we exclude from consideration works written by "Ukrainian" authors in Latin or Polish.

IV

In fact, in any serious study of the Baroque in Russia and Ukraine major source problems soon impose themselves. In the case of architecture, for instance, it is estimated that more than 70,000 cities, towns, and villages were devastated on Soviet territory in the course of the Second World War and some 3,000 individual monuments partially or completely destroyed. To this wholesale wartime destruction must be added that done to individual architectural monuments or to whole sites as a result of Soviet versions of "urban renewal". For until very recently the principles of architectural restoration and, still more, of historic preservation have enjoyed only sporadic and limited support among Soviet planners and policy–makers, support which has alternated with the deliberate destruction particularly of ecclesiastical monuments. In brief, numerous monuments testifying to Baroque influence on Russian building have been lost in this century, often with scarcely any graphic or documentary trace (I have in mind not only such a major monument as Patriarch Nikon's cathedral of the New Jerusalem monastery, which is now being laboriously restored, but countless urban and country churches of the eighteenth and nineteenth centuries). In Ukraine, if anything, the loss has been still more grievous—and is compounded by the relative sloth of restoration efforts. Not only were the three major examples of "Ukrainian Baroque" architecture in Kiev completely destroyed, but the loss of a "whole series of the most precious monuments" as well as of "certain archival materials" has meant that "only an approximate answer can be given to many important questions": I quote from the best study to date of eastern Ukrainian architecture of the period under review (Tsapenko, 1967; see also Hewryk, 1982).

Students of Baroque painting or sculpture in Ukraine are beset by comparable difficulties. In part these derive from the wartime architectural destruction just mentioned, in part from Soviet policy. Hordynsky (1973) points out, for instance, that only fifty of more than 10,000 icons collected in Lviv are accessible to researchers, while a recent study of early modern Ukrainian painting affirms both implicitly and explicitly that the loss of material has been simply enormous (Zholtovsky, 1978). The latter makes the melancholy point that not one of the "wondrous" paintings observed by Paul of Aleppo in his celebrated travels up the Dnieper basin in the middle of the seventeenth century survives. By contrast, the collection, restoration, study, and exhibition of Russian medieval and early modern painting, though far from ideal, have gone significantly further in Soviet times, especially in the last twenty years or so. Consider only the splendid two-volume catalogue of the relevant holdings of the Tretiakov Gallery in Moscow, where 1443 icons from a list of 4260 identified as then in the gallery are described (Antonova and Mneva, 1963).

Not all of the damage to the Russian and Ukrainian artistic heritage occurred in the twentieth century, to be sure. On the other hand, it was the relative meagerness of this heritage, quantitatively speaking, that makes this century's deliberate neglect and destruction so terrible. In England the Church Commissioners have to look after some 11,000 medieval stone edifices. This figure approaches the total of wooden and masonry churches known to have existed in Russia at the end of our period (about 1750) and of which a small fraction is now to be seen. In Norway and Sweden, fifty–six wooden or "stave" churches of the twelfth to the early fifteenth centuries have been preserved. In Russia and Ukraine, with but one or two debatable exceptions, the oldest surviving wooden churches, and a handful at that, date to the seventeenth century. One has only to tour the Soviet Union today, a copy of *Baedeker's Russia* of 1914 in hand, to sense the extent of the devastation to the built environment that has occurred since. And one senses that a comparably grim picture could be worked up for all of the plastic arts.

V

In the light of these multiple historiographical and source problems, not much can now be said with certainty regarding the career of the Baroque in Russia and Ukraine—not much more, generally speaking, than that the standard Western view, based on the pre-Revolutionary work in Russian of Grabar and others (1909), is no longer tenable. This is partly a tribute to the efforts of Soviet researchers, who in recent years have been setting aside the structures of an earlier time and are proceeding in their specialized studies to lay the groundwork for a new synthesis. Nor have one or two Western scholars been idle in the matter. We might consider some examples of this more recent research and fresher thinking in the primary field (for students of the Baroque) of architecture.

In the old view, Ivan Zarudny (or Zarudnev), an architect from Kiev who came to Moscow around 1700 and built one or more startlingly Baroque-like churches, was a key transmitter of the "Ukrainian Baroque" to Russia—indeed, the only one to be identified. But recent studies, in which further documentary as well as graphic evidence has been brought to bear, strongly suggest that the builders and decorators of the churches in question were Italians imported by Peter I. Zarudny, in this view, was an icon-painter and wood-carver whose only verifiable works are several triumphal arches and iconostases executed on the instructions, again, of Italian masters working in Moscow and St. Petersburg. At the same time, newly discovered documentary evidence suggests that Russian builders working in Kiev in the 1690s contributed decorative forms to the major monuments of the "Ukrainian Baroque" whose construction they either directed or assisted in. These builders were sent from Moscow to Kiev by Peter I at the urgent request of Hetman Mazepa, and pending still further investigations into the matter we must wonder whether the traffic in the Baroque was not two-way.

Then again, B.R. Vipper has argued, in essays written in the 1940s but only published in 1978, that there was no such thing as a "Moscow Baroque" in seventeenth-century Russian architecture. The decisive external influence on the latter's characteristically profuse decoration, he argued further, was not Ukrainian but Dutch, and that of a kind which had little or nothing to do with the Baroque but was rather Mannerist, even Gothic, in style. Given the relatively extensive commercial and other contacts between Russia and Holland in the period, this is a most promising suggestion. Meanwhile, the documentary and graphic evidence so far adduced on the penetration of Baroque—or Mannerist or Renaissance—motives in seventeenth-century Russian building points to two verifiable paths of diffusion, and only two: one, the elaborate iconostases fashioned by Belorussian craftsmen from about 1650 for patrons such as Patriarch Nikon and Tsarevna Sofia, numerous details of which were then copied, in their decorative schemes, by local church builders; and two, the illustrated books and individual prints flooding Russia from Ukraine, Poland, Germany and elsewhere in Europe in which local builders, in their rustic way, found a cornucopia of ornaments to imitate (Hughes, 1976; 1977). Indeed, we would seem to have here an excellent instance of the process of "rusticalization" in the transmission of art forms from a more to a less developed cultural community or "nation" (Stech, 1933).

In Russia, I would argue, Baroque architecture and the associated decorative arts arrived both directly and at once, in the space of a single generation—the work mainly of the thousand or more European builders of all kinds assisted by tens of thousands of local craftsmen who erected St. Petersburg, on the orders of Peter I, between 1703 and 1725 (Peter's death; intensive building resumed in the 1730s). This revolution in Russian architecture was eventually to reach into every corner of the Russian Empire. Particularly was this so during the reign of Peter's daughter, Empress Elizabeth, when a "Russian Baroque" in architecture is rightly said to have flowered, and again under Catherine II, when the Baroque in Russian building was overtaken, once more following European trends, by the relatively restrained tendency known as "Neoclassicism." This

Russian or, perhaps better, Imperial Baroque left its traces, and occasionally a major monument, in the Ukrainian parts of the Empire, too (Rastrelli's St. Andrew's church in Kiev). But it had virtually nothing to do, in its genesis or spread, with the "Ukrainian Baroque" of an earlier time.

Further, it may well be asked what the term "Ukrainian Baroque" itself can mean (cf. Ohloblyn, 1951). A "Belorussian Baroque" in architecture, it may be noted, is now a recognized phenomenon in Soviet scholarship, a matter less of ideological fashion than of plain fact. As a major work in the field makes clear, in Belorussia, owing to its complete incorporation in the Polish-Lithuanian state, the "basic trend in architecture of the seventeenth century and the first three–quarters of the eighteenth was Baroque" (Chanturiia, 1969). But the "Ukrainian Baroque" has been granted no such recognition. On the contrary, barely was it launched when Lukomsky proposed (1911) that the term had several and, to a degree, mutually exclusive meanings. There was, first of all, an early "Ukrainian Baroque proper . . . almost Catholic in feeling" that flourished in Lviv and elsewhere in Galicia, the work largely of Italian and Polish masters. In this sense the "Ukrainian Baroque" classifies readily, like its Belorussian cousin, as a species of the Baroque architecture—Italianate and Catholic—to be found throughout the territories of the seventeenth-century Polish-Lithuanian state (Miłobędzki, 1980). Next came, in Lukomsky's scheme, a "Mazepist" phase of the "Ukrainian Baroque": a "Mazepist Baroque" that was Germanic in its decorative details, both European and local in its structural forms, and pretty much confined, in its spread, to the towns and Cossack centres of the Dnieper river basin. But this architecture, now often called "Cossack Baroque," is not, I would insist, properly Baroque at all. Like the contemporary Orthodox church architecture of Belorussia or of the Moscow region, these were local structures festooned, in a rusticalizing way, with a miscellany of Baroque ornaments—or Mannerist or Renaissance or even Gothic—borrowed from who knows quite where. To call such buildings "Baroque" is both to misuse the term and to obscure their originality. A new stylistic term—simply "Cossack architecture?"—surely is needed here.

Finally, Lukomsky took note of—it could not be ignored—the Baroque of Rastrelli and his followers in Ukraine, a style emanating from St. Petersburg. This was indeed Baroque architecture properly so called. But it was confined to the Left Bank, and even there had only a limited impact on building, it seems. Moreover, historically as well as stylistically it was an imperial architecture, the first in a succession of Imperial Russian styles, and was not in any significant way specifically Ukrainian.

Thus with respect to architecture and the associated arts the term "Ukrainian Baroque" is something of a misnomer, and might be usefully eliminated in scholarly discourse in favour of a phrase such as "Baroque architecture in Ukraine," which provides for a variety of applications over both time and space. In literature, on the other hand, the situation is quite different. Whether one refers, narrowly, to writing readily classifiable as belletristic; or to, instead, the entire product of a given literary culture, including works of political, historical, religious, philosophical, and theological content (as I would prefer to do, in view of the time and the places under review): whether one uses "literature" in either the broader or the narrower sense, there is no question now that in the seventeenth century Baroque literary forms and themes were deployed, at times with remarkable skill, by Ukrainian writers. It is also clear that in so doing these writers drew heavily on Polish models; equally, that some of them carried Baroque norms to Moscow and St. Petersburg, where as teachers and preachers they contributed crucially to that modest flowering of Baroque literature in eighteenth-century Russia which was mentioned above.

Yet I would caution that it is at the least premature to speak of a "Ukrainian literary Baroque," if only because so much is still to be done in the matter of locating and establishing texts. I would also worry that the bilingual or even multilingual achievement of the most prominent writers in question itself vitiates against such a designation, since neither thematically nor biographically do these writers have enough in common to make up, as it were, for the linguistic deficit. To speak of "the Ukrainian Baroque" in literature is to imply both a unity and a frequency of phenomena which were not perhaps there. Nor should the importance of Ukrainian Baroque influence on Russian literature be exaggerated, as it sometimes is. Russian Baroque literature was a modest flower, to repeat, and the product also of direct German, Italian, and French influences.

VI

I began these remarks thinking to emphasize the importance of the Baroque in the cultural history of both Russia and Ukraine. I had thought to introduce at some point, for illustrative purposes, the career in those parts of Tasso's *Gerusalemme liberata* (1575), that epic of Italian Baroque literature which in Kochanowski's Polish rendition (1618) was probably the best–known literary work of foreign origin in seventeenth-century Poland. Around 1700 at least part of the Kochanowski version was translated into Ukrainian by Uniate monks, and as early as 1705, it seems, it was extensively quoted in a poetics course given at the Kiev academy. A version of this course was given at the Moscow academy in 1732, when a Russian translation of two verses of the Kocha-nowski/Tasso epic was achieved. Other instances could be adduced to illustrate this first or academic stage of the epic's career in Russia. A second stage is to be found in its influence, in the original Italian or in French or German translations, on the likes of Antiokh Kantemir, Trediakovsky, Lomonosov, Sumarokov, and Kheraskov. In 1772, M. I. Popov published his Russian translation of Mirabeau's French prose edition of the entire epic, which Catherine II judged "very fine" and which in 1787 was republished in a much larger run by Novikov. It was Popov who together with Chulkov did so much to create Russian fairy literature, one of their main sources having been, it seems, Tasso's epic. One could also point to the epic's having served as a source of theme or character or episode for several important operas and ballets produced in Russia during the last third of the eighteenth century. As a metaphor of the larger historical process, Tasso's complicated career in Ukraine and then in Russia—academic, literary, theatrical—is almost too neat.

I have not even mentioned music. In eighteenth-century Russia, both in church and at court, Baroque instrumental and especially choral music rapidly displaced the older, ultimately Byzantine norms—a process that had begun earlier in Ukraine, whence talented singers and composers went on to make exceptional careers in St. Petersburg. Analogous developments took place in painting (in portable or easel painting as well as in wall or decorative painting), with the result that in Russia icon-painting was rapidly reduced from a great state enterprise to a provincial, popular craft; in oratory, sacred and then secular, as is well known; and in what can only be called "thought." Here I mean that version of Jesuit Neoscholasticism (itself a typically Baroque combination of medieval Scholasticism and Renaissance-classical learning) perfected at the Kiev academy in the last decades of the seventeenth century which was then implanted elsewhere in Ukraine and in Russia—in the Moscow and St. Petersburg academies and in some twenty-six diocesan colleges—in the first decades of the eighteenth. It is not too much to say that Russians, like Ukrainians, first learned to think, in a formal, discursive, indeed in a logical way, under the tutelage of the Baroque.

When we consider, then, the history of Ukrainian and of Russian culture between about 1600 and 1750, it would appear that the Baroque influx had a major and at times revolutionary impact, particularly on the development of architecture and the plastic or decorative arts. This is as it should have been, once the political and aesthetic obstacles had been surmounted, given the essential nature of the Baroque in its homeland. And it might be agreed, in sum, that the term "Baroque" conveniently and properly designates a variety of European artistic and intellectual influences that were instrumental, sometimes crucially, in the formation of modern Russian and modern Ukrainian culture. It might be agreed that these influences were instrumental both extensively, by involving Ukrainians and Russians as never before in a dynamic, expansive civilization, and intensively, by giving impetus to the cultivation of national differences between them (political, religious, linguistic, etc.).

Yet I end these remarks fearing to have overstated the significance of the Baroque in Russian and especially Ukrainian history, a matter not alone of the historiographical and source problems already mentioned, but of the seemingly insuperable barrier of popular culture. For until the evolution of East Slavic popular culture in the last few centuries has been properly investigated, how can we really judge the impact on Russia or Ukraine of the Baroque (or, for that matter, of either Christianity or the Enlightenment)? I speak now as one who suspects that the impact of the Baroque on the East Slavic popular mind was considerable, a matter of everything from folktales to Christmas carols. But having myself been denied access, on occasion, to Soviet holdings of interest, I despair of Soviet scholars ever developing the capacity to study popular culture as historians in the West, notably in France and England, have begun to do (e.g. Burke, 1978; Muchembled, 1978). For now, the history of the Baroque in the East Slavic lands must remain a story told of, as well as by and for, a more or less appreciative cultural elite.

Works cited

Alekseeva, T.V. and others. *Russkoe iskusstvo barokko: Materialy i issledovaniia.* Moscow, 1977.

Angyal, A. *Die Slawische Barockwelt.* Leipzig, 1961.

Antonova, V.N. and N.E. Mneva. *Katalog drevnerusskoi zhivopisi XI-nachala XVIII v. v Gos. Tretiakovskoi galleree,* 2 vols. Moscow, 1963.

Białostocki, J. "Y eut-il une théorie baroque de l'art?" in A. Cielecka, ed., *Barocco fra Italia e Polonia.* Warsaw, 1977.

Braudel, F. *The Mediterranean and the Mediterranean World in the Age of Philip II,* 2 vols. Trans. S. Reynolds. New York, 1972.

Burke, P. *Popular Culture in Early Modern Europe.* New York, 1978.

Chanturiia, V. A. *Istoriia arkhitektury Belorussii: dooktiabrskii period.* Minsk, 1969.

Chyzhevsky, D. (Čiževskij). *History of Russian Literature from the Eleventh Century to the End of the Baroque.* The Hague, 1960. (Tschizewskij) "Das Barock in der russischen Literatur," in Tschizewskij, ed., *Slavische Barockliteratur I.* Munich, 1970. (Čiževsky) *Outline of Comparative Slavic Literatures.* Boston, 1952. *Istoriia ukrainskoi literatury.* New York, 1956.

Drage, C.L. *Russian Literature in the Eighteenth Century.* London, 1978.

Eremin, I.P. "Poeticheskii stil Simeona Polotskogo," in *Trudy otdela drevne-russkoi literatury* 6 (1948). *Simeon Polotskii. Izbrannye sochineniia.* Moscow, 1953.

Gorokhova, R.M. "Torkvato Tasso v Rossi XVIII veka," in M.P. Alekseev, ed., *Rossiia i zapad: iz istorii literaturnykh otnoshenii.* Leningrad, 1973.

Grabar, I.E. and others. *Istoriia russkago iskusstva,* vols. 2 & 4. Moscow, 1909, 1914. *Russkaia arkhitektura pervoi poloviny XVIII veka: issledovaniia i materialy.* Moscow, 1954.

Grabowicz, G. "Toward a History of Ukrainian Literature," in *Harvard Ukrainian Studies* 1, no. 4 (1977).

Hamilton, G.H. *The Art and Architecture of Russia.* Baltimore, 1975.

Hernas, C. *Barok.* Warsaw, 1973.

Hewryk, T.D. *The Lost Architecture of Kiev.* New York, 1982.

Hordynsky, S. *The Ukrainian Icon of the XIIth to XVIIIth Centuries.* Philadelphia, 1973.

Hughes, L.A.J. "Byelorussian craftsmen in late seventeenth-century Russia and their influence on Muscovite architecture," *Journal of Byelorussian Studies* 3, no. 4

(1976). "Western European Graphic Material as a Source for Moscow Baroque Architecture," *Slavonic and East European Review* 4, no. 4 (1977).

Likhachev, D.S. "Natsionalnoe edinoobrazie i natsionalnoe raznoobrazie," *Russkaia literatura*, no. 1 (1968). "Barokko i ego russkii variant XVII veka," *Russkaia literatura*, no. 2 (1969).

Lukomsky, G. "Ukrainskii barokko," *Apollon,* no. 2 (1911).

Miłobędzki, A. *Architektura polska XVII wieku,* 2 vols. Warsaw, 1980.

Morozov, A.A. "Problema barokko v russkoi literature XVII-nachala XVIII veka (sostoianie voprosa i zadachi izucheniia)," *Russkaia literatura,* no. 3 (1962). "Natsionalnoe svoeobrazie i problema stilei (K izucheniiu drevnerusskoi literatury i literatury XVIII veka)," *Russkaia literatura,* no. 3 (1967).

Muchembled, R. *Culture populaire et culture des élites dans la France moderne (XV-XVIIIe siècles).* Paris, 1978.

Nekrasov, A.I. and others. *Barokko v Rossii.* Moscow, 1926.

Ohloblyn, O. "Western Europe and the Ukrainian Baroque," *Annals of the Ukrainian Academy of Arts and Sciences in the U.S.* 1, no. 2 (1951).

Pumpiansky, N. "Trediakovskii i nemetskaia shkola razuma," in V.M. Zhirmunsky, ed., *Zapadnyi sbornik,* I. Moscow and Leningrad, 1937.

Rogov, A.I. and others. *Slavianskoe barokko: istoriko-kulturnye problemy epokhi.* Moscow, 1979.

Segel, H.B. "Baroque and Rococo in Eighteenth-Century Russian Literature," in *Canadian Slavonic Papers* 15, no. 4 (1973). *The Baroque Poem: A Compararative Survey.* New York, 1974.

Shmit, F.I. and others. *Russkoe iskusstvo XVII veka: sbornik statei.* Leningrad, 1929.

Součková, M. *Baroque in Bohemia.* Ann Arbor, 1980.

Stech, V.V. "Rustikalisierung als Faktor Stilentwickelung", in *XIIIe Congrès international d'histoire de l'art: Résumés des communications présentées au congrès.* Stockholm, 1933.

Tomassoni, I. *Per una ipotesi barocco.* Rome, 1963.

Tsapenko, M. *Arkhitektura Levoberezhnoi Ukrainy XVII-XVIII vekov.* Moscow, 1967.

Vipper, B.R. *Arkhitektura russkogo barokko.* Moscow, 1978.

von Faber du Faur, C. *German Baroque Literature: A Catalogue of the Collection in the Yale University Library,* 1, New Haven, 1958.

Zalozieckyj, "Die Barocharchitektur Osteuropas mit besonderer Berücksichtigung der

Ukraine," in *Abhandelungen des Ukrainischen Wissenschaftlichen Institutes in Berlin*, 2 (1929).

Zholtovsky, P.M. *Ukrainskyi zhyvopys XVII-XVIII st.* Kiev, 1978.

George G. Grabowicz

Ukrainian-Russian Literary Relations in the Nineteenth Century: A Formulation of the Problem

Since my avowed concern is with formulations, I should state at the outset that from my perspective the relation between Ukraine and Russia is not that of an "encounter," even a "historical encounter," but something much more intimate and long-lasting—in the language of Soviet pathos, a historical and indissoluble embrace or, as others might see it, a Sartrian *No Exit*. At the same time, since this article follows my earlier discussion of Polish-Ukrainian literary relations (which was also first presented in this same hospitable setting), I should stress that from the perspective of modern Ukrainian history and literature the Russian-Ukrainian relationship is undoubtedly the more central, and, especially in the nineteenth century, incomparably more complex.[1] My concern here, as stated by the subtitle, is not with the entire range and massive contents of this relationship, but with the principles and concepts by which we can systematize and facilitate our understanding of it; a comprehensive treatment, one which is sorely needed, would require the dimensions of a monograph. But even at this preliminary stage, the broad implications, and the difficulties, of this undertaking are clear. They are best indicated by the fact that, apart from the chronological designation,[2] all the terms employed to describe this investigation—not only "literary relations," but above all the meaning of the words "Ukrainian" and "Russian"—require fundamental re-examination.

It is undoubtedly quite revealing of the present political situation that for all the attention devoted to Russian-Ukrainian literary relations, this question is hardly ever constituted as a scholarly, or conceptual, or theoretical problem. This is primarily, of course, the case in Soviet scholarship, where the relationship between Ukrainian and Russian literature—like any number of larger and smaller issues—is understood only within the confines of official ideology, of *raison d'état*; the content and the dimensions of this subject, as well as the approaches to it, are strictly circumscribed and watched over by the highest organs.[3] One hardly needs to be enlightened as to the nature of these strictures; they are, above all, the teleological (and millenarian-utopian) notion of the drive to unification between the Russian and Ukrainian peoples, and the implicit and explicit older brother/younger brother relation between them.[4] The major corollary to these roles, one that is invariably applied in actual historical exegesis, is that it was the progressive forces in both nations that furthered, and the reactionary forces that impeded, this unification. These dogmas, of course, are never far from any Soviet literary criticism or scholarship, but they become particularly obtrusive and stultifying in discussions of this relationship. Two illustrations may be in order here. In an article on Lesia Ukrainka and Russian literature of the 1880s and 90s, Oleksandr Biletsky turns to one of her poems, "Napys v pustyni," a work clearly based on Shelley's "Ozymandias" (and in fact typifying her penchant for elaborating the "great," "Western" literary themes) and proceeds to argue that, if anything, the model here is provided by Nekrasov, not Shelley. "Before looking afar," he says,

> we must look closer to home, and here, after all, in immediate proximity to Lesia Ukrainka, was the democratic Russian literature, both the older and the contemporary, and this is what constitutes—along with the equally immediate Ukrainian literature—that closest of contexts, to which we must turn first when we study the poet.[5]

What is so telling here, along with the undercurrent of traditional xenophobia, is that this argument is made by an otherwise serious and conscientious scholar, and one who is particularly well acquainted with Western literatures. The second example concerns the relationship of Belinsky to Shevchenko, and particularly the ongoing attempt by the Soviet Ukrainian critic F.Ia. Pryima, among others, to attribute to Belinsky an unsigned, positive review of Shevchenko's *Kobzar* and thus, in contravention of all existing evidence, to show that the Russian critic did, in fact, also express favourable opinions on the Ukrainian poet.[6] In answer to those Soviet scholars who were not swayed by Pryima's tenuous reasoning (and these included such eminent figures as M.K. Hudzii and Oksman), the critic Ie. Kyryliuk noted, unambiguously, that "we, Soviet scholars, must not forget that this essentially academic problem also possesses a current political aspect."[7] The "theoretical" basis on which this not so subtle warning rests is precisely the dogma of the "progressive" writer and the imperative to trim the facts to the historiosophic scheme.

In non-Soviet scholarship the question of Russian-Ukrainian literary relations is also hardly posed as a *problem*. For nationalistically minded Ukrainian critics the relationship is largely perceived as one of national antagonisms and not so much a literary relationship as one of political and social oppression. In general, the occasional Western studies that impinge on this subject turn to discrete, individual moments, and not to the entire phenomenon. One may argue, in fact, that since the Revolution no real attempt has been made to conceptualize this relationship, to treat it as a complex literary, cultural and historical problem. The early Soviet (in a very real sense: non-Soviet) works of Zerov or Fylypovych or Sypovsky turn to selected aspects, but not to the whole.[8] The major non-Soviet history of Ukrainian literature, by Dmytro Chyzhevsky, which in its Ukrainian version extends only to the period of Romanticism, and in its English version treats "Realism" in a skimpy and idiosyncratic manner, is more attuned to the Western connections of Ukrainian literature, and is generally uninterested in the actual social and cultural context.[9] In short, a subject that attracted so much intelligent, unfettered and provocative attention in the pre-Revolutionary period—from Kulish, Kostomarov, Drahomanov and Franko, to name only the prominent Ukrainian critics—is now, a century later, either largely ignored or systematically distorted.

For the purpose of this discussion, and with the intent of making a provisional model for a future, more thorough investigation, I would propose treating the Russian-Ukrainian literary relationship in terms of five separate rubrics or aspects: 1) The legacy and influence that an individual writer, primarily the belletrist, but also the critic or scholar, of one literature may have on the other. 2) The simultaneous, or, more rarely, the sequential participation of individual writers in both literatures. (This bilingual bridging of the two literatures is almost exclusively a characteristic of Ukrainian writers and, again, it applies to both the creative artist and the critic and scholar.) 3) The major historical events and developments, primarily pertaining to cultural politics, that affect and mould both the individual literatures and the relationship between them. These are, to be sure, *extrinsic* factors or moments—the suppression of the Brotherhood of Saints Cyril and Methodius, the Ems ukase of 1876, and so on—but they are certainly more than mere "historical background." They are very much factors that determine the profile of Ukrainian literature and thereby, too, the nature of its relation to Russian literature. 4) The history of the various attitudes to this relationship, the attempts at conceptualizing the problem. This rubric is as fascinating as it is broad: it seems that anyone even remotely interested or involved in both Ukrainian and Russian literature also expressed an opinion on their interrelation, and these opinions range from scholarly and systematic studies to the occasional and scurrilous comments of publicists or agents provocateurs. A central theme here—one which cuts across such diverse fields as philology, linguistics, social and political ideology, administrative and educational policy, and so on—is the question of the "right" of Ukrainian literature and language to exist. The fifth and last rubric is a synthetic one, and its essence is not so much the historical data as the historiographic model. The specific concern here must be a functional periodization of nineteenth-century Ukrainian literature, in short, a means of systematizing the *intrinsic* history of the literature by focusing, on the one hand, on the appearance and disappearance of conventional literary norms and values (Classicism, Romanticism, Realism, and so on), and, on the other, even more intrinsically, on the underlying cultural sets and premises, the deep structures, so to speak. It is here, finally, that we can establish the more fundamental differentiae between the two literatures.

These five categories, of course, are not always clear-cut, and they differ in their importance for literary history. The third category, for example, the realm of cultural politics, so to speak, underlies all the others, and in some respects is more the canvas than the subject of the picture. The fourth category, the broad gamut of opinions on the Ukrainian language and literature, and their "right to exist," is as much a subject of Ukrainian intellectual history, or modern Ukrainian history *tout court*, as it is of literary history. It dramatically re-inforces the perception that the history of Ukrainian literature, and its relation to Russian literature, is much more than a literary matter. The second, seemingly natural and self-evident rubric, the content of which is the bilingualism of nineteenth-century Ukrainian writers, is actually profoundly problematical; the fact that until mid-century, and beyond, virtually all the Ukrainian writers also wrote in Russian suggests that in this period the distinc-tion made between Ukrainian and Russian as between two different, presuma-bly *national* literatures, may require rethinking. Each of these aspects, however, constitutes a valid frame of reference or strategy for approaching the many-faceted phenomenon in question; none of them can be ignored if the goal is a comprehensive treatment. And, indeed, with varying degrees of success, each has been so used at one time or another. In fact, there have even been attempts to examine the "deep structures," that is, differences in the essential nature, the "national profile," the make-up and function of the two literatures—but for the most part, these have been unsystematic and couched in metaphor rather than analytic judgment.

*

The first category mentioned is by far the largest in terms of actual studies. In a sense, it is quite natural that the study of literary relations be focused on such moments as the influence or, generally, the resonance of a writer of one literary tradition with or in another, particularly a neighbouring literary tradition; this, after all, not only subtends a *discrete* set of facts, but also, on the face of it at least, a set of *literary* facts. It would seem to offer, in short, the most intrinsically literary approach to the subject. As reflected, for example, by Holdenberh's survey of bibliographic sources for the study of Ukrainian literature, Soviet (i.e., Soviet Ukrainian) investigations of Russian-Ukrainian literary relations are totally dominated by this literary-historical paradigm: ex-cept for one bibliography of Russian literature in Ukrainian translation, and two bibliographies dealing with translations of the various literatures of the Soviet Union into Russian, all the works described are determined by the formula "N. N. and Ukraine" (the actual writers being, in alphabetical order, Gogol, Gorky, Korolenko, Lermontov, Maiakovsky, Nekrasov, Pushkin, Tolstoi, Turgenev, and Sholokhov).[10] There is also, of course, the obverse of this, whereby a Ukrainian writer is examined in terms of his contacts with, his interests and reception in Russian literature. Not surprisingly—given the objective, historical state of affairs, as well as the obligatory proportion of attention—the set is more circumscribed here, with the emphasis falling above all on Shevchenko;[11] beyond him, the focus is most often on such writers as Franko, Myrny, Hrabovsky, Kotsiubynsky, and a few others.[12]

In either case, the characteristic strength of the approach is the mass of factual data that is usually adduced. For example, in Pryima's study of Shevchenko in nineteenth-century Russian literature, which examines Russian literary influences on Shevchenko and on early nineteenth-century Ukrainian literature as such, which deals with Shevchenko's contacts with various Russian figures, his reception in Russian criticism and literary life, his legacy in Russian society and, in a word, the battle over Shevchenko, there is a wealth of useful references and facts.[13] Unfortunately, it is only raw data. That which purports to be the organizing theory or historiosophic conception is, as already suggested, only a reductive and crude dogma and teleology.

No less a problem is the narrowness and selectivity of the focus. In the various contemporary Soviet studies on Shevchenko and Russian literature, be it Pryima's monograph or the relevant article in the *Shevchenkivskyi slovnyk*, virtually all of the attention is devoted to the ideological side of the question (the critical pronouncements, the polemics, administrative or police measures, etc., etc.), but so central a moment—for the literary scholar—as the impact or resonance of Shevchenko's poetics is seldom addressed.[14] A more general statement of this problem is that Soviet critics invariably treat the relationship in question not as that of a literature to a literature, but of a "progressive" literature to a "progressive" literature. That which remains outside this exclusionary paradigm, i.e., the ideas or the roles of those deemed to be "reactionary" (be they Ukrainian or Russian), is bracketed out, reduced to a caricature, or, most frequently, ignored. To this we shall return.

One should, perhaps, qualify this judgment by noting that periods of political thaw bring with them a certain increase in critical and intellectual integrity, and veracity. Thus in 1961, in a striking example of critical housecleaning, O. Biletsky denounced, among other distortions, the absurd lengths to which some critics had gone to make Shevchenko a "faithful follower" of the Russian revolutionary democrats, which included making him a follower of Dobroliubov, who at the time in question was in his early teens.[15] These improvements, however, are only relative—and often very transitory. One can note, for example, that the same Biletsky, in an article on Pushkin and Ukraine that was originally written in 1938, but which received several redactions, the last, posthumously, in 1966, argued not only that Pushkin's true counterpart and ally in Ukrainian literature was Shevchenko, but that Kulish, for whom throughout his life Pushkin was a model and an ideal to whom he devoted poems and whose works he imitated, was, in fact, Pushkin's deceitful, ideological enemy.[16] So sweeping a distortion of historical and literary fact can only evoke our commiseration for the scholar who once felt obliged to make it, and later lacked the nerve to renounce it.[17]

The point of my argument is not ideological but methodological: the principal and unavoidable flaw of various studies juxtaposing the writer with neighbouring literature, be it *qua* "Pushkin and Ukraine" or "Panas Myrny and Russian literature," is not merely that their ideological premises are so simplistic and reductive, nor even that the influence always seems to be in one direction (while one need not accept the official Soviet metaphor that Ukrainians invariably "learned from" and "followed" their Russian counterparts, there is little doubt, and certainly no shame in admitting, that the flow of literary models, theories and ideas was precisely from the imperial centre to the provinces). The problem with the critical paradigm in question is that in its implementation it leaves no room for, nor does it show any consciousness of, a *literary system* that would underlie and make sense of the manifold facts that are strung together in the critic's narrative. A minor but telling illustration of the potential speciousness of a literary "fact" that is given without reference to its context occurs in the above-noted article on Myrny and Russian literature, in which the author argues that "one of the eloquent proofs of Panas Myrny's loving relation to the culture of the Russian people was his fervent wish to celebrate in Ukraine, in 1902, the fiftieth anniversary of Gogol's death."[18] It apparently never occurred to the author that for Myrny Gogol may have been a Ukrainian writer.

The system to which I am referring, of course, is not to be confined even to the whole set of the given *writer's* attitudes, values and convictions. It is precisely the given *literature's* values, norms and "interests" that must be conceptualized and, to the extent possible, reconstructed. In large degree this devolves on what the anthropologists would call "cultural readiness."[19] And this, of course, works in both directions: just as the first attempt to translate Pushkin into Ukrainian—Hrebinka's semi-burlesque rendition of "Poltava" —was a kind of cultural misunderstanding, so also the early (and indeed later) Russian perceptions of Shevchenko—even the extremely favourable ones— hardly perceived the qualities, the "cultural language," that was so stunningly manifest to virtually all Ukrainians. In sum, without a sense of the cultural code into which the given elements (ideas, models, etc.) are being transposed, a discussion in terms of the paradigm of influence, or interest, or resonance, runs the high risk of being arbitrary and mechanical; by its very focus on an individual writer rather than on a broad social process, or a readership, it can only give a selective picture.

Whereas the first rubric dominated discussions of Russian-Ukrainian literary relations, the second, pertaining to the manifest and unmistakable phenomenon of bilingualism, has been virtually ignored. Yet it is here, in the eloquent fact that to the middle of the nineteenth century, and beyond, virtually all the Ukrainian writers also wrote in Russian (frequently more than in Ukrainian), that we begin to see the outlines of the complexity of the problem before us.

The few critical and scholarly comments that have been devoted to this problem have been tentative at best. Soviet critics who discuss Shevchenko's Russian writings, for example, or those of Kvitka or Hrebinka, invariably see them as expressing an immanent (and "progressive") drive for "unification" (*iednannia*);[20] by way of further explanation, they may argue that turning to the Russian language was also motivated by practical concerns, in effect the desire for wider dissemination of their works. Every so often there appears the not insignificant argument that Russian was used (for example by the writers just named) to deal with themes that were broader and more general (e.g., social) than those usually dealt with in Ukrainian-language writings. Thus, for example, S.D. Zubkov says that the first reason that various early nineteenth-century Ukrainian writers turned to Russian when writing prose was that Ukrainian, confined as it then was to the level and style of burlesque, did not offer the breadth and subtlety of expression that the more developed system of Russian prose did. "The second reason," he goes on, "may have been the desire to turn society's attention to Ukraine. The recognition in Russian society of works by Ukrainian writers brought them out from a narrow, national frame and gave great social weight to the problems raised in these works."[21] An equally typical claim is that of N.E. Krutikova: "Collaboration in Russian literature was also valuable in that it became for Ukrainian writers one of the paths for directly joining in the democratic and humanistic ideas of progressive Russian society and in [working for] the desideratum of national character (*narodnist*) and realism. This could not be reflected in their Ukrainian creativity. It is interesting to note, [however,] that Kvitka and Hrebinka were often much more radical in their Russian works . . . the general tenor of Russian realist prose, its humanistic tendency, the spirit of challenging the destructive social norms had an emotional impact on the participants in this process and activated the better, democratic sides of their world-view."[22] Similar examples could be produced at will. At this juncture, however, two moments should be pointed out. One, of course, is the turgid, rhetorical and ultimately vague mode of expression. While facts are introduced (but seldom truly marshalled according to a hierarchy of criteria), the interpretative matrix, as already noted, is much too crude for anything but the broadest generalizations. This, unfortunately, characterizes not only discussions of Russian-Ukrainian relations, but much of contemporary Soviet Ukrainian literary scholarship. The more important moment, to be sure, is the content of these judgments. They are characterized, among other things, by a more or less unconscious shifting of essential criteria. As we see in the statements of Zubkov, and in the general line of reasoning, the distinction that is addressed is the one between the imperial centre, with its consciousness, literary culture and values, and the provinces. This distinction, however, is "nationalized," in effect, presented as that of "Russian" *vis-à-vis* "Ukrainian." As we shall see below, this leads to one of the most profound and widespread misconceptions in the approaches to the problem at hand.

For non-Soviet Ukrainian critics, the Russian-language writings of Ukrainian writers are most often treated as something of an embarrassment, like a skeleton in the closet; for some they are a hedging on the writer's national commitment. For many others, including most Western critics, this is largely a *terra incognita*. For virtually all, however, language is seen as determining literature: what is written in Russian belongs in the category of Russian literature. (While there is ambivalence about some works—for example, one detects a certain reluctance on the part even of Soviet critics to call Shevchenko's Russian-language *Zhurnal* [Diary] a part of Russian literature —there also seems to be a growing willingness in some recent works to designate such writings as part of Russian literature, pure and simple).[23] That this is not an ideological judgment, but a reflection of a much deeper cognitive set, is attested by the revealing fact that even in the very liberal 1920s, when any number of "sensitive" literary and cultural matters were investigated, the linguistic basis for the demarcation between Russian and Ukrainian literature remained unchallenged.[24]

The matter must now be addressed directly and forcefully: as important as it is, the linguistic basis cannot be accepted as the ultimate determinant of a national literature—and if it is, the inevitable result will be precisely the confusion we encounter in the history of Ukrainian literature and in the question of Russian-Ukrainian literary relations (particularly of the early nineteenth century). As I have argued elsewhere,[25] the use of the language criterion to determine a literature is not only faulty in its logic (and in effect a continuation of the Romantic, or, more precisely, Herderian identification of a people [*Volk*] and its spirit [*Volksgeist*] with its language), but is also, notwithstanding the absence up to now of a clearly articulated counter-argument, not at all followed in scholarly and literary-historical practice. For by relying solely on language as a criterion one would not be able to demonstrate the continuity of various literatures as they shift linguistic mediums (for example, from Latin to the vernacular, as in the case of Polish or Hungarian), or the separate identity of different literatures sharing the same language (e.g., English, American, Canadian), or, finally, the selfsameness of a literature, like Turkish, which, depending on its genre system, uses various linguistic vehicles (in this case Persian, Arabic and Turkish). In the case of Ukrainian literature—compounded as the matter is by the absence of an authoritative institution, be it a state or an Academy of Sciences—this confusion, which is essentially based on a dissociation of literature from its social context, has led to radical misconstructions of historical reality.

Having rejected the Romantic and quasi-metaphysical notion of literature as the emanation (the "spirit") of a "nation", i.e., a *Volk* and a *Volksgeist*, we must replace it with what I take to be a more rational, and certainly more empirical definition of literature as a reflection, product and function of a society. As such, "literature," or, more precisely, literary products and processes reflect that society and serve its needs; the structures and the mode of existence of a society are reflected in its literature. If that society is, among other things, bilingual, so too will be its literature. At various times in its history, this has been (not entirely uniquely) the peculiar fate of Ukrainian literature. In the multinational Polish-Lithuanian Commonwealth the use of the *lingua franca*, Polish—depending on genre and function—did not signify rejection of one's identity. (We see it used, for example, in a panegyric by one Ukrainian churchman [Ivan Velychkovsky] to another [Lazar Baranovych]. The "patriotism," the Ukrainian "national" and literary consciousness of the former can hardly be doubted.) The same applies to the Russian Empire and its *lingua franca*—it applies, that is, up to that time, somewhere in the last third of the century, when after the ground-breaking works of Shevchenko and Kulish, the system of Ukrainian literature came to shift to a monolingual basis.

To hold the contrary, I submit, is to misread history. If "Ukrainian literature" is understood simply as literature in Ukrainian, or, in other words, if no distinction is made between the literature in Ukrainian and the literature of Ukrainian society, then it must follow that since in the first three decades of the nineteenth century there is little Ukrainian-language literature to speak of, there was at that time little if any Ukrainian society. Now, although the question of when the modern Ukrainian nation came into being is arguable, there is no denying that a Ukrainian society—and not just a peasant mass—did exist and did satisfy its literary needs, although only partially and at first, as it were, only informally in the Ukrainian vernacular. And it is precisely the middle and upper levels of that society—and not the *narod*, the peasant mass—that produced (with but a few notable exceptions, primarily Shevchenko) the writers and activists who effected the national revival of the nineteenth century. It must be stressed, however, that the identification of "Ukrainianness" with "peasant-hood" or "muzhikdom" (i.e., the *narod*)—which is, in effect, the indentification that determines the equation of "Ukrainian literature" with literature written in the Ukrainian vernacular, the "language of the people"—was made not only by those, like Belinsky, who were hostile to the Ukrainian national revival, but by the very mainstream of that revival, i.e., the spokesmen of *narodnytstvo*, above all Kostomarov. To this, too, we shall return.

In sum, it is essential to recognize that a large body of works written in Russia, from the *Istoriia Rusov* to the later writings of Kulish and Kostomarov, are part of Ukrainian literature. Such a reformulation carries with it some important consequences. One is the task of determining the criteria of redefinition. As I have argued elsewhere,[26] this is a synthetic judgment, involving above all the cultural context, and not at all a mere discrimination of ethnic origins. To take one rather clear-cut example, V.G. Korolenko, who was ethnically Ukrainian, who lived much of his life in Ukraine and in his writings often turned to a Ukrainian subject matter, can hardly be considered, and indeed in no serious quarters is considered, a Ukrainian writer. A very different situation, however, obtains in the case of Gogol, the one writer who best exemplifies some of the complexities of Russian-Ukrainian literary relations. Gogol has been considered a Ukrainian (*as well as* a Russian) writer in the past (and not only, as we shall see, by nationalistic revisionists), and he indeed should be so considered now. Again, the basis for this judgment lies not in his ethnic origin or in his use of Ukrainian themes (although neither element is insignificant); still less is it a question of territorial ties. (After all, Shevchenko himself spent only a fraction of his mature, creative life in Ukraine.) In fact, while all these moments—language, thematic focus, ethnic origin and even territorial ties—may play a greater or lesser role, the issue of whether a given writer is, as in this case, a Russian or a Ukrainian writer must be resolved with finer tools than any one, or any combination, of these criteria can provide.

The case of Gogol is, of course, too involved to allow for a comprehensive answer in the framework of this overiew. At the same time, he is too important a presence for us not to attempt at least a preliminary resolution. It is clear, at any rate, that historically, in his own lifetime and throughout the nineteenth century, Gogol was considered a Ukrainian writer (as well as a Russian one). In one of the first academic histories of Ukrainian literature of the nineteenth century (written, it must be noted, from a position of all-Russian loyalism), Nikolai [Mykola] Petrov treats Gogol at length (along with such writers as Maksymovych, Bodiansky, Hrebinka and Storozhenko) in a chapter entitled "Ukrainian Nationalism or the National School in Ukrainian Literature." For Petrov, to choose only the most explicit formulation, "Gogol, who contains in his Ukrainian stories all the elements of earlier and contemporary Ukrainian literature, appears as a worthy culmination of the new Ukrainian literature in the first period of its development."[27] In his history, which takes the form of a book-length critique of Petrov's study, M.P. Dashkevych finds fault with many of his predecessor's formulations, but not those concerning Gogol as a Ukrainian writer. For him, "in the figure of Gogol Ukrainian creativity decisively directed all-Russian literature [*obshcherusskuiu literaturu*] onto the path of naturalism."[28] More than two decades earlier, the polemic between Maksymovych and Kulish concerning Gogol, carried on in *Osnova* and other journals, implicitly placed Gogol at the very centre of the Ukrainian literary process.[29] And some twenty-odd years before that, N.A. Polevoi, in his attack on Ukrainian literature as something artificial and anachronistic, singles out Kotliarevsky and Gogol as the culprits who started this futile and perhaps harmful exercise. "The followers of Kotliarevsky and Gogol," he argues, "revealed the comic side of the notion of the artificial creation of independent Ukrainian poetry, and of the idea that Ukraine can be the subject of drama, epic and lyrical poetry, the novel, and such narratives as would form a separate literature; [in fact] all this constitutes only a particular element of all-Russian poetry and literature."[30]

It should be obvious here that these various attitudes, while revealing a consistent climate of opinion, also raise as many questions as they answer. For one, on the level of methodology, they remind us that the historian's task is to critically re-evaluate the historiographic formulas of the past, and not merely accept them if they prove convenient.[31] Our concern here, however, is specifically with the existence of a consensus and not with the validity of the judgments it contains. In terms of the substance of these attitudes, it must be noted, of course, that for all these scholars or critics Gogol was also, and for some primarily, a Russian writer. (Kulish, perhaps more than others, was willing to stress this fact. In his various writings on Gogol, beginning with his "Ob otnoshenii malorossiiskoi slovesnosti k obshcherusskoi" (the epilogue to *Chorna rada*), he sees Gogol's greatest achievement in the fact that he opened the eyes of Great Russian, or "North Russian" society to Ukraine and its past, that through his talent he made his homeland an object of charm and interest,[32] that he furthered the friendship between the two peoples, and, not least of all, that he made a tremendous linguistic impact on the Russian language, expanding and indeed shifting its basis.[33]) For all of them, moreover, the central, though in varying degree conscious and explicitly stated premise is that being a Ukrainian writer and a Russian writer is not mutually exclusive, that like Gogol one can exist with such a *dvoedushie*. This consensus was manifest throughout much of the nineteenth century. In time, however, there came a shift in the mainstream of opinion and indeed in the operant categories. There occurred, in short, a fundamental "nationalization" of cultural and political life and consciousness. In his psychologically oriented study of 1909, D.N. Ovsianiko-Kulikovsky now speaks of Gogol as an *obshcheruss na malorusskoi osnove*.[34] Later, in Soviet treatments, and also in the West, even this *osnova* is hardly considered: Gogol is simply and straightforwardly seen as Russian writer who happens to be of Ukrainian origin.

To argue that Gogol is a Ukrainian writer does not, of course, mean that we are turning back the clock of history; we are not trying to resurrect the attitudes and the overall state of national consciousness in Ukraine and Russia of a century ago. It is essential, however, for us to be able to reconstruct these attitudes and consciousness, or, more generally, the prevailing cultural set precisely in order to reconstruct with any confidence the nature of the two literatures—Russian and Ukrainian—*as systems*. For it is only in terms of the overall system of the literature that we can answer the question of whether a given writer participates in it, or "belongs" to it. To approach the issue by attempting to determine whether the writer, in this case Gogol, is a "Ukrainian writer" is problematical not only because the criteria involved (blood, language, themes, etc.) are particular, but also because the very idea of what it is to be a Ukrainian writer (and indeed a "Ukrainian") is in a state of becoming.[35] The literature taken as a system—while clearly also a dynamic, evolving phenomenon—provides a much more concrete and testable set of criteria for resolving the problem at hand.

The most concrete evidence that Gogol is also a Ukrainian writer is provided by critical praxis: his writings—especially, of course, the early Ukrainian stories, but, to some extent at least, his later works, like *Revizor* or *Mertvye dushi* as well—are not fully comprehensible without reference to the context of Ukrainian culture and its traditions and Ukrainian literary culture and its traditions.[36] For our present purposes, more important than the adequacy of critical perception and interpretation is the literary-historical aspect—the literature as a set of norms and values, as a system. And here it is clear that in that historical period, roughly from Kotliarevsky to Shevchenko (and somewhat beyond), Gogol's work is quite consistent with the norms, values, and concerns of Ukrainian literature. The reliance in one set of genres of Ukrainian literature of that time—from the *Istoriia Rusov* to Shevchenko's *Zhurnal*—on Russian as a natural medium is quite evident (and these works have traditionally been considered—present Soviet revisionism aside—as part of Ukrainian literature). Gogol's gamut of literary, historical, and folkloric associations and subtexts, his formal and comic devices, his range of metaphor and symbolism, in short, any number of features of his poetics partake of the system of Ukrainian literature of the time. At the same time it must be noted that Gogol departs—with time, more consciously and consistently—from this system and moves into an all-Russian one. This movement is expressed not just by overt themes (the urban, above all) and concerns (the problem of the artist), or by conscious ideological formulations (the emphasis on an all-Russian patriotism as revealed, for example, in the second redaction of *Taras Bulba*), but most of all perhaps by his sense of a broad all-Russian audience, a sense, to be sure, that is already implicit in his Ukrainian stories. This shift does not invalidate our argument, however. As a writer Gogol participates in both literary systems. Beyond that it is clear that at that time it was in the nature of the all-Russian, imperial literary culture to include the Ukrainian, and for Ukrainian, conversely, to be part of, to participate, to a large if not total extent, in the imperial literary culture.

In the course of the second half of the nineteenth century this relationship was fated to undergo substantial change. At the turn of the century, around the time that the Russian Imperial Academy of Sciences determined officially that Ukrainian was a language and not a dialect, the all-Russian literary culture became simply the Russian literary culture, and the option of bilingualism ceased to exist.

A further, not unimportant, consequence of our focus on bilingualism is that of noetic precedent, so to speak: having performed this reformulation we may be more conscious of, and more ready to accept, the fact that such constructs as "national literature" (be it Ukrainian or Russian), just like the notions of "literary period" (Classicism or Romanticism), are above all historiographic formulas that periodically require rethinking.

*

The third rubric, as I have noted, is more the domain of social, political and intellectual historians. In touching upon it here we are again reminded to what extent the Ukrainian literary phenomenon is coterminous with the social and political one. Moreover, insofar as traditionally nothing that occurs in Russia is outside the interest of the government, the literary domain is also a state matter, indeed also a matter of state security. Clearly, though, what I am speaking of here are Ukrainian-Russian relations as they pertain to literature, that is, Ukrainian literature, and not specifically literary relations.

The range of moments that enter this picture, that is, the various events and decisions—political, administrative, educational, police, etc.—that affect and shape Ukrainian literature is both large and heterogeneous. It involves such matters as the decisions to open a university in Kharkiv and Kiev, to prosecute the Brotherhood of Sts. Cyril and Methodius, and of course the decision, first in 1863 and then more forcefully in 1876, to ban the use of the Ukrainian language and to stifle Ukrainian literature and the separatism that the government saw lurking in it. I shall focus briefly on the latter step and its profound literary implications.

In one sense, the Ems ukase of 1876 can be seen as the most definitive, unequivocal statement in the ongoing debate in Russia about the right of the Ukrainian language and literature to exist and develop. The damage this decision did to Ukrainian literature and culture, particularly mass education, is indubitable. But its ultimate effect was quite different from that originally intended. Without overdramatizing the matter, and with all due care not to oversimplify the complex historical picture, one could argue that the most important consequence of this act was to shift Ukrainian literature out of the provincial mode. This is not at all to argue that at that moment Ukrainian literature—in its thematic range, artistic sophistication, conscious *Weltanschauung*, etc.—became any less provincial than it may have been. In range and complexity and sophistication the ethnographic realism of a Myrny or a Nechui-Levytsky could still hardly be compared to the realism of a Tolstoi or a Dostoevsky. But this is not the point, nor is this the kind of comparativism that I consider productive. The point is twofold. In concrete practice Ukrainian writers from the Russian Empire now turn to Galicia to publish their works and in so doing not only begin the arduous process of unifying two heretofore separate Ukrainian literatures (and, to a certain extent, languages), but also— *volens nolens*—expand their consciousness, their field of vision, beyond the bounds of the Russian Empire. Probably as important, however, were what I would consider the structural implications of this act. For by deciding to proscribe (for all practical purposes, if not by law) the pursuit of Ukrainian literary activity the Russian government was implicitly removing it from the status of provincial literature and reclassifying it as something "subversive," "separatist," proto-nationalist. It goes without saying, of course, that these qualities must already have existed—more or less openly, as in Shevchenko, or *in potentio*. Only the time-table of their germination and fruition was unknown. But the administrative act, and its brutality, could not but bring this issue to a head: after the Ems ukase the option of being a Ukrainian-provincial writer in the mould of a Kotliarevsky or Kvitka, that is, reconciling one's language and themes and emotions (the "Ukrainian" component) with one's circumscribed political, social and intellectual horizons and one's loyalty to the state (the "provincial" component) was no longer feasible. It is highly ironic, of course, that precisely then, as an apparent response to this new situation, two new models of a provincial-adaptive response were being formulated—Kulish's "homestead mentality" *(khutorianstvo)* and Kostomarov's programme of "a literature for home use," primarily for the edification and education of the masses. These, however, were only defensive reactions; they were not a prognosis of the reaction of the coming generation of Ukrainian writers.

*

The issue we confront now, the range of conceptualization of the problem of Ukrainian-Russian literary relations, could easily take up, as I have suggested, an entire monograph, let alone a single paper. It would take that much merely to summarize the opinions of such thinkers and writers as Drahomanov, Kostomarov, Kulish or Belinsky, or of such scholars as Pypin, Petrov and Dashkevych, not to mention a host of minor publicists. Here again my task, as I see it, is to outline the major formulas.

The first subset in this broad category is, as already noted, the long-standing debate in both Russian and Ukrainian writings on the "right to life" question. It is quite paradoxical that the first voices expressing doubt about the future of the Ukrainian language (let alone literature) were those of Ukrainian writers— Maksymovych, Metlynsky, even Kostomarov, indeed even Kulish in his early novel *Mikhailo Charnyshenko*. This stance, which was largely a function of Romantic melancholy and nostalgia for a passing way of life, was dispelled by the appearance of Shevchenko. The Russian reactions to Shevchenko, particularly that of Belinsky, put the matter with new directness. While the opinions on the *Kobzar* of 1840 were largely favourable, the prospect of Ukrainian *literature*, especially a literature not merely confined to local colour or the low genres (travesty, burlesque, etc.), evoked more reservations than enthusiasm. Belinsky's consistently negative reaction to Shevchenko was occasioned precisely by his principled opposition to literary "separatism" and the political separatism that it necessarily implied.[37] In time the debate was joined by a host of major and minor figures,[38] but it soon became quite academic—not so much because of the decisions of 1863 and 1876, but because, as Drahomanov put it so well, discussing the *right* of Ukrainian literature to exist was beside the point—what mattered was whether it existed.[39] And however flawed or unsatisfactory its appearance, exist it did.

The actual discussions and conceptualizations concerning the nature of Ukrainian literature, and therefore, inevitably, also its relation to Russian literature can generally be divided into the analytical-descriptive and the prescriptive; not infrequently, especially in the writings of Drahomanov, the two categories overlap. The descriptive approach, beginning with Kulish's perceptive and provocative overview, "Ob otnoshenii malorossiiskoi slovesnosti k obshcherusskoi," culminated in time in a series of scholarly histories of Ukrainian literature, most of them written by Russians: Pypin and Spasovich, Petrov, and Dashkevych.[40] Already the second edition of Pypin and Spasovich's history shows a growing commitment to the discipline and, of course, the belief that its object is real, alive and permanent. By the time of Dashkevych's history, the discipline and the phenomena it deals with are treated as entirely self-evident.

The major prescriptive model, one that is in principle shared, despite various divergences, by all the major Ukrainian participants in the discussion (Kulish, Kostomarov, Drahomanov, Nechui-Levytsky, and Hrinchenko), is that Ukrainian literature is and should be a literature *for, by* and *of* the people. Russian literature, by contrast, is, in their general consensus, a *cosmopolitan* or *imperial* literature and one which largely, if not primarily, reflects the concerns and perspectives of a ruling class, indeed a state. Ukrainian literature is and should be *democratic* and concerned with the lot of its broad constituency. The most extensively argued and at the same time the most radical expression of this idea appears in the writings of Kostomarov, for whom the prime and sufficient cause for the birth and growth of Ukrainian literature is precisely this concern for speaking to and of the people, the *narod*, in a language they understand; this could not and cannot be done in Russian.[41]

Drawing on ideals posited earlier by Kulish and Kostomarov, Drahomanov proceeds to systematize the notion of a fundamental class-based (and class-oriented) differential between the two literatures into a model which, I would submit, still holds considerable heuristic validity. As formulated in a long article entitled "Literatura rosiiska, velykoroska, ukrainska i halytska" (1873), he argues that within the one Russian state there are two Rus' nations (an echo of Kulish and Kostomarov) and three literatures: the all-Russian *(obshche-russka)* imperial literature, one created by the combined efforts of Ukrainians as well as Russians; the Great Russian literature which expresses the ethnic nature, concerns and spirit of the Great Russians; and finally the Ukrainian literature.[42] For all its difficulties, the model is useful, particularly for highlighting the shift in literary systems that occurs in the course of the first half of the nineteenth century, that is, the "nationalization" of what had been an imperial supra-national literature (and, as Kostomarov would argue, a supra-national language as well) into its constituent national components. Again following Kulish and Kostomarov, Drahomanov believes that in this one respect—the shift to popular-based, "national" *(narodna)* literature—Ukrainian literature preceded Russian, and even, to some small extent, served as a model for this transition.

At the same time, however, more than any contemporary, Drahomanov is aware of the great differences in artistic quality and range, in simple matters of quantity, that exist between the two literatures. For him, nineteenth-century Ukrainian literature is undeniably a child of *Russian* (not Great Russian) literature, and for the foreseeable future destined to be its provincial appendage; as such its entirely honourable task is to learn from it and grow with it. The alternative, as he argues at length in his polemics with those, i.e., Nechui-Levytsky and Hrinchenko, who would hermetically separate Ukrainian literature from Russian and stress its national uniqueness, is both provincialism and self-induced stagnation.[43] This we shall now place in a broader context.

*

The final, and probably the most central issue in this discussion, is the interaction, and before that, even more basically, the differentiation between Russian and Ukrainian literature *as systems*. The importance of this for the history of nineteenth-century Ukrainian literature can hardly be overstated: while the conclusions drawn here may be far from insignificant for our under-standing of Russian literature, they are vastly more important for Ukrainian literature, for it is primarily in its relation to Russian literature, and especially in the changes that occur in this relationship, that the character of Ukrainian literature is defined.

The deep differences between the two literary processes become most appar-ent when we postulate a common scheme of periodization. Thus, while in Russian literature there is a well-established tradition of dealing with the nineteenth century simply by decades (a device that Iefremov borrows for his history[44]), the use of such arguably more intrinsic categories as Classicism, Romanticism, Realism, and so on is not only widely encountered in practice, but is also justified in principle. The same scheme can hardly be said to apply—certainly not with the same degree of "fit"—to Ukrainian literature.[45] Ukrainian Romanticism, to choose the one period that offers the greatest typological similarity, is still essentially different from Russian Romanticism;[46] the difference is even more pronounced in the case of Realism (and indeed has led some critics generally to qualify the Ukrainian phenomenon as "ethno-graphic realism"). In the case of Classicism, it is very much an open question whether that phenomenon—as a distinct period, as a distinct poetics and set of norms and values in *Ukrainian literature*—actually existed apart from Russian (i.e., all-Russian, imperial) literature.

What is really at issue here is not the invariable time lag, the "delayed" appearance, and the greater or lesser dependence of the Ukrainian phenomena on the analogous Russian phenomena, or indeed models; it is not a matter of the generally smaller, more circumscribed range of works and forms (the fewer talents, as some would say) appearing in Ukrainian literature; and it is not, speaking now on a more intrinsic level, the generally narrower register of themes and concerns (the Byronic theme and stance, for example, a central component in both Polish and Russian Romanticism, is scarcely evident in Ukrainian Romanticism). The issue is rather with the totality of the system, that is, with the operant dynamics or rules that are always, persistently, remolding all the constituent literary phenomena and relations.

Despite the twin dangers of tautology (the preceding is true of all systems, of course) and of nominalism (i.e., the ostensible willingness to see Ukrainian literature as something *sui generis)*, this assertion must be maintained: the system and the dynamics of Ukrainian literature differ much more from (in this case) those of Russian literature than the conventional literary-historical categories ("Romanticism," "Realism," etc.) allow us to perceive.

The differences in question are perhaps best revealed in the nature of the given system's transitions. In Russian literature, for example, the shift from Classicism to Romanticism, or Romanticism to Realism, is reflected, first of all, on a broadly differentiated gamut of genres and individual works; to speak of the movement from, say, Classicism to Romanticism is to speak about changes in the entire fabric and in the very essence of Russian literature. Secondly, it is a shift that is eminently *conscious*. It is argued and elaborated in a highly developed critical literature and in a host of programmatic statements, polemics, etc. Thirdly (and this may also be taken as an extension of the preceding moment), the given shift in values, norms and conventions resonates with an actively involved audience. There is, in short, a differentiated readership, considerable sectors of which are not only generally sophisticated but also specifically attuned to the aesthetic and formal aspects of literary creativity.

The picture in Ukrainian literature is radically different. In the analogous time-frame (for example, the onset of Romanticism), Ukrainian literature not only shows a narrower base, as I have already noted, but also one that has little if any differentiation. On the contrary, in the various publications of this time, especially the "almanacs,"[47] there is a marked tendency toward literary syncretism: all differences of style or approach are subordinated to the primary fact of participating in the new Ukrainian literature. By this same token, there is hardly any discussion, let alone polemic, concerning the premises and practice of the new poetics, be it Romanticism or Realism;[48] there is a small core of critical commentary, but it is almost exclusively focused on the basic "existential" questions—the validity of Ukrainian as a literary language, the need and the right of Ukrainian literature to exist—and not on such "secondary" matters as that literature's aesthetic or formal profile.[49] Finally (and this again is only the obverse of the same coin), the audience for Ukrainian literature is only peripherally attuned to the aesthetic and formal dimension. This is so, it must be stressed, only in their expectations, in their cognitive and emotional set, *with regard to Ukrainian literature*; in its sophistication and aesthetic requirements this same audience can be one with the all-Russian readership when the object is the overarching imperial literature. Thus, most importantly, it is the mental set and the function of literature that are different here, with the Ukrainian phenomenon expressing above all the thematic, the phatic, and the cathartic components of literary communication.

It is more than apparent, of course, that such categories as Classicism, Romanticism, and Realism do not adequately convey the internal dynamics of Ukrainian literature; they do not constitute genuine phases of its historical development, and to compare the two literatures, or even to speak of their interaction only, or even primarily, in this framework is to misconceive the historical reality.

What is the "historical reality" in nineteenth-century Ukrainian literature? Or, to return to the arguments begun above, what structures are revealed in this system's essential transitions? The answer, sketchy though it may be, must lie in a new model of periodization, the primary basis for which are precisely those factors—above all those reflecting the cultural context, but also the social and political—that are missing from the conventional schema of literary periods.

The three periods that I would postulate here are of very unequal duration.[50] The first, and by far the longest, lasts from the beginnings of modern Ukrainian literature to the time of Shevchenko; the traditional termini that one would invoke here are 1798, the year of the publication, in St. Petersburg (!), of Kotliarevsky's *Eneida*, and 1861. The former date, however, is only symbolic, for the publication of Kotliarevsky's travesty, without his knowledge or approval, was in many respects an anomaly, an accident, and *as a process* modern Ukrainian literature can be said to begin only around the 1820s. The latter date, 1861, does indeed mark a clear divide: not only the death of Shevchenko, but also the appearance of the first and highly important Ukrainian literary and cultural journal, Kulish's *Osnova*. The second period, therefore, has a clear beginning, but its end is much less distinct—it falls somewhere in the late 1880s or early 1890s. The last period thus also begins somewhat indistinctly, but it ends, quite clearly, with World War I and the Revolution.

The literary and cultural content of these periods is much more important, of course, than the dates of demarcation, and here, while risking some schematism, we can perceive the following general patterns. The first period, lasting well over half a century, is a time of beginnings and of self-discovery. It is the discovery of one's ethos (Kotliarevsky's *Eneida*), of literary forms and conventions (sentimental, pre-Romantic and Romantic), of history and folklore. This element of discovering or of initiating, where virtually every major literary work introduces a new form,[51] where the very potential of the language as a literary medium is being continually tested,[52] and where there are few if any literary traditions to fall back on, clearly supersedes, as I have argued above, any differentiation by literary style or *Weltanschauung*. (The writer Hulak-

Artemovsky, who is as willing to pattern himself on the Polish Classicist Krasicki as on the Polish Romantic Mickiewicz, is a telling case in point.) These features must also lead us to question the traditional recourse of subdividing this early period into the pre-Shevchenkian and the Shevchenkian, with 1840, the year of the appearance of the first *Kobzar*, as the date of demarcation. For while one cannot overestimate the importance of Shevchenko, his work, in terms of the criteria I am stressing here, only continues and culminates the process of literary and national self-discovery and self-assertion.

The essential and perhaps, at first glance, paradoxical concomitant of this process is that in this period Ukrainian literature reveals itself in many respects as a provincial phenomenon. All the Ukrainian writers also write in Russian; virtually all of them also publish in all-Russian periodicals. More to the point, they show quite clearly—at the very least in their choice of subject matter and of tone or level of discourse—that they write differently for the all-Russian and the Ukrainian audience. This is not to contradict our earlier conclusions concerning bilingualism; a great number of Russian-language works of Ukrainian authors should indeed be considered part of Ukrainian literature, and the author's sense of his audience should not by itself determine our understanding of the literary-historical phenomenon. At the same time, the sense that for virtually all these writers Ukrainian literature was a subset of imperial, all-Russian literature is inescapable, and this does define both their self-awareness and the nature of this literary phase. For that matter, in political terms, for all the Ukrainian writers of this period Ukraine is part of Russia. Characteristically, Shevchenko is the only exception, and a partial one at that: he rejects this verity in the visionary and mythical modality of his Ukrainian poetry, but he surely accedes to it in his Russian prose. What is more, his immensely influential poetic statement on the relationship of Ukraine to Russia, and, specifically, on the future of his nation, is couched in millenarian terms; as I have argued elsewhere, were it to be translated into the language of political thought it would constitute a radical anti-statist populism, or even anarchism.[53] Thus, in effect, the thought of this entire period, including the utopian-Slavophile program of the Brotherhood of Saints Cyril and Methodius, and including Shevchenko, is distinctly pre-political. As such it corresponds to the provincial, pre-national tenor of the literature of this time.

The real issue of this argument, however, is to be found not in the intellectual or political background but in the literature itself, in its internal make-up and distribution of functions. In short, the provincial character of early nineteenth-century Ukrainian literature is reflected above all in its system of genres, where, especially in the earliest phase, there is a specialization in the "low" or popular genres (mock-epic, travesty, fables, etc.) and a virtual absence of the "high" (ode, tragedy, epic, etc.). It is precisely this state of affairs that led Chyzhevsky to speak of this literature as "incomplete."[54] In time, this "imbalance" was redressed—on the one hand, by the normal broadening and development of the literature, and, on the other, more immediately, by the levelling and "democratizing" tendency of Romantic norms (which norms, even while not totally determining the overall profile of Ukrainian literature at this time, were never insignificant). Nevertheless, throughout this first period, some functions or genres were never represented: such "high" genres as, for example, the philosophical meditation that one associates with Tiutchev, translations of the broad range of literary forms (this despite the early interest in translations by such writers as Hulak-Artemovsky and Borovykovsky), and, above all, literary criticism and theory. The latter is the most revealing "structured absence." Not only was there little if any literary criticism, i.e., of the various discussions about the nature and function of literature that so characterized the Polish and Russian scene, but little if any polemics. If polemical notes are heard they are almost invariably reactions to skeptical remarks voiced by Great Russians[55]—and this absence of critical heterodoxy, and the concomitant (if not fully articulated) sense of external threat and internal self-sufficiency (with the strength and inspiration to come from the roots, the *narod*), are, again, the strongest indicators of the undifferentiated and provincial cast of the Ukrainian literature of this time.

Given this profile, we can speak of Ukrainian-Russian literary relations in this period only in a very qualified way; at any rate, this is emphatically not a relationship between two clearly defined national literatures, say English and French, or Polish and Russian, but rather one between two soft-edged entities, with one of them in many respects a subset of the other. It must be remembered, however, that just as Russian literature is at this stage an imperial literature with an ever more pronounced national basis, so also Ukrainian literature is then a provincial literature progressively discovering its national—not provincial—past, and future. Both entities, in short, are in a process of transition. In this configuration, moreover, it is most difficult to speak of the one moment in the relationship which has traditionally drawn the most attention—namely, the question of influence. In fact, it can be argued that as the two systems are crystallizing the issue of influence becomes marginal. On the one hand, it is clear that in Russian literature the interest in things Ukrainian is highest in the first decades of the nineteenth century, and reaches its apogee in the 1820s and—especially in terms of historicist interest—in the writings of the Decembrists; Gogol is the climax before a rapid decline. The subsequent, thorough discussion—above all by Belinsky—on the course of Russian literature as a national literature finds little room for questions of Ukrainian themes, models or influences. In Ukrainian literature, on the other hand, the very development of the awareness of a separate identity militates against accepting others' models—even, or perhaps especially, those of the "older brother." It is only in the subsequent period that this resistance to Russian literary influences was expressed consciously and programmatically; now it expresses itself informally and emotionally[56]—but it is no less real, and no less structurally central. And it is one of the clearest failings of Soviet scholarship that so central (and historically "normal") a structure in the literary process is either ignored or denounced as retrograde "nationalism."[57]

The second period in the schema I am proposing here is very much a transition: it is both a continuation of and a departure from the preceding period. Its onset plainly coincides with the activity of Kulish's *Osnova* (1861–2); indeed his "Ob otnoshenii malorossiiskoi slovesnosti k obshcherusskoi" (1857) is already a harbinger of a new stage in the literary process. The most important feature of this period, precisely as signalled by Kulish's epilogue-essay, is that what had only recently been largely an aggregate of literary works, and a relatively small circle of writers,[58] has now become a literature. It has become this not so much by sheer quantitative growth as by the emergence of new literary traditions (above all, Shevchenko's) which, while challenging older models (i.e., Kotliarevshchyna), introduce differentiation and new vitality. In general, many of the lacunae of the preceding period are filled in, most significantly, perhaps, in the range of translations (and in literary criticism).[59] The above-discussed Ems ukase of 1876, coming as it does at what is nearly the exact midpoint of the period, spells the end of the political option of a provincial literature; and the subsequent contacts with Western Ukraine, as well as the phenomenal growth of its journals and publications, signal the first stages of a truly national literature. Taken as a whole, however, the period from the early 1860s to the early 1890s shows a literature that is neither fully provincial nor fully national. In the matter of bilingualism, for example, the use of Russian by Ukrainian writers (in Russian Ukraine, of course) is much less pronounced than before, but it is not rare; it is still quite common in literary criticism (especially when a broad audience is intended—as, for example, in various articles by Drahomanov),[60] and it is occasionally used in belles-lettres, e.g., by Marko Vovchok, Kulish, Hanna Barvinok, Storozhenko, Svydnytsky, Hlibov, Konysky and others. (It is worth noting that all these are writers of the older generation; their younger colleagues, such as Nechui-Levytsky, P. Myrny, Karpenko-Kary, *et al.*, write only in Ukrainian. It is even more important to note, however, that this residual bilingualism is also to be found in Western Ukraine, where, for example, Iu. Fedkovych writes some early poetry in German and Franko some prose in Polish. We are thus dealing with a general structure in the development of Ukrainian literature, and not something specific only to the Russian sphere.)

The writers' attitudes on or conceptualizations of Ukrainian literature *vis-à-vis* the Russian also reveal this as an era of transition. The picture here, to use the favourite terms of Marxist-Leninist pseudo-exegesis, is complex and contradictory. But rather than leave it at that pass, or adjudicate it in terms of progressives vs. reactionaries, we can elaborate briefly on our preceding discussion of prescriptive stances by postulating a model that distributes the positions in question. As I see it, these positions—each of them fundamentally concerned with the relationship of Ukrainian to Russian literature—divide along two axes, which I will provisionally call the "political" and the modal. On the "political" axis the opposition is between "federalists" and "nationalists" (in effect, protonationalists), between those like Drahomanov and Kostomarov who saw Ukrainian literature, in the present and the foreseeable future, as having to exist in a partnership, indeed a professedly junior partnership with Russian literature, and those like Hrinchenko, Nechui-Levytsky and, to a lesser extent, Kulish, who saw the essence and future of Ukrainian literature in its opposition to Russian literature, and in a precondition of full autonomy and freedom from influences. (Again it must be stressed that the term "political" is used here more by way of analogy, to suggest the primacy of either coexistence or opposition in the respective positions, and not as a description of the intrinsic character of these positions.) Cutting across this axis and sharply separating the—in some respects—very unlikely bedfellows that are produced here is the modal axis, as I have called it. The opposing modes may be considered, again in a somewhat approximate way, as the Positivist and the Romantic. It is the opposition between, on the one hand, those like Drahomanov and Kulish who emphasize universal cultural and literary values, the world and attitudes of learning and Enlightenment, and who actively and indefatigably work on realizing concrete, "organic" achievements, who are, in a word, unalloyed *Kulturträgers*, and, on the other, those like Kostomarov, Hrinchenko, Nechui-Levytsky and others who are animated above all by an emotional, indeed nativist commitment to things Ukrainian and who in a very real sense (though characteristically not altogether consciously) place Ukraine, or rather the Ukrainian *narod*, on a separate, implicitly superior existential plane, where its cultural and literary existence becomes virtually self-sufficient. (It is quite clear, of course, that the major legacy animating this stance is that of Shevchenko, and that this perspective on the *narod* and its needs draws generically on his vision of a holy *communitas*.[61] It is also very indicative that the earliest, and to this day perhaps the sharpest challenges to this vision and its ominous implications for "normal," structured nationhood were made precisely by Kulish and Drahomanov.)

Thus we can postulate a fourfold schema produced by two intersecting and equally important axes of oppositions. In one quadrant, so to speak, is the position manned by Kostomarov. His idea of Ukrainian literature as a "literature for home use" is in this period the most conservative, old-fashioned and, very soon, the most discredited stance. Its origins are deeply rooted in Kostomarov's populism (*narodnytstvo*) and can be traced throughout his writings from the 1842 "Obzor sochinenii pisanykh na malorossiiskom iazyke," through his articles on Marko Vovchok (1859) and Shevchenko (1861), to his late works. It is presented most directly in his introduction to the section on Ukrainian literature in Gerbel's 1871 anthology of Slavic poetry.[62] The basic argument of this essay is one we have encountered before: Ukrainian literature is a literature for and about the people; its very *raison d'être* is to be accessible to the *narod* and to teach the educated about the *narod*. Thus for him the desire to raise the Ukrainian language to the level of an "educated" language, to present in it the works of a Byron or a Mickiewicz, is artificial since, on the one hand, the all-Russian language is as much Ukrainian as it is Great Russian, and, on the other, since the *narod*, in effect the peasantry, have no need for such writings. The elaboration of these positions in the several articles published in the early 1880s[63] is also clearly motivated by a desire to defend Ukrainian literature and the Ukrainian movement (*Ukrainofilstvo*)—if necessary by dissimulation—from official Russian harassment and persecution.[64] It is not surprising that this (all too typically Ukrainian) effort at mimicry and accommodation was seen, for example by Drahomanov, as a form of opportunism;[65] later, more nationalistic and more perfervid critics were much harsher in their judgement. And yet the balanced view, as signalled many times by Drahomanov himself, and later so eloquently by Hrushevsky, is to see Kostomarov above all as a major architect of the Ukrainian renascence of the first half of the nineteenth century. His later views, specifically on the role of Ukrainian literature in connection with the Russian, reflect not only the tenacity with which he held to his earlier Slavophile, federalist, and populist positions, but also his deeply emotional, almost nativistic and transnational understanding of the Ukrainian cause, and within that of Ukrainian literature.[66]

Drahomanov's position (our second, adjoining quadrant) is on the same side as Kostomarov's in view of his belief, as we have already seen, that Ukrainian literature is a "child" of all-Russian literature and that for the foreseeable future its opportunities for growth and development lie with the latter. At the same time, his position is on the other side of the modal axis by virtue of his quintessential rationalism and positivism. While he is a "federalist" like Kostomarov (though for him, of course, the overarching context is now socialism), and while he, too, places major stress on the obligation that Ukrainian literature has before the *narod*, Drahomanov is adamant about its need to grow and expand, to become as "educated" and sophisticated as possible—drawing *first* on the immediate and ready Russian model, but optimally on what for him is the universal standard, i.e., the European. In Drahomanov, and later *mutatis mutandis* in his disciple Franko, the cause of a creative interaction with Russian literature, an openness to the best—in effect the progressive and realist—strains that its highly developed tradition can offer, finds its strongest advocate.

The antithesis to this stance, in our scheme a quadrant that is diagonally opposite to Drahomanov's "positivist federalism" but adjacent to Kostomarov's nativist variant, is the position of such writers as Nechui-Levytsky and Hrinchenko. It was, of course, inevitable that it would be with them that Drahomanov conducted his most basic polemic,[67] for to his "federalism" and socialism they counterposed an elemental nationalism, while his rationalism and positivism were countered by their emotional and intuitive patriotism. As much as they could be charged, and were indeed so charged by Drahomanov, with a lack of any clear political program, their stance with regard to Ukrainian-Russian relations in the literary sphere was unambiguous: as expressed at greatest length by Nechui-Levytsky in his "Siohochasne literaturne priamovannia" (1878) and then *Ukrainstvo na literaturnykh pozvakh z Moskovshchynoiu* (1891), it was a program of separation and self-sufficiency. Far from being a potential model, Russian literature was alien in its cosmopolitanism and often the very weapon of denationalization. The essence and the racial (!) basis of Ukrainian literature is its native, folk poetry, and this literature will grow without the aid, and indeed despite the oppression, of the Russian state.[68] This, in fact, is a central thesis of the latter highly discursive and chaotically conceived essay (in effect a book-length polemic with Pypin's review of Ohonovsky's history of Ukrainian literature)[69]: Ukrainian literature can exist and develop without statehood, while a literature with the patronage of a state—emblematically the Russian—is not thereby rendered any more viable or attractive.[70] Here, both the facile compounding of the notions of literature and state, and, even more, the ultimately metaphoric understanding of nation and of national literature reveal a species of Romantic and nativist thought.[71]

The fourth position, occupied by Kulish, contiguous on one side with the "nationalist" position of Nechui-Levytsky and Hrinchenko and on the other with the positivism of Drahomanov, and constituting the total antithesis of Kostomarov, is in some respects quite problematical (and thus not a very proportionally situated quadrant). It presupposes that we focus primarily on Kulish's later views (and not on his early, seemingly unqualified *narodnytstvo*), and, beyond that, that we consider his actual literary efforts as more important than his various pronouncements. Given this, Kulish, for all his contradictions and inconsistencies, can be seen as a precursor of the later, essentially twentieth-century understanding of Ukrainian literature. Although his understanding of the national cause was certainly more cultural than political, his thinking, in its concern for the essentially Ukrainian, is in the final analysis more "nationalist" than "federalist"; much more clearly, his openness to literary influences and models, be they Russian or European, the range of his translations, and his fundamental concern for a rational and structured, not metaphysical and nativist, cast to Ukrainian literature and culture place him on the same side with Drahomanov and later writers and critics. It is not at all surprising that during the renascence of Ukrainian scholarship in the 1920s, precisely when a linkage was made between national culture and structures of statehood, Kulish was one of the most studied and commented figures of the nineteenth century.

For all their (to be sure, schematically highlighted) differences, these four positions all share a common basis—all are more or less determined by the premises of *narodnytstvo*, and the Ukrainian cause in general, and literary matters in particular, are perceived largely in terms of the *narod* and its needs. A shift from this state of affairs becomes evident in the 1890s and comes to characterize the last period of nineteenth-century Ukrainian literature. In the literary sphere the central movement is the growing differentiation of the literary audience and the literature itself: the central literary figure of this period, the prose (!) writer Kotsiubynsky, is no longer addressing the *narod*, but the sophisticated reader; the modernist (and, of course, still very tentative and timid) premises of Vorony and later the *Moloda muza* constitute an open break with the aesthetic ideals of *narodnytstvo* and the imperative of the writer's civic duty. In the political sphere this period is marked by nothing less than the crystallization of national consciousness; in practical matters this is the attainment of *sobornist*, the establishment of a consensus, and the co-ordination of efforts between Ukrainians living under Russian and Austro-Hungarian rule;[72] in symbolic terms this is the highly significant change in self-designation: "conscious" Ukrainians are no longer called, or call themselves, *Ukrainofily*—they are now simply "Ukrainians."[73] The Ukrainian cause is no longer the property of a small circle of intellectuals, the object of a sect, but a growing national movement.

The emergence of a national, differentiated literature, the disappearance —indeed the structural impossibility—of bilingualism, produces a radical transformation in Russian-Ukrainian literary relations. These relations continue to have and to increase their ramifications, their various points of contact, interaction, mutual influence, etc. But now the partners in this exchange are on more or less equal footing. For some decades—at least until the depredations of the Stalinist thirties—Ukrainian literature and Russian literature become commensurate entities.

Notes

1. Cf. "The History of Polish-Ukrainian Literary Relations: A Literary and Cultural Perspective," *Poland and Ukraine: Past and Present*, ed. Peter J. Potichnyj (Edmonton and Toronto, 1980), 107–31.

2. As we shall see below, in Ukrainian literature, as in so many others, the nineteenth century extends up to the period of the First World War.

3. Emblematic of this is the first chapter of L. I. Holdenberh's *Bibliohrafichni dzherela ukrainskoho literaturoznavstva* (Kiev, 1977), entitled "Osnovopolozh-nyky Marksyzmu-leninizmu pro literaturu. KPRS i ukrainska literatura."

4. Compare, for example, the very title of one milestone collection of articles: *Rosiisko-ukrainske literaturne iednannia* (Kiev, 1953). Characteristically, the rhetoric is always more turgid on the Ukrainian side: the earlier (slightly smaller)

Russian edition of this collection was simply *Russko-ukrainskie literaturnye sviazi* (Moscow, 1951).

5. Oleksandr Biletsky, "Lesia Ukrainka i rosiiska literatura 80–90–x rokiv," *Zibrannia prats u piaty tomakh* (Kiev, 1966), 4: 605.

6. A thorough discussion of this matter is given in Victor Swoboda's "Shevchenko and Belinsky," *Shevchenko and the Critics 1861–1980* (Toronto, 1980), 303–23.

7. Cf. ibid., 323.

8. Cf. M. Zerov, *Nove ukrainske pysmenstvo* (Munich, 1960) [originally published in Kiev, 1924]; P. Fylypovych, "Shevchenko ta ioho doba," in *Literatura* (New York, 1971) [originally published in Kiev, 1925]; and V. Sypovsky, *Ukraina v rosiiskomu pysmenstvi* (Kiev, 1928).

9. Cf. Dmytro Chyzhevsky, *A History of Ukrainian Literature* (Littleton, 1975) and my *Toward a History of Ukrainian Literature* (Cambridge, Mass., 1981).

10. Cf. Holdenberh, op. cit., 54–62.

11. Cf., e.g., F. Ia. Priima, *Shevchenko i russkaia literatura XIX veka* (Moscow, 1961).

12. Cf. the articles in *Rosiisko-ukrainske literaturne iednannia:* M. P. Pyvovarov's "Panas Myrnyi i rosiiska literatura," Ie. P. Kyryliuk's "Ivan Franko i rosiiska literatura," O. I. Kyseliov's "Pavlo Hrabovskyi i peredova rosiiska kultura," and L. D. Ivanov's "Literaturnyi protses v Rosii 90–900–kh rr. i tvorchist M. Kotsiubynskoho."

13. Op. cit.; cf. also his popularizing *Shevchenko i rosiiskyi vyzvolnyi rukh* (Kiev, 1966). This pattern, where the Ukrainian version is the popular, and the Russian the scholarly one, is not at all uncommon.

14. See, for example, *Shevchenkivskyi slovnyk u dvokh tomakh* (Kiev, 1977).

15. See O. Biletsky, "Zavdannia i perspektyvy vyvchennia Shevchenka," *Zbirnyk prats deviatoi naukovoi Shevchenkivskoi konferentsii* (Kiev, 1961), 13–25.

16. See O. Biletsky, "Pushkin i Ukraina," *Zibrannia prats u piaty tomakh* (Kiev, 1966), 219–28.

17. Timing, or, if one prefers, consonance with the latest stage of Marxist-Leninist teaching is of crucial importance here: Biletsky, who died in 1961, simply did not live to see, and take advantage of the—partial, to be sure—rehabilitation of Kulish in 1969 (i.e., with the publication of Panteleimon Kulish, *Vybrani tvory*, Kiev, 1969).

18. Pyvovarov, op. cit., 303.

19. The first to use this concept in Ukrainian literature, without naming it as such, was P. Fylypovych.

20. See for example, S. D. Zubkov, *Russkaia proza G. F. Kvitki i E. P. Grebenki v kontekste russko-ukrainskikh literaturnykh sviazei* (Kiev, 1979). The premises and the—to a large extent predetermined—conclusions of this study are stated succinctly at the end: "The analysis of the entire Russian corpus of Kvitka and Hrebinka, taken in its historical development and with due consideration of little-known publications and new material, gives irrefutable support to the thesis—which is important both in the literary-historical and the ideological

sense— that their turning to the Russian language was natural and organic and that their participation in Russian literature was fruitful. It also serves to persuasively reject bourgeois-nationalist conjectures that distort the true picture of the relation of the two brotherly literatures in the past, of their [drive to] unification" (p. 268).

21. Ibid., 12.

22. *Shliakhamy druzhby i iednannia: rosiisko-ukrainski literaturni zviazky* (Kiev, 1972), 19.

23. Cf. Zubkov, op. cit., passim.

24. See for example Fylypovych's review of Sypovsky's study (footnote 8 above), where a number of minor points are touched upon, but the major question of what literature and literary tradition some of the works belong to is not discussed; *Literatura: zbirnyk pershyi* (Kiev, 1928), 254–8.

25. Cf. *Toward a History of Ukrainian Literature*, 98–100.

26. Ibid., passim.

27. N. I. Petrov, *Ocherki istorii ukrainskoi literatury XIX stoletiia* (Kiev, 1884), 199–200.

28. N. P. Dashkevich, "Otzyv o sochinenii g. Petrova 'Ocherki istorii ukrainskoi literatury XIX stoletiia'," *Zapiski imperatorskoi akademii nauk*, vol. 59 (St. Petersburg, 1889), 99. On the next page Dashkevych speaks of Gogol as "a great Ukrainian writer"; cf. also p. 56, where he speaks of Ukrainian literature in general and mentions in one breath Gogol, Kvitka, Storozhenko and Levytsky. However, he does not agree with Petrov's inclusion of Gogol among the writers of the "national school"; cf. pp. 134–9 and passim.

29. Cf. M. D. Bernshtein, *Ukrainska literaturna krytyka 50–70–x rokiv XIX st.* (Kiev, 1959), pp. 116–17 and passim.

30. See *Biblioteka dlia Chteniia*, 1838, cited in Dashkevich, op. cit., 39.

31. Cf. my "Some Further Observations on 'Non-historical Nations' and 'Incomplete' Literatures: A Reply," *Harvard Ukrainian Studies* V, no. 3 (September 1981): 369–88.

32. Compare Kostomarov's comment: "That [the experience of reading Gogol's *Vechera na khutore bliz Dikanki* and *Taras Bulba*] was perhaps the first awakening of that feeling toward Ukraine which gave an entirely new direction to my activity. I read Gogol with a passion, I reread him and could not get enough of it: I don't know—it occurred to me—how I could not see what was so close and all around me! I shall really have to learn it all!" *Russkaia mysl,* no. 5 (1882): 202; cited in Dashkevich, op. cit., 72 n.

33. Panteleimon Kulish, *Vybrani tvory* (Kiev, 1969), 482–3. This is subsequently echoed by B. Eikhenbaum, *Lermontov* (Leningrad, 1924), 135.

34. See D. N. Ovsianiko-Kulikovsky, *Sobranie sochinenii*, tom I, *Gogol* (Moscow-Petrograd, 1923), especially chapter V: "Gogol—obshcheruss na malorosskoi osnove. K voprosu o natsionalnom-obshcherusskom znachenii ego," 126–33.

35. Thus, as seen above, the flexible, or indeed nebulous basis for determining Gogol's Ukrainianness: for Petrov he is a Ukrainian writer of the "nationalist"

orientation, i.e., one who focuses on the national past, on national-folk customs, etc.; for Dashkevych he exemplifies "Ukrainian creativity"; for Ovsianiko-Kulikovsky he is an ethnic Ukrainian presence in all-Russian literature and culture, etc.

36. Much has been written on this; cf., among others, I. Mandelshtam, *O kharaktere gogolevskogo stilia* (Helsingfors, 1902), V. Gippius, *Gogol* (Leningrad, 1924), V. Chaplenko, *Ukrainizmy v movi M. Hoholia* (Augsburg, 1948), George S. N. Luckyj, *Between Gogol' and Ševčenko* (Munich, 1971).

37. Cf. Swoboda, op. cit. Cf. also George S. N. Luckyj, *Between Gogol' and Ševčenko*, 70–71.

38. See P. K. Volynsky, *Teoretychna borotba v ukrainskii literaturi* (Kiev, 1959).

39. M. P. Drahomanov, "Po voprosu o malorusskoi literature," *Literaturno-publitsystychni pratsi u dvokh tomakh* (Kiev, 1970), 1: 371.

40. See A. N. Pypin and V. D. Spasovich, *Obzor istorii slavianskikh literatur* (St. Petersburg, 1865) and *Istoriia slavianskikh literatur* (St. Petersburg, 1879); N. I. Petrov, *Ocherki istorii ukrainskoi literatury XIX stoletiia,* op. cit. and N. P. Dashkevich, *Otzyv o sochinenii g. Petrova,* op. cit.

41. See his article, "Malorusskaia literatura," in Gerbel's *Poeziia slavian* (St. Petersburg, 1871), 157–63.

42. Op. cit., 80–220.

43. See, among others, his "Lysty na Naddnipriansku Ukrainu," "Chudatski dumky pro ukrainsku natsionalnu spravu," "'Nad Chornym morem: povist Ivana Levytskoho," and other essays in *Literaturno-publitsystychni pratsi u dvokh tomakh,* op. cit.

44. Cf. Serhii Iefremov, *Istoriia ukrainskoho pysmenstva* (Kiev-Leipzig, 1924).

45. Cf. *Toward a History of Ukrainian Literature.*

46. While stating this I still accept the literary-historical and typological validity of the notion of "Romanticism"; this is not the stand that René Wellek warns us about in his polemic with Arthur O. Lovejoy. Cf. "The Concept of Romanticism in Literary History" and "Romanticism Re-examined" in René Wellek, *Concepts of Criticism* (New Haven, 1963).

47. Compare, for example, *Lastivka* of 1841, the subtitle of which is "Sochineniia na Malorossiiskom iazyke." It includes such representatives of the classicist, burlesque tradition as Kotliarevsky and Porfyrii Korenytsky, the classicist-sentimentalist (and pre-Romantic) Kvitka, the early Romantics Borovykovsky, Chuzhbynsky, Zabila, and Pysarevsky (who also appears under his pen-name of S. Shereperia), Shevchenko and Kulish, and Hrebinka, the editor. The contents, as described on the title page, are also revealing: "Povesti i razkazy, nekotoryia narodnyia malorossiiskiia pesni, pogovorki, poslovitsy, stikhotvoreniia i skazki".

48. There is nothing resembling the "battle of the Classicists and the Romantics" that we see in Polish literature (cf. *Walka romantyków z klasykami,* Wrocław, 1960) or in Russian literature (cf. "Russia/ Romaničeskij-Romantičeskij- Romantizm," in *'Romantic' and its Cognates,* ed. Hans Eichner (Toronto, 1975), 418–74.

49. Cf., For example, Shevchenko's critical comments on Kotliarevsky in the preface

to the unpublished, 1847 edition of the *Kobzar*.

50. For present purposes, I am confining myself to Ukrainian literature in the Russian Empire. A consideration of western Ukrainian literature would require some adjustments, but the overall model does retain its validity.

51. Many of these—the literary ballad, the Byronic *poema*, etc.—are, of course, also being newly discovered in Polish and Russian literature.

52. The most frequently cited illustration of this is Kvitka's "Letter to the publishers of *Russkii vestnik*" (first published in *Moskvitianin* 6, no. 20 (1849): 327–34), where he notes that "I wrote *Marusia* to prove to one unbeliever that something gentle and moving can be written in the Ukrainian language." "I wrote *Soldatskyi patret*, he continues, "to stop critics from explicating that of which they know nothing." See Hr. Kvitka-Osnovianenko, *Tvory u vosmy tomakh* (Kiev, 1970), 8: 96. Cf. also his letters to P. O. Pletnev (15 March 1839), A. O. Kraevsky (25 October 1841) and others elaborating this same issue; ibid., pp. 140–42, 258–60 and passim. At the same time, one cannot but notice that these statements were made only in private correspondence, or, as in the case of the first letter, published posthumously. The forthright personal opinion did not translate into a literary-historical fact.

53. Cf. my *The Poet as Mythmaker: A Study of Symbolic Meaning in Taras Ševčenko* (Cambridge, 1982), 134.

54. My reservations regarding this term, and the theory behind it, are given in *Toward a History of Ukrainian Literature* and "Some Further Observations on 'Non-historical Nations' and 'Incomplete' Literatures: A Reply," op. cit., passim.

55. Cf. P. K. Volynsky, *Teoretychna borotba v ukrainskii literaturi (persha polovyna XIX st.)* (Kiev, 1959), 141–210 and passim. Shevchenko's above noted criticism of Kotliarevsky is the exception that proves the rule.

56. The quintessential examples here—characteristically expressed in poetry, not in critical discourse—are Shevchenko's biting comments on Russian literary models in the prologue to his *Haidamaky*, e.g., "Spivai pro Matrioshu,/Pro Parashu, radost nashu,/Sultan, parket, shpory,—/Ot de Slava!!!" Cf. also Hrebinka's introduction and epilogue to *Lastivka*, Kvitka's letters, and so on.

57. To be sure, the fetishization of such resistance by the nationalistically minded, its elevation to the role of prime determinant in the Ukrainian literary process, is equally wrong-headed.

58. Cf. M. Maksymovych's letter to D. Zubrytsky (22 April 1840), where he—still at this late date—states, "In our country one cannot have a literature in the South Russian language, we can only have, and do have, individual works—of Kotliarevsky, Kvitka (Osnovianenko), Hrebinka and others," *Halychanyn* 1, no. 2 (1863): 107–9; cited in P. D. Tymoshenko, *Khrestomatiia materialiv z istorii ukrainskoi literaturnoi movy* (Kiev, 1959), 1: 204.

59. Kulish, with his translations of the Bible, of Shakespeare, of a host of contemporaries and classics is, of course, the prime *Kulturträger*.

60. It goes without saying that it is still the exclusive language of scholarship and theory—cf. the writings of O. O. Potebnia.

61. Cf. *The Poet as Mythmaker*, passim.
62. *Poeziia slavian. Sbornik luchshikh poeticheskikh proizvedenii slavianskikh narodov v perevodakh russkikh pisatelei*, ed. N. V. Gerbel (St. Petersburg, 1871).
63. See "Malorusskoe slovo," *Vestnik Evropy*, 1881, no. 1; "Ukrainofilstvo,' *Russkaia starina*, 1881, no. 2; "Zadachi ukrainofilstva," *Vestnik Evropy*, 1882, no. 2.
64. Already in his article in *Poeziia slavian* (op. cit., 162), Kostomarov speaks of the 1863 Valuev administrative decision forbidding the use of Ukrainian in non-belletristic writings as destroying Ukrainian literature; the 1876 Ems ukase was much more drastic, of course. See Fedir Savchenko, *The Suppression of the Ukrainian Activities* (Munich, 1970).
65. Cf. "Lysty na Naddnipriansku Ukrainu," *Literaturno- publitsystychni pratsi*, 1: 452. Cf. S. Iefremov's critical comments in his *Fatalnyi vuzol* (Kiev, 1910), and Dmytro Doroshenko, *Mykola Ivanovych Kostomarov* (Kiev-Leipzig, n.d.), 72–80 and passim.
66. Cf. Mykhailo Hrushevsky, "Kostomarov i Novitnia Ukraina," *Ukraina*, vol. 3 (12) (1925): 3–20. It is interesting to note, however, that there are some similarities in Drahomanov's and Kostomarov's positions. They both share the belief that the Ukrainians were the first (and the Great Russians only followed suit) in rebelling against the lethargy of great-power bureaucracy, the ossification of structured society, etc.—in short, the above-discussed premise of the democratic principle in Ukrainian literature and culture (cf. Hrushevsky, ibid., 15). Both of them share a profound sense of disgust with Russian despotism, and though less pronounced in Drahomanov, he, too, shares with Kostomarov an undercurrent of anarchism.
67. Cf. footnote 43, above. Joining the polemic, very much in the spirit of Drahomanov, was Ivan Franko; cf. his "Literatura, ii zavdannia i naivazhnishi tsikhy," *Molot*, 1878, 209–15 (Ivan Franko, *Tvory v dvadtsiaty tomakh* [Kiev, 1955,] 16: 5–13), an answer to Nechui-Levytsky's "Siohochasne literaturne priamuvannia," *Pravda*, 1878, nos. 1 and 2.
68. I. Bashtovy [Nechui-Levytsky], *Ukrainstvo na literaturnykh pozvakh z Moskovshchynoiu* (Lviv, 1891), 122 and passim.
69. See Omelian Ohonovsky, *Istoriia literatury ruskoi* (Lviv, 1878–93) and Pypin's review: "Osobaia russkaia literatura," *Vestnik Evropy*, September, 1890.
70. *Ukrainstvo na literaturnykh pozvakh z Moskovshchynoiu*, 124–5. Indeed, Nechui-Levytsky is willing to draw on any source that supports his anti-statist argument. Thus: "The first founder and architect of the first temporal kingdom—so St. Augustine tells us—was Cain, the fratricide. He began building cities and laid the basis and the beginning of human statehood. On just such a fratricide was founded the city of Rome, which later became the capital of the world and which united in one state all the kingdoms of the world," etc.; ibid., 142–3. Here, the connection to Shevchenko's mythical thought, his dichotomy of structure and *communitas* as tantamount to the opposition of good and evil (cf. his "Saul"), is striking.
71. For example: "The state has the power only to expand the form and not the spirit or essence of literature, for the state is in itself only a form, while the nation, in the broad sense of the term, is a living force which has the power to create the

very content, the very spirit of literature, for it is in its nature a kind of living, creative force, a life force, like the life force of nature, which in ways unknown to us, drawing on its inexhaustible life forces, created forever and ever living beings, living creatures, living plants and living flowers." Ibid., 124.

72. Emblematic of this may be Hrushevsky's transfer, in 1907, of the *Literaturo-naukovyi vistnyk* from Lviv to Kiev.

73. Cf. the conclusion of Lesia Ukrainka's letter to her uncle, Drahomanov, 17 March 1891: "Speaking of which, I must say that we have rejected the term 'Ukrainophiles,' and simply call ourselves Ukrainians, for that is what we are, without any "philism." Lesia Ukrainka, *Tvory v desiaty tomakh* (Kiev, 1965), 9: 63.

Bohdan R. Bociurkiw

The Issues of Ukrainization and Autocephaly of the Orthodox Church in Ukrainian-Russian Relations, 1917–1921 *

Among the principal characteristics of Eastern Christianity has been a close interdependence of religion and ethnicity on the one hand, and a positive relationship between church and state on the other hand. Wherever state and nationality coincided (which was rare until the nineteenth century), the Orthodox Church in its institutional and social aspects has become a national church. Under such circumstances, sooner or later, the national state intervened to end ecclesiastical dependence on the "mother church" abroad, usually by unilaterally proclaiming autocephaly of the national church, since the previous ruling church centre often opposed the diminution of its flock.[1]

The doctrine of "symphony" of spiritual and temporal powers, given the state's claim to sovereignty over its subjects, has generally led to a situation in which the physical preponderance of an autocratic state would result in the Orthodox Church's subjection to the powers that be. Hence the caesaro-papist pattern of Byzantine history or the transplanted "Erastian" pattern of Peter the Great's ecclesiastical reforms.

Such a confluence of political and ecclesiastical authority could not but generate serious problems, both political and religious, whenever the Orthodox Church happened to exist in a multi-national empire—Byzantine, Ottoman, or Russian—since the church generally identified itself with the dominant or favoured nationality (e.g., the Greeks in the Ottoman Empire) within the state. It was thus inevitable that, with the crystallization of national consciousness and the rise of nationalist movements among subject Orthodox peoples, strivings for national independence should sooner or later also produce

*This paper is part of a larger project on contemporary Ukraine. The author would like to acknowledge the financial support received for this project from the Canadian Institute of Ukrainian Studies at the University of Alberta, the Shevchenko Foundation, and the Iwachniuk Ukrainian Studies and Research Fund at the University of Ottawa.

All dates in the text will be given according to the New Style (Gregorian calendar), which was officially introduced by the Soviet Government on 1 February 1918, by redating it 14 February. Dates of periodicals are listed in the end notes in both the Old Style (Julian calendar) and the New Style until the adoption of the latter.

demands for a separate, "national" and autocephalous church organization. Similarly, a nation's loss of statehood tended to result in the surrender of its ecclesiastical independence and the transfer of church authority to the new political centre, as had happened, for example, with the Georgian Church following Georgia's annexation by Russia, or with an autonomous Ukrainian Church thirty-two years after the Treaty of Pereiaslav.[2]

As can be illustrated from Ukraine's historical experience, this interdependence of ecclesiastical and political institutions had not only been caused by the church's traditional dependence on the state for material support and protection against schisms and rival religions. It derived mainly from the integrating and legitimizing social functions performed by religion and the church with respect to political organization, structure and rules—functions crucially important in ethno-culturally heterogeneous empires as yet untouched by modernization and secular ideologies. From the viewpoint of political rulers of Ukraine, native or alien, their control of the church's organization and political orientation was, therefore, deemed essential to the consolidation of their regimes. Depending on the location of the supreme political power, the church has played for the Ukrainian people, politically speaking, both "nation-building" and "nation-destroying" roles. As a rule, despite the church's basic dogmatic and structural continuity, its canons have objectively served to reinforce the successive powers that be (expect for the first decade of Bolshevik rule). There is, accordingly, a peculiar ambiguity in the relationship between the Orthodox Church and nationality in modern Ukrainian consciousness, which, I believe, owes a great deal to the church's increasingly "symphonic" relationship to the Russian state after the latter's absorption of Ukraine.

This article will focus on the period from 1917 to 1921, which witnessed the emergence of the national church movement that paralleled Ukraine's evolution from autonomy to short-lived independence. The movement's goals of Ukrainization (or de-Russification), autocephaly, and conciliarism *(sobornopravnist)* of the Orthodox Church in Ukraine brought it into an escalating confrontation with the powerful Russian ecclesiastical establishment. This conflict culminated in the secession from the Russian Orthodox Church of the main, if not all, elements of the movement and the formation, in 1921, of an independent Ukrainian Autocephalous Orthodox Church with a hierarchy and constitution that broke with established Orthodox canons. The issues of Ukrainization and autocephaly of the Orthodox Church, while "resolved" by Soviet fiat in Ukraine in favour of the Moscow Patriarchate, continue to divide Ukrainian and Russian churches in the West, as well as to separate the "nationally conscious" Ukrainians from their "non-conscious" brethren. These differences are not matters of merely theological and historical interest. They go to the very roots of Ukrainian-Russian relations, to the two-pronged question of the consummation of the modern nation-building process among the Ukrainian people, on the one hand, and the change *from* the Russian perception of the Ukrainian people as a prodigal "younger brother" destined to be "reunited" with his "older brother" in one Russian "family" *to* the perception of Ukrainians as another, separate Slavic nation with a birthright to its own nation-state and its own, unique historical destiny, on the other hand. Only the resolution of these two interrelated questions can offer a firm foundation for a Ukrainian-Russian dialogue and co-operation, including the settlement of their ecclesiastical disputes. This article attempts to shed some light on the genesis, initial circumstances and self-perception of the movement for the Ukrainization and independence of the Orthodox Church in Ukraine, in the hope that a frank exchange of views and a better knowledge of each other will enhance the chances of mutual understanding between Ukrainians and Russians.

The Church and the Ukrainian Revolution

The legacy of the long Russian domination over the Orthodox Church in Ukraine not only placed the latter outside the mainstream of the Ukrainian cultural and national revival but also made it into an ideological and institutional weapon of forces determined to block the evolution of the Ukrainian people toward nationhood and political independence. In the words of a prominent Ukrainian student of ecclesiastical affairs, Oleksander Lototsky,

> In the course of more than two centuries a system of Russification operated in Ukraine mainly by filling influential ecclesiastical posts with Russsifying elements—either native Muscovites...or Russified Ukrainians, who thanks to their natural ties with the Ukrainian environment excelled the Muscovites in carrying out the policy of Russification within the church in Ukraine. Metropolitans and bishops, without exception, belonged to this category of ecclesiastical leaders strained though the bureaucratic-Russificatory sieve. This category of administrators filled all positions in the ecclesiastical administration with their adherents—people of the same ideology of ecclesiastical Russification—largely their relatives from Muscovy. During two centuries, especially over the past seventy-five years, there emerged in the cities of Ukraine a ruling class of Russian ecclesiastical bureaucrats who assumed exclusive influence over all aspects of church life.[3]

Russified theological schools and monasteries in Ukraine zealously guarded against the infiltration of "Ukrainophile" influences and produced a clergy that was largely alien to Ukrainian national and social aspirations. This state of affairs reflected, too, the degree of submergence of national identity in the Ukrainian masses and the weakness of the national movement which, arrested by legal and administrative restrictions,[4] was largely restricted to the small stratum of Ukrainian intelligentsia until the early 1900s. As Mykola Kovalevsky points out,

> One could find in Volhynia or Podillia priestly families which, while not using the Russian language at home and retaining certain overt characteristics of their Ukrainian nationality, politically stood completely and without reservation on the

platform of Russian unity and Muscovite autocracy. [Nationally] conscious individuals among our Orthodox clergy were simply lost in the sea of Muscovite reaction *(chornosotenstvo)* that predominated among our Orthodox parish priests *(batiushky)*. Church organization, too, was Russified to an absurd degree in our country, making no concessions to Ukrainian rites and popular customs, even where such concessions could have been made without undermining ecclesiastical unity with Moscow.[5]

After the collapse of the tsarist regime in March 1917, the Ukrainian church movement emerged as a reaction against this state of affairs in the Orthodox Church. Its principal objectives were formulated at the congresses of the clergy and laymen that met in all Ukrainian dioceses during the spring of 1917. The most elaborate statement of Ukrainian demands was given by Archpriest Feofil Buldovsky[6] at the May congress of the Poltava diocese:

1. In a free, territorially autonomous Ukraine, there should be a free, auto-cephalous church independent of the state in its internal order...

3. The Autocephalous Ukrainian Church shall have a conciliar constitution which should permeate the entire organization of the church.

4. Church services in the Ukrainian Church shall be celebrated in Ukrainian...[7]

Similar resolutions were adopted at other, if not all, diocesan congresses, in-cluding that of the Kiev diocese (chaired by Archpriest Vasyl Lypkivsky),[8] where the Ukrainian liberal majority called also for the convocation of an all-Ukrainian congress of clergy and laymen.[9]

An opportunity for united action presented itself to the Ukrainian church movement when an All-Russian Congress of Clergy and Laymen met in Moscow in June. Sixty-six Ukrainian delegates persuaded the congress to give its overwhelming support to the proposition that "should Ukraine become an independent state, the Ukrainian church, too, should be autocephalous; should there be an autonomous Ukraine, the church should also be autonomous." The Moscow gathering approved also, in principle, the use of national languages in the church and offered its support to the proposed *sobor* of the Ukrainian dioceses.[10] However, when the Kiev diocesan council undertook to elect a commission for the convocation of a Ukrainian Sobor, it met stiff opposition from the local episcopate and, in July, the Petrograd Synod flatly rejected all Ukrainian demands:

The Synod refuses to consider the question of establishing a separate Ukrainian church; it is not intended to raise this question at the All-Russian Local Sobor, since there was never an autocephalous church in Ukraine; the Kiev Metropolitan has been subordinated to the Patriarch of Constantinople and, since the end of the seventeenth century, to the Moscow Patriarch and, by succession, to the Synod.[11]

Having failed to receive blessings from the episcopate, the Kiev commission nevertheless proceeded with the convocation of a Ukrainian Church Congress to be held in Kiev in mid-August 1918,[12] but at the last moment this gathering was prohibited by the new Ober-Procurator of the Holy Synod, A. V. Kartashev.[13] Soon afterward, the Kiev Metropolitan Vladimir (Bogoiavlensky) counterattacked with a pastoral letter condemning liberal tendencies in the church and challenging the *bona fides* of the Ukrainian movement:

> Combined with the general misfortune visiting the Russian land is our local concern about the significantly increasing spiritual unrest. I am speaking of the mood which is revealing itself in Southern Russia, and which endangers the peace and unity of the church. It is dreadful for us to hear them speak of the separation of the South Russian Church from the One Orthodox Russian Church. Have they, after such a long life in common, any reasonable grounds for these endeavours?... None whatsoever. I testify, on the basis of my personal experience, that in all dioceses and metropolies in which the Lord has honoured me to serve, everywhere the teachings and customs of Orthodoxy are preserved pure and un-changed, everywhere there is unity in church doctrine, liturgy and rituals. Who strives toward separation? Who benefits by it? Naturally it brings joy only to domestic and foreign enemies. The love of one's own fatherland must not overshadow and overcome our love for all Russia and the One Orthodox Russian Church.[14]

The Metropolitan's message failed to answer the grievances and demands of the Ukrainian movement, which were addressed not to the doctrinal but to the *national* and *political* orientation of the Orthodox Church in Ukraine. Vladimir's phraseology and reasoning reflected well the extent of the episcopate's alienation from the national and cultural aspirations of their Ukrainian flock, in fact their failure to recognize a distinct Ukrainian national identity,[15] let alone appreciate the potential strength and viability of the Ukrainian church movement. Novel and impatient of the canonical and juris-dictional obstacles raised by its opponents, this movement appeared to the Russian episcopate as an artificial, politically inspired, "unchurchly" fringe group that was alien to the "South Russian" believers and destined to pass away with the return of peace and order to Holy Russia.

The repeated failures of the Ukrainian movement to secure by canonical means any of its objectives and the growing pressure applied by the bishops on the Ukrainian clergymen caused some defections from the movement's ranks. No less discouraging was the refusal of the socialist-dominated Central Rada to intervene on behalf of the Ukrainian church movement, a refusal that was rationalized in terms of a yet-to-be-realized separation of church from state.[16] The combined effect of these frustrations was a marked radicalization of the movement's mood and its growing conviction that the only alternative left to the advocates of ecclesiastical Ukrainization, democratization and independence was to break away from the Russian Church by "revolutionary means."[17] In early November, the autocephalist cause received a sympathetic response from the Third Ukrainian Military Congress in Kiev, which voted, on 9 November, that

> In a free, democratic Ukrainian Republic there must be a free autocephalous Orthodox Church independent of the state in its internal order, with a conciliar constitution... In Ukraine, the liturgy should be celebrated in the Ukrainian language.[18]

The quickened pace of developments in Russia and Ukraine appeared now to improve the autocephalist prospects. On the night of 6/7 November, Lenin's Bolsheviks seized power in Petrograd and, on 20 November, the Central Rada issued its Third Universal proclaiming the Ukrainian People's Republic, which was soon given *de facto* recognition by the representatives of France and Great Britain. Meanwhile, having defeated the liberal faction at the Local Sobor of the Russian Church in Moscow, its conservative majority voted, on 10 November, to re-establish the Moscow Patriarchate, a decision that was perceived by the Ukrainian circles as a victory for the reactionary, centralist forces within the Russian Church.

In response to these developments, a joint meeting of three principal organizations espousing the causes of the Ukrainization and independence of the Ukrainian church[19] constituted, on 6 December, a Provisional All-Ukrainian Orthodox Church Council (*Tserkovna Rada*) headed by an army chaplain, Oleksandr Marychiv, with the retired Archbishop Oleksii (Dorodnytsyn) as its honorary chairman.[20] Pointing to the "separation of the Ukrainian State from the Russian State" and to the election of Patriarch Tikhon, "who might also extend his power to the Ukrainian Church," the *Tserkovna Rada* took the revolutionary step of proclaiming itself a provisional administration of the Orthodox Church in Ukraine until the convocation of an All-Ukrainian Sobor, to which it would surrender its powers. In an intensely nationalistic pro-clamation, the Rada called for the Sobor to meet in Kiev on 10 January, and de-termined the mode of representation at the projected Sobor with the proviso that its membership should be restricted to "Ukrainians by birth and invariably sympathetic to the Ukrainian cause."[21] Although local Russian circles con-demned its initiative, the Rada dispatched a delegation to Patriarch Tikhon to plead for a compromise that would assure a canonical solution of the conflict.[22] The subsequent negotiations, in Moscow and Kiev, with Metropolitan Platon and Archbishop Evlogii as representatives of the Patriarch and the All-Russian Sobor, started to bear fruit only after the Ukrainian government belatedly intervened in the ecclesiastical dispute by setting up a Commissariat for Religious Affairs and granting official recognition to the Tserkovna Rada.[23] After a compromise formula was accepted by both sides, providing *inter alia* for the episcopate's veto over all decisions of the forthcoming Sobor, the latter now received "blessings" from the Patriarch and the Moscow Sobor.[24]

As the First All-Ukrainian Church Sobor convened in Kiev on 20 January, its prospects were effectively doomed by the invasion of Ukraine by Soviet Russian forces, the setting up of a puppet Bolshevik Ukrainian Government in Kharkiv, and the shrinking of the territory under the Central Rada's control. In anticipation of an imminent collapse of the Ukrainian Republic, the episcopate and their centralist and autonomist followers among the delegates now adopted delaying tactics, joining in lengthy procedural and organizational confrontations; by the time Muravev's troops threatened Kiev, forcing the adjournment of the Sobor until late May, not a single substantive question on its agenda had been resolved. Hectic attempts of the Ukrainian delegates to secure a vote on the crucial question of autocephaly at the last session of the Sobor were frustrated by the now more numerous supporters of the Moscow Patriarchate.[25]

Russian-Ukrainian Polarization under the Hetman Regime

The Ukrainian-Russian confrontation within the church entered a new phase in spring 1918, with the German dispersal of the Central Rada and the installation of the conservative Hetman regime, which lacked broad support among the Ukrainian intelligentsia and incurred increasing hostility among the peasantry and workers. The necessities of political survival made the Skoropadsky regime seek a compromise with Russian interests in Ukraine, flooded at that time by a mass of politically vocal refugees from Soviet Russia. Taking advantage of the strong Russian influence in the new government and its vacillating ecclesiastical policy, the opponents of the church's Ukrainization and autocephaly were now able to turn the balance of forces in their favour.

This was well illustrated by the proceedings of the May 1918 Sobor of the Kiev Diocese; not only did this gathering elect a staunch opponent of the Ukrainian movement, Antonii Khrapovitsky, as Metropolitan of Kiev, but it also resolved against autocephaly for the church in Ukraine, condemned the use of Ukrainian in church services, and called for the removal of the Tserkovna Rada members from among the First All-Ukrainian Sobor delegates before the resumption of the Sobor.[26]

By the time the Sobor reconvened in June, the supporters of autocephaly and their liberal allies found themselves short of a majority among the delegates, without a single spokesman among the bishops, and with little effective support from the Hetman government.[27] The chief task before the summer session of the Sobor was the adoption of a constitution for the Ukrainian Church. Despite its endorsement by the government, a compromise draft constitution introduced by the autocephalist and liberal delegates, which provided for broad autonomy of the Ukrainian Church while preserving its canonical subordination to the All-Russian Sobor,[28] was defeated by the conservative majority. Professor

Pokrovsky, one of the liberal co-authors of the draft, later observed that

> the last opportunity was lost to devise the kind of autonomy that could yet have
> been accepted by the nationally conscious *(shchirye)* Ukrainians. From that
> moment on, the ecclesiastical aspirations of the Ukrainians could no longer be
> accommodated in the framework of even the broadest autonomy, but deviated
> sharply toward autocephaly.[29]

Before turning to an alternative draft endorsed by the episcopate, the pro-Russian majority voted to expel 45 members of the *Rada* from the Sobor, which in turn provoked the liberal opposition into a walkout in protest against this violation of the compromise representation formula accepted in December 1917 by the Patriarch, the bishops, and the Rada.[30] Soon afterwards, on 9 July, the Sobor adopted "The Statute of the Provisional Supreme Administration of the Orthodox Church in Ukraine." The "Statute" offered a rather limited autonomy to the Church, to be governed henceforth by a triennial Ukrainian Church Sobor and, between Sobors, by a Holy Sobor of Bishops and a Supreme Church Council—both to be chaired by the Metropolitan of Kiev and Halych. Although it provided for the election of bishops at diocesan sobors and of the Kiev Metropolitan at an All-Ukrainian Sobor, the Statute left the Patriarch of Moscow and the All-Russian Sobor with wide powers over the Church in Ukraine, including the Patriarch's authority to "confirm and bless" the Metropolitan and all diocesan bishops, to receive complaints against the Kiev Metropolitan, to exercise appellate jurisdiction over all diocesan bishops, and to ratify the Statute itself.[31]

In his letter of 26 September to Metropolitan Khrapovitsky, Patriarch Tikhon (speaking on behalf of the All-Russian Church Sobor as well) introduced a number of important revisions which further narrowed the modest autonomy of the church in Ukraine:

> 1. The Orthodox dioceses in Ukraine, while remaining an inseparable part of the One Russian Orthodox Church, shall form an ecclesiastical province of the former, enjoying special autonomous privileges.
>
> 2. Autonomy of the Ukrainian Church shall extend over local church matters—administrative, educational, missionary, charitable, monastic, economic, judicial in subordinate instances, and shall not include matters of general church significance.
>
> 3. Decisions of the All-Russian Church Sobors, as well as decisions and directives of the Holy Patriarch, shall have obligatory force for the whole Ukrainian Church.
>
> 4. The bishops and representatives of clergy and laymen of the Ukrainian dioceses shall participate in the All-Russian Church Sobors in accordance with the existing Sobor rules. The Metropolitan of Kiev *(ex officio)* and one of the

bishops of Ukrainian dioceses...shall participate in the Holy Synod.

5. The Holy Patriarch shall have the right to send his representatives to the Ukrainian Church Sobor.

6. The Holy Patriarch approves both the Metropolitan and governing bishops of Ukrainian dioceses.

7. The Holy Patriarch retains with regard to the Ukrainian Church all rights provided for in the All-Russian Sobor's resolution on the rights and duties of the Holy Patriarch of Moscow and All Russia.[32]

The revised "Statute" was presented for final approval at the fall session of the Ukrainian Sobor, which met in late October. The proposed church constitution was by then condemned both by the Ukrainian church movement[33] and by the Ukrainian National Union (Soiuz), an alliance of the Ukrainian opposition parties. Neither their opposition nor the short-lived insistence of the Hetman government on Ukrainian autocephaly[34] would sway the now solidly pro-Russian Sobor; its mood was voiced by D. Skrynchenko, one of the closest collaborators of Metropolitan Antonii, who challenged the very legitimacy of the Ukrainian government:

> The Sobor expresses the will of the people. This will is clear. Only the Government fails to understand it. The ground is already prepared; now is the time to realize it, and, having extended [the Government's] hand to the Sobor, to admit: we erred; we shall now join the people who do not desire separation from Russia and her church. But if the Government even now fails to comprehend the events, if it still intends to violate the Sobor's decision, who knows whether the Sobor would not have to resort to the means which had sometimes been used by the church in defence of its positions, that is, the excommunication of the violators.[35]

The threat of a church-state confrontation was suddenly dissipated by a political *volte-face* on the part of the Hetman regime, which reacted to Germany's capitulation by proclaiming Ukraine's federation with Russia, an act that signalled the beginning of an anti-Hetman uprising. The news of the "restoration of a united Russia and the fall of the cabinet of independentists" was received at the Sobor "with tremendous enthusiasm."[36] The gathering now hastened to vote, without discussion, on the issue of autocephaly, which was rejected by a nearly unanimous vote (against three opposed) in favour of the Statute as amended at Moscow.[37]

The meeting resolved to announce the Sobor's decision to the clergy and believers in a special message, condemning "any attempts at arbitrary (*samochinnoe*) proclamation of autocephaly." According to *Golos Kieva*,

> Leaving the Sobor, its members congratulated, kissed one another and crossed themselves. The 15th of November shall become a great historical day. The

ecclesiastical unity with Russia will become a guarantee, no doubt, of state unity as well.[38]

The Sobor's message, published on 22 November, attested to the intensity of the passions guiding this body. After declaring that the "preservation of our filial unity with the supreme Russian archpastor and the entire Russian Church" was in accordance with the historical traditions and spiritual interests of the Ukrainian people, the seventeen bishops who signed this document threatened with "divine punishment"

> those unwise men [who] attempt to sow chaos and to separate the Ukrainian Church from unity with the Holy Patriarch, who nurture hope to enhance by such evil deeds the unity of the Ukrainian people and strengthen its independent 'sovereign' statehood. Not by these means, however, should one strengthen the life of the people, not by ecclesiastical separation and hatred of the fraternal Russian people, but through love of and faithfulness to God's Church...

> Therefore, do not listen, brothers, when they speak to you such unwise words: We are Ukrainians and we do not need an alien Moscow Patriarch but will recognize only our Ukrainian pastors. Do not listen to them: no benefits came to those peoples that have separated themselves from the great patriarchal sees and enclosed their life within the borders of their states; virtue and religious teaching grow scarce among these peoples and everything is absorbed by the struggle between political parties. Thus it happened in the kingdoms of Romania and Serbia, in Greece and Montenegro, and the Bulgarian people, having illegally separated themselves from the Patriarch, were subjected justly to exclusion from the Orthodox Church and ceased to be an Orthodox people, becoming a schismatic people. This fate now awaits also the Georgian people, who separated themselves from the All-Russian Church. May the Lord preserve from such disaster for the sake of her present and future life our Orthodox Ukraine... May he preserve her from evil splitters; they speak of their love for Ukraine, but in fact many of them want to drag our people into the nets of the Uniate heresy, that is, completely to split it away from the Church of Christ and, consequently, from eternal salvation.[39]

As the Hetman regime was waging a losing war against the Ukrainian insurgents, the Sobor voted, on 12 December, to retain the Church-Slavonic language on historical, aesthetic, and linguistic grounds, as well as to satisfy

> ...the spiritual need of every people to pray in a different tongue than the everyday, ordinarily spoken language; the general and unanimous wish of the entire Ukrainian population expressed through their representatives at diocesan congresses in 1918; as well as the fact that the Church-Slavonic language...unites all Slavic churches and peoples...[40]

On 18 December, after the capture of Kiev by the Directory, the Sobor of Ukrainian Bishops resolved:

> ...should any members of the government dare to repudiate the significance of this

[Ukrainian Church] Sobor and consider its resolutions null and void, they should be excluded from the Church. ...any official, secular or clerical, who would dare to convoke an [illegal Ukrainian] Sobor or participate therein, shall by this decision of ours be excluded from the Church if he is a layman or defrocked if he is a bishop or clergyman.

　　And we, Orthodox bishops, remaining faithful to the Holy Orthodox Church, do reaffirm the canonical and obligatory nature of the recent All-Ukrainian Church Sobor and by [our] oath accept the obligation both to conform to its decisions and submit in everything to the Holy Patriarch Tikhon, and, after his death, to his legitimate successor, and also to the representative of the All-Ukrainian Church, His Grace the Metropolitan of Kiev, Antonii, and, in the event of his death or voluntary departure from the see, to his successor, legally elected by the Sobor and approved by the Patriarch, and until the election of such, to His Grace Metropolitan Platon of Kherson.[41]

This important resolution signed by eighteen bishops was clearly intended to frustrate any attempts by the victorious Directory to implement its plans for the autocephaly and Ukrainization of the Church and indeed to threaten the entire Ukrainian autocephalous movement with wholesale excommunication from the Orthodox Church. This document was destined to play a fateful role in the subsequent Russo-Ukrainian struggle for control of the Ukrainian Church.

The Directory's Proclamation of Autocephaly

Following Skoropadsky's abdication, an interim Ukrainian Revolutionary Committee arrested, on 18 December, in a general round-up of the principal anti-Ukrainian leaders, Archbishop Evlogii, and, on the next day, Metropolitan Antonii, confining them to a Uniate monastery in Western Ukraine.[42]

　　The reversal of political fortunes and the anxiety created by the arrest of the two hierarchs evidently broke the united political front of the episcopate, with Archbishop Ahapit (Vyshnevsky) of Katerynoslav and Bishop Dionisii (Valedinsky) of Kremianets joining in cooperation with the Directory Government.[43]

　　Under the new regime, the Ukrainian autocephalist movement emerged stronger than ever before, with its members assuming important positions in the government.[44] The new Government made the realization of autocephaly one of its first priorities. On 1 January 1919, the Council of Ministers decreed "The Law on the Supreme Authority of the Ukrainian Autocephalous Orthodox Conciliar Church." Paradoxically resembling in some respects the pre-revolutionary ecclesiastical legislation, the new law severed the church's links with the Moscow Patriarchate. While retaining close links between the church and the Ukrainian state, it invested the latter with extensive powers over ecclesiastical affairs, designed, no doubt, to compensate for the weakness of Ukrainian elements in the upper echelons of the church. Accordingly, the law provided that:

　1. The supreme ecclesiastical authority in Ukraine—legislative, judicial, and

administrative—shall belong to the All-Ukrainian Church Sobor; its decisions,
whenever they relate to church-state relations or require expenditure of funds
from the state treasury, shall be submitted for consideration and approval to the
state's legislative organs.

2. A Ukrainian Church Synod shall be created to direct the affairs of the
Ukrainian Autocephalous Orthodox Church...

6. The Ukrainian Autocephalous Church with its Synod and clergy shall not be
subordinated in any way to the All-Russian Patriarch.[45]

Attempting to implement the law on autocephaly, the Ukrainian Government
entered into protracted negotiations with the episcopate to secure its co-
operation in setting up a Ukrainian Church Synod. Despite the bishops'
reluctance to commit themselves without approval from Patriarch Tikhon or
Metropolitans Antonii and Platon, a tentative agreement was reached to establish such a body on a provisional basis, although, in order to conciliate the
episcopate, the term "Synod" was dropped in favour of the designation "All-
Ukrainian Supreme Sacerdotal *(Osviachena)* Council." Two hierarchs,
Archbishop Ahapit, as chairman of the Council, and Bishop Dionisii were selected to serve on this temporary council, together with several priests (including Archpriest V. Lypkivsky) and several laymen.[46] The Council, which
managed to meet only once, ceased to exist when the Directory was forced to
evacuate Kiev in early February.[47] The Ministry's plans for the consecration of
the new nationally conscious bishops had to remain unfulfilled.[48] Once again,
the changing fortunes of war frustrated Ukrainian attempts to secure control of
the Church "from above."

While some members of the newly formed autocephalous Church Council
left Kiev, following the Directory in its retreat westward, several leaders of the
Ukrainian church movement (rejoined, in November 1919, by Archpriest Vasyl
Lypkivsky), remained in Kiev, where under the Bolshevik regime they
successfully continued their activities, using a new tactic of "grassroots
Ukrainization." [49]

The Rise of the Ukrainian Autocephalous Orthodox Church

Paradoxically, it was only after the Soviet takeover of Ukraine that the
autocephalist movement could successfully challenge Russian control of the
Church by means of an ecclesiastical "revolution from below." During the
spring of 1919, having "recognized" the Soviet Separation Decree[50] (even as
the Moscow Patriarchate continued its confrontation with Lenin's regime), the
Ukrainian autocephalists took advantage of the new legislation by promptly
"registering" several "Ukrainized" parishes under a re-established All-
Ukrainian Orthodox Church Council.[51]

After the interval of Denikin's rule, which brought about the virtually complete suppression of the autocephalist movement,[52] the autocephalists re-
emerged. By early 1920 the Soviet Ukrainian authorities had formally recognized the "Union of Ukrainian Orthodox Parishes" as a separate ecclesiastical
organization in Ukraine under the All-Ukrainian Council. Soon afterward the
Russian episcopate suspended all clergy of the Ukrainized parishes, to which
the Council responded, in May 1920, with a formal proclamation of
autocephaly for the Ukrainian Orthodox Church.

The Council's "declaration of independence" argued that the proclamation of
Ukrainian ecclesiastical independence from Moscow was merely the
reaffirmation of the "virtual autocephaly," conciliar constitution, and national
character of the Orthodox Church in Ukraine which the latter possessed before
its unlawful annexation by Moscow in 1686. For subsequently, the "Muscovite"
church authorities, with the help of the tsars,

> used prohibitions, banishments, violence and terror to abolish step by step not
> only the independence and conciliar constitution of the Ukrainian Church, but
> almost everything in it that contained any characteristics of the national creativity
> peculiar to the Ukrainian people.

The Russification, centralization and bureaucratization of the Orthodox
Church—claimed the All-Ukrainian Council—had alienated the Ukrainian
people, denying them the full satisfaction of their religious needs. Accordingly,
the autocephalist movement wanted to bring the church back to the Ukrainian
people and the people into the church. But since 1917, the "Muscovite
ecclesiastical authorities" had been sabotaging all legitimate attempts to revive
the Ukrainian Church and had shown themselves to be "not a good pastor, but
an enemy of the Ukrainian people."[53]

The All-Ukrainian Orthodox Church Council was now left with the crucial
problem of providing an episcopate for the Autocephalous Church; unlike the
Georgian Orthodox Church, which was led by its own bishops when it broke
away from the Russian Church in 1917, the former failed initially to attract a
single bishop in Ukraine. By August 1920, however, Archbishop Parfenii
(Levytsky) of Poltava had agreed in somewhat vague terms to assume the
spiritual leadership of the Autocephalous Church, admittedly in the hope of
averting a "schism" while seeking again for a canonical solution to Ukrainian
demands.[54] In the spring of 1921, however, Parfenii was forced by the
Patriarchate to cut his links with the autocephalists after he was elected *(in
absentia)* an "All-Ukrainian Metropolitan" by the Kiev *guberniia* sobor in May
1921, a gathering which also adopted a series of radical resolutions challenging
the established canons of the Church.[55]

Having already announced the convocation of an All-Ukrainian Sobor for
October 1921, the Council now searched in vain for an Orthodox bishop
willing to ordain the autocephalist episcopate. On 15 August, the autocephalist

leaders appealed, despite their previous repudiation of the authority of the Moscow Patriarchate, to the "Sobor of Bishops of 'All Ukraine'," which was then in session, for the recognition of an All-Ukrainian Council, the creation of an extraterritorial diocese for the autocephalists, and the ordination of a Ukrainian bishop for such an independent diocese.[56] When, predictably, the bishops rejected the Ukrainian request, two episcopal candidates (S. Orlyk and P. Pohorilko) were dispatched late in August to the Georgian Orthodox Church, reportedly sympathetic to the Ukrainian cause. With Russian-Georgian hostilities under way, they were detained by the authorities in Kharkiv. They made last-minute attempts to obtain consecration from Parfenii of Poltava and Archbishop Ahapit of Katerynoslav, but neither would consent to undertake this task.[57]

As the Sobor assembled on 14 October 1921 in the ancient St. Sophia Cathedral, the last frantic appeal for a canonically ordained bishop was addressed by the gathering to the newly appointed Patriarchal Exarch of Ukraine, Mikhail (Iermakov), who came to the Sobor on 19 October, but only to denounce it as lacking any canonical validity. In desperation, the Sobor "moderates" continued negotiations with Mikhail and his two vicars throughout the next day, but without any success.[58] This ended any remaining illusions about the prospects of compromise with the Russian hierarchy. The Autocephalous Church was thus left with an agonizing dilemma: either it could recognize its failure to acquire a canonically ordained episcopate and return to the ranks of the Russian Church or it could do away with those Orthodox canons which were invoked by the episcopate to frustrate the Ukrainian demands and resolve the question of the hierarchy in a revolutionary manner.

The Sobor debate that followed focused on the crucial question: should the Sobor itself, in the absence of bishops, ordain the episcopate for the new church and, if this came to pass, would the church remain Orthodox? A positive answer to these questions was offered in the papers read to the Sobor by Archpriest Vasyl Lypkivsky and layman Volodymyr Chekhivsky—the two prominent figures who were to dominate the future course of the Ukrainian Autocephalous Church—who appealed to the long—abandoned practice of the early church and opposed the "natural right" of the Ukrainian believers to the positive canon law of the church.[59] The negative was argued by an Orthodox missionary, Ksenofontii Sokolovsky, who charged that the consecration of bishops by the Sobor delegates would amount to a "Protestant deviation and betrayal of the Orthodox faith";[60] however, he offered no alternative solution to the autocephalist predicament. In the vote that followed, the majority—its size disputed in the literature—voted for the motion to ordain the first two bishops (Vasyl Lypkivsky and Nestor Sharaivsky)[61] by the laying on of hands of the clergy and laymen in attendance, but to have subsequent bishops consecrated by bishops alone, as had been the practice of the Orthodox Church. This compromise formula, forced upon the Sobor by the refusal of the canonical bishops to ordain an autocephalist episcopate, did not satisfy the minority of delegates who left the Sobor, insisting on the literal observance of the Orthodox canons.[62] This departure from the established canons, as well as a series of reforms adopted by the 1921 Sobor, not only alienated some clerical supporters of the Ukrainian Church movement but also resulted in the subsequent isolation of the Ukrainian Autocephalous Church from other Orthodox churches that refused to recognize the canonical validity of its episcopate.

Conclusion

The Ukrainian church movement that emerged after the collapse of the tsarist regime in March 1917 combined Ukrainian nationalism with ecclesiastical radicalism and fundamentalist religious zeal. On the one hand, it represented a projection of renascent Ukrainian nationalism upon the ecclesiastical-religious scene, sharing with the political forces of the day the ultimate aim of the Ukrainian Revolution—the recovery of national identity, tradition and freedom through emancipation from Russian control. On the other hand, it paralleled the evolution in Ukrainian aspirations by moving from demands for ecclesiastical autonomy and the Ukrainization of the liturgy toward demands for the autocephaly of the Ukrainian church. As the same time, the movement expressed in the *Ukrainian context* the strivings of a progressive current within the Russian Orthodox Church toward the democratization of the Church on a conciliar basis, equalization in status of the parish and monastic clergy, and the curtailment of episcopal domination; the renovation of the Church, especially at its parish grass roots; and the establishment of harmony between the Church and the aspirations of the people.

The core of the Ukrainian church movement consisted of people of such diverse backgrounds as urban parish priests (e.g., Vasyl Lypkivsky, Feofil Buldovsky, and Petro Tarnavsky); military chaplains (Oleksander Marychiv, Pavlo Pohorilko, Iurii Zhevchenko); theological seminary teachers (Vasyl Bidnov, Petro Tabinsky, and Volodymyr Chekhivsky). Ivan Ohiienko was a university professor, and Mykhailo Moroz was a landowner. Oleksandr Lototsky's pre-revolutionary career combined government service with literary work, while Serhii Shelukhyn was a jurist. Among them there were almost none with experience of ecclesiastical administration (one exception was Petro Sikorsky [future bishop Polikarp]) and, surprisingly, very few village priests. Some, like Lypkivsky, Chekhivsky and Bidnov, had long espoused the Ukrainian cause in ecclesiastical circles, and their careers had been thwarted by official antagonism. Others revealed their Ukrainian convictions only after the fall of the autocracy, and a handful, such as Nestor Sharaivsky, were converts from the Russian nationalist camp. Most leading members of the movement came from priestly families or attended theological schools. Nationalist and religious motives were closely intertwined in bringing them into the movement; with some, personal ambition and career expectations might have carried additional weight.

Probably the main sources of the movement's strength were its intense faith in the righteousness of its course, its optimism and energy. Its weaknesses were many: its lack of access to the levers of ecclesiastical power; its precarious and limited base among the rank-and-file clergy; and emotionalism, impatience and inexperience of its members in the art of ecclesiastical politics.

Arrayed against the national church movement was the entire episcopate of Ukraine, supported by the administrative ecclesiastical apparatus and nearly all the monastic clergy, and commanding considerable material resources of the local church. This formidable force, including some of the outstanding representatives of political reaction and militant clericalism in Russia, was headed from 1918 by an old enemy of the Ukrainian movement, Metropolitan Antonii Khrapovitsky, a powerful figure with considerable gifts of leadership and persuasion, vast ambition and authority, who maintained a remarkable hold on the loyalties of the ecclesiastical elite in Ukraine. This leading stratum of the church was motivated by a combination of nationalism and conservatism that shaped their perception of the Ukrainian problem. Hence their disdain for and ridicule of the Ukrainian language as either a crude dialect of "Little Russian" peasants or a "Galician invention"; they viewed the Ukrainian people as an integral part of a single Russian nation, without a distinct past or future; perceived Ukrainian nationalism as an artificial and unpopular creation of misguided intellectuals and enemy-inspired troublemakers; and saw the Ukrainian church movement solely as a politically inspired venture of a handful of priestly malcontents and radicals devoid of true faith and alien to the pious "South Russian" masses.[63] Hence, too, their insistence on both the indivisibility of the Russian Orthodox Church and on its greatest possible freedom from the Ukrainian state's intervention.

It seems that this perception of the Ukrainian church movement shaped to a great extent the strategy of the Russian Orthodox Church leadership *vis-à-vis* the Ukrainian autocephalists. More specifically, this strategy sought, by denying any meaningful concessions to the movement's demands for Ukrainization, to stimulate the radicalization of its goals and methods so as to frighten away moderate supporters of the Ukrainian church movement and, perhaps, ultimately to push the so-called "extremists" into a schism, thereby purging the church of Ukrainian "trouble-makers" and "agitators."

On the other hand, it is clear that the absence of bishops sympathetic to the cause of the Ukrainian church movement seriously weakened the support it initially enjoyed among the Orthodox clergy and led it to place special emphasis on a "democratization" of the church through the participation of laymen in ecclesiastical administration, as well as to seek the support of the Ukrainian state authorities in ending the dependence of the church in Ukraine on the Moscow Patriarchate.

The nearly complete monopoly of power enjoyed in the Ukrainian dioceses by the Russian or Russian-oriented episcopate,[64] which was equally opposed to the Ukrainization and the democratization of the church, made the tasks of the Ukrainian church movement both simpler and more difficult. It tended to submerge the contradictions among the conservative, moderate and radical elements of the autocephalist movement and enabled it to draw its support from both the nationalist and, eventually, the socialist elements of Ukrainian society, as well as from the progressive stratum of the Russian clergy and church intelligentsia in Ukraine. The movement's cause thus reflected the blending of national and social aspirations that typified the early stage of the Ukrainian Revolution.

Yet, at the same time, the canonical framework and hierarchical structure of the Orthodox Church supplied the Russian episcopate, as the exclusive repository of apostolic succession and canonical authority, with formidable weapons against the opponents of the *status quo*. Not only could the bishops resort at will to ecclesiastical sanctions against the "anti-canonical" clergy and believers; on their side they also had the forces of inertia and habit, the conservative spirit of the church, and last but not least the vigorous support of the powerful nationalist and reactionary Russian elements strategically entrenched in the Ukrainian cities, both within the church and outside it, in the bureaucratic and military strata, and among the middle class. Believers or not, these elements of the hitherto dominant Russian minority in Ukraine shared the episcopate's view that the retention of the church's subordination to Moscow, its Russian orientation and leadership were of prime importance in preparing for the restoration of "one and indivisible Russia." With the break-up of the imperial power structure and the dispersal or suppression of the political organizations of the Russian Right in Ukraine, the church remained the principal institutional link with the past around which these forces could rally and combat, from the church's privileged sanctuary, the forces of Ukrainian "separatism" and radicalism.

While the majority of some eight thousand "white" parish priests in Ukraine were Ukrainian by origin, the nationally conscious clergy among them were a distinct minority and, as a rule, were deprived of positions of ecclesiastical authority. On the whole, the rank-and-file clergy tended to resent the heavy hand of the monastic bishops, and here the appeals of both the church liberals and autocephalists for improvement in the status of the parish clergy could not but strike many sympathetic chords. As long as they could be effectively protected either by the state or by an alternative *de facto* ecclesiastical authority from episcopal sanctions or rejection by their parishioners, many "white" clergymen were willing to challenge their bishops by openly supporting ecclesiastical reformers. This was amply demonstrated by the early successes of spokesmen for progressive church reforms, including Ukrainization, when they enjoyed the direct support of the progressive Ober-Procurator V.N. Lvov and the local civil authorities. The subsequent loss of this relative immunity to their superiors' reprisals combined with the realization of dangers to their individual welfare inherent in laymen's control of church affairs to cause a large-scale defection of the parish clergy from the ranks of the liberal and national church movements.

The Ukrainian Revolution provided the autocephalist movement with the historically tested, if not necessarily canonical, alternative of relying on state legislation and administrative measures to establish harmony between the church and the Ukrainian national interest. Unfortunately for the movement, the Central Rada government, which probably stood the best chance of enforcing the Ukrainization of the church, intervened belatedly and only half-heartedly in support of this cause. The Hetman regime, though taking a positive attitude toward ecclesiastical affairs and professing sympathy for the Ukrainization of the church, was too dependent on the acquiescence of the conservative Russian strata to break by state power the open defiance of the Ukrainian cause by the Russian episcopate. Eventually, in a futile attempt to salvage his regime, Skoropadsky sacrificed the cause of the emancipation of the Ukrainian Church along with that of Ukrainian independence. The Directory acted promptly and forcefully to implement by law the objectives of the Ukrainian autocephalist movement, but this regime's life-span was simply too short to implement its decree on autocephaly effectively. Of several causes that prevented the autocephalists from breaking the opposition of the ecclesiastical authorities, the instability of the Ukrainian national governments was the most obvious one.

As the Ukrainian-Russian struggle for control of the church increased in bitterness, the chances for a compromise solution espoused by Russian church liberals—broad autonomy of the Ukrainian Church under the limited authority of Moscow, coupled with the gradual Ukrainization of the Church—rapidly decreased with the polarization and growing rigidity in the attitudes of the contending camps. The two major documents of this period, the "autonomous" Statute as finally adopted in November 1918 by the All-Ukrainian Church Sobor and the January 1919 decree of the Directory on autocephaly, illustrated the irreconcilability of the positions taken on the one hand by the Moscow Patriarchate and its spokesmen in Ukraine and, on the other hand, by the Ukrainian autocephalists and their governmental supporters. Neither of these two documents could be said to have finally settled the controversy; they were rather declarations of the mutually exclusive attitudes of the respective contending parties. The Ukrainian side, with some support from the Russian church liberals, had persistently denied the validity of the 1918 Statute on such grounds as the arbitrary composition and procedures of the second and third sessions of the All-Ukrainian Sobor and the failure of this document to secure the required approval of the Ukrainian state. The supporters of the Moscow Patriarchate, for their part, rejected the Directory's law on autocephaly as a unilateral act of the Ukrainian government which had never been approved by the canonical leadership of the church. While the Bolshevik victory prevented the implementation of the 1919 decree on autocephaly, the former document—the 1918 *Polozhenie* as amended by the Patriarch—was of some practical significance in guiding the internal affairs of the Russian Orthodox Church in Ukraine until its nearly complete destruction by the late 1930s; later, in 1941–3, the nominal autonomy provided in this document was claimed and expanded in practice by the pro-Russian wing of the church in German-occupied Ukraine.

As the hopes for the survival of Ukrainian statehood faded away, the Ukrainian autocephalist movement came to face with a momentous decision. Having been frustrated in its attempts to de-Russify the church from above, it had either to admit defeat and disband, perhaps to work slowly toward these aims within the church, or it had to resort to a church revolution, sever its canonical links with the Russian Church and establish a separate church organization that would undertake Ukrainization from the grass roots by winning over the Ukrainian believers and progressively depriving the Russian Church of its parishes in Ukraine. The passionate faith of the Ukrainian autocephalists in the righteousness of their cause made most of them choose the second alternative.

*

Looking at Ukrainian-Russian relations within the Orthodox Church from the perspective of our time, it should be noted that the shared experiences of religious persecution in the Soviet Union and, in pre-1939 Poland, Warsaw's Polonization policies *vis-à-vis* the Orthodox Church, have had the effect of both moderating the ecclesiastical radicalism of the Ukrainian autocephalists and breaking down the once united opposition of the Russian episcopate to an effective Ukrainization and autocephaly of the Orthodox Church in Ukraine. It is not without irony that the resurgence of the Ukrainian Autocephalous Church in German-occupied Ukraine would have not been possible without the decisive support it received from the two senior Russian hierarchs of inter-war Poland, Metropolitan Dionisii (Valedinsky) of Warsaw and Archbishop Aleksandr (Inozemtsev) of Pinsk.[65]

It is also significant that the revived Ukrainian Autocephalous Orthodox Church has broken with its predecessor's "revolutionary" approach to Orthodox canons and that it followed them in consecrating its episcopate, although it admitted, without reordaining, some surviving priests of the "old" Ukrainian Autocephalous Church—an act which has earned it lasting condemnation by its Russian critics.[66] In fact, its only hierarchical link with the inter-war church in Soviet Ukraine was supplied by Metropolitan Feofil Buldovsky of Kharkiv, one of the early pioneers of ecclesiastical Ukrainization in 1917 who had left the ranks of the Patriarchal episcopate in 1925 to establish, together with four other canonically ordained bishops, a "canonical alternative" to the Ukrainian Autocephalous Church (in the form of the so-called "Conciliar-Episcopal Church").[67]

Beginning in the early 1940s, the religious policy initiated by Stalin accorded the Russian Orthodox Church the status of the relatively most favoured, most "patriotic" religious organization in the USSR. Once again recognized as an integrating, anti-separatist force, the Moscow Patriarchate joined the regime in combating Ukrainian nationalism in religious and political fields, beginning with a series of wartime appeals and measures against the Ukrainian Orthodox Autocephalous Church (but not against its pro-Russian rival in occupied Ukraine, the Autonomous Church). With the return of the Soviet authorities, the sole remaining autocephalist bishop (Metropolitan Buldovsky) was removed from office, while the autocephalist parishes were instantly annexed to the Russian church. Simultaneously, the Ukrainian language disappeared from liturgical use, even in those areas of Volhynia where it had been entrenched for a generation. The role played by the Moscow Patriarchate in the Soviet suppression of the Ukrainian Greek Catholic Church in Galicia and Transcarpathia, in the persecution of its bishops and clergy, and in the annexation of its parishes and flock to the Russian Orthodox Church could not but deepen Ukrainian-Russian differences in the ecclesiastical field.[68] Whether by choice or by compulsion, the Russian Church has assumed a role not unlike the one it performed in pre-1917 Russia—that of guardian of imperial unity against the "unchurchly" designs of Ukrainian nationalism.

One should not, however, assume that the Soviet concern about the unity of the Russian Church is entirely patriotic or unselfish: from the Kremlin's point of view, it is far easier to control, manipulate and progressively strangle a centralized church organization sufficiently alienated from the national, cultural and social aspirations of the believers. Even continuing Ukrainian-Russian confrontation in the ecclesiastical field may not be completely adverse to the Kremlin's interests, as long as it serves to bring the Russian church closer to the regime and helps prevent any effective co-operation between the Ukrainian and Russian faithful who oppose the existing regime.

Notes

1. E.g., Constantinople's refusal to recognize (until 1589) the autocephaly of the Russian Church proclaimed in 1448, and, in more recent times, that of the Bulgarian Church (1870); Moscow's opposition to the autocephaly of the Orthodox churches of Georgia (1917) until 1943 and Poland (1924); and the Serbian Patriarchate's refusal to recognize Macedonian autocephaly (1967).

2. On the annexation of the Kiev Metropoly to the Moscow Patriarchate in 1685–6,

see Oleksandr Lototsky, *Avtokefaliia*. Vol. II: *Narys istorii avtokefalnykh tserkov* (Warsaw, 1938), 368–80; Ivan Ohiienko, *Pryiednannia tserkvy ukrainskoi do moskovskoi v 1686 r.*, 2d ed. (Tarnów, 1922); and Ivan Vlasovsky, *Narys istorii Ukrainskoi Pravoslavnoi Tserkvy* (New York and Bound Brook, N.J., 1957), II, Pt. 1, 330–43.

3. Lototsky, op. cit., Vol. I: *Zasady avtokefalii* (Warsaw, 1935), 459.

4. Including the ban on publishing in the Ukrainanian language that lasted from 1876 to 1905.

5. Mykola Kovalevsky, *Pry dzherelakh borotby* (Innsbruck, 1960), 557–8.

6. 1865–1943(?). Ordained in 1923 as an auxiliary bishop for Lubni and Myrhorod, Buldovsky seceded along with two other bishops from the Russian Orthodox Church in 1925 in an attempt to form a "canonical" Ukrainian autocephalous Orthodox church. See this writer's "Ukrainization Movements within the Russian Orthodox Church, and the Ukrainian Autocephalous Orthodox Church," *Harvard Ukrainian Studies* III/IV (1979–80): 102–10.

7. [Feofil Buldovsky], *Pro ukrainizatsiiu tserkvy. Doklad prochytanyi na Poltavskomu Eparkhiialnomu Z'izdi dukhovenstva i myrian, 3–8 travnia 1917 roku*, 3rd ed. (Lubni, 1918), 8.

8. 1864–1938(?). Having presided over a diocesan congress of clergy and laymen in Kiev following the 1905 Revolution, Lypkivsky re-emerged in this capacity in the spring of 1917 and was elected chairman of the Kiev diocesan council. The principal clerical leader of the Ukrainian church movement from 1917, Lypkivsky was consecrated in a moving if not canonical manner by clergy and lay members of the 1921 Autocephalist Sobor as Metropolitan of Kiev and All Ukraine. He presided over the Ukrainian Autocephalous Church until his removal from the leadership of the U.A.O.C. in 1927, which was demanded by the Soviet authorities in return for the restoration of the church's legal status. For his short autobiography written in December 1933, see Vasyl Lypkivsky, *Istoriia Ukrainskoi Pravoslavnoi Tserkvy*. Part 7: *Vidrodzhennia Ukrainskoi Tserkvy* (Winnipeg, 1961), lxxvi–lxxvii [cited hereafter as *Istoriia*].

9. *Russkiia vedomosti*, 18 April/1 May 1917; Iu. Samoilovich, *Tserkov ukrainskogo sotsial-fashizma* (Moscow, 1932), 28; Lypkivsky, *Istoriia*, 7.

10. *Odesskii listok*, 23 June/6 July 1917; *Odesskiia novosti*, 23 June/6 July 1917; see also a memorandum of the Ukrainian Renovationist Synod, *Dokladnaia zapiska Sv. Sinoda Ukrainskoi Pravoslavnoi Tserkvi Ego Sviateishestvu Sv. Vselenskomu Patriarkhu...ob istorii i kanonicheskikh osnovaniiakh avtokefalii Ukrainskoi Pravoslavnoi Tserkvi* (Kharkiv, 1926), 1.

11. *Rech*, 13/26 July 1917.

12. *Bezvirnyk* (Kharkiv), no. 1 (1931): 45.

13. *Russkiia vedomosti*, 2/15 August 1917.

14. *Kievskiia Eparkhiialnyia Vedomosti* LVI, no. 32–33 (20–27 August/12–19 September 1917): 261–2; cited in Friedrich Heyer, *Die Orthodoxe Kirche in der Ukraine von 1917 bis 1945* (Cologne and Braunsfeld, 1953), 37.

15. One of the participants in the Ukrainian church movement in Kiev, the priest

P. Korsunovsky, relates that, when accused by a Ukrainian Rada delegation in December 1917 of being alien to Ukrainian aspirations, Metropolitan Vladimir (Bogoiavlensky) of Kiev "simply could not understand what they were talking about. Astonished, he asked: What kind of Ukraine? What kind of Ukrainian people? Is not the Little Russian people the same as the Russian people?" ("Tserkovnyi rukh na Ukraini v pershi roky revoliutsii," *Dnipro* [Trenton, N.J.], 21 November 1925).

16. O. Lototsky, "Znevazhena sprava," *Tryzub* (Paris) III, no. 12 (20 March 1927): 7.

17. See S. Hai, "Polozhennia dukhovenstva," *Nova Rada*, 10/23 September 1917.

18. P. Khrystiuk, *Zamitky i materiialy do istorii ukrainskoi revoliutsii 1917–1920 rr.* (Vienna, 1921), 1: 194.

19. Convened by the "Organizational Committee for the Convocation of the Ukrainian Church Sobor" (constituted by the Third Ukrainian Military Congress a short time previously), the meeting was also attended by leaders of the *Bratstvo Voskresennia* (Brotherhood of the Resurrection), the new organizational form assumed by the "mainsteam" Ukrainian church movement, as well as by some members of the old Church Congress Committee elected by the Kiev diocesan congress in the spring of 1917. See Samoilovich, 36–8; Heyer, 40–41; and Korsunovsky, 15 August 1925.

20. A Ukrainian by origin, Dorodnytsyn was dismissed by the Synod in March 1917 on a charge of collaboration with Rasputin, and was subsequently living in retirement in Kiev. For Dorodnytsyn's denial of the charge, see *Novoe vremia*, 25 March/7 April 1917. Dorodnytsyn explained his motives for joining the Ukrainian movement in a letter to *Kievlianin* (6/9 December 1917) in response to this paper's attacks on his "Ukrainophilism."

21. Cited in full in Dmytro Doroshenko, *Istoriia Ukrainy 1917–1923 rr.* (Uzhhorod, 1930), 1: 408–09; cf. *Vserossiiskii Tserkovno-Obshchestvennyi Vestnik* (Petrograd), 1 December 1917, 3; and Heyer, 40–41.

22. *Kievlianin*, 25 November/8 December 1917; *Odesskii listok*, 12 December 1917; Korsunovsky, 29 August 1925; Vlasovsky, IV, Pt. 1, 17. While the Ukrainian delegation reported upon its return to Kiev that Patriarch Tikhon had given his blessings to the All-Ukrainian Sobor, according to Metropolitan Antonii (Khrapovitsky) of Kharkiv, Tikhon told the delegates that "I shall never give my consent to any autocephaly of the Ukrainian Church, but autonomy, even the widest, is in your hands" (Bishop Nikon [Rklitsky], *Zhizneopisanie Blazhenneishago Antoniia, Mitropolita Kievskago i Galitskago* [New York, 1958], IV, 234). On the hostile reaction of the Kiev bishops and clergy to the proposed Ukrainian Sobor, see Peter T. Sheshko, "The Russian Orthodox Church Sobor of Moscow and the Orthodox Church in the Ukraine (1917–1918)," Pt. 2, *Analecta Ordinis S. Basilii Magni* (Rome), sect. 2, X (XVI), no. 1–4 (1979), 239–48; and *Kievskiia Eparkhialnyia Vedomosti*, nos. 44–5 (29 October-5 December/11 November-18 December 1917); on the opposition at the All-Russian Sobor in Moscow against the Sobor and its Rada initiators, see Sheshko, 251–324; *Russkiia Vedomosti*, no. 258 (25 November/8 December 1917); Korsunovsky, 21 and 28 November 1925.

23. *Kievskiia   Eparkhiialnyia   Vedomosti*   LVI,   nos.   48–49–50   (Dec. 3–10–17/16–23–30, 1917): 365–6.

24. See "Sozyv Vseukrainskago tserkovnago soboru," *Kievlianin*, 22 December 1917/4 January 1918, signed by V. Lypkivsky and N. I. Luzgin; and *Russkiia Vedomosti*, no. 259 (28 November/8 December 1917). Cf. Samoilovich, 37–41; and A. I. Pokrovsky, "Avtokefaliia Pravoslavnoi Tserkvi na Ukraine," *Ukrainskyi Pravoslavnyi Blahovisnyk* (Kharkiv), no. 18 (15 September 1925), 4.

25. D. Skrynchenko, "Vseukrainskii Tserkovnyi Sobor," *Kievskii Pravoslavnyi Vestnik*, no. 1 (1/14 October 1918), 88–94; Korsunovsky, 19 December 1925; Lypkivsky, 10; Pokrovsky, 4; Samoilovich, 44–5.

26. *Kievskii Eparkhiialnyi Vestnik*, no. 1 (2–15 May 1918), 1–4; and no. 23 (17–30 June 1918), 91; *Golos Kieva*, 29 May 1918; *Nova Rada*, 16 June 1918; Samoilovich, 54–6; and Doroshenko, 2: 323–5. According to the then Minister of Confessions in the Hetman cabinet, V. V. Zenkovsky (Zinkivsky), who favoured autonomy but not autocephaly of the Ukrainian church, the Kiev diocesan sobor was designed to bypass the Ukrainian Sobor and to place Metropolitan Antonii at the helm of the Ukrainian church by a *fait accompli* masterminded by the "Ukrainophobe" Bishop Nikodim (senior Kiev vicar who temporarily replaced Metropolitan Vladimir after the latter was murdered by Bolshevik soldiers in February 1918) ("Vospominaniia [1900–1920]: Piat mesiatsev u vlasti [Moe uchastie v ukrainskoi zhizni]," unpublished 1952 manuscript in Columbia University's Archive of Russian and East European History and Culture, 22–5, 33–9). At Zenkovsky's insistence, the Hetman Government refused to recognize Antonii as the *Kiev* Metropolitan until he was subsequently confirmed in this capacity by the Second Session of the All-Ukrainian Sobor. Meanwhile, a meeting of six bishops of the Ukrainian dioceses who were participating in the Moscow Sobor was held on 2 April 1918 under the chairmanship of Metropolitan Antonii Khrapovitsky. At this meeting, according to Pokrovsky (op. cit., 4), "the decision was reached not to make haste, if possible, with the opening of the second session of the Ukrainian Sobor and to postpone it indefinitely, i.e., not to continue this Sobor at all." See "Akt soveshchaniia episkopov Ukrainskikh eparkhii," *Kievskii eparkhialnyi vestnik*, no. 1 (2–15 May 1918), 2–4. This "Act" clearly seeks to change unilaterally the mode of representation at the All-Ukrainian Sobor agreed upon in the course of negotiations between the Rada and the delegation of the All-Russian Sobor in December 1917. The bishops instruct dioceses to hold conferences of the clergy and laymen *prior* to the resumption of the Ukrainian Sobor sessions, at which such crucial questions are to be decided as the selection and funding of Sobor delegates (with the bishops clearly hinting at the reduction of the number of diocesan delegates at the expense of the likely supporters of autocephaly); and the desirability of "autocephaly or autonomy of the Church in Ukraine, Ukrainization of the liturgy, etc." (p. 3). Urged by Ukrainian church circles, Zenkovsky had to apply government pressure, including a meeting with Hetman Skoropadsky, to persuade the episcopate to reconvene the All-Ukrainian Sobor (op. cit., 37–8).

27. Archbishop Iosif [Krechetovich], *Proiskhozhdenie i sushchnost samosviatstva lipkovtsev* (Kharkiv, 1925), 6n; Lototsky, "Znevazhena sprava," 8; Doroshenko,

2: 324–5. See in particular P.V.L. [Lypkivsky], "Tserkovne zhyttia na Ukraini v 1918 rotsi," *Trybuna*, no. 13 (2 January 1919).

28. Pokrovsky, 4; Doroshenko, 327–8; Lototsky, "Tserkovna sprava na Ukraini," *Literaturno-naukovyi visnyk* XXII, no. 5 (1923): 66; Zenkovsky, 45–7. According to Zenkovsky, "the right-wing [Academy] professors and higher clergy [at the Ukrainian Sobor] did not want to solve any question of principle until the restoration of all Russia" (ibid., 66–7).

29. Pokrovsky, 4.

30. Korsunovsky, 27 February; 6, 13, 20 March; 10, 17 April; 1 May 1926; P. V. L. [Lypkivsky], op. cit.; Metropolitan Evlogii, *Put moei zhizni* (Paris, 1947), 313; *Dokladnaia zapiska Sv. Sinoda*, 2; Lypkivsky, 11–12. See also Oleksandr Lototsky, *Ukrainski dzherela tserkovnoho prava* (Warsaw, 1931), 130 (cited hereafter as *Ukrainski dzherela)*.

31. The complete text of the statute is reproduced in Doroshenko, 2: 328–30. Following its adoption of the statute, the Sobor elected to the Supreme Church Council Metropolitans Antonii of Kiev (as *ex officio* chairman) and Platon (Rozhdestvensky) of Odessa, Archbishop Evlogii (Georgievsky) of Volhynia and Bishop Pakhomii of Chernihiv, as well as several priests and laymen; none of them could be considered sympathetic to the Ukrainian autocephalist movement (*Kievlianin*, 25 August 1918).

32. Cited in full in Doroshenko, 2, Appendix XI, p. lxii. Patriarch Tikhon turned down the request from the Hetman Government not to ratify Article 2 of the Statute defining the Patriarch's powers over the Ukrainian Church until this matter had been given more consideration by the Ukrainian Sobor and the Government (ibid., 331–2). Professor Pokrovsky, one of the leading spokesmen of the liberal "moderates" at the Sobor, who opposed both "centralist" and "autocephalist" tendencies in favour of a "broad ecclesiastical autonomy of the Ukrainian church," commented on the amended statute that "of the autonomy of the Ukrainian church, almost nothing has been left [in it] except for a hollow sound" (A. Pokrovsky, "Vseukrainskii tserkovnoi sobor," *Odesskii listok*, 3 November 1918).

33. Samoilovich, 59–68.

34. Toward the end of October, Hetman Skoropadsky had a new cabinet formed which included nominees of the Ukrainian opposition, among them Oleksander Lototsky as the new minister of confessions. On 12 November, Lototsky addressed the third session of the Ukrainian Sobor, informing the latter that the Government was now firmly in favour of complete independence of the Orthodox Church in Ukraine (for the full text of his address, see Lototsky, *Ukrainski dzherela*, 133–4. Two days later, however, Lototsky and his Ukrainian fellow ministers were dismissed by the Hetman in connection with his proclamation of federation with Russia, a step designed to save his regime in the wake of Germany's capitulation.

35. *Golos Kieva*, 16 November 1918. Cf. Oleksander Lototsky, "Na svitanku tserkovnoho vyzvolennia," *Kalendar-almanakh "Dnipro" na perestupnyi rik 1928* (Lviv, 1928), 106.

36. *Golos Kieva*, 16 November 1918.

37. *Russkii golos*, 16 November 1918.

38. *Golos Kieva*, 16 November 1918.

39. Ibid., 22 November 1918.

40. Cited in Lototsky, *Ukrainski dzherela*, 49n. On other Sobor resolutions, see *Kievskaia mysl*, 10 and 13 December 1918; and *Mir*, 12 December 1918. Before Skoropadsky abdicated on 14 December, the Sobor issued two appeals to the population to unite around the Hetman for the sake of "the salvation of all Russia" and to fight against the "Petliurite bands" (i.e., the forces of the Directory that led an uprising against Skoropadsky triggered by his proclamation of federation with Russia). See *Vidrodzhennia*, 21 November 1918; and *Trybuna*, 19 December 1918.

41. "Pravoslavie i ukrainofilstvo," *Tserkovnyia vedomosti* (Ekaterinodar), no. 7, 1919, reproduced in the Karlovtsi Synod's *Tserkovnyia vedomosti izdavaimyia pri Arkhiereiskom Sinode Russkoi Pravoslavnoi Tserkvi zagranitsei*, no. 1–2 (1930): 14–15. Cf. Nikon (Rklitsky), 4: 239.

42. *Trybuna*, 19 December 1918. The bishops (also arrested were Bishop Nikodim and the Pochaiv monastery abbot, Vitalii [Maksymenko]) were charged but not tried for their appeals to the population to fight the "Petliurite bands." The principal consideration on the part of the Ukrainian authorities may have been to isolate the main opponents of the Ukrainian autocephaly that was soon to be proclaimed by government decree. After confinement in a Basilian monastery in Buchach (where they were joined by Archbishop Dorodnytsyn, who came to plead for their release), the bishops were liberated by the advancing Poles and, travelling by way of Lviv (where they were guests of the Uniate Metropolitan Andrei Sheptytsky), they eventually joined the Denikin forces in Novorossiisk. By the end of the summer of 1919 Antonii and Nikodim resumed their posts in Kiev after its capture by the "Whites." See Evlogii, 318–44; cf. Vlasovsky, IV, Pt. 1, 78–82. To fill in the hiatus in ecclesiastical authority, Metropolitan Platon—evidently reluctant to act as Khrapovitsky's deputy—convened in late December the Sobor of Bishops, which decided to transfer ecclesiastical administration temporarily to the Kiev office (*kontora*) of the Bishop's Sobor, to be headed by Bishop Dionizii (Valedinsky) of Kremianets (*Nash Put*, 29 December 1918). Platon himself left for Odessa to plead with the local French vice-consul, Hainnot, to assume "the protection of the interest of the Orthodox Church in Ukraine" (*Trybuna*, 1 January 1919).

43. See memoirs of Lototsky's successor in the Ministry of Cults, Ivan Lypa, "Iak ia pishov v revoliutsiiu," *Kalendar-almanakh "Dnipro" na perestupnyi rik 1928* (Lviv, 1927), 98. Archbishop Ahapit, assisted by V. Lypkivsky and other Kiev clergy, presided over a solemn service in St. Sophia Square in Kiev on 19 December, welcoming the victorious Directory upon its official arrival in the capital (*Trybuna*, 21 December 1918; Korsunovsky, 12 June 1926).

44. Members of the autocephalist Brotherhood of Sts. Cyril and Methodius (formed in the wake of the first session of the All-Ukrainian Sobor), Volodymyr Chekhivsky and Serhii Shelukhin, became Premier and Minister of Justice respectively in the

new Ukrainian Government, Ivan Lypa from Odessa became Minister of Cults, while Lototsky was soon to be dispatched as the Directory's envoy to Turkey with the special task of securing support for Ukrainian autocephaly from the Ecumenical Patriarchate of Constantinople. See Lototsky, "Tserkovna sprava na Ukraini", 68; Iosif (Krechetovich), 9. *Trybuna*, 24 and 27 December 1918; and Oleksandr Lototsky, *V Tsarhorodi* (Warsaw, 1939), 94–9.

45. Ukrainska Narodna Respublika, *Vistnyk Derzhavnykh Zakoniv* 1, no. 5 (18 January 1919), reproduced in full in Lototsky, *Ukrainski dzherela*, 297–8; cf. *Trybuna*, 2 January 1919.

46. Lypa, 98; cf. Samoilovich, 76.

47. Lypa, 98; for the next eight months the Ministry of Cult in fact ceased functioning as the Directory retreated westward before superior Soviet forces, eventually establishing itself in Kamianets Podilskyi in the Podillia region.

48. Two Ukrainian candidates for episcopal consecration were selected by Lypa. Bishop Dionisii was requested for arrange for the consecration of one of them, Archpriest Iurii Zhevchenko, as bishop-administrator of the Kiev diocese (to replace Antonii's vicar, Nikodim). Convened by Dionisii, the *kontora* of the Episcopal Sobor (three bishops) turned down the government's request on the grounds that only the sobor of bishops was empowered to select new bishops (*Poslednyia novosti*, 11 January 1919).

49. Lypkivsky, 13–20. Following the liberation of Kiev by the Ukrainian army at the end of August 1919 and the loss of the capital to the Denikin forces (which remained in the hands of the "Whites" until December), Lypkivsky and some other Ukrainian autocephalist leaders escaped to the Directory's temporary "capital," Kamianets Podilskyi, where in October 1919, under the new Minister of Confessions, Ivan Ohiienko, Lypkivsky was elected chairman of the reconstructed Ukrainian Holy Synod; the latter's activities were cut short by the Polish occupation of Kamianets in mid-November, with Lypkivsky soon returning to Kiev. Oleksander Dotsenko, *Litopys Ukrainskoi Revoliutsii. Materiialy i dokumenty do istorii Ukrainskoi Revoliutsii, 1917–1922*, 2, Bk. 4 (Lviv, 1923), 117–18; V. Bidnov, *Tserkovna sprava na Ukraini* (Tarnów, 1921), 26–32.

50. "The Decree of the Provisional Worker-Peasant Government of Ukraine on the Separation of the Church from the State and of the School from the Church" of 22 January 1919 (published in *Sobranie Uzakonenii Ukrainy*, no. 3, 1919, art. 37), closely followed the earlier Soviet Russian decree of 5 February 1918, except for omitting the provision depriving churches and religious associations of the rights of a judicial person. This deliberate omission was later "corrected" by a resolution of the Council of People's Commissars of the Ukrainian SSR of 3 August 1920 (*Sobranie Uzakonenii Ukrainy*, no. 22, 1920, art. 435). On the autocephalists' rationale for "recognizing" the Separation Decree, see Lypkivsky, 13–14.

51. The "Second" All-Ukrainian Orthodox Church Council (Rada) was organized in April 1919, with Mykhailo Moroz as chairman, Lypkivsky as vice-chairman, and Ivan Tarasenko as secretary. See ibid., 14–20; and V. Lypkivsky, *Pravoslavna Khrystova Tserkva ukrainskoho narodu* [1927] (Munich, 1951), 24–5. Initially, in March 1919, a group of Ukrainian clergy and laymen sought permission from

Bishop Nazarii (temporarily administering the Kiev diocese) to assign them a Kiev church where Gospels could be read in the Ukrainian language during the Lent and Easter services. After the bishop turned down this request on the grounds that the Ukrainian Sobor of 1918 had banned the Ukrainian language from church services, the group constituted itself as a "parish association" under the new Soviet legislation. Following the "registration" of its parish statute, the authorities assigned the first Ukrainian parish one of the parishless Kiev churches (the "military" church of St. Nicholas). Cf. Ivan Sukhopliuev, *Ukrainski avtokefalisty* (Kharkiv, 1925), 7–9.

52. Lypkivsky, *Istoriia*, 20; cf. K. V. Fotiev, *Popytki ukrainskoi tserkovnoi avtokefalii v XX veke* (Munich, 1955), 27. With Metropolitan Antonii's return to Kiev, the Kiev Consistory instructed the deans: "...All [church] services which were previously celebrated in the 'Ukrainian' language should be conducted in Church-Slavic; books in the 'Ukrainian' language, if there are such in churches, should immediately be collected and deposited into the church archive under the special responsibility of the church warden. All church business should be conducted only in the Russian state language; all vital and confessional records and other books that were written in the 'Ukrainian' language should at once be rewritten in Russian; you are ordered to pay special attention to this instruction" (cited in Dotsenko, 2, Bk. 4, 237).

53. "Vid Vseukrainskoi Pravoslavnoi Tserkovnoi Rady do ukrainskoho pravo-slavnoho hromadianstva. Lyst pershyi," *Tserkva i zhyttia*, no. 1 (1927): 120–23. This declaration was adopted at an enlarged Rada meeting on 5 May, just two days before the capture of Kiev by the now allied Polish and Ukrainian forces and the return of the government of the Ukrainian People's Republic. As the latter was committed to Ukrainian autocephaly, it is likely that the proclamation was bound up with the expectation of decisive government action to solve the question of Ukrainian ecclesiastical independence and the consecration of bishops for the Ukrainian Autocephalous Orthodox Church. Few would have expected at that time that the Bolsheviks would be back in Kiev within a month.

54. See *Tserkva i zhyttia*, no. 1 (1927): 25, 123–4; Lypkivsky, *Istoriia*, 27–30; and Ivan Shram, "Iak tvorylas Ukrainska Avtokefalna Tserkva," *Na varti* (Volodymyr Volynskyi), nos. 7–8 (May 1925): 2–5. See also Vlasovsky, 4: 83–7.

55. Shram, op. cit.; A. Richytsky, *Problemy ukrainskoi religiinoi svidomosty* (Volodymyr Volynskyi, 1933), 12; "Materiialy do istorii borotby za avtokefaliiu ukrainskoi tserkvy," *Relihiino-naukovyi visnyk* (Aleksandrów Kujawski), 3, nos. 7–8 (February-March 1923): 47–55; Sukhopliuev, 11–15, 36–42; and especially Iosif (Krechetovich), 13–19. For a popular outline of the autocephalist ideology and programme, see a brochure by the All-Ukrainian Orthodox Church Rada circulated prior to the pre-Sobor Conference of the Kiev *okruha* (district) which met on 27–9 March 1921 in Kiev and was subsequently published by I. Ohiienko in Poland (*Pidvalyny Ukrainskoi Pravoslavnoi Tserkvy* [Tarnów, 1922]).

56. Iosif (Krechetovich), 24.

57. Lypkivsky, *Istoriia*, 31–4.

58. Iosif (Krechetovich), 26.

59. Lypkivsky, *Istoriia*, 39–40. An extended autocephalist argument in favour of the legitimacy of the episcopate ordained by the priests and laymen at the 1921 Sobor appears in Ivan Teodorovych, *Blahodatnist iierarkhii U.A.P.Ts. (Ukrainskoi Avtokefalnoi Pravoslavnoi Tserkvy)* (Regensburg, 1947), originally written in 1922 and previously published in Philadelphia in 1941. Ironically, Archbishop Teodorovych, who had been assigned to head the Ukrainian Orthodox Church in the United States in 1924 and who had himself been ordained by Metropolitan Lypkivsky and Archbishop N. Sharaivsky at the 1921 Sobor, eventually became sufficiently doubtful of the validity of his consecration to submit to another episcopal ordination after World War II, this time by the canonically ordained Orthodox bishops.

60. Ibid., 40; Vlasovsky, 4, Pt. 1, 117–18. According to Heyer (p. 83), Sokolovsky represented the position taken by the conservative "Poltava tendency."

61. Vlasovsky, 4, Pt. 1, 118; Lypkivsky, *Istoriia*, 40–42; for an eyewitness account of the consecration, see Archbishop Ivan Pavlovsky, "Pershyi Vseukrainskyi pravoslavnyi sobor," *Tserkva i zhyttia*, nos. 2–3 (1927): 197–205.

62. The secessionists were led by priests K. Sokolovsky, Serhii Pylypenko and Pavlo Pohorilko (Vasyl Potiienko, *Vidnovlennia iierarkhii Ukrainskoi Pravoslavnoi Avtokefalnoi Tserkvy* (Neu-Ulm, 1971), 23, 36–8; Heyer, 83; Vlasovsky, 4, Pt. 1, 118).

63. Metropolitan Antonii Khrapovitsky, in the words of his biographer, "was not and could not be a separatist, since he, like many [people] then, was hoping that Ukraine liberated from the Bolsheviks would serve as a basis for the salvation of Russia, when again a union of Great and Little Russia would take place" (Nikon [Rklitsky], 4: 224). Antonii's treatment of the autocephalists at the first session of the Ukrainian Sobor abounded in more or less veiled accusations of "shtundism," "Catholicism," and "Uniate" tendencies (Skrynchenko, 91–3); Archbishop Evlogii characterized his position at the 1918 sessions of the Ukrainian Sobor as follows: "I was passionately for 'the one, indivisible Russian Church,' admitting, however, that some concession could be made to Ukrainians" (Evlogii, 313). Characteristic of the attitudes of the "centralist" Kiev clergy in late 1917 was a resolution adopted on 24 November by the Union of the Kiev parish councils (embracing some 60 clergymen and four local bishops): "(a) to protest to the utmost against the arbitrary, anti-canonical attempt to establish an autocephalous Ukrainian church; (b) to consider the establishment of such a church very dangerous for Orthodoxy and likely to lead it first into Union [with Rome], against which the South Russian population fought for centuries, and subsequently to complete subordination to the Vatican and the Pope; (c) to present a complaint to the Holy All-Russian Sobor against the masterminds of [these] troubles in order for the Sobor to summon them to trial and to defrock them unless they repudiate their designs; (d) to ask the church authorities not to allow the convening of the All-Ukrainian Sobor; and (e) to consider the absence from Kiev of the Kiev Metropolitan undesirable at such a dangerous moment, the more so since he could be replaced at the Sobor by one of the Kiev vicar bishops." (*Vserossiiskii Tserkovno-Obshchestvennyi Vestnik*, no. 156, 1 December 1917, 3).

64. In 1915, of the nine diocesan bishops in Ukraine, eight were Russians, and only one bishop, Ahapit (Vyshnevsky) of Katerynoslav, was of Ukrainian origin. Of the fifteen vicar bishops, eleven were Russians, and only two were of Ukrainian origin (Kievan vicars Vasylii Bohdashevsky and Dymytrii Verbytsky). Sviateishii Pravitelstvuiushchii Sinod, *Spiski sluzhashchikh po Vedomstvu Pravoslavnago ispovedaniia za 1915 god* (Petrograd, 1915).

65. Joining Ukrainian church circles in opposing the continued canonical submission to the Moscow Patriarchate of the majority of Orthodox bishops in Volhynia (imposed during the Soviet occupation of 1939–41), Metropolitan Dionisii appointed Archbishop Polikarp (Sikorsky) of Lutsk "Provisional Administrator of the Orthodox Autocephalous Church in the Liberated Lands of Ukraine" on 24 December 1941. In February 1942, Archbishop Aleksandr of Pinsk joined Archbishop Polikarp in ordaining two bishops for the Autocephalous Church in Ukraine, and subsequently participated in the sobors of Ukrainian bishops (see Vlasovsky, 4, Pt. 2, 199–248).

66. Fotiev, 58. Reflecting attitudes widespread among Russian Orthodox churchmen, the same author characterizes *lipkovshchina* (i.e., the Ukrainian Autocephalous Church headed by Metropolitan Lypkivsky and his successors) as follows: "At its [*lipkovshchina's*] root are the same [as the Renovationists'] caste resentments of the white [married] clergy, and therein lies the secret of its relative and short-lived success. Nationalist ideas may have gratified representatives of the Ukrainian 'intelligentsia' who had not found their place in the construction of the Great Empire and were suffering from [the sense] of their offended folkloric particularities. This chauvinist operetta has [however] remained alien to the people. *Lipkovshchina* was a parish clergy (*popovskoe*) movement which was maintained by the Petliurite administration, just as twenty years later the "autocephaly" of Bishop Polikarp derived its support from the German occupiers-dismemberers and Galician policemen appointed by them" (ibid., 20). An even less subtle account appears in S. Raevsky, *Ukrainskaia Avtokefalnaia Tserkov* (Jordanville, N. Y., 1948). For analogies with the current Soviet characterization of the Ukrainian Autocephalous Orthodox Church, see K. Ie. Dmytruk, *Pid shtandartamy reaktsii i fashyzmu* (Kiev, 1976), 162–72, 190–224.

67. See this writer's "Ukrainization Movements within the Russian Orthodox Church," 101–10. It is significant that Buldovsky was joined at the 1925 "Lubni sobor" by two other veterans of the Ukrainian church movement—former members of the All-Ukrainian Church Rada who seceded from the 1921 Sobor—K. Sokolovsky (ordained in the autumn of 1921 Bishop Ioannikii of Bakhmut by the Kievan bishops) and P. Pohorilko (ordained in 1923 as a Renovationist vicar bishop for Podillia).

68. See, e.g., a 1966 petition of a persecuted Ukrainian Catholic priest, Hryhorii Budzynsky, to the Soviet Procurator General, reproduced in full in *Ukrainskyi Visnyk*, nos. I-II (January-May 1970) (Paris and Baltimore, 1971), 64–71. See also this writer's "The Uniate Church in the Soviet Ukraine: A Case Study in Soviet Church Policy," *Canadian Slavonic Papers* 8 (1965): 89–113.

ECONOMY AND DEMOGRAPHY

Ralph S. Clem

Demographic Change among Russians and Ukrainians in the Soviet Union: Social, Economic and Political Implications

Relations among ethnic groups may take any number of forms and will involve a wide range of interconnected factors.[1] Thus, in their historical encounter one might expect ethnic groups to engage along political, economic and linguistic lines, with the intensity of their interaction and the relative strength of the contestants fluctuating over time. In concrete terms, however, what is perhaps the ultimate manifestation of inter–ethnic contact is that which occurs between or among the populations of the different groups, the patterns of settlement and territoriality, and the manner in which these patterns shift. One might even say that the geography of ethnic groups is a function of—that is, determined by—the interplay of forces on the more abstract levels of politics, economics and culture. In this sense, demographic trends may be seen as the outcome of broader conflicts. This is not to say, of course, that population change will not in and of itself be fraught with potentially serious consequences.

In this paper I shall describe the manner in which the population of the dominant nationality of the USSR—the Russians—and that of the numerically largest minority—the Ukrainians—have interacted geographically since the advent of the Soviet regime. Unfortunately, it is not possible to go much beyond this period retrospectively, as the empirical evidence required is not suitable for our purposes; where practicable, figures from the only census of the *ancien régime*, that conducted in 1897, will be adduced. Beyond this description, I shall attempt an explanation of these ethnodemographic patterns and the changes therein by reference to specific events or by relating them to longer-term determinants of population trends, most notably those concomitant with economic development. In conclusion, some implications of the ethnodemography of the Soviet Union are suggested.

Because the issue of territoriality is of particular importance in ethnic group relations, we will focus attention on the extent to which Russians and Ukrainians have penetrated each other's homelands. As defined here, the respective ethnic homelands are the Russian Soviet Federated Socialist Republic (RSFSR) and the Ukrainian Soviet Socialist Republic (UkSSR) as they are presently constituted. Clearly, the sub-national political unit structure of the USSR is not the perfect expression of ethno-territoriality. For one thing, the inter-republic boundaries are not now nor have they ever been exactly coterminous with the area of settlement of their given titular nationalities. Further, the RSFSR contains a host of subordinate non-Russian ethnic units, which serves to dilute the "Russianness" of that vast republic. Nevertheless, the fact that for more than a half-century the RSFSR and the Ukrainian Republic have been formally, constitutionally recognized as ethnic homelands renders them meaningful representations of ethnoterritoriality and, as will be argued later, lends them a certain legitimacy.

Data and Methods

Heretofore, the principal obstacles connected with a study such as that proposed here have been the many problems attendant to the data required to describe and analyze the historical economic and demographic trends that have taken place in the various regions and among the different ethnic groups of the USSR. An example of such problems would be the changes which have occurred in both the national territory and in the internal political-administrative unit structure of the Soviet Union from time to time, changes which effectively rule out any longitudinal analysis at a relatively fine geographical scale based directly on the census data as published. Further, such seemingly unambiguous terms as "urban" or ethnic identification were defined differently from census to census and even within the same census. Hence, although the broad outlines of population change and its correlates in the USSR have been apparent for some time, the censuses of the USSR—which are our chief sources of information on Soviet society—have been underutilized owing to these and other technical difficulties.

To overcome these obstacles we have derived from the original census figures a unique data set which allows for a description and analysis of social and demographic trends in the USSR from the early years of Soviet power (as evidenced in the 1926 census) through the post-World War II era (as manifested in the 1959 census) to the present (represented by the 1970, 1979, and 1989 censuses). This data set is based on consistent definitions and the figures have been ordered into territorially comparable units.[2] As a spatial framework for purposes of description and analysis we chose 141 krai/oblast/ASSR level units as they were defined in the 1959 census.[3]

In order to solve the problem of internal territorial comparability, data from the 1926 Soviet census were fitted into the 1959 base units by means of two area allocation procedures (one primary and one as a check). In those few instances in which 1970 and 1979 census units differed from those of 1959, the 1970/1979 data were likewise ordered into the 1959 units. Finally, the territory equivalent to the present-day USSR had to be "reconstructed" for the 1926 benchmark by utilizing census data from various East European countries which ceded territory to or were incorporated into the Soviet Union in the years before and after the Second World War.[4]

The data derived by this procedure include variables for each of the territorially comparable units for the censuses of 1926, 1959 and 1970 and partial figures for the censuses of 1979 and 1989; even at this writing, complete results of the 1979 census are not available. Data from the 1989 census are as yet available only at the republic level. The variables and their availability are:

(1) *Ethnic Composition*, as enumerated in the Soviet censuses (mainly on the basis of self-identification), by oblast/krai/ASSR/republic, for 1926, 1959, 1970 and 1979.

(2) *Urban Population*, defined here as the number of people in each unit enumerated in cities with populations of 15,000 or more, by oblast/krai/ASSR/-republic, for 1926, 1959 and 1970.

From these variables in turn we calculated two types of indices for the purpose of describing demographic patterns and trends:

(1) *Distribution Indices*, which are simply the percentage of the nation-wide population of a given variable found in each of the 141 territorially comparable units. For each intercensal period (1926–59, 1959–70 and 1970–79) we also have a matrix of percentage–point change by unit for the variables. Of special significance in this category are figures which show the extent to which the different nationalities are concentrated in their respective ethnic territories.

(2) *Composition Indices*, which indicate the percentage of the population of each unit accounted for by a given variable (or sub-population). Of particular interest among these indices is the *level of urbanization*, which—based upon the operational definition of "urban" given above—is the percentage of the population of each unit living in urban centres. Also, the *ethnic composition of the urban*[5] population is of special significance owing to the importance of the urban sector in the USSR; data on this aspect of population composition are available for 1926, 1959 and 1970.

Using this data set to provide the empirical evidence, we hope in the following sections of this paper to shed some light on the historical ethnodemography of Russians and Ukrainians in the USSR. Specifically, we will attempt to answer the following questions:

(1) How many Russians and how many Ukrainians—both in absolute numbers and as a percentage of the total group— lived in their respective ethnoterritories and in each other's ethnoterritories at the different census dates? These figures are found in Tables 1 and 2.

(2) What percentage of the population of each nationality's ethnoterritory was accounted for by the titular group and by the other group for the census years? These figures are found in Table 3.

(3) What percentage of the urban population of each nationality's ethnoterritory was accounted for by the titular group and by the other group for the various censuses? These figures are found in table 4.

(4) For sub-republic units of the RSFSR and Ukraine, what percentage of the total

population was accounted for by Russians and Ukrainians at the census dates? These figures are found in Tables 5 and 6.

It should be understood here that the ethnodemographic history of Russians and Ukrainians involves groups and regions other than the two principals and their given ethnic homelands. Thus, it would be ill-advised to omit references to third–party groups—such as the Jews—because at certain times and in some areas these other actors were important to the interethnic drama. Likewise, Ukrainians and Russians have interacted in regions other than Ukraine and Russia; Kazakhstan is an obvious example. Accordingly, although our study will follow the framework outlined above, peripheral considerations will of necessity be drawn into the discussion when appropriate.

A Note on the Size of the Russian and Ukrainian Population

One reason why the study of the relationship between Russians and Ukrainians assumes considerable importance is the simple fact that between them they have always dominated, numerically, the Soviet population. In 1926, according to one estimate, Russians and Ukrainians combined accounted for 68.9 per cent of the total population on the territory of the present-day USSR.[6] Although this figure cannot be compared directly to the 1897 census data—because the population was enumerated by native language rather than ethnic identification in the 1897 count—this apparently represents an increase over the comparable figure (63.8 per cent) for the later tsarist period, probably owing to higher than average natural increase among Russians and Ukrainians at that time. By 1959, the Russian-Ukrainian share had increased still further to 72.4 per cent of the national total, and then began a slow decline to 70.3 per cent in 1970, 68.6 per cent in 1979, and 66.2 per cent in the most recent census, that taken in January 1989.[7] It is interesting to note, therefore, that the publicity concerning the rapid growth of the Soviet Muslim population notwithstanding, the Russians and Ukrainians still comprise a larger portion of the country's population than they did at the turn of this century. We have estimated, in another study, that even by the year 2000 approximately 2 out of every 3 Soviet citizens will be either Russians or Ukrainians.[8]

1926: Geographical Patterns of Russian and Ukrainian Settlement in the Early Soviet Period

The spatial distribution of the nationalities of the USSR in 1926 reflects the cumulative influence of the "normal" processes of demographic change as well as the vagaries of war, civil war and border changes. In this discussion, we will consider these patterns of ethnic population settlement in 1926 on the territory of the USSR as it is now configured. There are advantages and disadvantages to this approach. The actual boundaries of the Soviet Union in its early years were, of course, considerably different from those of today, particularly in the Western regions, where—in 1926—much of contemporary Ukraine and Belorussia, and Estonia, Latvia, Lithuania and Moldavia were not part of the USSR.[9] As was noted earlier, for this study the population of these truncated areas was "reconstructed" from contemporary non-Soviet census data to derive a territorially comparable geographic framework. Although it is certainly advantageous to be able to trace demographic trends within standardized spatial units, some interpretational difficulties will arise. Most importantly, the ethnic composition of the excluded lands will be strongly influenced by the simple fact that they were not part of the USSR in 1926. That is, when these areas became part of the Soviet Union, population shifts occurred on the basis of that change alone. Not only did the populace realign (i.e., through migration), but one must assume that many persons re-identified themselves in ethnic terms subsequent to the change.

On the present-day territory of the USSR in 1926 there were slightly more than 78 million Russians and almost 35 million Ukrainians (see Table 1). Of these totals, some 72 million Russians (92 per cent) lived in the RSFSR and about 27.5 million Ukrainians (78.9 per cent) lived in the Ukrainian Republic. However, the most important aspect of the Russian and Ukrainian settlement patterns involves the population of each group *not* living in its given ethno-territory. Here it is interesting to note that a much larger absolute number of Ukrainians were enumerated in the RSFSR (6.1 million) than there were Russians in Ukraine (3.2 million); see Table 1. This imbalance is further reflected in the distribution figures for each group (Table 2), which show a considerably higher percentage of the total Ukrainian population in Russia (17.5 per cent) than vice versa (4.1 per cent).

In order to put these ethnic population distributions in their proper perspective, it is necessary to look at the patterns on a larger geographical scale (Tables 5 and 6). Within the RSFSR, for instance, one finds that in 1926 the vast majority of Ukrainians resided in oblasts contiguous with or very close to Ukraine; Belgorod, Kursk, Voronezh and Rostov oblasts and Stavropol and Krasnodar krais contained almost 4 million Ukrainians in 1926, about two-thirds of the Ukrainians in the RSFSR or approximately 11 per cent of all Ukrainians in the USSR in today's borders. Rostov oblast alone had over one million Ukrainians in 1926, more than in all but 11 of the 25 oblasts of the Ukrainian Republic proper. No doubt much of the "exclusion" of Ukrainians from their own republic in this sense derives from the manner in which the inter-republic borders were drawn and is, therefore, artificial. Thus, it may not be correct to speak of many Ukrainians in the category "living beyond the boundaries of the Ukrainian SSR" as residing outside Ukrainian ethnoterritory for other than statistical purposes. Nevertheless, as will be seen later, this "ex-cluded" group of Ukrainians experienced considerably different demographic tendencies than did their brethren in the Ukrainian Republic. In addition to this arc of dense Ukrainian settlement along the Russo-Ukrainian frontier, in 1926 comparatively large numbers of Ukrainians were to be found across the steppe zone of the RSFSR through the Volga region (Saratov and Volgograd oblasts) and into West Siberia (Orenburg, Omsk and Novosibirsk oblasts and Altai krai).

Determining the ethnic composition of the Ukrainian Republic itself retrospectively is a more complicated undertaking, because the border changes involving territorial losses and gains were much more extensive than in the case of the RSFSR. Our estimates for the 1926 population in the 1959 boundaries suggest a total population for Ukraine of approximately 37.95 million, which compares with the figure of 38.57 million given by the Ukrainian demographer V. I. Naulko.[10] Of the republic total, we assessed the number of Ukrainians as 27.5 million and Russians as 3.19 million (Table 1). Naulko derived a higher estimate for Ukrainians (28.63 million) and a datum almost identical with our own for Russians (3.16 million). By our reckoning, Ukrainians thus accounted for 72.5 per cent and Russians for 8.4 per cent of Ukraine's population in 1926 (Table 3), whereas Naulko reported 74.2 per cent and 8.2 per cent respectively.

Such differences notwithstanding, the point must be made again that these republic–level figures disguise more meaningful sub-republic patterns. The reason why this distinction is so important in the case of Ukraine is that the Russians were highly concentrated in the heavy industrial and mining districts of the eastern part of the republic. Thus, in 1926 one found almost half (47.8 per cent) of the Russians in Ukraine in the five oblasts of Donetsk, Voroshy-lovhrad (Luhansk), Kharkiv, Dnipropetrovsk and Zaporizhzhia, where they comprised almost one-fifth of the population. Even more importantly, the Russians in Ukraine occupied a disproportionately large share of the republic's urban population (23.6 per cent; Table 4). By comparison, it can be seen that the Ukrainian population of the RSFSR was overwhelmingly rural; that is, Ukrainians constituted a much smaller percentage of the urban population than of the total population of Russia (see tables 3 and 4). In addition to those areas mentioned, Russians were also present in large numbers in oblasts bordering the RSFSR (Sumy and Chernihiv), in Kiev oblast, in the Crimea and in the area around Odessa. There were very few Russians in western Ukraine in 1926, mainly because these lands were not Soviet territory at the time.

Two other points concerning ethnic population distribution in the early Soviet period must be made. First, the large Jewish population in Ukraine in 1926—the "third-party" phenomenon to which we referred above—complicates the ethnic settlement pattern further. We calculated the 1926 Jewish population of Ukraine in its present borders at 2.39 million; Naulko gives a figure of 2.49 million. The key here, however, is that the Jews exhibited a strong presence in cities of Ukraine; in 1926, Jews accounted for 24.43 percent of the republic's urban population, a larger share than that of the Russians. Secondly, the contact and mixing of Russians and Ukrainians was evident in areas other than Russia and Ukraine. This was especially true in Kazakhstan, where 1.3 million Russians and about 800,000 Ukrainians were found in 1926, primarily in the agricultural areas in the north.

1959: Russian and Ukrainian Demography in the Postwar Period

The period of Soviet history between the censuses of 1926 and 1959 encompasses dramatic social and economic change as well as the traumatic events of collectivization, famine, the Great Patriotic War, and the realignment of international frontiers. All these factors resulted in major alterations of the ethnodemographic landscape, with significant consequences for both the Russian and Ukrainian populations. Unfortunately, as the intercensal period was of such long duration, it is difficult to separate causes from effects; the census of 1939 is of little value because it has never been published in its complete form and is now largely discredited. In any case, the two outstanding ethnodemographic trends of the 1926–59 time frame were: (1) the drastic reduction of the Ukrainian population in the RSFSR; and (2) the rapid growth of the Russian population in Ukraine. We will focus our discussion of the 1926–59 periods around these two phenomena.

The sharp decline in the number of Ukrainians in Russia occurred primarily in that area of the RSFSR contiguous with or close to Ukraine, stretching from Kursk through Belgorod, Voronezh, Rostov, Krasnodar and Stavropol. This zone of formerly dense Ukrainian settlement, where some 3.8 million Ukrainians lived in 1926, contained only 587,000 Ukrainians in 1959. Accounting for this precipitous drop is problematic and contentious. It is known with certainty that the famine which struck many agricultural areas of the USSR in the early 1930s was particularly devastating in the North Caucasus, a factor that obviously would have reduced the number of Ukrainians in this region. A comparison of census figures for 1926 and 1939 revealed virtually no growth in the population of the Kursk-Stavropol zone; Lorimer estimated population growth in this area as the lowest in the USSR between 1926 and 1939.[11] Not all of the deficit in population for this region can be attributed to calamitous events, however, as many of these oblasts—especially those of the Central Chernozem region—and krais have been characterized by out-migration throughout the Soviet era. War losses after 1939 through much of this zone must also have been appreciable. Although there was some increase in population from 1939 to 1959, it was modest indeed and not nearly what would have been expected under normal circumstances.

Yet, the most important aspect of this situation is that the number of Russians in this same area did not decline at all; rather the Russian population in the six units listed above jumped from 8.3 million in 1926 to 12.8 million in

1959. The increase in Russians was especially noteworthy in Rostov oblast and Krasnodar krai, the very units in which the Ukrainian decrease was most pronounced. These changes are of such magnitude as to warrant explication. In 1926, our estimates show about 1.3 million Russians and 1 million Ukrainians in Rostov oblast; by 1959 there were more than 3 million Russians but only 138 thousand Ukrainians. Similarly, in 1926 the Ukrainian population of Stavropol krai stood at 558,000, a figure which dropped to a mere 43,000 in 1959; meanwhile the Russians increased from about a million to 1.6 million. For Krasnodar krai, the Ukrainians went from 694,000 to 146,000 between 1926 and 1959, whereas the Russian population grew from 1.25 million to 3.36 million.

This countervailing trend among Russians might be explained in one of two ways: (1) it is possible that the Ukrainian population was reduced through famine and war and/or out-migration and was subsequently replaced by a huge Russian in-migration; or (2) some reduction in the number of Ukrainians as in (1) occurred, but a portion of their losses involved assimilation (ethnic re-identification) of Ukrainians to Russians. Although there is no way of resolving this question definitively, we believe that the evidence favors the second argument. The 1926 census showed, for example, that nearly one-half of Ukrainians in the North Caucasus declared Russian as their native tongue; it is generally considered that adoption of another language as the native tongue is conducive to ethnic re-identification.[12] Another factor promoting Russification among Ukrainians outside their own republic has been the almost total absence of educational and cultural institutions employing the Ukrainian language.[13] This is the most important consequence of the border delimitation that excluded so many Ukrainians from their official ethnoterritory, where such services would be provided. Without these supporting institutions, it must be assumed that the Ukrainian ethnic identity was eroded more quickly than would usually have been the case.[14] On balance, it would appear that the assimilation of at least several hundred thousand Ukrainians to Russians explains in some measure the decline in the Ukrainian population of the RSFSR.[15]

The second outstanding feature of the 1929–1959 period was the proliferation of Russians throughout the Ukrainian Republic. The size of the Russian increase was of such proportions (3.9 million) as to almost equal the growth of Ukrainians in their own ethnoterritory (4.7 million); see Table 1. Consequently, the Russians' share of Ukraine's population jumped from 8.4 per cent in 1926 to 16.9 per cent in 1959 (see Table 3). The ethnic Russian presence in Ukraine, however, became even more pronounced in the eastern region of the republic than it had been earlier (see Table 6). Thus, the five oblasts of eastern Ukraine (Dnipropetrovsk, Donetsk, Zaporizhzhia, Voroshylovhrad and Kharkiv) experienced an increase in the Russian population from 1.5 million in 1926 to over 4 million by 1959. As a result of this dramatic growth, Russians comprised 30 per cent of the combined population of these units in 1959, up from 19 per cent in 1926. More importantly, the Russians' share of the urban sector in the eastern region also soared, to the extent that in the five oblasts listed above, Russians formed between one-quarter and one-half of the city population. In addition to the substantial Russian growth in eastern Ukraine, they also became much more numerous in the Crimea (where they comprised 71 per cent of the population) and in Kiev. Further, the Russians established at least a small presence in the various units of western Ukraine (see Table 6), where they had been virtually absent in 1926.

Despite the tremendous increase in the Russian population of Ukraine, there actually occurred something of a demographic "Ukrainization" of the republic between 1926 and 1959. That is, the Ukrainians increased their proportion of the total and of the urban population over this period, with the rise in the Ukrainian share of the urban sector being especially significant (see tables 3 and 4). This seeming inconsistency—whereby both Ukrainians and Russians accounted for larger shares of the population—is explained by the huge drop in the "third–party" groups in Ukraine, particularly Jews and Poles. The number of Jews fell from about 2.4 million in 1926 to 840,000 in 1959, and the Polish population on the territory of the present–day Ukrainian SSR shrank from approximately 2.2 million to 363,000 over the same period.

Ethnodemographic Trends in the Contemporary Period: 1959–89

Demographic trends among Russians and Ukrainians and in their specific ethnoterritories can be characterized for the most part as a continuation of earlier tendencies. The principal exception to this generalization is the levelling off of the Ukrainian population in the RSFSR. Apparently, in the 1970s the previous trend (evident during the 1960s) toward net in-migration of Ukrainians to Ukraine was reversed, and perhaps 150,000 Ukrainians moved out of their own republic to the RSFSR, Belorussia and the Baltic republics.[16] Thus, there was a small decline in the percentage distribution figure for Ukrainians enumerated in the Ukrainian SSR (Table 2). This trend continued through the 1980s, as the Ukrainian population shifted increasingly toward the RSFSR.

Otherwise, the number of Russians in Ukraine continued to grow apace, exceeding the 11 million mark in 1989 and accounting for more than one-fifth of Ukraine's population in that year (tables 1 and 3). In fact, for the first time, the intercensal growth of Russians in Ukraine between 1970 and 1979 actually exceeded that among Ukrainians, resulting in a relative decline in the proportion of Ukrainians in the republic's population. Within Ukraine, the Russian share of the industrial east increased to 35.3 per cent by 1979 and the Russian population of the Crimea jumped from 858,000 in 1959 to 1.46 million in 1979.

One interesting point which runs counter to the foregoing is the growing share of Ukrainians in Kiev. Between 1959 and 1970 and again between 1970 and 1979 the Ukrainian component of Kiev's population increased from 60.1 per cent to 64.8 per cent and then to 68.7 per cent by 1979. Even though the Russian population in Kiev increased in absolute terms, they lost ground to the Ukrainians, and the Russian share has fallen from 23 per cent in 1959 to 22.4 per cent in 1979.

Toward an Explanation of Ethnodemographic Trends in Russia and Ukraine

Clearly, the most important trend in the demographic history of the Soviet nationalities has been the spatial redistribution of the Russians. This redistribution occurred mainly to regions of economic development in the USSR, regardless of whether or not the developing regions were Russian ethnoterritory or non-Russian lands. Thus, the proliferation of Russians in the official Ukrainian ethno- territory is part of a country-wide pattern to which there are few exceptions.[17] We have suggested elsewhere that it is fruitful conceptually to view the Soviet Union as an ethnically stratified society, one in which the dominant group (i. e., the Russians) will enjoy a favored position.[18] One aspect of this privileged status is a greater geographical mobility, facilitated by the use of the Russian language as a *lingua franca* and the spread of Russian culture into the non-Russian ethnoterritories.

Another factor at work in promoting the migration of large numbers of Russians to non-Russian lands has been the ability of the Russians to fill the need for skilled labour as regions develop economically. The influx of so many Russians to the heavy industrial zone of the eastern Ukraine is an example of this phenomenon. Owing partly to chance and partly to their superior position in the Russian and Soviet state, the Russians were among the very first ethnic groups to be exposed to the social and economic updrafts engendered by industrialization. Hence, from their ranks could be drawn the cadres of workers required by expanding industry and related activities.[19] Once their presence was established, a certain inertia set in, because areas of economic growth would take on an ethnic Russian character which would in turn attract additional Russians (and repel other groups).

This large-scale movement of Russians to non-Russian areas has—without much doubt—impeded the socio-economic development of the non-Russian peoples indigenous to those areas. Simply put, in many cases the Russian migrants have taken jobs which otherwise might have gone to the local populace. There are, unhappily, no census data available directly which provide details of the ethnic composition of the work force in Ukraine (or, for that matter, in any other area of the USSR). A Soviet scholar, however, utilizing unpublished census materials, has furnished information on the share of the total and indigenous employed population of 13 republics—including Ukraine—in white-collar and blue-collar (i.e., non-agricultural) jobs.[20] The figures for Ukraine indicate that about 6.6 percentage points fewer employed Ukrainians worked in the non-agricultural sector in Ukraine than was true for non-Ukrainians in the republic, and that this discrepency was essentially unchanged over the Soviet period. Furthermore, because the Russians have steadily augmented their share of the total population of Ukraine, their numerical dominance in the modern sector of the republic's economy has actually increased. Consequently, in 1970—the latest year for which we have data on the subject—the majority of Ukrainians in the USSR remained rural dwellers despite the fact that their republic was one of the most advanced economically in the Soviet Union, a testimony to the prevalence of Russians in the urban centres of Ukraine.

As was noted earlier, in the first years of Soviet power there were actually more Ukrainians in Russia than Russians in Ukraine. By 1979, this situation had been dramatically reversed, not just because of the Russian migration to Ukraine, but also owing to the drastic reduction in the number of Ukrainians living beyond the borders of Ukraine. Originally, most of the Ukrainians outside the Ukrainian Republic were rural dwellers in predominantly agricultural areas; Ukrainians formed an important component of the migration stream eastward across the steppe in the late nineteenth and early twentieth centuries.[21] More recently, however, the "excluded" Ukrainians are considerably more urbanized than those in Ukraine proper, and are more highly educated as well. This attests to what may be an increasingly more prominent role for Ukrainians as what Pokshishevsky called "sputniki peoples," or surrogates for the Russians in non-Russian, non-Ukrainian ethnoterritories.[22]

The political implications of the shifting ethnic patterns of settlement I leave to others. Suffice it to say here that greater ethnic mixing has often led to heightened tensions; the notion that such contacts increase understanding among peoples seems to be unfounded. As Roman Szporluk has pointed out, Russians in Ukraine are a minority only in the statistical sense, and the impact of their ever-increasing numbers on the ethnic dynamic in the republic, including the sensitive language issue, is profound.[23] On the other hand, the presence of 4.4 million Ukrainians in the RSFSR (1989 population: 147 million) would not seem to represent much of a challenge to the maintenance of Russian ethnic indentity. In conclusion, we might say that the consequences of ethnodemographic trends have been and will likely continue to be of much greater import to the Ukrainians and their homeland than to the Russians.

TABLE 1

Number (thous.) of Russians and Ukrainians in Given Units, USSR: 1926, 1959, 1970, 1979, and 1989[a]

	RSFSR					UkSSR				
	1926	1959	1970	1979	1989	1926	1959	1970	1979	1989
Russians	72,208	97,863	107,748	113,522	119,807	3,187	7,091	9,126	10,472	11,340
Ukrainians	6,116	3,359	3,346	3,658	4,364	27,503	32,158	35,284	36,489	37,370

	Other Areas					USSR Total				
	1926	1959	1970	1979	1989	1926	1959	1970	1979	1989
Russians	3,058	9,160	12,141	13,403	14,250	78,453	114,114	129,015	137,397	145,072
Ukrainians	1,263	1,736	2,123	2,200	2,402	34,882	37,253	40,753	42,347	44,136

[a] Sources: For 1926, 1959, and 1970 figures, see: Ralph S. Clem, "The Changing Geography of Soviet Nationalities and Its Socioeconomic Correlates: 1926," Unpublished Ph.D. Dissertation, Columbia University, New York, 1975, Chapter II; for 1979 figures, see *Vestnik Statistiki*, No. 7 (1980) pp. 41-44, and No. 8 (1980), p. 64; for 1989 figures see Gosudarstvennyi komitet SSSR po Statistike, *Statisticheskie materialy ob ekonomicheskom i sotsialnom razvitii soiuznykh i avtonomnykh respublik, avtonomnykh oblastei i okrugov* (Moscow: Finansy i Statistika, 1989), pp. 3-59.

TABLE 2

Percentage Distribution of Russians and Ukrainians in Given Units:
1926, 1959, 1970, 1979, and 1989[a]

	1926	1959	RSFSR 1970	1979	1989	1926	1959	UkSSR 1970	1979	1989
Russians	92.0	85.9	83.5	82.6	82.6	4.1	6.2	7.1	7.6	7.8
Ukrainians	17.5	9.0	8.2	8.6	9.9	78.9	86.3	86.6	86.2	84.7

	1926	1959	Other Areas 1970	1979	1989
Russians	3.9	8.0	9.4	9.8	9.6
Ukrainians	3.6	4.7	5.2	5.2	5.4

[a] Sources: see note, Table 1.

Ralph S. Clem

TABLE 3

Percentage of Russians and Ukrainians of the Total Population of Given Units, USSR: 1926, 1959, 1970, 1979, and 1989[a]

	RSFSR						UkSSR				
	1926	1959	1970	1979	1989		1926	1959	1970	1979	1989
Russians	77.6	83.3	82.8	82.6	81.5		8.4	16.9	19.4	21.1	22.0
Ukrainians	6.6	2.9	2.6	2.7	3.0		72.5	76.8	74.9	73.6	72.6
Others	15.8	13.8	14.6	14.7	15.5		19.1	6.3	5.7	5.3	5.4

	Other Areas						USSR total				
	1926	1959	1970	1979	1989		1926	1959	1970	1979	1989
Russians	8.7	18.5	18.8	17.9	16.0		47.2	54.7	53.4	52.4	50.8
Ukrainians	3.6	3.5	3.3	2.9	2.8		20.9	17.8	16.9	16.2	15.4
Others	87.7	78.0	77.9	79.2	81.2		31.9	27.5	29.7	31.4	33.8

[a] Sources: see note, Table 1.

TABLE 4

The Percentage of Russians and Ukrainians of the Urban Population
of Given Units, USSR: 1926, 1959, 1970, and 1979[a]

	RSFSR				UkSSR			
	1926	1959	1970	1979	1926	1959	1970	1979
Russians	84.5	87.2	87.3	N/A	23.6	30.7	30.9	N/A
Ukrainians	4.1	3.2	2.9	N/A	36.7	60.6	62.0	N/A
Others	11.4	9.6	9.8	N/A	39.7	8.7	7.1	N/A

	Other Areas				USSR Total			
	1926	1959	1970	1979	1926	1959	1970	1979
Russians	19.2	N/A	32.2	N/A	57.4	N/A	65.8	N/A
Ukrainians	1.6	N/A	4.2	N/A	11.1	N/A	13.7	N/A
Others	79.2	N/A	63.6	N/A	31.5	N/A	20.5	N/A

[a] Sources: see note, Table 1.

TABLE 5
Ukrainians in the RSFSR
(Major Areas of Settlement Only)[a]

Unit	1926 (thous.)	% of Pop.	1959 (thous.)	% of Pop.
Briansk	108.4	6.5	18.3	1.2
Belgorod	376.0	24.8	68.2	5.6
Voronezh	785.4	29.1	176.8	7.5
Kursk	384.9	19.1	15.6	1.1
Volgograd	184.8	10.1	77.4	4.2
Saratov	223.5	7.7	112.2	5.2
Krasnodar	693.7	22.8	145.6	3.9
Stavropol	557.5	30.7	43.1	2.3
Rostov	1,011.9	40.9	137.6	4.2
Orenburg	160.6	10.4	128.5	7.0
Altai	321.2	12.5	111.9	4.2
Novosibirsk	201.4	13.0	62.3	2.7
Omsk	159.9	15.3	128.0	7.8
Primor'e	163.5	26.4	182.0	13.2
Other Areas	783.3		1,951.5	

[a] 1926 estimates from: Ralph S. Clem, "The Changing Geography of Soviet Nationalities and Its Socioeconomic Correlates: 1926-1970," Unpublished Ph.D. Dissertation, Columbia University, New York, 1975, Appendix I. 1959 figures from: *Itogi Vsesoiuznoi Perepisi Naseleniia 1959 goda—RSFSR* (Moskva: Gosstatizdat, 1963), pp. 312-337.

TABLE 6
Russians in the RSFSR[a]

Unit	1926 (thous.)	% of Pop.	1959 (thous.)	% of Pop.
Dnipropetrovsk	155.2	8.9	465.9	17.2
Donetsk	404.6	25.6	1,601.2	37.6
Zaporizhzhia	176.0	18.3	379.1	25.9
Voroshylovhrad	351.4	26.5	950.0	38.7
Poltava	52.6	2.4	83.2	5.1
Sumy	167.2	9.2	167.6	11.1
Kharkiv	436.8	18.3	665.5	26.4
Vinnytsia	42.5	1.7	93.5	4.4
Volyn	8.8	.9	37.1	4.2
Zhytomir	35.4	2.2	86.9	5.4
Zakarpattia	17.1	2.4	29.6	3.2
Ivano-Frankivsk	nil	0.0	37.9	3.5
Kiev	144.2	5.8	336.7	11.9
Kirovohrad	83.5	6.0	102.2	8.4
Lviv	nil	0.0	181.1	8.6
Rivne	11.9	1.3	39.1	4.2
Ternopil	1.8	.1	26.9	2.5
Khmelnytsky	22.4	1.2	61.6	3.8
Cherkasy	15.7	.8	66.9	4.5
Chernihiv	129.4	6.8	61.2	3.9
Chernivtsi	39.4	5.1	51.3	6.6
Krym	301.4	39.2	858.3	71.4
Mykolaiv	107.0	9.9	139.2	13.7
Odessa	338.4	19.4	440.3	21.7
Kherson	142.9	17.1	128.2	15.6

[a] 1926 estimates from: Ralph S. Clem, "The Changing Geography of Soviet Nationalities and Its Socioeconomic Correlates: 1926-1970," Unpublished Ph.D. Dissertation, Columbia University, New York, 1975, Appendix I. 1959 figures from: *Itogi Vsesoiuznoi Perepisi Naseleniia 1959 goda—Ukrainskaia SSR* (Moskva: Gossitatizdat, 1963), pp. 174-178.

Notes

1. In this paper, the terms "ethnic group" and "nationality" are considered synonyms and used interchangeably. In this regard, see Walker Connor, "A Nation is a Nation, is a State, is an Ethnic Group, is a...," *Ethnic and Racial Studies* 1, no. 4 (1978): 377–400.

2. For a more complete description of these procedures, see R.S. Clem, "Estimating Regional Populations for the 1926 Soviet Census," *Soviet Studies* 29, no. 4 (1977): 599–602. For a full list of data sources, see Ralph S. Clem, "The Changing Geography of Soviet Nationalities and Its Socioeconomic Correlates," unpublished Ph. D. dissertation, Columbia University, New York, 1975, Ch. III.

3. Republics not subdivided into oblast/krai/ASSR level units were considered as individual units in their entirety. These units are the Estonian, Latvian, Lithuanian, Moldavian, Azerbaidzhan and Armenian SSRs. The Azerbaidzhan SSR does include an ASSR (Nakhichevan), but this unit is so defined only because it is not territorially contiguous with the republic.

4. Specifically, the countries involved and the year of the census used were: Finland (1930); Estonia (1922); Latvia (1925); Lithuania (1923); Poland (1931); Czechoslovakia (1939); and Romania (1939). Because these census dates did not correspond exactly to the 1926 Soviet census, data from these enumerations were projected forward or backward to 1926 by interpolation with earlier or later censuses.

5. Adna Ferrin Weber, *The Growth of Cities in the Nineteenth Century* (Ithaca, N. Y., 1963), Ch. 3; Jack P. Gibbs and Walter T. Martin, "Urbanization, Technology, and the Division of Labor: International Patterns," *American Sociological Review* 27, no. 5 (1963): 667–77.

6. For a more complete discussion, see Robert A. Lewis, Richard H. Rowland and Ralph S. Clem, *Nationality and Population Change in Russia and the USSR* (New York, 1976), Ch. 7.

7. Ibid. For 1979 figures, see *Vestnik Statistiki*, no. 7 (1980): 41–2.

8. Ralph S. Clem, "Population Growth Among Soviet Ethnic Groups: Recent Trends, Possible Causes and Implications," Paper presented at the 13th National Convention of the American Association for the Advancement of Slavic Studies, Asilomar, California, September 1981.

9. There were, of course, some other, more minor changes. For details, see Clem, "Changing Geography of Soviet Nationalities...," Ch. III.

10. V.I. Naulko, *Etnichnyi sklad naselennia Ukrainskoi RSR* (Kiev, 1965), 78–82.

11. Frank Lorimer, *The Population of the Soviet Union: History and Prospects* (Geneva, 1946), 162–72.

12. Brian D. Silver, "Ethnic Identity Change Among Soviet Nationalities: A Statistical Analysis," Unpublished Ph.D. dissertation, University of Wisconsin, 1972, 25–41.

13. Ivan Dzyuba, *Internationalism or Russification?* 2nd ed. (London, 1968), 109.

14. Regarding the role of institutions in supporting ethnic identity, see Raymond

Breton, "Institutional Completeness of Ethnic Communities and the Personal Relations of Immigrants," *American Journal of Sociology* 70, no. 2 (1964): 193–205.

15. Robert A. Lewis, Richard H. Rowland and Ralph S. Clem, "The Growth and Redistribution of the Ukrainian Population in Russia and the USSR: 1897–1970," in Peter J. Potichnyj, ed., *Ukraine in the Seventies* (Oakville, 1975). The estimate of the decline in the Ukrainian population does not take into account expected natural increase from the base 1926 population; there is no reasonably accurate way of estimating natural increase for this period because vital statistics are lacking. This means, of course, that the deficit in the Ukrainian population discussed here should be considered a minimum, the actual figure no doubt being somewhat higher.

16. Theodore Shabad, "Ethnic Results of the 1979 Soviet Census," *Soviet Geography: Review and Translation* 21, no. 7 (1980): 463–5.

17. Clem, "Changing Geography of Soviet Nationalities...," Ch. IV.

18. For the definitive treatment of the concept of ethnic stratification, see Tamotsu Shibutani and Kian M. Kwan, *Ethnic Stratification: A Comparative Approach* (New York, 1965). Regarding the application of the concept to the Soviet case, see Lewis, Rowland and Clem, *Nationality and Population Change*, 83–128.

19. V.V. Pokshishevsky, "Etnicheskie protsessy v gorodakh SSSR: Nekotorye problemy ikh izucheniia," *Sovetskaia etnografiia*, no. 5 (1969): 3–30.

20. Iu. V. Arutiunian, "Izmenenie sotsialnoi struktury sovetskikh natsii," *Istoriia SSSR*, no. 4 (1972): 3–20.

21. Lorimer, *Population of the Soviet Union*, 2–5.

22. Pokshishevsky, "Etnicheskie protsessy...," 6.

23. Roman Szporluk, "Russians in Ukraine and Problems of Ukrainian Identity in the USSR," in Peter J. Potichnyj, ed., *Ukraine in the Seventies* (Oakville, 1975), 195–217.

Peter Woroby

Socio-economic Changes in the USSR and Their Impact on Ukrainians and Russians

The purpose of this study is to investigate the demographic and economic relationships between Russians and Ukrainians that cover the period of the last fifty years. It is important to find out how each of these ethnic populations fared in relation to the other, what their natural gains and losses were, and how much they have been affected by famine, war and assimilation. One would expect that the Russians, being the dominant group, should have a better record than the Ukrainians, but how much better?

The subsidiary question is that of regional distribution. What has happened to Ukrainians who lived outside the borders of the republic? Did their share increase or diminish, and how much? How do these results compare with the influx of Russians into Ukraine? Can one objectively speak about the intensified effects of Russification?

The numerical changes in population which apply to both ethnic groups can be amplified by discussing the qualitative differences which exist between Russians and Ukrainians, such as occupational status, level of education, urban-rural settlement, etc. These qualitative differences are mentioned in our study, but do not receive the coverage they deserve because of the broad scope of our discussion and the primary emphasis placed on quantitative data.

Along with demographic problems, one could investigate the economic relationships between the ethno-political territories of Ukraine and Russia. One can discuss the structural differences of both economies, their strengths and weaknesses, their degree of dependence on each other and the levels of their development. It should be of great interest to find out to what extent the two units have participated in economic progress and whether the benefits have been equitably distributed between them.

The student of Soviet affairs can easily anticipate the forthcoming conclusions. This paper supports the thesis that Russia and Russians have been favoured in comparison with other ethnic groups and ethnic territories; they record significant demographic and economic gains. Compared with them, the Ukrainians have suffered significant biological and ethnic losses, and the economic growth of their country has been greatly retarded.

A. Demographic Changes

Past Trends

It is not difficult to reconstruct the past pattern of population growth for the principal ethnic groups in the USSR. Table 1 illustrates the point in question. It is confined to three ethnic groups and three enumeration dates—1897, 1926 and 1979.[1] Since there is a discrepancy in the political-administrative territory associated with these years, the statistical information has been adjusted for the common core territory, which is that of 1926.[2]

TABLE 1

Composition and Growth of Ethnic Groups in the USSR,
1897-1979

| | Millions of Persons | | | Annual Rate of Growth | |
	1897	1926	1979	1897/1926	1926/1979
Russians	54.6	77.7	136.1*	1.23	1.06*
Ukrainians	20.2	31.2	33.4	1.50	.13
Other	31.2	38.1	70.9	.69	1.18
TOTAL	106.0	147.0	240.4	1.13	.93

* Included are one-half of Russians (1.4 millions) who reside in the Western territories which were annexed to the USSR after 1939.

The results show that Ukrainians had the highest rate of growth in the 1897–1926 period and by far the lowest rate—recording virtually no growth—in the 1926–79 period. One is easily tempted to equate this absence of growth with the effects of war, of famine during collectivization, and of assimilation. If these factors do indeed account for the lack of growth, one is anxious to know how they are interrelated and how much each contributed to the decline. Two related questions come to mind: can we determine what the increase in the Ukrainian population would have been if these events had not occurred? How would their numbers have compared with those of other leading nations of Europe?

One can attempt to answer these questions by making a realistic assessment of the probable rate of growth under more favourable circumstances—such as those enjoyed by the Russians—taking into consideration war losses, but not the effects of collectivization. The rate of growth of Russians would appear to be a logical choice for such a comparative evaluation, except for one important component in that growth rate—assimilated persons. If, however, adjustments were made for this factor, one could readily accept the adjusted rate as an approximation of the natural increase applicable to Ukrainians.[3]

There are no records which would show the extent of assimilation among Ukrainians or other ethnic groups. In the absence of such records, however, one can study the increase in the numbers of ethnic nationals who consider the Russian language their mother tongue. Some authors think that these groups represent the first stage in the assimilation process.[4] Although such an interpretation might be disputed, the quantitative data measuring the extent of cultural transformation are useful for our purposes.

TABLE 2

Effects of Linguistic Conversion in the USSR,
1926-1979

	Cultural Russians		Cultural Assimilation		Cumulative Increments		
	Ethnic (Mlns)	Linguistic (Mlns)	(Mlns)	Percent	Ethnic (Mlns)	Linguistic (Mlns)	Percent Shares
1926	77.7	84.1	6.4	8.2	-	-	-
1970	129.0	141.8	12.8	9.9	51.3	6.4	12.5
1979	137.4	153.5	16.3	11.9	59.7	9.9	16.6

Table 2 shows that 9.9 million persons among non-Russians have adopted the Russian mother tongue in the 1926–79 period. If we accept that the same intensity applied to the process of ethnic assimilation which is not recorded, then one must adjust the figure for the Russian population in 1979 accordingly, i.e., subtract 9.9 from 137.4 million. This procedure yields 127.5 million Russians inhabiting the present administrative territory and 126.1 million if adjusted downward to 1926 political boundaries. Translated into the rate of natural growth this is equivalent to .92 per cent per annum (lower than 1.06 per cent) or 62.5 per cent, if applied to the cumulative effects over the entire period (instead of an unadjusted figure of 75.0 per cent). These, then, are the rates to which one would refer when projecting the growth of the Ukrainian population.

One should hasten to add that the above calculation would not yield a final result. One must reduce the figure further by subtracting the amount of assimilation. The last column reveals the magnitude of linguistic transfer, which accounts for 16.6 per cent in the total increase of ethnic Russians. When applied to the non-Russian population, which is smaller than the Russian, this rate changes to 18.8 per cent.[5] In the subsequent calculations we have assumed the incremental rate of assimilation to be 15 per cent for Ukrainians in Ukraine and twice as high (30 per cent) for Ukrainians outside the republic's boundaries. The combined avarage of the two components yields the exact avarage rate of 18.8 per cent.

Russian Gains and Ukrainian Losses

We have already alluded to Russian gains in the period 1926–79, which were estimated at 9.9 million. This represents a surplus of 7.8 per cent of the total population, which would have been secured through natural growth (127.5 million). One assimilated person has been added to 13 persons of Russian extraction at the end of the period under analysis. When related to the increase of ethnic Russians (49.8 million), assimilation assumed the abnormally high ratio of 1:5.

TABLE 3

Estimated Changes of Ukrainian Population by Regions,
1926-1979
(Millions of Persons)

	All Ukrainians	Ukraine and Moldavia	Other Regions
1939 Political Boundaries:			
Population, 1926	31.19	23.28	7.91
Natural Increase (1926-79, .92% per year)	19.37	14.45	4.92
Transfer of Population	-	-2.34	2.34
1979 Estimate, 1939 Boundaries	50.56	35.39	15.17
Territories Added after 1939:			
Western Ukraine	8.19	8.19	-
Western Belorussia	.05	.05	-
Moldavia	.51	.51	-
1979 Estimate, Present Boundaries	59.31	44.14	15.17
1979 Actual Population	42.31	37.06	5.25
Total Deficit	17.00	7.08	9.92
Magnitude of Assimilation	3.65	1.83	1.82
Incremental Rate (%)	18.8	15.0	25.1*
Unexplained Deficit	13.35	5.25	8.10

* Consists of 30% of natural increase and 15% of transferred population.

We find it advisable to reconstruct the Ukrainian gains and losses in greater detail, specifying them by geographic region and functional type.

Peter Woroby

TABLE 4
Estimate of Ukrainian Gains and Losses in Outer Regions, 1926-1979
(Thousands of Persons)

	1926	1979 Estimate[1]	1979 Actual	Percent Ratio	Immigration[2]	Assimilation	Remaining Deficit
A. Expanding Settlements							
Baltic States	-	159	135	84.9	159	24	-
North West	15	554	465	83.9	529	82	-
Moscow Region	50	634	520	82.0	553	92	22
Belorussia	35	228	181	79.4	172	32	15
Transcaucasia	35	110	80	72.7	53	14	16
Turkestan	98	392	296	75.5	233	53	43
TOTAL	233	2,077	1,677	80.7	1,699	297	103
B. Diminished Settlements							
Far East	315	650	434	66.8	140	73	143
Kazakhstan	861	1,625	898	55.3	229	195	532
Siberia	878	1,699	893	52.6	275	205	601
Volga Region	724	1,174	606	51.6	-	135	433
TOTAL	2,278	5,148	2,831	55.0	644	608	1,709

C. Annihilated Settlements							
Black Soil	1,790	2,902	290	10.0	-	334	2,278[3]
Don and North Caucausus	3,310	5,041	450	8.9	-	579	4,012[3]
TOTAL	4,900	7,943	740	9.3	-	913	6,290
GRAND TOTAL	7,911	15,168	5,248	34.3	2,348	1,818	8,102

[1] Includes the effect of natural growth (.92% per annum) and new immigration.

[2] Considered to be the difference between the 1979 and 1926 populations in expanding settlements. In Group B (diminished settlements) the immigration figures have been deduced from the population increase of smaller regions in the 1959-1979 period.

[3] These figures include also collectivization losses assessed at 430,000 for the Black Soil Region and 595,000 for Don and North Caucausus.

From the statistical information listed above one can conclude that there should be close to 60 million Ukrainians today—a figure which appears quite reasonable in comparison with the past numbers and growth of other European nations, such as Great Britain, France, and Italy. One–third of this total consists of a moderate growth of less than 1 per cent per annum covering the period of 53 years. This is a net rate which makes allowance for war losses at least to the same extent as they applied to the Russian population. The actual increase barely exceeds 2 million, which amounts only to one-eighth of the expected growth (it is calculated by subtracting the total deficit of 17.00 million from the natural increase of 19.37 million). Losses due to assimilation, estimated at 3.6 million, are evenly split between Ukraine and other regions. They represent 5.5 per cent of the potential Ukrainian population within the political borders of the 1926 republic and 12.0 per cent of the expected number of Ukrainians outside these borders. These are new additions to those who were assimilated previously and whose estimated numbers in 1926 were of the same magnitude.[6]

Most revealing, however, are the residual deficits, which amount to 5.25 million in Ukraine. If the rate of assimilation has been adequately assessed, as well as the outflow of 2.3 million migrants to territories outside the political borders of the republic, then this number might represent the biological loss of the Ukrainian nation due to collectivization and excessive war losses. The remaining shortage of population would still be very significant, even if more liberal allowances have been made for assimilation and emigration. As accounted here, the residual loss represents 15 per cent of the estimated Ukrainian population within the 1926 boundaries. The effects of collectivization apply also to the Ukrainians settled in the neighbouring regions of Kursk, Voronezh, Don and Caucasus; they yield one additional million, which raises the total loss to the enormous figure of 6.25 million—one-third of the natural increase.

The other alarming result of the analysis is the deficit of Ukrainians outside the republic's boundaries. It amounts to 7 million, after one allows for 3 million lost to assimilation and collectivization. This figure does not represent the biological loss and cannot be identified with accelerated assimilation, even under the worst possible circumstances. It exceeds the natural growth by 2 million and cuts deeply into the original ethnic substance. Out of a population of 8 million in 1926, the 1979 census shows the retention of 5.25 million, actually 3.25 million when one excludes 2 million unassimilated immigrants from this figure. This is equal to a 60 per cent reduction of the initial number of Ukrainians, which is scarcely credible. In view of such an improbable result, one must draw the conclusion that the figures for ethnic Ukrainians outside the republic are fraudulent and have been artificially doctored. These figures are intended to suggest that Ukrainians have ceased to exist outside the boundaries of their republic, particularly in their traditional block settlements and border territories. This is evident from the statistical information in Table 4, which breaks down the results into various settlement regions.

The results (Table 4) show that areas which absorbed an influx of new immigrants have retained 80 per cent of the estimated population and the settlements in Asia and the Volga region 50–65 per cent, while the neighbouring territories of the Black Soil region, Don and North Caucasus account for less than 10 per cent of the 1926 population. Approximately 5 million persons are missing in the latter region after one has allowed for losses due to assimilation and collectivization, with one million persons attributed to each factor. This result is unbelievable. If it were caused by increased assimilation, one would expect a different pattern: greater intensity of Russification in the remote territories and lesser intensity in the areas surrounding Ukraine. It appears that the Soviet statistic is meant to make the point that the administrative boundaries of Ukraine coincide with its ethnic territory, and that Ukrainians should make no claims to the neighbouring territories. This underlying objective is also evident in the ethnic atlases of the USSR, which show the progressive shrinking of Ukrainian settlements in areas bordering Ukraine.

Russification of Ukraine

The demographic annihilation of Ukrainians outside the borders of the republic has been accompanied by the numerical increase of Russians in Ukraine. The global dimensions of this process are listed in Table 5. The re-

TABLE 5

Ethnic Composition of Ukraine,
1926 and 1979
(Millions of Persons)

| | | Eastern Ukraine 1926 | 1979 | | |
			Eastern Ukraine	Western Ukraine	Ukraine
A.	Millions of Persons				
	Ukrainians	23.22	28.30	8.20	36.50
	Russians	2.98	10.01	.46	10.47
	Other	5.63	2.05	.59	2.64
	TOTAL	31.91	40.36	9.25	49.60
B.	Percent Shares				
	Ukrainians	73.0	70.1	88.5	73.6
	Russians	9.3	24.8	5.1	21.1
	Other	17.7	5.1	6.4	5.3
	TOTAL	100.0	100.0	100.0	100.0

sults apply for comparable territories, which are confined to the political borders before 1939, including the Crimea. They show a tremendous increase of Russians, who now amount to one-quarter of the total population and exceed a 1:3 ratio vis-à-vis Ukrainians. This is almost a threefold increase when compared with the ratio that obtained in 1926. The significance of this increase diminishes somewhat when viewed in relation to Ukraine's present territory, including the western regions. The Russian share of population in Western Ukraine is insignificant in spite of concerted efforts to increase their presence. The other interesting feature of the tabulated results is the decline by two-thirds of other ethnic groups (Jewish, German and Polish, for example) which enhances the polarization between Ukrainians and Russians.

One should also stress that the rate of increase of Russians in Ukraine has become ever more significant in recent years. In the period 1959–70, the composition of increments was 61 Ukrainians vs. 39 Russians; in 1970–79 the ratio was 47 to 53 (see Table 6). Translated into compound rates of annual growth, the results show that the Russian increase was three times as great as the Ukrainian in the period 1959–70 and four times as great in 1970–79.

TABLE 6

Growth of Ukrainians and Russians in Ukraine,
1959-1970

	Ukrainians	Russians	Ukrainians and Russians
Population (Mlns)			
1959	32.16	7.09	39.25
1970	35.28	9.13	44.41
1979	36.49	10.47	46.96
Increases (Mlns)			
1959-70	3.13	2.03	5.16
1970-79	1.21	1.35	2.56
Percent Shares			
1959-70	60.7	39.3	100.0
1970-79	47.3	52.7	100.0
Annual Rate of Growth			
1959-70	.85	2.32	1.13
1970-79	.37	1.54	.62

An important factor is the concentration of Russians in urban centres (see Table 7).

The results of 1970 show the share of Russians in urban areas to be five times higher than in rural areas. This in turn reflects the weak representation of Ukrainians in cities and towns as compared with the rural areas (62.9 per cent

TABLE 7

Rural-Urban Composition of Ukrainians and Russians
in Ukraine 1970

	Millions of Persons			Percent Shares		
	Ukrainians	Russians	Total	Ukrainians	Russians	Total
Rural	19.12	1.42	21.44	89.2	6.6	100.0
Urban	16.16	7.71	25.69	62.9	30.1	100.0
Rural/Urban	35.28	9.13	47.13	74.9	19.4	100.0

vs. 89.2 per cent).

Additional insights into the role of Russians in Ukraine can be gained when one analyzes their geographical distribution. Table 8 reveals their massive presence in certain areas, which is very inconvenient, if not dangerous, to the economic and political integrity of the republic.

It is apparent from the table that the primary area of Russian concentration in the East is the Donbas, along with the surrounding Kharkiv, Dnipropetrovsk and Zaporizhzhia oblasts. The Russian population in these areas exceeds 35 per cent, and its urban share must be more than 40 per cent (three to four points higher than in 1970). The oblasts of Donetsk and Voroshylovhrad approach the 45 per cent mark, and a relatively high representation can be observed in Kharkiv and Zaporizhzhia oblasts (more than 30 per cent in total and more than 25 per cent in urban centres). The "weakest" link, although with strong Russian representation, is the political-administrative area of Dnipropetrovsk (more than 20 per cent and 25 per cent). The eastern region accounts for more than one-half of the Russian population in Ukraine (close to 6 million).

The other area of Russian density is the south, which is anchored by the Crimea on one side (Russians make up more than two-thirds of its population) and the Odessa region on the other. Although the latter administrative unit has only 36 per cent Russians in urban centres, it also has fewer Ukrainians than one would expect (48 per cent).[7] Between these two poles are the oblasts of Mykolaiv and Kherson, where Russians have a 20 per cent share of the total and 25 per cent of urban population. There are more than 2.5 million Russians in this region, which is exactly one-quarter of their total number in the republic.

One-fifth of the Russian population (2 million) is distributed over the remainder of the territory, which comprises 16 oblasts (out of a total of 25) and has a population of 26.0 million (out of a total of 49.6 million). The overall Russian share in these areas is less than 8 per cent, with the only significant concentration, exceeding 20 per cent, occurring in the capital city of Kiev. The urban component in other centres, although stronger than in rural areas, does not exceed 15 per cent.

TABLE 8

Geographical Distribution of Russians in Ukraine,
1970-1979

	Urban & Rural, 1979		1970 Urban	
	Millions	Percent	Millions	Percent
I High Concentration:				
A East				
1 Core Area				
Donetsk	2.23	43.2	1.88	43.9
Voroshylovhrad	1.22	43.8	1.02	45.0
TOTAL	3.45	43.4	2.90	44.3
2 Adjoining Area				
Kharkiv	.96	31.8	.67	34.2
Dnipropetrovsk	.83	22.9	.65	25.2
Zaporizhzhia	.61	31.1	.40	34.6
TOTAL	2.40	27.9	1.71	30.2
Core & Adjoining Areas	5.85	35.3	4.62	37.8
B South				
1 Core Area				
Crimea	1.46	68.4	.84	72.9
2 Adjoining Area				
Odessa	.66	25.9	.47	35.6
Mykolaiv	.22	18.0	.14	23.8
Kherson	.23	19.6	.14	24.3
TOTAL	1.11	22.5	.75	30.2
Core & Adjoining Areas	2.57	36.3	1.59	43.7
Total East & South	8.42	35.6	6.21	39.2
II Low Concentration				
Kiev	.47	22.4	.38	22.9
North Central Areas	1.11	7.6	.72	13.9
Western Area	.47	5.1	.43	14.4
TOTAL	2.05	7.9	1.53	15.6
All Ukraine	10.47	21.1	7.74	30.1

The preference of Russians for settlement in urban centres and in specific geographic areas has produced a dangerous situation for Ukrainians. Deliberate acceleration of the same type of immigration is capable of changing the ethnic composition of the territories in question and tilting them toward the Russian majorities in urban centres.

Most vulnerable are territories where Russians have high numerical rep-

resentation and a high percentage of the total population. The foremost
candidates are the oblasts of Voroshylovhrad, Donetsk and Odessa. Slightly
more than half a million new immigrants are required for Russians to gain complete dominance in urban centres. The next line of attack appears to be the
oblasts of Zaporizhzhia and Kharkiv, which would require an increase of
800,000 Russians. One would have to add about 1,350,000 persons to the 4.5
million Russians now living in these five administrative areas. This would be
an increase of exactly 30 per cent.

TABLE 9

Russian Deficits in Urban Centres in the Selected Areas
of Ukraine, 1970

	(Thousands of Persons)			Russians per 100 Ukrainians
	Ukrainians	Russians	Russian Deficit	
A. Low				
1. Voroshylovhrad	1,159	1,022	137	88.2
2. Odessa	634	475	159	74.9
	1,793	1,497	296	83.5
B. Moderate				
1. Donetsk	2,137	1,879	258	87.9
2. Zaporizhzhia	702	403	299	57.4
3. Mykolaiv	419	144	275	34.4
4. Kherson	394	135	259	34.3
	3,652	2,561	1,091	70.1
c. High				
1. Kharkiv	1,171	669	502	57.1
2. Dnipropetrovsk	1,766	643	1,123	36.4
	2,937	1,312	1,625	55.3

Relatively resistant to such pressures appears to be the oblast of Dnipropetrovsk; it would require more than one million Russian immigrants to
balance the ethnic Ukrainians. Because of their size the oblasts of Mykolaiv
and Kherson require a modest immigration input, which amounts to one-half of
that required for Dnipropetrovsk. They have a low level of urbanization and a
relatively high share of Ukrainian urban population. It can be assumed that
future economic development (i.e., industrialization) would absorb more of the
Ukrainian rural population and favourably affect the strength of Ukrainians in
urban centres. Barring the increases in immigration the Russian deficits might
become numerically larger.

The analysis of the geographical distribution of Russians in Ukraine reveals a geopolitical situation that is liable to bring about a shrinkage of Ukrainian ethnic territory in two strategic areas: territories of the east, which are highly industrialized, and of the south, which is an indispensable access to the Black Sea. Should established patterns and trends of Russian immigration continue, present-day Ukraine could easily become a much smaller and weaker state. This possible development appears to be a logical extension of the previously discussed disappearance of the Ukrainian population outside the eastern borders of Ukraine (Black Soil, Don and North Caucasus regions). Thus the advantages gained through the extension of the ethnic territory in the past are now being forcibly taken away by the Soviet regime.

The numerical strength of Russians in urban centres and specified territories is closely related to their occupational and social standing, which is higher than that of Ukrainians. This can be deduced indirectly from their levels of education as they apply to urban dwellers and the entire population. For comparative purposes the same information has been provided for Russians and Ukrainians in Russia (See Table 10.)

Taking the Russian population in Russia (urban and rural combined) as a reference point, one can observe that the Russians in Ukraine exceed the comparative standings by 40–50 per cent, particularly in the four top classifications. Ukrainians in turn are 30 per cent below the applied standard in the three highest categories and 10 per cent below in the remaining two. Relating the two ethnic groups in Ukraine to each other, one can see the overwhelming superiority of Russians at high levels of education (special intermediate and above), exceeding a 1:2 ratio. This effect, which can be attributed largely to the urban-rural patterns of settlement, is nevertheless still pronounced among the urban population. The participation of Ukrainians in higher educational groups is 25–30 per cent below the comparable rates of Russians. Undoubtedly this must be related to differences in social status between these two ethnic groups.

The surprising fact revealed by this comparison is the educational profile of Ukrainians in Russia. They exceed the level of Russians in a fashion similar to that of Russians in Ukraine. The applicable spreads are even larger in both the entire and the urban population, indicating that Ukrainian immigrants must occupy responsible administrative and professional positions to a greater degree than one would expect from their numerical representation. One might also speculate here about the level of resistance to assimilation, which appears to be positively correlated to educational achievement.

Although the demographic relationship between Russians and Ukrainians cannot be described exhaustively in this article, it should be noted here that Russian strength in Ukraine is also qualitatively reflected in the overrepresentation of Russians among academics, candidates and Ph.D.s, members of the Academy of Sciences, scientific workers, editorial staff of journals, etc.[8] All these features enhance their social and political position and place them at a

TABLE 10

Educational Level of Russians and Ukrainians
in Ukraine and Russia, 1970

(per Thousand Persons 10 years old and over)

Cumulative Level of Education	Entire Population				Urban Population			
	Ukraine		Russia		Ukraine		Russia	
	Russians	Ukrainians	Russians	Ukrainians	Russians	Ukrainians	Russians	Ukrainians
A. Number of Persons								
High	66	30	43	73	75	52	57	92
Incomplete High	86	39	56	91	97	68	74	115
Special Intermediate	186	97	132	196	205	156	167	238
General Intermediate	361	224	242	329	396	344	306	394
Incomplete Intermediate	608	458	494	595	644	605	580	667
B. Ratios:								
High	1.53	.70	1.00	1.70	1.74	1.21	1.33	2.14
Incomplete High	1.54	.70	1.00	1.63	1.73	1.21	1.32	2.05
Special Intermediate	1.41	.73	1.00	1.48	1.55	1.18	1.27	1.80
General Intermediate	1.49	.93	1.00	1.36	1.64	1.42	1.26	1.63
Incomplete Intermediate	1.23	.93	1.00	1.20	1.30	1.22	1.17	1.35

higher level than one would expect from the analysis of quantitative data.

B. *Economic Changes*

It is difficult if not impossible to appraise the relationship between two inter-mixed ethnic groups that populate each other's territory. The proper method of proceeding appears to be to identify them with their political-administrative units, which they dominate, and to concentrate on an economic analysis of the regions. Thus, Ukrainian fortunes can be assessed by determining the rank and role of Ukraine, while the welfare of Russians can be identified with the economic status of Russia.

When comparing two regions, it is customary to review the structures of their economies and assess the intensity of their growth and development. Normally, this treatment should devote equal space to both component parts, Ukraine and Russia. This essay departs somewhat from the ideal of even-handedness, discussing the problems of Ukraine at greater length than those of Russia, since our purpose here is to assess in greater detail the results associated with the economic dependence of the small region on the large one. No less important is the need to reduce the voluminous statistical material required for such a presentation. Notwithstanding this decision, the economic interests of Russia are adequately appraised, and the structure and development of Russia or the USSR are consistently used as an evaluation benchmark for the smaller region, Ukraine.

Structural Effects

The ultimate goal of politically independent states seems to be economic self-sufficiency or autarchy. In most cases this goal is pursued by larger countries that have a sufficiently diversified economic base. Viewed from this perspective, Ukraine is big and rich enough to fall into this category, fully comparable with the principal nations of Western Europe. The same applies, to an even greater degree, to ethnic Russia.

Regardless of its size, no country in the world can rely solely on its own resources and its capacity to deliver all economic goods and services. There will always be some deviations from the desired objective—deficits or surpluses of various kinds—which can be rationally explained and tolerated. Some might be due to the lack of natural endowment, while others may be caused by a deliberate economic policy. This latter aspect is particularly important when evaluating the structure of the Ukrainian and Russian economies.

Soviet statistical sources do not provide integrated indicators that measure the contribution of various republics in the main fields of economic activity. Their information refers to selected branches of industry and agriculture expressed in terms of physical output and therefore not properly comparable with one another.[9] They do, however, reflect the approximate strength or weakness of each of the republics in specific sectors of the economy. The proper method of analysis is to calculate regional shares for various types of industry and to compare them with the corresponding shares of population. The resulting discrepancies, appraised for the size of their variation, can then be identified as abnormal deficits or surpluses. They are listed in tables 11–13.

Before undertaking a detailed interpretation of the compiled information, we would like to stress the existence of potential conflict between the well-being of the part (Ukraine) and the whole (the USSR or Russia). Their optimization goals are not necessarily the same. As a rule, the smaller region must subordinate its functioning to the interests of the larger region. In practical terms, this means taking over the assigned role of economic specialization and moving away from the desired self-sufficiency. Thus the structure of industry in a small region might significantly vary from the structure that would exist under conditions of political or economic independence. The rationale for allocation of economic activities within a large region and the resulting advantages need not necessarily correspond with the requirements and interests of its constituent part.

There are two suitable examples for this argument. First, when natural gas was discovered in Dashava in Western Ukraine and a pipeline was built to transport it to urban centres, the first beneficiary of this project was not Kiev, the capital of Ukraine, but Moscow, the capital of the USSR and Russia. The second example concerns two coal basins in Ukraine, the Donbas and the Lviv-Volhynia deposits. To minimize the cost of transportation, one would expect that the western source of coal would supply all oblasts of Ukraine located west of Kiev. This, however, is not the case. Donbas coal moved as far westward as Zhytomyr and Rivne, while Lviv-Volhynia coal went to the Baltic republics and Leningrad.[10] From the point of view of a large region, this probably makes good sense, but judged in terms of benefits to the Ukrainian economy it makes sense of a different kind.

The effect of dominance, integration and specialization can best be observed when reviewing the structure of various sectors of economic activity in Ukraine. In the case of agriculture (Table 11), Ukraine is well endowed with natural resources and occupies a leading role in Soviet production. This applies to all the main products of land and livestock operations with the exception of rye, rice and wool. Also relatively low is the output of potatoes, while such technical cultures as sunflower, maize, millet and beans are twice as strong as one would expect them to be on the basis of the participating rural population. The greatest concentration occurs in sugar-beet production (three times as strong). Historically the spread in proportions has been altered in a positive way through decline in such products as sugar beets, maize, buckwheat and fruit and increases in flax and rice. One undesirable effect is the decline in the production of potatoes, rye and wool.

TABLE 11

Intensity of Agricultural Activities in Ukraine,
1975 and 1940
(Expressed as Percent of USSR Production)

	1975	1940
Entire Population	19.2	21.3
Rural Population	19.9	20.9
A. Land Products		
Sugar Beets	57.8	72.4
Sunflower	47.8	35.9
Maize	42.0	49.3
Millet	38.7	31.9
Beans	35.8	37.1
Wheat	27.6	26.5
Buckwheat	27.4	44.2
Fruit	25.9	40.0
Flax	23.9	5.4
Potatoes	18.5	27.1
Rye	12.2	19.4
Rice	10.8	1.6
B. Livestock Products		
Meat	23.5	24.0
Milk	23.4	21.1
Eggs	21.6	26.8
Wool	6.2	8.3

Moving into the industrial sector of the Ukrainian economy (Table 12), we observe the relative dominance of food and black metallurgy, the latter being recorded in the category of "other." On the deficit side there is a significant underrepresentation of textiles, machines, pulp and paper, and chemical production. While the relative levels of output in such industries as food, black metallurgy, and pulp and paper are understandable, being associated with the surplus or lack of natural resources, the low level of textiles, machinery and chemicals in Ukraine is not justified. The reference to sectoral rates of growth indicates that lags in these industries have existed for some time and are not likely to disappear in the near future. These negative findings apply also to the overall growth rate of industry in Ukraine, which is approximately 15 per cent lower than that of the USSR. Compared with Russia, for which data were temporarily not accessible, this spread must be even wider.

TABLE 12

Structure and Growth of Industrial Production in
Ukraine and the USSR in 1975
(Based on Gross Value of Production)

Industry	Percent Shares		Annual Rate of Growth*	
	Ukraine	USSR	Ukraine	USSR
Electrical Power	2.7	2.8	8.8	9.8
Fuel	5.8	5.7	4.3	6.3
Chemical	5.9	6.9	11.1	11.4
Machines	24.4	27.8	11.3	12.8
Pulp and Paper	2.7	4.6	6.0	5.4
Building Materials	4.1	4.1	10.9	11.0
Textiles	12.2	14.9	5.9	4.2
Food	24.2	19.0	3.4	5.0
Other	18.0	14.2	7.1	7.0
	100.0	100.0	7.3	8.4

* Covers a period of 35 years with 1940 production serving as a basis of evaluation.

Deep insight into the structure of individual industries can be gained from the next three tables. Table 13 shows Ukraine's participation in the heavy industrial sector, while Tables 14 and 15 deal with the production of household and personal goods. Concentrating on the findings of Table 13, we can see the leading role of Ukraine in extractive industries such as coal, pig iron and steel. The contribution of Ukraine to the USSR economy approximates the 1.5:2 ratio of the population. In the past these shares were from 2.5 to 3 times as high. Ukraine depends completely on imported oil, since its own resources, although developing, are still insignificant. Its output of natural gas, on the other hand, is increasing and can be regarded as adequate if judged by the standard of all-union production.

Of special interest is the structure of the machine industry, which is charac-terized by a very high concentration of such machines as locomotives, boxcars and bulldozers. These products are bulky and require significant volumes of steel or iron. To minimize the cost of production and transportation, they must be produced in the vicinity of supply and, insofar as possible, of demand as well, hence the assigned role of specialization for Ukraine. The story is much the same for the production of turbines, tractors and excavators.

Concentration of this kind is more than offset by the lack of industrial output in trucks, buses and passenger cars, carriage wheels, metal-pressing and cutting machines, etc. Further inspection of data not listed here reveals additional types of machines not produced in Ukraine or produced in very insignificant volume.

TABLE 13

Ukraine's Contribution to the Major Lines of
Industrial Production in the USSR, 1975 and 1940
(Expressed as Percent of USSR Production)

	1975	1940
Entire Population	19.2	21.3
Urban Population	18.7	22.2
1. Power Generation	18.8	25.3
2. Fuel		
Coal	30.8	50.5
Natural Gas	23.8	15.4
Oil	2.6	1.1
3. Metallurgy		
Pig Iron	45.0	64.7
Steel	37.5	48.8
4. Chemicals		
Mineral Fertilizers	20.2	30.8
Sulphur Acid	21.6	25.6
Calcium Soda	18.6	81.1
Caustic Soda	13.7	44.3
Synthetic Material	13.5	27.5
5. Machines		
Turbines	24.6	11.6
Locomotives	95.2	NA
Boxcars	53.4	33.1
Passenger Cars	11.9	NA
Trucks and Buses	5.3	NA
Tractors	26.0	32.9
Bulldozers	44.2	100.0
Excavators	22.9	5.7
Metal Cutting Machines	15.4	20.0
Pressing Machines	15.0	36.8
Carriage Wheels	13.5	8.9*
6. Pulp and Paper		
Cut Wood	2.5	3.1
Lumber Products	8.2	8.4
Paper	4.5	3.3

7. Construction		
Cement	18.4	21.1
Bricks	24.0	24.9
Window Glass	22.8	33.4
8. Textile Fabric		
Cotton	5.5	.3
Linen	9.1	.7
Wool	9.9	9.9
Silk	10.5	NA

* 1950 Data.

This is the category of machines and equipment for industrial plants, shipyards, mines and power stations, electric locomotives, railway coaches, grain combines, and so on. Taken together, the underrepresented and missing industries are more sophisticated in nature and serve as the hard core of industrial development.

There is evident a deliberate reduction of Ukraine's chemical output, particularly of soda and synthethic materials. These products were produced at a high level in the past and have a favourable resource base even today. The downward adjustment has created significant deficits.

Neither the pulp and paper industry nor the textile industry has shown much development. The weak status of the first is quite understandable because of the lack of wood in Ukraine. This situation has not changed appreciably in the last thirty or forty years. Textiles, however, can be successfully developed in Ukraine. Some improvement has been recorded in the production of silk, linen and cotton fabric, while wool production has remained unchanged. Textiles have been regarded historically as an exclusive domain of Russian industry, and this is still evident today.

The established pattern of machine and textile industries is wholly reflected in the production of consumer goods for personal and household needs (Table 14). The figures show that Ukraine has been assigned the specific role of producing disproportionly large numbers of television sets, vacuum cleaners, electric irons and record players, but at the same time is denied the opportunity of delivering significant numbers of refrigerators, washers, electric stoves, radio receivers, cameras and motorcycles. Judging by the weight of the Ukrainian population in the total population of the USSR (approximately 20 per cent), the production of these goods is one-half to three-quarters short of maximum potential. This appears to be a recent development, since (as Table 14 indicates) there was a drastic falling off between 1965 and 1975. To trace the historical trend back to 1940 is impossible because of the

TABLE 14

Production of Selected Household Goods in Ukraine,
1975 and 1965
(Expressed as Percent of USSR Production)

	1975	1965
Entire Population	19.2	19.6
Bicycles	20.7	20.4
Motorcycles	6.8	3.7
Refrigerators	10.4	16.8
Washers	6.8	8.6
Electric Stoves	6.5	25.5
Electric Irons	26.3	34.5
Vacuum Cleaners	28.5	23.3
Radio-Receivers	4.2	10.7
Record Players	25.7	19.0
T.V. Sets	34.5	14.2
Cameras	11.8	12.9
Pianos	16.7	18.0
Accordians	19.7	21.9
Zinc Utensils	22.4	28.7
Enamel Utensils	28.5	26.7
Aluminum Utensils	17.0	13.8
Tables	23.4	24.2
Chairs	24.8	25.9
Cabinets	20.9	28.5
Wardrobes	20.4	23.5

unavailability of statistical data and low levels of electrical-goods production at that time. Also entirely missing among Ukraine's manufactures are such products as watches, various types of musical instruments, phonograph records, etc.

The production of consumer goods (see Table 15) such as food corresponds more or less to the proportions recorded in the agricultural sector–an abundance of sugar, vegetable oil and salt, with other products oscillating around the share of population. The output of fish products, as one would expect, seems least

TABLE 15

Production of Selected Consumer Goods in Ukraine,
1975, 1965 and 1940
(Expressed as Percent of USSR Production)

	1975	1965	1940
Entire Population	19.2	19.6	21.3
A. Food			
Sugar	58.1	60.6	73.0
Meat	22.5	21.1	19.4
Sausages	19.7	18.4	16.6
Fish	10.6	10.2	9.8
Butter	25.5	26.2	13.2
Milk	20.3	19.2	NA
Cheese	20.2	16.1	9.2
Vegetable Oil	34.2	31.5	19.7
Margarine	20.2	20.6	12.6
Canned Goods	25.1	23.4	30.3
Flour	17.1	19.7	23.7
Confectionery	21.3	20.1	24.1
Macaroni	19.1	17.8	24.4
Wine	18.8	27.4	25.9
Beer	23.4	21.3	21.9
Salt	42.9	40.1	45.2
B. Clothing			
Stockings	21.7	20.0	16.2
Shirt and Underwear	20.3	20.6	23.9
Outer Clothing	15.8	17.3	20.4
Leather Shoes	23.7	19.6	19.2

developed, and Ukraine has an unjustifiably low share in the production of flour. Garment industries adequately maintain their weight in the production of stockings, shirts and underwear, but fail in the production of outer clothing. One must add that most of the required fabric (one-half or more) is imported from Russia. The production of leather shoes appears to be adequate.

Generalizing these findings, we can state that the USSR practices a territorial specialization of production which is unfavourable to Ukraine. It forces her to produce disproportionately large amounts of goods in industries based on natural resources and deliberately deprives her of more sophisticated machine, chemical, textile and household-goods industries. The latter facilities are predominantly concentrated in Russia; this is a well-known fact, although we are unable to support it with statistical evidence.

Such specialization leads to the dependence of the regions on one another, which is reflected in the internal exchange of goods among them. The types of exported and imported products closely follow established patterns of surplus and deficit industries. Thus Ukraine exports raw materials such as iron, coal and natural gas, some products of the chemical industry (unspecified), heavy machinery (e.g., locomotives and tractors) and agricultural products (e.g., sugar). The main imports, in turn, consist of machinery and equipment, textiles, timber, pulp and paper, coloured metals and oil. No statistical information was available to enable the author to illustrate the volume and composition of this trade.[11]

TABLE 16

Regional Participation in the Exchange of Goods
with Ukraine, 1969
(Expressed as Percent of Total)

Import from:		Export to:	
Russia	87.0	Russia	62.4
Belorussia	3.2	Belorussia	15.5
Baltic States	3.1	Baltic States	8.2
Moldavia	1.8	Moldavia	6.2
Transcaucasia	1.4	Transcaucasia	4.3
Kazakhstan and Asia	3.5	Kazakhstan and Asia	3.4
	100.0		100.0

In addition to the composition of material exchanges one can analyze their origin and destination. This is recorded in Table 16, reproduced from a Soviet Ukrainian publication which in turn has been reconstructed on the basis of railway freight statistics.[12] It shows the overwhelming dependence of Ukraine on imports from Russia (87 per cent). This also applies, although to a lesser degree, to exports (62 per cent). The second place in Ukraine's exports belongs to Belorussia and the Baltic republics (24 per cent), which import four times as much from Ukraine as they export.

As a postscript to a discussion of the global structure of the Ukrainian economy one should consider the question of internal differences. Customarily the country is divided into three economic regions, east, south and west, which show extremely disparate levels of industrialization. The eastern region comprises eight oblasts (Voroshylovhad, Donetsk, Zaporizhzhia, Dnipropetrovsk, Kirovohrad, Kharkiv, Poltava and Sumy), accounts for more than 40 per cent of the total population (21.0 million), and is the most advanced economically. Endowed with rich natural resources (coal, iron, manganese and natural gas), it has developed a very strong industrial base in machine-building, metallurgy and chemical production. In the southern region, which consists of four oblasts (Crimea, Kherson, Mykolaiv and Odessa) and has a population of 7.1 million, industry is concentrated in the major urban centres, most of which are important naval ports. It has machine-repair shops and shipyards, food-processing enterprises (sugar refining, canned goods and fruit), and fish and wine industries. The least developed region is the western (the remaining 13 oblasts, with a population equal to or exceeding that of the eastern region). It has insignificant processing of locally mined coal, oil and natural gas. The same applies to pulp and paper mills, which are supplied with resources drawn from the surrounding areas. The strength of the region is a highly developed industry (sugar, alcohol beverages) that reflects its predominantly agricultural character. There is also a considerable surplus of under-employed labor. Strangely enough, the level of development of the three economic regions coincides with the concentration of Russian settlements which were discussed previously.

Economic Growth

In evaluating the economic position of a major region such as Ukraine, one should not only look into the level of goods and services produced but also investigate its rate of economic growth. To counterbalance inherited in-equalities, one could expect the strong region to grow more slowly than the weak one. The same applies to individual economic sectors, which would aim to achieve reasonable parity through growth. Unfavourable conditions exist, however, when this is not the case, when the strong region and strong sector grow faster than their weak counterparts. A classical example of this situation can be found in comparing the rate of growth in Ukraine with that of Russia.

References have been made previously to the increase of industrial production in these two economic and political regions which showed Russia at a definite advantage (Table 12). Economic development extends, however, beyond this orbit. It also comprises agricultural production, transportation, distribution and other related services. Normally one can measure the contributions of these sectors and their growth through values added to the national product (gross or net), but information to which we are accustomed in the West is not readily available for the USSR. A painful effort of reconstruction would be required, with many important links still missing in the final results. Information required for a regional comparison would be particularly incomplete and inadequate.

The high rate of growth in a certain region may be self- sustained, drawn from the wealth of the region's own natural resources, or it may be achieved with the assistance of other regions. In the latter case growth relies heavily on the import of capital from other territories. This assistance is highly beneficial to the receiving region, accelerating its growth of investment and production, but it is detrimental to the exporting region, whose rate of economic growth and development is thereby diminished. The question of capital flow between Ukraine and Russia has been discussed by various economists.[13] The consensus is that Ukraine has subsidized the development of Russia at an annual rate of 10–20 per cent of capital earnings. The rate has fluctuated, of course. In fact, this trend was briefly reversed during the period of post-war reconstruction. Overall, however, the magnitude of the subsidy exceeds significantly the export of capital to Imperial Russia, which oscillated between 3 and 5 per cent.

The influx and outflow of capital is only normal in dealings between two sovereign nations. It is an economic transaction with a debit and a credit side, in which the importing country must retire its obligation. It does so through the export of domestically produced goods, or it allows the other country to acquire a share of its own assets in the form of foreign ownership. Whatever the virtues of such an exchange, the receiving country benefits by adding the borrowed capital (i.e., external savings) to its own, thus accelerating the growth of its investments and production. In the relationship between Ukraine and Russia the values of imported and exported goods were not properly counted and the transfer of ownership was completely ignored. What took place was the systematic economic exploitation of the junior partner by the senior one.

The author of this study has approached the problem of economic relations between Russia and Ukraine—the evaluation of their gains and losses—in a somewhat unusual way. He started by searching for a standard that would substitute for capital flow and yet render a suitable denominator for all economic transactions. He found it in the level of urbanization. After all, urban centres play a very important role in the economic and non-economic life of the country; they provide location and employment for industries, transportation, finance and trade; they are also cultural, political and administrative centres. High levels of urbanization must always be associated with more advanced development of the above activities, and low levels with less advanced.

Evaluating these effects in 1939 and 1979 in Ukraine and Russia, which comprise the comparable if not fully identical territories in both time periods, we find that both countries started from the identical position of 33.5 per cent urban population.[14] Forty years later, Ukraine has reached 61.3 per cent, while Russia has advanced to 69.3 per cent. This is a spread of 8 points, which reflects a potential urban deficit in Ukraine of 4 million persons—a very significant result. Translated in terms of employment, it means a lack of 2 million workers in manufacturing and related urban activities. This represents a shortage of some 1.5 million living quarters and numerous industrial establishments. It also has a weakening effect on the development of cultural and recreational infrastructure.

If four million additional urban dwellers were properly distributed in Ukraine, they would double the population of 40 urban centres with 100,000 persons each, or alternatively they would do the same for 80 centers that now have only 50,000 inhabitants. One should stress that these are very important centres; they can be considered thresholds or "growth poles" of industrial development and are relatively weak at present.

Not only did Russia experience a high rate of urbanization, which is identical with its high rate of economic growth, but it did so with the added advantage of regional equalization. This did not apply to Ukraine, which endured both a low level of urban growth and the continuation of existing disparities.

TABLE 17

Progress and Variation of Urbanization in
Ukraine and Russia, 1939-1979

	Ukraine		Russia	
	1939	1979	1939	1979
Upper Quartile	54.1	77.3	51.9	81.1
Mean	33.5	61.3	33.5	69.3
Lower Quartile	18.7	44.7	20.8	57.9
Range of Variation	35.4	32.6	31.1	23.2
Coefficient of Variation	48.6	26.7	42.8	16.7

Table 17 shows the upper and lower levels of urbanization for Ukraine and Russia in 1939 and 1979. They have been computed as arithmetical means for the administrative areas which had a higher or a lower share of urban population than the general area. The spread between them, which is called range of variation, is almost identical in Ukraine and Russia in 1939, as is the coefficient of variation.[15] But these conditions had changed dramatically by 1979. The range of variation in Russia had narrowed to two-thirds of the variation in Ukraine. This was achieved by a deliberate effort to intensify the urbanization

Peter Woroby

TABLE 18

Locational Effects of Urbanization in
Ukraine and Russia, 1979

Percent Urban	Ukraine			Russia		
	No. of Admin. Areas	Population (Mlns)	Percent	No. of Admin. Areas	Population (Mlns)	Percent
76 and over	3	11.6	23.3	18	49.2	35.8
61-75	5	13.8	27.7	26	47.1	34.2
46-60	6	9.4	19.0	23	37.9	27.6
Under 45	11	14.9	30.0	4	3.3	2.4
	25	49.7	100.0	71	137.5	100.0

process in the economically backward areas. The incremental gains in these areas exceed the gains in the upper quartile; in practical terms, this brought about a narrowing of economic disparities among individual regions.

The same effects can be measured through a frequency distribution of administrative units and their populations in relation to a level of urbanization (Table 18).

The data reveal a disproportionate tilt in the distribution of total population in Russia above and below the 60 per cent level of urbanization which is the mean in Ukraine. While in Ukraine the applicable split is as one would normally expect—a 50:50 ratio—in Russia it is a 70:30 ratio. Most interesting is the very end of the distribution, the class interval of 45 per cent urbanization and less. In Ukraine it has an abnormal share of 30 per cent of the total population, while in Russia it barely exceeds 2 per cent. It applies to four small autonomous republics, and in Ukraine it comprises eleven oblasts whose territory constitutes more than 36 per cent of the total area of the republic. The least urbanized administrative unit in Russia is Dagestan, with 39 per cent urban population; in Ukraine the last rank belongs to Ternopil oblast, with 31 per cent. Altogether there are seven provinces in Ukraine (18.6 per cent of total population, 19.2 per cent of total territory) which are below the lowest level of urbanization in Russia.

TABLE 19

Geographical Pattern of Urbanization
in Ukraine, 1979

Region	No. of Admin. Areas	Population (Millions)			Percent Urban	
		Urban	Admin. Centres	Total	All Centres	Non Admin. Centres
East	8	15.8	5.5	21.0	75.4	66.7
South	4	4.5	2.1	7.1	62.8	47.2
West	11	10.2	4.9	21.6	47.1	31.5
	25	30.5	12.5	49.7	61.3	48.3

In geographical terms the most urbanized part of Ukraine is the most industrialized region of the east, with 75.4 per cent urban population (see Table 19). Next in rank is the south with 62.8 per cent, which closely approximates the republic's average. The least urbanized is the west, with 47.1 per cent urban dwellers. In addition to the regional inequality, most urban residents are concentrated in administrative-political centres which are also the largest centres in the given areas. They comprise more than 40 per cent of the total urban population. Taking them out of the scope of analysis, i.e., out of the urban and total population, one can calculate the reduced rate of urbanization for the remaining centres. While the overall rate drops below 50 per cent, the most significant downward adjustments apply to the southern and western regions. Eastern Ukraine still holds a relatively strong position. From the point of view of urbanization one can split Ukraine into two halves along the Kiev-Odessa axis, the economically advanced and urbanized east and the underdeveloped, predominantly rural west.

On the basis of this analysis one can draw very painful conclusions regarding the Ukrainian-Russian relationship. It has never been satisfactory. Imperial Russia favoured industrial development (e.g., textiles) in her own ethnic territories and suppressed Ukrainian national development. It pursued a deliberate policy of Russification and Russian settlement in Ukraine. On the positive side, Ukrainians had the opportunity to extend their ethnic territory to the south (access to the sea), east (Black Soil region) and beyond the natural boundaries, moving in great numbers into North Caucasus. Less beneficial was immigration into the Volga region and Asia, which are far removed from the mother country. In spite of these disadvantages and political pressures the Ukrainian settlers were able to preserve their ethnic and cultural identity, as was confirmed in the results of the 1926 census.

Compared with these results, which are almost benevolent, Soviet rule brought a tragic biological and ethnic annihilation of Ukrainians within and outside the present political boundaries. The scars of collectivization are still with us. They reflect a cumulative loss of more than six million people, with an additional eleven million apparently having been assimilated. The latter results are scarcely credible; at least one-half or two-thirds of this total must have been statistically falsified. In Ukraine the ratio of Russians increased three times to a point where they exceed 10 million today.

Economically Ukraine has been assigned the role of supporting the development of the Russian territories, and is doing so by exporting significant surpluses of capital. The republic's industrial production, which is subordinated to the needs of other parts of the union, is highly unbalanced. This causes Ukraine to depend economically on imports. While some progress has been made, it does not measure up to the standard of economic growth and rate of urbanization that apply to Russia. If we extrapolate the past trend in these two fields, we will find that Russia is eight to ten years ahead of Ukraine. One can regard this disparity as a cumulative result of past and present exploitation.

Notes

1. The sources of this tabulation are the census data of 1897 and 1926 as recorded in *Vsesoiuznaia perepis naseleniia 1926* and partial results of the 1979 census published in *Vestnik Statistiki*, 1980.

2. Population of 1979 was reduced by subtracting the following figures (millions of persons):

	Ukrainians	Russians	Other	All Groups
Western Ukraine	8.19	.47	.59	9.25
Western Belorussia	.05	.20	2.25	2.50
Moldavia	.56	.51	2.88	3.95
Lithuania	.03	.30	3.06	3.39
Latvia	.07	.82	1.61	2.50
Estonia	.03	.41	1.02	1.46
All Territories	8.93	2.71	11.41	23.05

3. The natural increase (numerical excess of births over deaths per thousand persons) of the two ethnic groups was approximately the same in the 1926–79 period. The figures in Table 1 show that Ukrainians had a considerably higher rate of growth than Russians between 1897 and 1926. This trend must have continued until the Second World War. In 1940 Ukraine recorded 1.30 per cent and Russia 1.24 per cent annual increase. This situation drastically deteriorated in the period 1950–59 and then improved again in the last twenty years, assuming the following pattern:

	Annual Rate of Growth[*]	
Period	Russia	Ukraine
1950-59	1.68	1.34
1960-69	.99	.93
1970-79	.58	.53

[*] This information has been reconstructed from *Naselenie SSSR*, 1973, pp. 70-71 and the annual *Narodnoe Khoziaistvo SSR* for successive years.

One can reasonably argue that the recent decline in Ukraine as compared with Russia must have been offset by the higher rate of growth in the past, probably yielding the same rates of natural increase for both countries in the 1926–79 period.

4. B. Krawchenko, "Society in Ukraine in 1970," unpublished paper (1981), 17. R. Szporluk, "Urbanization in Ukraine since the Second World War," in *Rethinking Ukrainian History*, ed. I.L. Rudnytsky (Edmonton, 1981).

5. This rate represents the percentage of 9.9 million persons subtracted from the natural increase of non-Russian ethnic groups. The Ukrainian population in 1979 has been estimated to have had an average growth rate of .92 per cent per annum, others 1.18 per cent as recorded.

6. The 1926 census shows 31.19 million ethnic Ukrainians in the USSR, out of whom 27.57 million considered Ukrainian their mother tongue.

7. This information and the statistical material listed in the preceeding tables has been derived from the last two censuses. The relevant sources for 1970 are *Itogi vsesoiuznoi perepisi naseleniia*, vols. I-VIII (Moscow, 1972), and partial results of the 1979 census published in various issues of *Vestnik statistiki* (1980).

8. Reported in various demographic and economic yearbooks of the USSR and Ukraine.

9. They are published in annual volumes of *Narodnoe khoziaistvo SSSR* and *Narodnoe khoziaistvo Ukrainskoi RSR*; the most recent available at the time this essay was written were the issues for 1976 and 1977.

10. See the related discussion and criticism in P.V. Voloboi and V.A. Popovkin, *Problemy terytorialnoi spetsializatsii i kompleksnoho rozvytku narodnoho hospodarstva Ukrainskoi RSR* (Kiev, 1972).

11. There is considerable coverage of this topic in P.V. Voloboi and V.A. Popovkin.

12. Ibid., 171.

13. There are numerous investigations dealing with the subject; the most notable among them are the studies of V.N. Bandera and Z.L. Melnyk in *The Ukraine within the USSR: An Economic Balance Sheet*, ed. I.S. Koropeckyj (New York, 1977). See also the findings of H.T. Wagener (ibid.), and T.W. Gillula, "The Economic Interdependence of Soviet Republics," in *Soviet Economy in a Time of Change*, Joint Economic Committee (Washington, 1979).

14. The missing link in 1939 was the oblast of Transcarpathia, which belonged at that time to Hungary. The exclusion of this territory from the comparison does not alter the rate of urbanization in Ukraine.

15. Coefficient of variation is the difference between quartiles divided by their sum and expressed as per cent ratio.

$$\text{Formula:} \quad \frac{Q_3 - Q_1}{Q_3 + Q_1} \times 100$$

N. V. Riasanovsky

Conclusion

First hearing and later reading the fifteen papers assembled in this volume, I was impressed, first of all, by their richness and by the number of truly interesting problems and materials they contained. Because students in my introductory classes are not likely to read this learned volume, I can even afford to confess that I learned very much from it, both in terms of basic information and in terms of a fundamental understanding of the issue of "Ukraine and Russia in Their Historical Encounter."

Professor Jaroslaw Pelenski's initial contribution, both learned and lucid, deals with "The Contest for the 'Kievan Inheritance.'" It is an excellent introduction to a central and controversial problem, a problem which emphasizes, as perhaps no other, the remarkable historical and cultural closeness of the Ukrainians and the Russians, a key factor in the past, the present and presumably the future relationship of the two peoples. I would only broaden the author's third view of the inheritance, neither simply Russian, nor simply Ukrainian, but belonging fully to both peoples, to include non-Soviet historians, often much less biased than Soviet specialists. In more personal terms I am thinking of my father, Professor Valentin A. Riasanovsky, of my Harvard teacher, Professor Michael Karpovich, and indeed of Professor Jaroslaw Pelenski himself, who—although he prefers to treat the Kievan state and people not as firm entities from which other such entities were later derived, but as transitional phenomena in the process of evolution—splendidly apportions throughout his article and especially in its last two pages the Kievan inheritance between the Russians and the Ukrainians.

Pelenski's fundamental contribution is followed by five other historical papers: Professor Edward L. Keenan's original "Muscovite Perceptions of Other East Slavs before 1654: An Agenda for Historians"; Professor H.J. Torke's erudite, up-to-date, and critical discussion of "Muscovite-Ukrainian Relations in the Seventeenth Century" and in particular of the *ungeliebte Bund* of 1654; Professor Marc Raeff's presentation of the Russian-Ukrainian "Intellectual and Political Encounter from the Seventeenth to the Nineteenth Centuries," with special attention to the universities of Kiev and Kharkiv; Professor E. Hoesch's depiction of "The Ukrainian Policy of Paul I," part of the ongoing reconsideration by a number of specialists of the historical role of that unfortunate emperor; and Professor Martha Bohachevsky-Chomiak's pioneering study of "Ukrainian and Russian Women: Cooperation and Conflict." While Professor Pelenski guides his listeners and readers to the very emergence of the

Ukrainian-Russian problem and the resulting togetherness and also apartness of the two peoples in subsequent periods, Professor Raeff offers them particularly sound example and advice for treating Ukrainian-Russian relations in these later times. Ukraine and Russia, the Russian state, Ukrainian and Russian peoples meant quite different things at different points in history and in different contexts. Professor Raeff's own treatment of his subject is a model of historical awareness: of the distinction between the elites and the masses, of the changes in intellectual climate, of evolving self-definitions. The author also gives explicit directives: "nationalism" in our usual sense is a phenomenon that

> makes its appearance strictly in the nineteenth century (or at the earliest in the late eighteenth century in some instances). It should be sharply distinguished from the claims of regional and estate autonomies of ancien-régime states and societies. It cannot be extrapolated backward into the earlier period. Not only did ancien-régime regionalism refer to specific historical and legal events to justify its claims to autonomy, if not outright independence, but its concern was not the "nation"; it was only interested in the sense of identity and self-image of particular élites that were in existence at the moment the claims were raised. It was not an all-embracing psychological, political and cultural notion, but the limited pragmatic demand for the maintenance of traditional modes of public life. It is uncritical and anachronistic to project the concerns and basic assumptions of the new nationalism onto the earlier forms of regional and social autonomy. [1]

Professor Raeff's admonition is all the more relevant because it can well be argued that the greatest single failing and bias in the treatment of Russian-Ukrainian relations has been an anachronistic ascription and application to times past of modern romantic and integral nationalism, whether Russian or Ukrainian.

Three papers on politics follow the six on history. Professor John A. Armstrong, more theoretically inclined than other contributors to the volume, deals with "Myth and History in the Evolution of Ukrainian Consciousness" and pays special attention to "Myth, Symbol and Communications." By contrast, Professor John S. Reshetar, Jr. is soberly factual and pragmatic, as well as a little sad. His "Ukrainian and Russian Perceptions of the Ukrainian Revolution" is essentially an expert examination of the much-discussed failure of that revolution, both because of the weakness on the Ukrainian side and especially because of the total Russian inability to appreciate the Ukrainian cause. Finally, Professor Yaroslav Bilinsky's "Political Relations between Russians and Ukrainians in the U.S.S.R., the 1970s and Beyond" takes up the star-crossed relations between the two peoples fifty years after Professor Reshetar's period. It is a fascinating piece—perhaps especially for an ignorant outsider such as myself—which ranges from facts and interpretations of the current Soviet policy in regard to the nationalities to relations between Russian and Ukrainian dissenters. In contrast to a certain finality characteristic of Professor Reshetar's contribution, Professor Bilinsky's reads like an ambivalent prolegomenon to an uncertain future.

The three papers on "Culture and Religion," which follow, have on the whole clearer foci than the political pieces, and they are all masterfully presented. First in order comes Professor James Cracraft's elegant "The Mask of Culture: Baroque Art in Russia and Ukraine, 1600–1750," followed by Professor George Grabowicz's basic contribution, "Ukrainian-Russian Literary Relations in the Nineteenth Century: A Formulation of the Problem," and Professor Bohdan Bociurkiw's expert study of a limited but highly relevant subject, "The Issues of Ukrainization and Autocephaly of the Orthodox Church in Ukrainian-Russian Relations, 1917–21." Language and the written word playing the role they have played in modern nationalism, Professor Grabowicz's discussion of such topics as the four nineteenth-century views of Ukrainian literature goes *ipso facto* beyond questions of literary genre or literary criticism and indeed makes his piece one of the most important in the volume. As to the perennial problem of the closeness of the Ukrainians and the Russians, Professor Grabowicz begins his paper as follows:

> Since my avowed concern is with formulations, I should state at the outset that from my perspective the relation between Ukraine and Russia is not that of an "encounter," even an "historical encounter," but something much more intimate and long-lasting, in the language of Soviet pathos, a historical and indissoluble embrace, or, as others might see it, a Sartrian *No Exit*.[2]

The last section of the symposium contains two papers on "Economy and Demography": Professor Ralph S. Clem's "Demographic Change among Russians and Ukrainians in the Soviet Union: Social, Economic and Political Implications" and Professor Peter Woroby's "Socio-Economic Changes in the USSR and Their Impact on Ukrainians and Russians." More technical than others, they illuminate an extremely important aspect, or rather aspects, of Ukrainian-Russian relations, and carry major implications beyond their immediate contexts. The authors' conclusions elucidate demographic trends unfavorable to the Ukrainians, who both suffered enormous population losses, especially during collectivization, and have been increasingly subject to massive Russian immigration.

As an appendix the volume contains A.I. Solzhenitsyn's "Open Letter to the Conference on Russian-Ukrainian Relations and to the Conference of Peoples Enslaved by Communism (Strasbourg)" and Professor Pelenski's extensive commentary on it.

At the risk of praising my associates, if not myself directly—a frequent academic risk—I would maintain that the excellent papers in this volume need no further justification than their particular contributions to their specific themes. Yet, as I tried to suggest in this brief conclusion, they also contain common threads and recurrent emphases which make them comprise indeed a joint volume. And such a volume in such a field is very welcome and makes one hope for others to follow.

The papers and the volume may also have ramifications beyond their immediate scholarship. Professor Omeljan Pritsak's resounding introduction hails it as the first step in the Ukrainian-Russian dialogue. Professor Pritsak's forceful declaration needs no amplification. It might be worth pointing out, however, to the casual reader that German contributors to the volume and, to use a telling phrase, "real Americans" (or Canadians) belong here as much as participants with more obviously Russian or Ukrainian names. They, too, provide some of the most convincing and some of the most controversial accounts and interpretations of the Ukrainian-Russian problem. Moreover, they, too, frequently are part of Russian or Ukrainian historiography, because for scholars at least, the issue, of course, is intellectual and not ethnic.[3]

It is also worth reminding readers and writers alike that historians and other scholars have been very bad prophets. It is apparently of the essence of history to be unique at each point and to defy prediction. On the subject of nations and nationalism, glorious states and nations have disappeared, while other appear historically, so to speak, from nowhere. I am referring not only to certain new states of the Third World, but also, for instance, to Finland, which had no independent historical past as a nation until 1917. Nor is this a derogatory remark, unless the scholar's view of history is mandated to legislate for the future, a claim which has no justification. Worse yet, all of us, especially those engaged in intellectual history, know very well how scholarly opinions and objective determinations of one age become deeply ingrained prejudices for the next—there is no reason to exclude the 1980s and the years to follow from that process. Still, these and other such qualifications do not amount to proclaiming any opinion as good as any other, to denying all validity to the scholar's work, or to objecting to the scholar's and, indeed, the human being's unceasing search for truth. Therefore, in a minor key, but as firmly as Professor Pritsak, I endorse a Ukrainian-Russian scholarly dialogue, and wish it every success.

Notes

1. See p. 81 above.
2. See p. 215 above.
3. How "outsiders" join Russian or Ukrainian historiography is a varied and involved process. I remember a colleague in the field who baffled me because, without any Russian background or any religious, ideological or cultural sympathies for Russia, he invariably followed the main line of Russian historiography, sternly dismissing minority opinion. I decided in the end that, having finally learned Russian very well, he was determined not to have to study any other East European language.

Appendix

On Ukrainian-Russian Relations

The Organizing Committee of the First Conference on Ukrainian-Russian Relations, entitled "Ukraine and Russia in Their Historical Encounter," which was held on 8–9 October 1981 at McMaster University, Hamilton, Canada, invited Aleksandr Solzhenitsyn to participate. Mr. Solzhenitsyn responded to the invitation with an "Open Letter" and an additional statement to the conference. Both were published before the conference took place, first in the Russian-language press, including *Novoe russkoe slovo* on 21 June 1981 (no. 25,541) and, in Ukrainian translation, in *Svoboda* on 5, 6, and 7 August 1981 (nos. 145, 146, 147). Mr. Solzhenitsyn's open letter was read at the conference. Professor Jaroslaw Pelenski commented on this letter on behalf of the conference organizers.

The English-language texts of Aleksandr Solzhenitsyn's open letter and Jaroslaw Pelenski's commentary are published here as documents relevant to Ukrainian-Russian relations.

April 15, 1981

To the Conference on Russian-Ukrainian
Relations in T o r o n t o [and]
Harvard Ukrainian Research Institute

Gentlemen:

May I express my sincere appreciation for inviting me to attend your conference. Unfortunately, my intensive work schedule makes it impossible for me to leave at this time and participate in any social activity.

However, I should like to seize this opportunity to expound certain ideas in writing to which, I feel, your invitation has entitled me.

There is no doubt that the Russian-Ukrainian problem is one of the major current issues and, certainly, of crucial importance to our peoples. Yet, it seems to me that the red-hot passion and the resultant sizzling temperatures are pernicious to that cause.

In the Stalinist camps my Russian friends and I always stood up like one man with the Ukrainians—a solid wall against Communism with no room for denunciations and accusations. And the Russian Social Fund which I have created in recent years extends help broadly to Ukrainian and Lithuanian political prisoners, certainly to no less an extent than to the Russians and no difference is made between nationalities—all that matters are the victims of Communism.

Is not this current intense rage of passions an émigré affliction—the loss of a sense of direction? In fact, very little is done to combat Communism (some major émigré groupings are still contaminated by socialist utopias) and the thrust of passions is wasted on accusing one's brothers. I venture to suggest that the emigration reveals a certain tendency to overestimate its understanding and its perception of the true sentiments in the homeland, in particular, those who left their homeland long ago or were not even born there. And should your conference initiate a fundamental dialogue on Russian-Ukrainian relations, you must never, for a minute, forget that relations between peoples and not between émigrés are involved.

Moreover, this issue, unfortunately, quickly slides down from a moral height, loses all conceivable depth and its historical perspective is reduced but to the cutting edge: separatism or federation (as if all problems ended on this side of that chord). Am I, perhaps, supposed to react to this question alone?

I have repeatedly stated and am reiterating here and now that no one can be retained by force, none of the antagonists should resort to coercion towards the other side or towards its own side, the people on the whole or any small minority it embraces, for each minority contains, in turn, its own minority. And the wishes of a group of fifty people should be heeded just as much as the wishes of 50 million. Whatever the circumstances, the *local* viewpoint should be sought and implemented. And therefore, all problems can only be truly settled by the local population and not in remote émigré disputes tainted by a distorted judgement.

This unrealistic atmosphere is, alas, well known. Just one characteristic example: last year I published an article in the American *Foreign Affairs* journal; its content and purpose: to warn the West against being lulled into the assumption that the greatest Communist evil that beset mankind for the past half century (even two centuries, beginning with the Jacobins) was a national Russian phenomenon. I emphasized that *all* peoples who have been enslaved by Communism during any decade and in any part of the planet Earth are (or may become) its victims. It would seem that in our time and age when Communism has been swarming in the festering hotbeds of all four continents, seized half of the world and found volunteers to do its bidding in *each* of the nations—there would be no room for such false prejudice, particularly, among those peoples and nations who had contact with Communism. However, I was stunned by the vehemently hostile and utterly paradoxical reaction to my article (not a word in it against Ukraine) on the part of a certain segment of the Ukrainian public in the United States of America. By way of example: there is L. Dobryansky's article in the *Congressional Record* of June 1980, then, the pamphlet "The Captured Nations in the 1980's", published by the Ukrainian Congress Committee. Yet, I was castigated for my statement that the Russian people *like all the others* were enslaved by Communism (and no special rights were claimed for the Russian people)—for this alone, I was blasted with a shower of accusations such as being a champion of "militant Russian nationalism", "Russian chauvinism" and, by implication, a "Communist quisling". Professor Dobryansky's article teems with a frenzied obsessively redundant hatred of Russians while Russia is spoken of in Marxist terms and modern Communism is referred to as *mythical* Communism! The pamphlet also resorts to the popular Leninist formula about Russia. To the present day, the authors of the pamphlet persist in referring to Mainland China and Tibet as countries seized by Russians and to the Russian people as the oppressors of the world (we wonder whether by inference the Russians themselves are supposed to thrive....). In the summer of 1980, at a Ukrainian meeting in Buffalo during the "Captive Nations Week" the main speaker laboured the idea as follows: Solzhenitsyn is indifferent to the enslaved peoples, he is *sick and needs treatment* (excellent Soviet phraseology!). *Communism is a myth!* he proclaimed.—Beware, not of the Communists, but of the Russians who want to conquer the world. (Russians—whose birth rate fell below a critical level, whose millions are starving, whose advocates of religious and national consciousness are flung into prison).

These emphatic professions of a "mythical Communism" may lure us all yet into becoming slaves on five continents and for ten successive generations. Apparently, there is no need for America to sober up and take stock of World

Communism, there being no such problem *per se*.

Indeed, in such an atmosphere and in *such* a state of benightedness there is no point in discussing the issue— any dialogue and conference would be fruitless. A sound assessment of the present and the future can only be deduced from an understanding of Communism as an international, historical and metaphysical evil and not simply as Moscow's doings. (And any socialist aspect invariably camouflages and diminishes the villainous irreversibility of Communism).

Listening to these smug assailants one wonders: do they really take themselves to be Christians? But sowing hatred among peoples has never done any good to any side. Mutual goodwill should supersede and transcend razor-edged controversies. The principle of self-restraint and repentance must underlie any approach to national problems.

I am particularly pained by the fierce intolerance that rages around the Russian-Ukrainian question (detrimental to both nations and beneficial only to their enemies) because of my Russian-Ukrainian origin and because I was raised under the combined influence of both cultures and I have never experienced, nor do I now, even the slightest antagonism between the two. On various occasions I wrote and publicly spoke of Ukraine and her people, of the tragedy of the Ukrainian famine. I have quite a few old friends in Ukraine and to me the sufferings of Russians and Ukrainians alike invariably occupy equal space in the Communist-enslaved peoples. In my heartfelt perception there is no room for a Russian-Ukrainian conflict and should, heaven forbid, the issue ever come to a head I can safely affirm: under no circumstances and at no time shall I participate in a Russian-Ukrainian clash or allow my sons to do so—whoever the reckless hotheads who would try to drag us into it may be.

But in the thick of the population which suffers from Communism daily there is *no* mutual intolerance, all problems are viewed in depth and with a greater sense of responsibility. And our mutual twentieth century problems are not solved solely by the fact that once one of our branches fell under the Tatars and the other under the Poles or by arguing whether Ilya Muromets served Kiev as a Russian or a Ukrainian. The Russian-Ukrainian dialogue cannot simply follow the line of divergencies and divisions but should also embark upon the path of common characteristics which are not readily dismissed. We should draw on the plight and the national ordeals of our peoples (all peoples of Eastern Europe, in fact) and not on the experience of discord. Six years ago I already attempted to express this concept in an address to the Strasbourg conference of Communist-enslaved nations and am enclosing it now with the request to make it public at your conference.

Thus, so much for my comments in the suggested discussion.
This communication may be considered as an open letter.

With best wishes,
Sincerely yours,

Aleksandr Solzhenitsyn

Open Letter to the Conference on Russian-Ukrainian Relations and to the Conference of Peoples Enslaved by Communism (Strasbourg)

This is to convey to you my heartfelt support for your attempt at making yourself heard in the parliament center of Western Europe which, at this juncture, maintains a precarious freedom, and for your attempt at speaking with the concerted voice of Eastern Europe. The unity of the peoples of Eastern Europe may be the last hope of this continent. The Western world is still holding its own but in its ossified arrogance it does not realize that it has been losing ground steadily on all levels of its current strength and intellectual endeavor and is becoming a provincial corner of the planet Earth. Eastern Asia fell in with the chorus of voices from Eastern Europe but a world which has not experienced the depths of suffering is deaf until it is directly hit and driven into the ground by the shock of extermination.

You and I know that Communism is not some national figment of imagination but an organic pervasive gangrene on the body of mankind. By a callous and ignorant substitution of the term "Russian" for the term "Soviet" the crimes and new designs of World Communism are attributed to a people who were the victims of Communism earlier than others and longer than others, and who lost together with their brothers in sorrow—the peoples of the USSR—sixty million people! (in addition to forty three million lost by negligence in conducting war operations, see Prof. I. Kurganov).

Steeled by our ordeals we must not let our national anguish get the upper hand on our sense of unity. Having experienced so much cruel suffering let us never inflict it upon our neighbors; let us seek the establishment of relations which would transcend those known to the modern world: not relations of mutual tolerance but of mutual magnanimity.

My best wishes for success in the cause of rallying oppressed peoples and expanding the circle of those you will be representing in the future. The émigrés from enslaved nations alone amount to millions of people. By uniting in mutual trust, by never yielding to the slackening and lulling temptation of a false security, by never forgetting our brothers at home, we shall speak up in a voice and with a force that will affect the course of world events.

Aleksandr Solzhenitsyn
September 27, 1975

On the Need of Russian-Ukrainian Dialogue
(Commentary on Aleksandr Solzhenitsyn's "Open Letter to the Conference on Russian-Ukrainian Relations")

Before I address myself to the substance of Aleksandr Solzhenitsyn's open letter to the Conference on Russian-Ukrainian Relations, I would like to say a few words about the reasons why the conference organizing and advisory committees invited him to participate in this unprecedented scholarly event.

As a Russian prisoner of conscience, a man of letters, an intellectual, and, above all, a human being, Aleksandr Solzhenitsyn has demonstrated extraordinary courage in speaking out without constraint on the crucial issues of our time. Both in his native Russia and abroad, he has dared to expound highly unpopular views and to bring to our immediate attention the most tragic and appalling twentieth-century upheavals and conditions experienced by the nations of Eastern Europe. His courage to voice dissident opinions is acknowledged not only by his admirers, but also by those who, otherwise, do not share his views on many fundamental issues.

Solzhenitsyn belongs among the few prominent contemporary Russians who have chosen to address themselves in their writings to the problems of Russian-Ukrainian relations, which are the principal subject of today's conference. Although his contribution to the understanding of Russian-Ukrainian relations may not be impressive in quantitative terms, the opinions he has ventured to express on the relations between the two peoples, as they are most explicitly revealed in Part V of his monumental *Gulag Archipelago* (English translation [New York: Harper & Row, 1976], 44–6), bespeak a caring and sharing individual who is deeply involved in and sincerely concerned with the destinies of the two peoples and of the relations between them.

For this reason, the members of the organizing and advisory committees of the conference felt it only natural that a discussion of Russian-Ukrainian problems would be more fruitful if the views of Solzhenitsyn as an individual and as the most distinguished representative of that current in Russian cultural and social thought which, for lack of a better term, can be described as national, populist-conservative, and Orthodox-religious, were publicly aired at this first scholarly conference of its kind.

Solzhenitsyn's attitudes toward the Ukrainian people and Russian-Ukrainian relations are characterized by an ambivalent approach, symptomatic of the intellectual and cultural traditions from which he descended. His predisposition toward Ukrainians as a people and Ukraine as a country is humane and compassionate. In contrast to many Russians, both at home and abroad, he not only speaks with empathy of the Petliurovites (*petliurivtsi*), who in his own words "were merely Ukrainian townsfolk and peasants who wanted to order their lives without our [Russian] interference," and openly admits that during the revolutionary period of 1917–20 "we [the Russians] immediately crossed the border which we had recognized and imposed our rule on our blood brethren," but he also has kind words to say about the Ukrainian nationalists with whom he shared the Gulag experience and whom he credits with having played an important role in organizing strikes and mutinies that were undertaken in the most notorious of the Soviet camps.

Both in his major work, the *Gulag Archipelago,* which is permeated with observations indicative of a fertile mind with a keen sense of history, and in the open letter to the conference, he has openly acknowledged the significance of the Ukrainian problem ,and the crucial importance of Russian-Ukrainian relations. On the other hand, some of his political propositions, such as ascribing equal moral standing to the protagonists of the federalist and independent solutions to the Ukrainian problem and his ambivalent advocacy of the plebiscite in Ukraine on a province by province basis, provide grounds for skepticism concerning the extent of his genuine commitment to the ideas of self-determination and independence for Ukraine.

Moreover, Solzhenitsyn should not have been "stunned by the vehemently hostile and utterly paradoxical reaction to his article on the part of a certain segment of the Ukrainian society in the United States of America" ("Misconceptions about Russia Are a Threat to America", *Foreign Affairs* 58, no. 5 [Summer 1981]). Like any other public figure who takes a stand on important and controversial issues, he should have expected adverse reactions. There always will be those individuals and groups in the Ukrainian community who, on account of some dreadful personal or familial past experiences, or because of sufferings of their compatriots, will be antagonistically predisposed to any Russian-Ukrainian dialogue or, for that matter, to any kind of historical compromise, just as there always will be plenty of Russian, as well as Ukrainian, extremists and professional patriots who will seek to build careers on the anxieties, frustrations, and failures of their societies.

It is true that the problem of Russian-Ukrainian relations is often debated in an atmosphere of emotion, passion, and mutual intolerance. But is Solzhenitsyn's conclusion justified when he argues that "in such a state of benightedness there is no point in discussing the issue" and that "any dialogue and conference would be fruitless?" On the contrary. It is precisely because of the existence of such an unhealthy atmosphere, and because of the seriousness of the problem, that reasonable men and women on both sides should have the moral responsibility to engage in a dialogue and to search for at least theoretical answers to questions Solzhenitsyn himself acknowledges as "extremely painful." Is it not precisely the function of intellectuals and academics, who are best equipped with the necessary knowledge and capacity to analyze complex problems, to provide explanations to their societies of these problems and to offer some alternatives for their solution? Finding a solution to problems of Russian-Ukrainian relations is too serious a matter to be left to the antagonistically inclined forces in both societies, or to the proverbial Slavic destiny (*sudba, dolia*).

Solzhenitsyn and, for that matter, a number of former dissidents who arrived in the West display understandable difficulty in comprehending certain assumptions under which open societies function. They expect their opinions to be accepted at face value, almost as if they were pronouncements *ex cathedra*, and seem to resent their being subjected to questioning and debate. Furthermore, they insist that emphasis be placed only on those issues and concerns that strengthen the sense of unity among the various national groups at home and in the diaspora. That approach may not be altogether in the best interest of all the parties involved. This has been well understood by leading figures in the Polish political opposition even before the developments which led to the founding of the independent trade union movement and the sociopolitical transformations in today's Poland. In the late 1970s, a protracted debate took place among the representatives of various political factions in the Polish opposition. Some emphasized the need for avoiding controversial subjects and the necessity for stressing unity as the more desirable operative goal. The prevailing majority, however, came to the conclusion that it was much more important to exemplify to the Polish society the values of an open debate and of a democratic process. By analogy, what the Russian and Ukrainian societies, both at home and in the diaspora, need most at the present time is to follow that example and to encourage ideas in free and unencumbered debate even on the most painful subjects, provided, of course, that this debate be conducted in a civilized manner.

Let me now comment briefly on Solzhenitsyn's well-known position on the issue of communism and its intricate relationship to the political system and political culture of Russia's past and present, as he raises them in his letter to the conference and elaborates upon them in detail in the aforementioned article, published in *Foreign Affairs*, to which he refers in the same letter. In summary, Solzhenitsyn rejects any connection between communism as ideology and political practice and the historical experience of Russia. He refuses to accept the possibility of any link between traditional Russian imperial, and contemporary Soviet imperial, policies. Concretely, he argues in favor of an approach that stresses the exclusively totalitarian and internationalist nature of the Soviet communist system, a perfectly plausible approach that, incidentally, prevailed in the West in the 1950s and early 1960s, but was abandoned in the mid-1960s even by those who had originally devised it.

However, the problem in question can as well be discussed from the historical, cultural, and comparative perspectives. There is absolutely nothing prejudicial in observing, for example, that except for brief periods in her history, Russia, both Muscovite and imperial, had no representative institutions of her own, or that throughout the long years of the ancien regime, the absolute majority of the elite, and most likely a majority of the population as well, accepted an autocratic regime and firm authoritarian methods of governing a society as natural and even appropriate conditions. There is also nothing wrong with establishing systemic similarities in institutional history or political culture between imperial Russia and the Soviet Union, nor is there any inherent anti-Russian sentiment implied in studying the policies of Russia's ancien regime toward the non-Russian nationalities of the empire and reaching the conclusion that they had been repressive. After all, the implementation of the *privislanskii krai* doctrine on the Polish territories after the mid-1860s and the enactment of the *Emskii Ukaz* of 1876 in Ukraine, both undertaken during the reign of one of the more benevolent Russian emperors, to name only two examples, cannot be viewed as evidence of enlightened and progressive policies on the part of the Russian imperial government. And they certainly cannot be blamed on international communism.

The same comparative approach applies to the vexed question of continuity or discontinuity between traditional Russian imperialism and modern totalitarian or authoritarian Soviet expansionism and hegemonism. The inquiry into this question and attempts to ascertain in which areas the policies of the two systems have differed and in which they have displayed similarities represent a perfectly acceptable and respectable academic and intellectual endeavor which cannot simply be dismissed in the name of national sentiment or a devotional approach to national history.

In short, drawing historical parallels and analogies between the policies of two different regimes of any given country, including Russia, or even conducting a rigorous critique of traditional Russian imperialism, should not be interpreted as evidence of hostility or intolerance toward the Russian people. Russian imperialism does not represent an isolated phenomenon; other European states also engaged in imperialist policies in the past and the discussion of these policies is not regarded by the absolute majority of their citizens as detrimental to the reputation of their countries. I have always rejected the concept of collective responsibility when it is applied to any people, including the Russian people, for the deeds committed by their governments or elites. Nonetheless, there must have existed some powerful forces in the old Russian elite and society which made the building and maintaining of that gigantic bicontinental empire possible. And without some similar forces the Soviet Union would not be able to function as a modern empire today. The fact that elite groups and even some sizable segments of the subordinate nationalities have participated in the functioning of the two imperial systems, and that Russians have often suffered because of their country's involvement in imperialist policies, does not undermine the validity of the comparative approach.

In conclusion, let me emphasize once again the importance of the Russian-Ukrainian dialogue in the future. I sincerely hope that Solzhenitsyn, a man of strong moral commitment and of a deeply felt sense of justice, will be able to overcome his ambivalent attitudes towards the possibility of attaining a normalization of Russian-Ukrainian relations at least in the diaspora, and will join the efforts of his Russian compatriots, and of those Ukrainians, who have already committed themselves to this noble cause. In Solzhenitsyn's own words, "since the two peoples have not succeeded over the centuries in living harmoniously, it is up to us to show sense."

Jaroslaw Pelenski
October 1981

Contributors

JOHN A. ARMSTRONG, professor emeritus of political science, University of Wisconsin-Madison, resides in his native city, St. Augustine, Florida. During 1965-67, he was president of the American Association for the Advancement of Slavic Studies, and at the University of Wisconsin at various times headed the Russian Area Studies Program and the Western European Area Studies Program. He is the author of seven books (including *Nations before Nationalism*, 1982, and *Ukrainian Nationalism*, 3d edition, 1990) and numerous articles.

YAROSLAV BILINSKY is professor of political science at the University of Delaware. He is the author of *The Second Soviet Republic: The Ukraine after World War II* (1964) and numerous articles and book chapters on Soviet nationality policy. Currently he is preparing a major work on Gorbachev's policy toward Germany.

BOHDAN R. BOCIURKIW is professor of political science at Carleton University in Ottawa. A specialist in Soviet politics, he has published numerous studies on religion and politics in the Soviet Union, especially in Ukraine, including "The Orthodox Church in Ukraine since 1917" in *Ukraine: A Concise Encyclopedia* 2 (1971); *Religion and Atheism in the USSR and Eastern Europe* (co-edited with J.W. Strong, 1975); *Ukrainian Churches under Soviet Rule: Two Case Studies* (1984); and *Historische Perspektive der sowjetischen Religionspolitik in der Ukraine* (1986).

MARTHA BOHACHEVSKY-CHOMIAK has published widely on Russian and East European history. Having taught history at Manhattanville College and Johns Hopkins University, she has joined the National Endowment for the Humanities in Washington. Her books include *S. N. Trubetskoi: An Intellectual among the Intelligentsia in Prerevolutionary Russia* (1976), *A Revolution of the*

Spirit: Crisis in Value in Russian Thought, 1890-1924 (1982), and *Feminists despite Themselves: Women in Ukrainian Community Life, 1884-1939* (1988).

RALPH S. CLEM is professor of geography at Florida International University, Miami. He is the author, co-author, or editor of several books, chapters, and articles dealing with the population geography of Russia and the USSR.

JAMES CRACRAFT is professor of history at the University of Illinois at Chicago. He has published *The Church Reform of Peter the Great* (1971) and edited *For God and Peter the Great: The Works of Thomas Consett, 1723-1729* (1982) and *The Soviet Union Today: An Interpretive Guide*, 2d ed. (1988).

GEORGE G. GRABOWICZ is director of the Harvard Ukrainian Research Institute and president of the International Association of Ukrainianists. He has written on literary theory and on Polish and Ukrainian literature. His books include *Toward a History of Ukrainian Literature* (1981) and *The Poet as Mythmaker: A Study of Symbolic Meaning in Taras Ševčenko* (1982).

EDGAR HÖSCH is professor of history at the University of Munich and head of the Department of History at the East European Institute in Munich. He is editor of "Schriften zur Geistesgeschichte des Östlichen Europa" and "Veröffentlichungen des Osteuropa-Institutes München, Reihe: Geschichte" and co-editor of *Jahrbücher für Geschichte Osteuropas*. His books include *Orthodoxie und Häresie im alten Russland* (1975), *Die Kultur der Ostslaven* (1977), and *Geschichte der Balkanländer* (1988).

EDWARD L. KEENAN is chairman of the Department of History at Harvard. He has published *The Kurbskii-Groznyi Apocrypha* (1972) and contributed articles to professional journals.

JAROSLAW PELENSKI is professor of history at the University of Iowa. His writings deal with ideologies, political and legal thought, and comparative sociopolitical systems of Russia, Poland and Ukraine in the medieval and early modern periods, as well as in the twentieth century. He is the author of *Russia and Kazan: Conquest and Imperial Ideology, 1438-1560s* (1974) and of more than 100 articles. He has edited several books, including *The Political and Social Ideas of Vjačeslav Lypyns'kyj* (1987).

PETER J. POTICHNYJ is professor of political science at McMaster University in Hamilton, Ontario. He has edited or co-edited many volumes on Soviet and East European affairs, including *Ukraine in the Seventies* (1975), *Poland and Ukraine, Past and Present* (1980), *The Soviet Union: Party and Society* (1985), and *Ukrainian-Jewish Relations in Historical Perspective*, 2d ed. (1991). He is co-editor of the multi-volume series *Litopys Ukrains'koi povstans'koi armii.*

OMELJAN PRITSAK is Mykhailo S. Hrushevs'kyi Professor of Ukrainian History Emeritus at Harvard University. He has published widely in Ukrainian and European history and in Turkic philology, and is the author of *The Origin of Rus'*, vol. 1 (1981). He is a fellow of the American Academy of Arts and Sciences and an honorary member of the Atatürk Academy and other institutions.

MARC RAEFF is Bakhmeteff Professor of Slavic Studies Emeritus, Columbia University. His many publications include *Origins of the Russian Intelligentsia: The Eighteenth-Century Russian Nobility* (1966), *The Well-Ordered Police State: Social and Institutional Change through Law in the Germanies and Russia, 1600-1800* (1983), *Understanding Imperial Russia: State and Society in the Old Regime* (1984), and *Russia Abroad: A Cultural History of the Russian Emigration, 1919-1939* (1990).

JOHN S. RESHETAR, JR. is professor emeritus of political science at the University of Washington (Seattle). He previously taught at Princeton University and was a visiting lecturer at Yale University. He is the author of *The Ukrainian Revolution, 1917-1920* (1952); *A Concise History of the Communist Party of the Soviet Union* (1960); *The Soviet Polity: Government and Politics in the USSR* (1971), and various other works.

NICHOLAS V. RIASANOVSKY is professor of history at the University of California, Berkeley. His books include *Nicholas I and Official Nationality in Russia, 1825-1855* (1959), *A Parting of Ways: Government and the Educated Public in Russia, 1801-1855* (1976), *A History of Russia*, 4th ed. (1984), and *The Image of Peter the Great in Russian History and Thought* (1985).

HANS J. TORKE is professor of Russian and East European History at the Free University of Berlin. He has published books on the Russian bureaucracy in the first half of the nineteenth century and on state and society in seventeenth-century Muscovy, as well as articles on Russian absolutism and on Russian and Soviet historiography. He is editor of and contributor to *Lexikon der Geschichte Russlands* (1984) and of the series "Forschungen zur osteuropäischen Geschichte."

PETER WOROBY is professor of economics at the University of Regina. He was previously in the employ of the Saskatchewan Power Corporation in charge of research and planning. His areas of study include resource economics (energy, water and agriculture) and urban research. His current research concerns the hierarchy of urban systems in Ukraine.

GLEB ŽEKULIN is professor emeritus, Department of Slavic Languages and Literatures and former Director of the Centre for Russian Studies, University of Toronto. He has taught at the University of Liverpool, the University of Glasgow, McGill University and, since 1968, at the University of Toronto. He has published widely in the fields of Russian and Czech literature.